PROGRAMME MUSIC

IN

THE LAST FOUR CENTURIES

A CONTRIBUTION TO THE HISTORY OF

MUSICAL EXPRESSION

BY

FREDERICK NIECKS, Mus.D.,

Reid Professor of Music in the University of Edinburgh.
(Author of 'Frederick Chopin as a Man and Musician '; &c.)

———

HASKELL HOUSE PUBLISHERS Ltd.

Publishers of Scarce Scholarly Books

NEW YORK. N. Y. 10012
1969

First Published 1907

HASKELL HOUSE PUBLISHERS Ltd.
Publishers of Scarce Scholarly Books
280 LAFAYETTE STREET
NEW YORK. N. Y. 10012

Library of Congress Catalog Card Number: 68-25299

Standard Book Number 8383-0311-0

PREFACE.

As the subject of programme music is almost always treated controversially, or at least with a *parti pris*, it may not be an unnecessary precaution to state that the present book is neither a defence nor an attack, but simply an historical account. I entered on my task as an impartial inquirer. The proof of my having kept true to my purpose may be found in the fact that the results of the inquiry modified to some extent my previous notions and judgments. If there was one matter to which I gave my attention more than to any other, it was the views of the composers themselves. And it was a great satisfaction to me to find that materials of this kind were much more plentiful, interesting, and instructive than I had expected. I am sure that the harvest here garnered will cause not a little surprise, and give not a little pleasure.

The primary difficulty in the discussion of programme music has always been the non-existence of a correct and adequate definition. As a rule the definitions are too narrow, often indeed dictated by prejudice and even hostility. They should embrace all possible kinds, degrees, and characters : the outward and the inward, the simple and the complex, the general and the particular, the lyrical, epic, dramatic, melodramatic, descriptive, symbolical, &c. They should embrace also music with the programme merely indicated by a title, and music the programme of which is unrevealed. The absence of programme and title does not prove the music to be absolute. This will explain my classing so much as programme music that is more generally classed as absolute music. Indeed, my opinion is that whenever the composer ceases to write purely formal music, he passes from the domain of absolute music into that of programme music.

On the title-page this book is called ' a contribution to the history of musical expression.' This is not saying too much, but perhaps too little. Programme music as I understand it is so comprehensive that a history of it goes far towards being a History of Musical Expression.

Next I wish to refer briefly to certain principles that have guided me in the execution of my task—principles that experience teaches me do not enjoy excessive popularity either with authors or with readers. In the first place, it has been my endeavour to place the facts so before the reader that he can control my argumentation and form his own conclusions when mine do not please him. As man is constituted, individual judgments, even those of the wisest, are precarious. My second endeavour has been to be as objective as possible in the characterization of men and artists, and their actions and works, taking care not to draw conclusions from one-sided evidence. For fantastic idealizations evolved from inner consciousness, in which imagination takes the place of fact, and poetry of truth, I have a thorough contempt in history and biography. ' Il ne faudrait pas prendre ce portrait tout à fait au pied de la lettre, car il est vu à travers la peinture et à travers la poésie, et embelli par une double idéalisation ; mais il n'en est pas moins sincère et fut exact à son moment.' Thus writes Théophile Gautier of an idealized portrait of Charles Baudelaire, painted by Emile Deroy, subsequently further idealized in poetic prose by Théodore de Banville. What is the good of the sincerity if the outcome is a falsehood ? Of course there is the cant about the poet's insight, and our readiness to accept as true what is beautiful. My third endeavour has been to be in the translations loyal to the authors, even at the price of some loss in the idiomatic expression of the English. You cannot render Wagner's involved and figurative periods in Johnson's, De Quincey's, Macaulay's, Ruskin's, or Froude's language. And if you tried to do so, you would denaturalize the author's prose, which both in form and content is out and out un-English. Again, if one were to translate Lesueur's lame French into elegant English, correcting the bad logic and grammar, would that not be tantamount to misleading the reader ? A fourth point, perhaps not superfluous to mention, is something I have *not* endeavoured to do—namely, to write a *catalogue raisonné* of all the programme music written during the last four centuries. I have not emptied my note-books in these pages. The record of all the battle and hunting pieces alone would fill a goodly volume. But, although critics may often say ' Why did the author not mention this or that composition?' I am more likely to be blamed for having told too much than too little.

In conclusion I must express my heartfelt thanks to all who have assisted me in my labours by giving me information and by reading the proofs. Special thanks are due to the composers who were so exceedingly kind as to enrich the value of the publication by statements of their views and practice.

EDINBURGH, *October*, 1906.

CONTENTS.

BOOK I.

EARLY ATTEMPTS.

BOOK II.

ACHIEVEMENTS IN SMALL FORMS AND SERIOUS STRIVINGS IN LARGER FORMS.

CHAPTER II.

CHAPTER III.

CHAPTER IV.

CHAPTER V.

BOOK III.

FULFILMENTS.

BOOK IV.

OTHER FULFILMENTS.

BOOK V.

CONTEMPORARIES AND SUCCESSORS OF THE PROGRAMMATIC PROTAGONISTS OF THE LAST TWO PERIODS (1830-1900).

BOOK I.

EARLY ATTEMPTS.

CHAPTER I.

INTRODUCTION: SURVEY AND DIVISION OF THE SUBJECT.

The history of programme music may be said to be the history of the development of musical expression; at any rate, it presents itself as such if programme music is not understood in too narrow a sense. But what is programme music? The current notions concerning it are so vague and varied that it will be advisable to consider, before commencing our story, the term and the things signified by it. Some think that programme music is music which imitates sounds—the song of birds, the purling of the brook, the bustle and noises of war, &c. Others, allowing it somewhat larger scope, think that it is music which, besides the audible, imitates by analogy also the visible—effects of light, darkness, and colour, and all kinds and degrees of movement. Others again, with a more adequate conception, go much farther than this, and think that programme music is music which imitates not only the outward, but also the inward; which not only describes, but also expresses; which has to do with emotions and thoughts as well as with sense-impressions, with soul-painting as well as with body-painting. To not a few the last view seems absurd. They hold that nothing of the kind is within the capacity of music. But the pretension is by no means unreasonable. On the contrary, it is obviously and strikingly reasonable. Why should not music be able to express and excite emotions by imitating the sounds and movements by which they demonstrate themselves? A discussion of the expressional power of music I reserve for another volume, here it will suffice to enumerate the means of expression at the disposal of the composer :—

(1) Imitation of the human cries and the accents of speech as regards pitch, rhythm, loudness, and quality of tone.

(2) Imitation of the movements of the internal and external bodily organs that accompany the emotions—action of the heart, breathing, gestures, &c.

(3) Imitation of the sounds in nature, which are expressive directly and indirectly, indirectly by association.

(4) Imitation of rest and motion, strain and relaxation, pleasure and pain, by certain musical means— namely, consonance and dissonance, and the tendencies of tonality.

The prejudices as to programmes are many. That absolute music—by which we are to understand pure music, music with none but æsthetical qualities, music unconnected with anything definite in thought or nature, according to some a mere formal play with tones—is the only legitimate instrumental music, was long the orthodox and all but universal doctrine, and even now has not become a wholly extinct belief. Then, we find people who approve of a title, but object to a poem or a prose narrative prefixed to a piece of music. And yet, a title may imply a great deal more than a poem or a prose narrative. What vast subjects, for instance, are indicated by single words such as Faust, Hamlet, Manfred, Hebrides, Eroica, Hungaria, &c.! It is a mistake, although in accordance with a time-honoured definition, to say that programme music is music with an explicit verbal programme prefixed to it. Many of the compositions of Berlioz, Liszt, and Richard Strauss, the most famous masters in this *genre* of music, have nothing but simple titles. In fact, you may have programme music without even as much as a title. If the composer had a programme in his mind while composing, the composition is programme music, whether he reveals his programme or not. It used to be very common with composers to conceal their programmes. They were either afraid of the prejudiced critics, and kept their secret, like Weber in the *Concertstück;* or were themselves affected by the prevailing prejudice, and tried, like Schumann, to excuse their practice by explanations intended to allay their own doubts as well as the wrath of others.

The prejudice, however, which has led to the largest amount of misconception and to an infinitude of preposterous criticism is the assumption that the composer gives in his music all that is set forth in the programme, whereas in reality the music is intended only as a commentary and illustration, not as a duplicate or translation of it. Indeed, the programme would be a superfluity if it did not contain something that music is unable to express at all or equally well. We cannot reason, give orders, and tell stories in music. It cannot name persons, times, and places connected with what it communicates, although it may characterize them and hint at them. On the other hand, we can express the

infinite shades and degrees of moods and emotions better
by tones than by any other medium.   Of course,
composers have often, from ignorance or presumption,
attempted the impossible.   But misuse does not justify
the condemnation of use.

There are several other considerations worth pointing
out.   Usage reserves the term programme music for
instrumental music with a prefixed verbal programme.
But this should not prevent us from seeing facts as
they are.   A programme may be recited or sung
before or with the music as well as printed.   This
difference in the enunciation of the programme does not
make an essential difference in the character of the music.
In fact, all good, that is, all expressive vocal music is
programme music.   Further, the programme need not
be verbal at all, it may also be pantomimic or pictorial.
Next, let us note the various characters of programmes.
Three main divisions are easily distinguishable—the
predominatingly   descriptive,   the   predominatingly
emotional, and the predominatingly symbolical.   The
descriptive (the materially descriptive) is the lowest
kind of programme music, and is best used in combination
with and subordination to one of the others.   To make
up for the absence of the emotional element is a difficult
and rarely successful task.   It is the musical element
par excellence.   Lastly, although a programme invites
and admits deviation from the structural methods
of absolute music, it neither necessarily demands
abandonment of the classical forms, nor in any
conceivable case excuses formlessness.

What shall be the starting point of our history?
We may pass over the beginnings of the art, which are
matters of conjecture, the antique and early medieval

music, of which our practical knowledge is extremely scanty, and the polyphonic art-music of the 14th and 15th centuries, in which emotional and descriptive expression does not seem to have been, indeed, could not have been, a chief aim. Where expression was not altogether excluded from the old polyphonic compositions by the love of ingenuity of combination, it did not often go beyond the general, unspecialized states of feeling, such as calm, dignity, liveliness, agitation, vigour, languor, &c. A different state of matters began to develop in the 16th century. A striving after greater freedom, ease, lucidity, and suppleness became more and more noticeable, and consciously aimed at greater expressiveness or unconsciously contributed to the attainment of that aim. The cultivation of the madrigal and the more popular villanella and villota, the endeavour so to set the words to music as to remain intelligible, the experiments in chromaticism, tonality, solo song, instrumental music, and theatrical performances—all these had one origin, arose from one impulse, and tended one and all to the great revolution brought about towards the end of the century by the evolution of the instrumentally accompanied solo song (monody) and the musical drama. The 16th century, then, must be our starting point.

To escape the danger of losing ourselves in a multitude of isolated facts, we will endeavour to group them in periods corresponding to stages of evolution. Do not look, however, for perfect continuity and progression in one straight line; instead of it you will often see leaps, sporadic phenomena, zigzag movements, and retrogression as well as progression. Childish programme music, such as we find in the earliest stages,

B

we still find in the last stage beside the highest developments. Observe that my periods overlap. Observe also that the early periods are to the last two what steps, porch, and vestibule are to a house or a temple.

First Period, 16th century: *Vocal programme music.*

Second Period, from the latter part of the 16th to the beginning of the 18th century, opening with the Englishmen Byrd and Mundy and ending with the German Kuhnau: *Isolated and tentative cases,* at first without exception crude and childish, and even later on mostly so, at least partially if not wholly.

Third Period, from the 17th to the middle of the 18th century, that of the French masters (lutenists and clavecinists) of musical miniature *genre* and portrait painting, which culminated in François Couperin: *First artistically satisfactory achievements in programme music.*

Fourth Period, the 18th century: Spreading of the cultivation of programme music and *more general striving after expressiveness in instrumental music,* as seen (*a*) in Overtures, *Entr'actes,* and incidental music to plays and operas, and the instrumental *ritornelli* and accompaniments of vocal compositions; (*b*) in Melodrama (instrumental accompaniment to the spoken word); and (*c*) in Symphony and Sonata.

Fifth Period, from the close of the 18th century: *Programme music in the larger classical forms and vitalization of the lesser forms.* First appears Beethoven, who, at least as regards the larger classical forms, is the principal inspirer of those who come after him.

Sixth Period, from about the fourth decade of the 19th century: *Departure from the classical forms and wider scope of subjects.* The inspiring geniuses of this period are Berlioz, Liszt, and Wagner.

CHAPTER II.

FIRST PERIOD (16TH CENTURY): VOCAL PROGRAMME MUSIC—
JANNEQUIN, GOMBERT, JOSQUIN DEPRÈS, LASSO, PALESTRINA,
MARENZIO, ETC.

In connection with the history of Programme Music allusions are generally made to descriptive vocal compositions of the 16th century, but they are mostly inadequate and not infrequently incorrect. The number of works composed and the number of editions of many of them prove the great popularity enjoyed by this kind of music. CLÉMENT JANNEQUIN, of whose life we know next to nothing, was, as far as our knowledge goes, not only the most prolific and successful composer in this *genre*, but also one of the earliest. His works appeared in the second and third quarter of the 16th century. As we cannot be sure that we have the first editions of these works, and some editions do not bear the year of issue, it is inadvisable to be more explicit. The descriptive vocal pieces of Jannequin's first published are *La Guerre*, or *La Bataille*, *La Chasse du Lièvre*, *Le Chant des Oiseaux*, and *L'Alouette*. Here we have at once the favourite subjects of the programme music of that age, and of all ages for a certain class of the public—namely, War, the Chase, and the imitation of Animal Voices, especially Bird Voices. Battle pieces, however, are so decidedly in the majority that the first subject must be recognized as the prime favourite.

In addition to the compositions already mentioned, Jannequin gave to the world: *Le Rossignol, La Prise de Boulogne, La Réduction de Boulogne, Le Siège de Metz, La Chasse au Cerf, Le Caquet des Femmes,* and *Les Cris de Paris.* A few words have to be said of at least two of the most famous of the descriptive pieces by Jannequin, who was undoubtedly the cleverest, liveliest, and most interesting and pleasing of all those who tried their strength in this *genre.* No one could question the appropriateness of the title given to the edition of some of them in 1544—'Inventions musicales.' In the *Bataille,* with the subtitle *Défaite des Suisses à la journée de Marignan* (Marignano or Melegnano)—the battle of 1515, where Francis I. beat the Swiss—there are to be found imitations of fifes, drums, bugles, cannon and musket reports, and all the bustle and noises of war. Jannequin's *Cris de Paris* begins with the words: 'Listen to the cries of Paris' ('Voulez ouyr les cris de Paris'), after which a wonderful variety of these cries are introduced, and made to form a harmonious whole —red and white wine, hot pies, delicious tartlets, fresh herrings, fine mustard, old shoes, milk, vegetables, and every imaginable thing.*

Among these Chansons of Jannequin's we found a 'Lark,' a 'Nightingale,' and a 'Chanson des Oiseaux.' The last named, a four-part composition, was famous, but the three-part composition with the same title by the contemporary NICOLAS GOMBERT (1544) was no' less, if not more, famous.†   It is a complete bird concert

---

* Reprints of *La Bataille, Chasse du Lièvre,* and *Cris de Paris* are to be found in F. Commer's *Collectio operum musicorum batavorum sæculi XVI.,* vol. xii. ; and of *La Bataille* and *Chant des Oiseaux* in the Prince de la Moskowa's *Recueil des Morceaux de Musique ancienne,* vol. v.

† In Commer's *Collectio,* vol. xii.

a revelling in bird music. Of all the birds the one
enjoying the greatest favour was the harmonious cuckoo,
and next to it came the tuneful nightingale. Lorenz
Lemlin's *Der Gutzgauch* (1540) is full of cuckoo calls.*
The later Leo Leone gives a good imitation of the
nightingale in his madrigal 'Dimmi, Clori gentil'
(1609). But even the sounds of the least musical
animals have been utilized by composers. Antonio
Scandelli, for instance, imitates in a part-song (1570)
the cackling of hens. Adriano Banchieri has in his
carnival farce, in madrigal form (1608), a 'contrapunto
bestiale alla mente' (an improvised bestial counterpoint),
where, above the fundamental bass melody, a dog, a
cuckoo, a cat, and an owl, barks ('babbau'), calls
('cuccu'), mews ('gnao'), and cries ('chiu'). *À propos*
the cat, the much later Adam Krieger composed a
four-part vocal fugue (1667), in which a characteristic
chromatic subject is sung to 'miau, miau.'

A few more specimens of vocal programme music
may yet be mentioned : Tomaso Cimello's *Battaglia*, in
his *Canzone Villanesche* (1545) ; Matthias Fiamengo's
(le Maistre's) *La Battaglia Taliana* (Italiana), a
counterpart to Jannequin's *Bataille française*, published at
Venice in 1551,† having for its subject the battle of Pavia
in 1525, where Charles V.'s army vanquished Francis I.
and took him prisoner ; Thomas Mancinus's *The Battle
of Sievershausen* (1608), fought in 1553 by Moritz of Saxony
and Albrecht of Brandenburg-Kulmbach ; and Massimo
Trojano's *Battaglia della Gatta e la Cornacchia* (Battle of
the cat and the crow) of 1567. Very different in subject
is the first of the last compositions of this kind I shall

---

* In C. F. Becker's *Hausmusik.*

† Reprinted in L. O. Kade's *Mattheus le Maistre* (1862).

mention, Alessandro Striggio's *Il Cicalamento delle donne al bucato et la Caccia* (the Chattering of the Women at the wash, and the Chase), published in 1567. As to Johannes Eccard's *Zanni et Magnifico* (1589),[*] in which Winterfeld saw a scene of the life in St. Mark's Square, at Venice, a picture rising before the mind of the hearer even without his understanding the words, it is quite possible to see in it nothing but a *Quodlibet* in which five voices sing simultaneously four different sets of words and four contrasting melodies, the characters being two beggars, a grandee, a tippling foreign soldier, and a fifth personage more difficult to characterize. Many have repeated Winterfeld's opinion, but without examining Eccard's composition.

From what has been said the reader may already have gathered that in so far as the vocal compositions mentioned can be called programme music at all, they are programme music of the lowest type—body-painting, not soul-painting: imitation of tones and noises, not interpretation of moods and emotions, that is, not real programme music. Here and there, however,—for instance, where something of the spirit and excitement of war is represented—we get an approach towards a higher type. But, of course, these compositions ought not to be taken too seriously. They are things intended for pleasant pastime, for jovial social entertainment. They are not high art, although, as with Jannequin, they may be good and delightful art.

In the more serious *genres* of the vocal music of that time we get not only approaches towards a higher type,

---

[*] Reprinted in vol. xxi. (No. 14) of the *Publikationen* of the Gesellschaft für Musikforschung (edited by R. Eitner).

but actual attainments. Although on the whole music
did not then greatly surpass architecture in
expressiveness,—expressing, if anything at all, only
generalities, and even most of these only in a
rudimentary, merely indicative manner—full-blooded
geniuses of the type of JOSQUIN DEPRÈS (d. 1521) and
ORLANDO LASSO (1532-1594) did not rest content with
this, but specialized the expression, and sometimes even
characterized down to the least detail, following not
only the text as a whole, but its every phrase and word.
Of the 'indescribable genius' Josquin Deprès, the
contemporary theorist Glareanus said that no one had
more expressed the moods of the soul in song than this
master. And another contemporary, Luther, was wont
to grow eloquent over the expressiveness of the works of
this most admired among his favourite composers. No
one has written with more insight and enthusiasm of
Lasso than that excellent connoisseur of the old
·ecclesiastical art, Carl Proske, who saw in this most
glorious of the Netherland masters a universal mind,
and in his works a range from ecclesiastical
contemplativeness to the gayest of worldly strains, and
traits of epico-dramatic force and truth that breathe
upon us like the spirit of Dante and Michelangelo.
That the less impassioned and more restrained
PALESTRINA (d. 1594) was not indifferent to
expression may be proved, without going to his works, by
a passage in a letter addressed to Duke Guglielmo of
Mantua,* where he commends his noble patron, who had
sent him for criticism a mass of his own composition,
for the vivid expression he gives to the words according
to their significance. Indeed, if it were not for their

* A. Bertolotti's *La Musica in Mantova,* p. 49.

unfamiliarity with the old musical idiom, and their taste
blunted by too strong and too much seasoning, modern
audiences would find a great deal more of expressiveness
in the music of Palestrina and his contemporaries than
they now perceive. And they would find there not
only generic, but now and then also specific expression
of feeling. Even under the obtaining conditions, a
little attention would lead to surprising revelations.
Nothing need be said about the material illustrations of
' ascend ' and ' descend,' of ' high ' and ' low,' and other
externalities; nor of the expression of contrition,
jubilation, devotion, ecstasy, &c. But it is not superfluous
to point out the distinctly programmatic touches, such
as we meet with, for instance, in what we may call the
dramatized portions of the Credo and the settings of the
Psalms.

Secular music afforded wider scope for expression than
sacred music. Indeed, the words of madrigals were a
continuous challenge to composers in this respect.
That the challenge was courageously and successfully
taken up, no one illustrates more fully than the greatest
of all the madrigal composers, LUCA MARENZIO
(d. 1599). G. B. Doni of the 17th century boldly declares
that Marenzio was the first to endow the parts with
beautiful melody and beautiful grace, and to make the
words more expressive and intelligible; and W. Ambros
of the 19th century enthusiastically praises his music for
its noble sentimentality, tones of most inward feeling,
tender beauty of soul, local colouring, warm tinge of life,
occasional delicate word-painting, in short, for the
breath of modern expression that flows from it. And,
although pre-eminent, Marenzio was not singular among
the madrigalists. THOMAS MORLEY, himself a

distinguished master cultivating the *genre,* tells the
musicians of his time (in *A Plaine and Easie Introduction
to Practicall Musicke,* 1597) that if they wish to be
successful in the composition of madrigals, they must
possess themselves with an amorous humour, must be
wavering like the wind, now wanton, now drooping, now
grave and steady, now effeminate.

CHAPTER III.

SECOND PERIOD (FROM THE LATTER PART OF THE 16TH TO THE BEGINNING OF THE 18TH CENTURY): ISOLATED AND TENTATIVE CASES OF INSTRUMENTAL PROGRAMME MUSIC—BYRD, MUNDY, MONTEVERDI, FROBERGER, KUHNAU, PURCELL, ETC.

Let us now turn to Instrumental Music, our real subject. The first examples of instrumental programme music are two pieces for the virginal by the English musicians JOHN MUNDY (d. 1630) and his greater contemporary WILLIAM BYRD (1543-1623). Of the first we have a Fantasia* in which he describes successively, 'Fair weather,' 'Lightning,' 'Thunder,' 'Calm weather,' 'Lightning,' 'Thunder,' 'Fair weather,' 'Lightning,' 'Thunder,' 'Fair weather,' 'Lightning,' 'Thunder,' 'A clear day.' The tone-painting here is by no means striking, indeed is of a very primitive and childlike nature. Without the labels no one could possibly recognize the lightning and thunder, and hardly the fair weather and the clear day. There is, however, a contrast between the character of the figures —the rolling bass figure expressive of thunder, the brisk figures of disjunct notes expressive of lightning, and the quieter gait of the rest. Byrd's piece, contained in

* No. 3 of the Fitzwilliam Virginal Book. edited by J. A. Fuller Maitland and W. Barclay Squire.

My Ladye Nevells Booke in the possession of the
Marquess of Abergavenny and still unpublished, is a
battle piece with the following contents: 'The march
before the battle; the soldiers' summons; the march of
footmen; the march of horsemen; now followeth the
trumpets; the Irish march; the bagpipe and the drone ·
the flute and the drum; the march to the fight; here the
battle be joined; the retreat; now followeth a galliard
for the victory.' Of this work I have seen only a later
copy, of about 1656 (British Museum, Add. MS. 10,337),
which seems to differ in some respects from the older
manuscript. Instead of the 'Irish march' it has a
'Quick march' which may be only a difference of title;
instead of the 'Galliard for the victory' it has 'The
Burying of the dead,' which one cannot very well imagine
to be merely a difference of title; and between the 'March
for the fight' and 'Battle joined' there occurs a 'Tarra-
tantarra.' This composition is more valuable as music,
and more interesting as programme music, than Mundy's.
The marches are no doubt characteristic specimens of
the time, and probably contain tunes then popular. The
imitation of the trumpets, fifes, and drums is striking,
which cannot be said of the bagpipes, if the English and
Irish bagpipe music was in any way like what we know
of the Scottish. The tone-painting is chiefly to be found
in 'The Battle joined' and 'The Retreat.' No one can fail
to recognize in the former the bustle and tussle of the
contest, and in the latter the giving way, first slowly,
then quicker and quicker, until it ends in a wild flight.
This venerable instrumental battle-piece, the oldest one
known, proves that the type reached perfection almost at
once. Then the strength lay in the marches and
popular tunes and the weakness lay in the childish

tone-painting; now strength and weakness are still
where and as they used to be.

To these two compositions there ought perhaps to be
added *Lachrymae, or Seven Tears figured in seven
passionate Pavans, for Lute, Viols, or Violins, in five parts*
(1605), by JOHN DOWLAND, the delightful composer of
songs, of whom a poet has said that his ' heavenly touch
on the lute doth ravish human sense.' The virginal pieces
of the Elizabethan and Jacobean age frequently have
titles, but in most cases these are derived from the
popular ballads or other vocal compositions on which
they are founded—'The hunt's up,' 'The Carman's
Whistle,' 'Walsingham,' 'Daphne,' &c. Sometimes
they contain a patron's name or the name of a person
with whom the piece was an especial favourite. Nor
need we look for profound significance in titles like
' His Humour,' 'Giles Farnaby's Dream,' and
' Dr. Bull's Myself.'

Dramatic music furnishes a wide field for programme
music. How well it has been cultivated we learn from
the works of Gluck, Mozart, Beethoven, Weber, Rossini,
Meyerbeer, Gounod, and above all Wagner, whose
dramas, especially his later ones, are colossal symphonic
poems. The earliest occurrence of programme music in
the musical drama is of the first decade of the 17th
century; and to CLAUDIO MONTEVERDI (1567-1643),
that daring genius and great innovator, belongs the
honour of the origination. The characteristic, though
short and simple, orchestral pieces, and some of the
instrumental accompaniments and interludes of the
vocal pieces in his *Orfeo* (performed at Mantua in 1607
and published in 1609) have an indisputable claim to a
place in the history of programme music. In the only

other opera of Monteverdi's that is known to have come
down to us, *L'Incoronazione di Poppea* (Venice, 1642),
the instrumental portions are few and insignificant.   On
the other hand, his *Combat of Tancred and Clorinda*
(*Il Combattimento di Tancredi et Clorinda*), a setting of
some stanzas from the 12th book of Tasso's *Gerusalemme
liberata*, performed in 1624 and published in 1638 in the
8th book of his madrigals,* is again of the greatest
interest and importance, more especially on account of
its instrumental accompaniments written for four viols,
with *tremolo* and *pizzicato* effects among others.   This
was his first composition in the *stile concitato* (agitated,
passionate style), which he claims as his invention.   He
says that there are three principal grades in the
expression of the emotions, to which correspond three
styles, the agitated or passionate (*concitato*), the
temperate (*temperato*), and the gentle (*molle*).   'In all
the works of the preceding composers I found examples of
the last two styles, but not of the agitated, although that
manner of expression had already been described by
Plato in the third book of the Rhetoric [he meant
Republic] ; "Take that harmony which in tone and voice
imitates that of a brave man going into battle."'   The
importance of such views, and their realization in
practice in general for the development of musical
expression and programme music in particular needs no
pointing out.

Monteverdi's pupil and successor, the most famous
opera composer and the most brilliant representative of the Venetian school in the 17th century,

---

* *Orfeo* is to be found in the *Publikationen* of the Gesellschaft für Musikforschung (edited by R. Eitner), *L'Incoronazione* in H. Goldschmidt's
Studien zur Geschichte der Italienischen Oper, II. ; and *Il Combattimento*
in C. v. Winterfeld's *Johannes Gabrieli*, Part III.

FRANCESCO CAVALLI (c. 1600-1676), often introduces characteristic instrumental pieces in his works. I shall note here only the *Sinfonia infernale* and the *Chiamata alla caccia* in *Le Nozze di Teti e di Peleo*, the *Passata dell' armata* and the *Sinfonia navale* in *Didone*, and the music descriptive of the billowing and roaring of the sea in *Nettuno e Flora festeggianti*.* Cavalli's great, though less prolific rival, MARC ANTONIO CESTI (c. 1620-1669) ought likewise to be named in this connection, and also the distinguished woman composer FRANCESCA CACCINI, whose *La Liberazione di Ruggieri dall' Isola d'Alcina*, performed in 1625, contains independent instrumental pieces.

In Italian instrumental music apart from the opera we find hardly anything in the nature of programme music. The *Capriccio stravagante* (1627) by the Italian CARLO FARINA, Court violinist at Dresden,—with its inartistic imitations of the cackling of hens, mewing of cats, barking of dogs, the *flautino*, the *fifferino della soldadesca*, and the *chitarra spagnola*, &c.—does not deserve the name. Again, BIAGGIO MARINI'S *La Martinenga* and *Il Priulino* (dances of 1622), G. B. VITALI'S *La Graziani* and *Capriccio detto il Molza* (1669), and LEGRENZI'S *La Cornara, La Fugazza* (1663), and *La Rosetta* (1671) point to patrons and admirers, not to subjects. If there were an exception, it could only be the last piece, the first movement of which might perhaps, with an effort of the imagination, be regarded as the portrait of a sweet pretty maid worthy of the name Rosie. We have, however, an instance of unmistakable programme music in MARCO UCCELLINI'S

---

* See H. Kretzschmar's essay on *Die Venetianische Oper* in *Vierteljahrsschrift für Musikwissenschaft*, vol. viii. (1892).

Wood Symphonies (*Sinfonie Boscareccie*, 1669), one of
which is entitled *La Suavissima* and another *La Gran
Battaglia*. Although called grand, this battle does not
produce a very terrifying effect, indeed it amounts to no
more than that two violins alternately throw a snappish
figure at each other, and have some tussles, runs, and
rushes together. All the compositions mentioned in this
paragraph are written for violins and a figured bass.* Of
Italian composers for keyboard instruments of this period
only one calls for notice, ALESSANDRO POGLIETTI,
who, however, on account of residence abroad and
foreign influences, will find a more appropriate place
further on. That FRESCOBALDI (d. 1644) utilizes
the cuckoo notes as a motive in one of his capriccios,
and imitates the pifferari in another—the *Capriccio fatto
sopra la Pastorale*—does not constitute him a composer of
programme music. Some of the titles of his pieces
might seem to point to programmes—for instance,
La Battaglia, which, however, is merely a variated bugle
call, and *La Frescobalda, Fra Jacopino*, &c., which are
no more than names of tunes. More weighty arguments
could be drawn from the master's recommendation of
varied and elastic *tempo*, his allusion to difference of
passages and expression, and the superscription 'Let him
who can understand me follow me, I understand myself';
but generally speaking, Frescobaldi was too much
preoccupied with technical problems and outward effects
to think of anything else.

Now we will transport ourselves from Italy to
Germany, where our attention is first attracted by
JACOB FROBERGER (d. 1667), a pupil of Frescobaldi's,

---

* J. W. von Wasielewski's *Instrumentalsätze vom Ende des XVI. bis
Ende des XVII. Jahrhunderts* (1874).

one of the most notable figures in the history of instrumental music, eccentric as a man, inimitable as a player of and composer for the harpsichord and organ. Mattheson says of him : ' This composer knew well how to represent on the clavier alone whole stories with the portraiture of the persons that had been present and taken part in them, together with their characters.' The same writer relates in the *Ehrenpforte* (1740) that he had in his possession a manuscript composition of Froberger's entitled, ' Plainte, faite à Londres, pour passer la mélancolie,' in which the composer describes ' what he experienced between Paris and Calais, and from Calais to England, from robbers on land and sea, and how the English organist had abused him, taken him by the arm to the door, and kicked him out.' Mattheson had also of Froberger an ' Allemande, faite en passant le Rhin dans une barque en grand péril, with a detailed description.' This *Allemande,* with what belongs to it,—as the same author relates in *Der vollkommene Capellmeister* — was a pretty clear description, in 26 *Noten-Fällen,* of Count Thurn's passage across the Rhine, and the danger experienced by the company, among whom was Froberger himself. But Froberger's compositions generally, although without titles and programmes, give one the unmistakable impression that he aimed at something more than a clever and pleasing putting together of notes. The vivid expression of moods, feelings, and fancies, both serious and humorous, is truly remarkable, especially if we consider the character of the instrumental music of his time. But although as a rule his aims were praiseworthy, they were occasionally mistaken ; as, for instance, in the beautiful Lament on the death of the Emperor

Ferdinand IV. (*Lamento sopra la dolorosa perdita della R. M. di Ferdinando IV. Re de Romani. Per il Cembalo,* 1649), where at the end occurs a *glissando* C major scale which, according to Ambros's interpretation, represents the Jacob's ladder on which Ferdinand IV. ascends to heaven.

The Italian ALESSANDRO POGLIETTI, who in 1661 became chamber organist to the Emperor Leopold I., and perished in 1683 during the siege of Vienna by the Turks, gave to the world a *Capriccio* entitled *Il Rossignolo,* a *Petit Air gay pour imitation de Rossignole,* and a *Capriccio* on cock-crowing and hen-cackling. The imitation of the animal voices is here excellent, probably better than anything of the kind that had been done before.   But after all it is of the lowest kind of tone-painting, and can hardly be called programme music. Specimens of a somewhat higher order are to be found in some of Poglietti's variations in *Aria Allemagna con alcuni variazioni sopra l' età della Maesta* (the number of the variations being the same as that of the years of his Majesty the Emperor), one of the pieces 'pour le Clavecin ou l'Orgue' (1663). Here we find among others the following really significant superscriptions : Bohemian Bagpipe, Dutch Flageolet, Hungarian Fiddles, Juggler's Rope-dance, and French Baiselemens (*baisemains,* compliments).   The three last-named are the most interesting of the variations, the movements of the Juggler, French *élégant,* and Hungarian Fiddler being hit off most happily and musically.

Not to fatigue the reader, I shall close my enumeration of instances of programme music belonging to the second period by proceeding at once to the latest and most important specimens—the Six Bible

c

Sonatas (1700) of JOHANN KUHNAU (1660-1722), J. S. Bach's predecessor as Thomas cantor at Leipzig. From the preface to these works we gather that programme music was then more common than is generally supposed, and also that much of what was then produced is unknown to us, either having perished or being hidden in dusty uncatalogued heaps in libraries. Kuhnau tells us that if he pretended to be the first to compose such an 'invention,' he would prove himself ignorant of the celebrated Froberger's and other excellent musicians' Battles, Waterfalls, and Tombeaux (*i.e.*, elegies on the death of persons), and of whole sonatas (evidently meaning what we call suites) composed in this manner, with words added to discover the meaning. Of the sonata species he mentions one by a celebrated Prince-Electoral Chapelmaster, which the author calls *La Medica*, and in which, among other things, he sets forth the moaning of the patient and his relatives, how they run to the doctor and state their distress, &c., &c., and concludes with a *Gigue* bearing the superscription : 'The patient is doing well, but is not yet fully restored to health.' The composer alluded to is very probably JOHANN CASPAR KERL, from 1656 to 1673 Chapelmaster at Munich. This composition, of which we have no further knowledge, reminds me of another lost work, DIETRICH BUXTEHUDE'S Seven Suites, in which, according to Mattheson, the nature and qualities of the planets were prettily pictured (*artig abgebildet*). This loss is to be regretted for more than one reason—for the eminence of the composer, the character of the subject, and the fact that it was unique among the master's works, his strength lying above all, to quote Spitta's words, in absolute instrumental music uninfluenced by any poetical idea. I must yet, parenthetically as it were, allude to one other composition, one by the famous organist JOHANN PACHELBEL (d. 1706), the younger contemporary of Buxtehude (d. 1707). It is entitled *Musikalische Sterbensgedanken, aus vier variirten Chorälen bestehend* (Musical Dying Thoughts, consisting of four variated Chorales—1683), to the composition of which the impulse was given by the plague at the time raging in Erfurt, where Pachelbel resided from 1678 to 1690. No copy of the original edition is known to exist, but three of the four variated chorales have been republished, after manuscript material, in the *Denkmäler der Tonkunst in Bayern* (II. 1), edited by M. Seiffert. If these compositions can be called programme music at all, it can be only in the sense of an outpouring of sadness and piety by a man who had lost wife, child, and happiness at one fell swoop.

To return to KUHNAU'S preface to the Bible Sonatas. It shows that the composer was well aware of the difficulties and dangers of the *genre*, and had considered them carefully. If he did wrong, he did so with *malice prepense*. He is of opinion that the imitation by instrumental music of the songs of birds, the ringing of bells, the report of cannon, and trumpets and kettle-drums, can be understood without the help of words; and that this is also the case with the expression by instrumental music of the general feelings of joy and sadness, unless they are to be connected with particular individuals—that is where, for instance, the lament of Hezekiah is to be distinguished from that of the weeping Peter, or from that of the complaining Jeremiah. On the other hand, verbal indications of the intentions of

the composer become a necessity when the hearer
himself is to be moved, now to joy now to sadness, now
to love now to hate, now to cruelty now to mercy, the
reason being that the dissimilarity of their temperaments
causes the hearers to be differently affected, both in kind
and degree, by one and the same thing. In fact, this
preface is an apology for instrumental programme music,
and being the first apology is of historical as well as of
æsthetical interest.

The general title of Johann Kuhnau's publication of
1700 with which we are concerned runs as follows:
*Musikalische Vorstellungen einiger Biblischer Historien in
6 Sonaten auf dem Clavier zu spielen* (Musical
Representations of some Biblical stories in six sonatas,
to be played on the clavier). The titles of the six
sonatas are respectively (1) *The Combat between David
and Goliath;* (2) *David curing Saul by means of music;*
(3) *Jacob's marriage;* (4) *Hezekiah sick unto death and
recovered of his sickness;* (5) *The Saviour of Israel,
Gideon;* and (6) *Jacob's death and burial.* These sonata
titles, however, are not the only verbal indications of the
subjects; each sonata is provided with a lengthy
argument which at the end is tersely summarized; and
in addition to this superscriptions are placed above the
different parts of the sonatas. The summary of the
argument of the first sonata runs: (*a*) The boasting and
defying of Goliath; (*b*) The terror of the Israelites; and
their prayers to God at sight of the terrible enemy;
(*c*) The courage of David, his desire to humble the pride
of the giant, and his child-like trust in God; (*d*) The
contest of words between David and Goliath, and the
contest itself in which Goliath is wounded in the
forehead by a stone, so that he falls to the ground and

is slain; (*e*) The flight of the Philistines, and how they
are pursued by the Israelites, and slain by the sword;
(*f*) The exultation of the Israelites over their victory;
(*g*) The praise of David, sung by the women in alternate
choirs; (*h*) and finally, the general joy, expressing itself
in hearty dancing and leaping. The summary of the
argument of the second sonata is not so many-membered:
(*a*) Saul's sadness and madness; (*b*) David's refreshing
harp-playing; (*c*) Tranquillity restored to the King's
mind. It would take up too much space to quote the
contents of the four remaining sonatas. The curious
will find them in Seiffert-Fleischer's new edition
(the third) of Weitzmann's *Geschichte der Klaviermusik*
(I., 247). The music of the first two sonatas has
been recently put within the reach of everybody by
J. S. Shedlock's edition of them (Novello).*

Kuhnau's sonatas, the most ambitious attempts at
programme music up to 1700, are not sonatas in the
modern sense of the word, nor are they suites, but a
series of movements differing in length, tempo, measure,
structure, and not infrequently also in key, which lead
one into the other, each having at the beginning a
superscription indicating what it is intended to express.
While the second sonata consists of a few sustained
movements, the first contains short as well as long ones.
A rapid scale and some twirls depict ' the pebble is sent
by means of the sling into the forehead of the giant ';
and five bars suffice for the depicting of ' Goliath falls.'
On the other hand, the terror and prayers of the
Israelites, the courage of David, the joy of the Israelites

* All the six sonatas have been reprinted, edited by K. Päsler, in the
Denkmäler deutscher Tonkunst, vol. iv., 1901. A careful biography of
*K*uhnau by Richard Münnich will be found in the *Sammelbände* of the
Internationalen Musikgesellschaft (year III.—April-June, 1902).

over their victory, are expressed leisurely. That Kuhnau's subjects are not always judiciously chosen may be judged from the following headings. 'Laban's deceit in taking Leah instead of Rachel to the honest cousin and bridegroom' (third sonata); 'Gideon's doubts in God's promises of victory made to him'; and 'The blowing of trombones and trumpets, as well as the breaking of the pitchers, and the war-cry' (fifth sonata); and 'The journey from Egypt to the land of Canaan' (sixth sonata). Kuhnau himself tells us that he has expressed the deceit of Laban by an interrupted cadence (called by the Italians *inganno*), and Gideon's doubts by repeating again and again the opening of subjects a degree higher and higher.

Although we may here and there smile at the mistaken choice of subject,—or rather the mistaken selection of the points of a subject—and the *naïveté* and the inadequacy of the means of expression, it would be downright foolishness to laugh at these sonatas contemptuously. They are remarkable achievements, daring, and often successfully daring, in their efforts at expressiveness, and full of musical beauties apart from expression. Novel in their ideas, means, and form, these sonatas enjoyed great popularity in their day. But they must have done more than please, entertain, and edify the general public; they also must have exercised a great influence upon the composers of the master's own and succeeding generation. Who, knowing these sonatas and the music of Kuhnau's time as well, could doubt their suggestiveness and stimulative qualities? Their importance, I am convinced, has not so far been fully recognized. On account of the influence that Kuhnau's Bible Sonatas

must have exercised, they have a good claim to a
place in our fourth period. But, all things considered,
their proper place is here, for they are interesting
and powerful attempts rather than altogether satisfactory
achievements.

Having reached what I intended to be the end of this
period, it strikes me that many, at least in Great
Britain, will ask: ' But what of Purcell ? ' One cannot
help wondering that HENRY PURCELL (1658-1695),
with his passionate, we may even say violent, striving
after expressiveness, has not left us among his
instrumental works—sonatas, suites, &c.—specimens
of programme music. In his accompanied vocal
music there is, however, plenty of tone-painting of all
sorts, material and spiritual, good and bad, great and
little. It is to be found oftener in the vocal than in
the instrumental parts, and for that reason is not
infrequently reprehensible, because of its giving undue
prominence to the subordinate—to the material at the
expense of the spiritual, to the word-expression at
the expense of the thought-expression. It is not only
psychologically wrong, but also comical rather than
seriously impressive, to sing the word 'round' to a
smooth, twirling series of eighteen semiquavers, and the
word 'spread' to a long extent of coloratura. The
tremulous execution of portions of the vocal parts asked
for by the composer in the Frost-Scene of *King Arthur*
—to express the quivering and shivering and the
chattering of teeth caused by cold—must have given rise
to much misgiving. Sir Hubert Parry is not too severe
in saying that, in spite of his powerful genius, Purcell
carried to excess the tendency of the later Madrigal
period towards realistic expression, that he fell not

infrequently into the depth of bathos and childishness, was impelled to make experiments quite astounding in crudeness, and that he adopted in secular solo music realistic devices of a quaintly innocent kind. In view of this, one cannot help speculating. What grand and perfect works might Purcell not have given to the world if, like Handel, he had been able to spend a year or two in Italy, and had afterwards, again like Handel, found in England worthy opportunities for the exercise of his powerful genius! Now our admiration cannot be unmixed with regrets.

BOOK II.

ACHIEVEMENTS IN SMALL FORMS AND SERIOUS STRIVINGS IN LARGER FORMS.

CHAPTER I.

THIRD PERIOD (FROM THE 17TH TO THE MIDDLE OF THE 18TH CENTURY): FRENCH LUTENISTS AND CLAVECINISTS— DENNIS GAULTIER, CHAMBONNIÈRES, COUPERIN LE GRAND, RAMEAU, ETC.

On entering the Third Period—that of French Musical Miniature *Genre* and Portrait Painting, as practised by the lutenists in the 17th century and by the clavecinists in the 17th and first half of the 18th century—we leave the time of isolated cases of programme music behind us. Another point about this period calls for notice. It was the French School of clavecinists, culminating in François Couperin, that achieved the first artistically satisfactory results in programme music. The source of what we may call the programmatic movement may be traced back to the earlier flourishing School of French lutenists. In their music we find already pieces with titles, partly mythological and partly idyllic. Of the sixty-two pieces, *La Rhétorique des Dieux*, by the 'illustrious' DENNIS GAULTIER (d. about 1660-1670), contained in the splendid 'Hamilton Codex' now in Berlin, about one half have titles. Here are a few: *Phaéton foudroyé*,

Minerve, Mars superbe, Junon ou la Jalouse, &c.; and *La Coquette virtuosa, La Caressante, L'Homicide,* &c. Now the question arises : Are these titles vain ornaments, mere affectations, artful allurements, or are they truly significant ? It is difficult for us, strangers as we are to the effects of the lute well played, to measure the extent to which these compositions reach the height, depth, and breadth of their subjects. The limited means of the instrument as shown by the notes seem to promise little. But there can be no doubt that the French composers for the lute often, though not in the majority of cases, indicated by the titles of their pieces what they intended to illustrate. The writer of the preface to the 'Hamilton Codex' states that Gaultier represents the passions perfectly, and that he elevates the most abased spirits to the sublimest virtues. 'This manner of expressing himself may justly be called *La Rhétorique des Dieux.*' Of the first-mentioned piece (*Phaéton foudroyé*) it is said that it 'bears witness to Phaeton being, by his imprudence and ambition, the cause of the conflagration of the half of mankind, to the punishment meted out to the rash youth by Jupiter, and to the sorrows of his father Apollo on account of his loss.' And of *La Coquette virtuosa* we read that 'this fair one, who makes as many lovers as there are men that understand her, proves by her priceless discourse the sweetness she finds in the love of virtue, the great esteem she has for those who adore it, and that she will give herself to him who will have first attained the title of the magnanimous.' Without further concerning ourselves with the lutenists, we will turn to the father of the School of French clavecinists, CHAMPION DE CHAMBONNIÈRES, who died about 1670. Of him we have two books of *pièces* (dances).

He, too, makes use of titles, but more sparingly than Gaultier. Only ten of his sixty-one pieces are thus provided for. And the titles of these ten are very vague, and less likely to mean much than little or nothing. Judge for yourself: *La Rare, Iris, La Dunkerque, La Loureuse, La toute belle, L'Entretien des Dieux, La Villageoise, La Verdinguette,* and *Les Jeunes Zéphirs.* The clavecinists that come immediately after Chambonnières—Le Bègue, the elder Couperins (Louis and François), D'Anglebert, and others—offer us in the present inquiry no matter of interest. And thus we may hasten onward to the FRANÇOIS COUPERIN of a later generation, the most distinguished of a musically most richly gifted family, which in France formed a counterpart to the Bachs in Germany.

The composers of the French harpsichord School of the 17th and 18th centuries are either entirely ignored or greatly underrated in the history of programme music. At any rate, I am not aware that they ever received their due in this respect. The prevalent opinion about them is that their compositions are pretty trifles, and that the titles are for the most part fancy titles and—even when they are not altogether that—need not be taken seriously. An unprejudiced study of the works of François Couperin, called 'le grand' (1668-1733), and acquaintance with his intentions, will show that this view is quite wrong, and that the master's miniatures, slight in form and light in texture, but perfect in execution, are masterpieces not only of musical composition, but also of tone-painting. Of all the masters of the School, Couperin is the most important, both on account of the quantity and the quality of his programme music. The compositions that chiefly concern us here are four books of harpsichord pieces—*Pièces de Clavecin* (1713, 1716, 1722, 1730)—grouped not in Suites or Partitas, but in 'Ordres.' There are altogether twenty-seven orders. The number of pieces in the orders varies greatly. The second order, for instance, contains twenty-three, the fourth only four. All the pieces of an order have the same key-note ; the mode, however, is sometimes major and sometimes minor. But the orders are distinguished from suites and partitas not only by the number, but also by the nature of their constituents, for although they contain many dances, they contain more pieces that are not dances. The pieces not in dance form are in a primitive kind of *Rondo* form, in which a principal thought alternates with secondary thoughts (called *Couplets*) ; in short, the forms of these pieces are forms of cumulation, not of development. Of the dances some have names, others have not ; the other compositions are all named.

In the preface to Couperin's first book of *Pièces de Clavecin,* published in 1713, there occurs the following passage : ' I have always had an object in composing all these pieces : different occasions have furnished me with it—thus the titles correspond to the ideas I have had. I may dispense with giving an account of them ; nevertheless, as among these titles there are some which seem to flatter me, it is well to warn people that the pieces which bear them are a species of portraits that have been sometimes found like enough under my fingers, and that the greater part of these prepossessing titles are rather given to the amicable originals whom I wished to represent than to the copies I have drawn of them.' This cannot leave any doubt in our minds as to the composer's intentions. Couperin's pieces are now

sentimental, now characteristic, now humorous, now
descriptive. The tone-painting in them is now
soul-painting and now body-painting—that is, now
concerned with the inward, and now with the outward.
A few of the pieces paint states of feeling, such as
*Les Regrets, Les Langueurs tendres, Les Sentiments, Les
Idées heureuses,* and *Les Agréments.* Very many pieces
are portraits, the sitters of which are variously indicated
—by proper names, by predominant quality, by a
combination of the two, or by moral or national character :
La Couperin, La Princesse Marie, and *La Sœur Monique;
La Superbe, La Ténébreuse, La Pateline, La Voluptueuse,
La Terpsichore, La Badine,* and *L'Enchanteresse;
L'aimable Thérèse, La douce Janneton,* and *La tendre
Fanchon; La Basque, L'Ausonienne, La Castelane, La
Boulonnaise,* and *Les Chinois.* Some of the pieces are
impressions from nature : *Les Lis naissans, Les Roseaux,
Les Pavots, Le Verger fleuri, Les Guirlands, Le Réveille-
matin, Le Point du Jour, Les Bergeries, Les Ondes,
L'Anguille, Les Abeilles, Les Papillons, Le Moucheron, Le
Gazouillement, Les Canaries, La Linotte effarouchée, Les
Fauvettes plaintives, Le Rossignol en amour,* and *Le
Rossignol vainqueur.* Not a few of the pieces are *genre*
pictures, in which there is even more than in the
preceding classes a great deal of imitation of the
outward (movements, tones, and noises) : *Le Bavolet
flottant, Les petits Moulins à vent, Le Tic-Toc-Choc, ou
Les Maillotins, Le Gaillard-boiteux, Les Tours de passe-
passe, Le Drôle de corps, Les Timbres, Le Carillon de
Cythère, Les Ombres errantes, Le Turbulent, La Harpée*
(*pièce dans le goût de la Harpe*), *Les Tambourines, La
Musette de Choisi, La Musette de Taverni, La Commère, La
Fileuse,* and *Les Tricoteuses* (with the 'mailles lachées'

near the end). A considerable number of the pieces
consist of two, three, four, and more parts; they
represent or depict groups of scenes: *Les Pèlerines*
(1. *Caritade ;* 2. *Le Remerciment*), the alms-asking and
the thanksgiving of female pilgrims; *Les Calotins et les
Calotines, ou La Pièce à tretous* (1. *Les Calotins ;* 2. *Les
Calotines*), the comic performance of buffoons (male and
female) on a trestle-stage, in short, of a company of
strolling players; *Les Bacchanales* (1. *Enjouemens
Bacchiques ;* 2. *Tendresses Bacchiques ;* 3. *Fureurs
Bacchiques*), different effects of wine; *La Triomphante*
(1. *Bruits de guerre et Combat ;* 2. *Allégresse des
vainqueurs ; Fanfare*), three phases of war; *Les petits
Ages* (1. *La Muse naissante ;* 2. *L'Enfantine ;* 3.
L'Adolescence ; 4. *Les Délices*). A larger programme
is set forth in *Fastes de la grande et ancienne
ménestrandise* (Records of the grand and ancient
minstrelsy). It comprises five pieces, called by the composer 'acts':—Act I. The minstrel notables and jurymen;
Act II. The hurdy-gurdy players and the beggars;
Act III. The jugglers, tumblers, and mountebanks
with their bears and monkeys; Act IV. The invalids, or
those crippled in the service of the grand minstrelsy;
Act V. Disorder, and defeat of the whole troop, caused by
the drunkards, the bears, and the monkeys. Couperin in
his titles often reminds one of Schumann, but in no case
more than in the piece which he calls 'Les folies françaises
ou les Dominos,' which brings at once to mind the more
recent composer's *Carnaval*. This composition consists
of twelve *couplets*, in which the harmony remains the
same, on which, however, a new characteristic structure
is again and again raised. The several *couplets* are
entitled : (1.) Virginity under the domino of the colour

of the invisible; (2.) Pudicity under the rose-colour
domino; (3.) Ardour under the carnation domino; (4.)
Hope under the green domino; (5.) Fidelity under the
blue domino; (6.) Perseverance under the drab domino;
(7.) Languor under the violet domino; (8.) Coquetry
under different dominos; (9.) The old Galants and the
superannuated female Treasurers under purple and
withered-leaves dominos; (10.) The kind Cuckoos under
yellow dominos; (11.) Taciturn Jealousy under the
mauve-grey domino; and (12.) Frenzy or Despair under
the black domino. *Les Folies françaises* are followed by
what may be described as an epilogue, *L'âme en peine*,
Lent repentance after the Carnival indiscretions.

Thus far only Couperin's *Pièces de Clavecin* have been
noticed; but we have also works of the master for
harpsichord combined with other instruments (stringed
or wind), which, however, he allowed to be played on two
harpsichords or spinets. I shall mention the *Concerts
Royaux* written for Louis XIV.'s Sunday concerts and
published with the third book of harpsichord pieces
(1722); *Les Goûts réunis ou nouveaux Concerts à l'usage
de toutes sortes d'instruments de musique, augmenté d'une
Sonade en Trio intitulée: Le Parnasse ou L'Apothéose de
Corelli* (1724); and the *Concert instrumental sous le titre
d'Apothéose, composé à la mémoire de l'incomparable
monsieur de Lully* (1725).* Only the two Apotheoses
concern us here. Couperin says that with regard to the
Italian and the French style he occupies a neutral
position: 'I have always esteemed meritorious things
irrespective of author or nation.' He says also that,

---

* A transcription of these works for stringed instruments and
pianoforte by Georges Marty has been published by A. Durand et Fils,
Paris.

when thirty years earlier the first Italian sonatas made
their appearance in Paris, he was encouraged to compose
some himself. *Le Parnasse, ou L'Apothéose de Corelli,*
comprises seven movements, the first forming an introduction to the second; they bear the following superscriptions : (1.) Corelli, at the foot of Parnassus, asks the
Muses to receive him among them; (2.) Corelli, charmed
by the good reception given him on Parnassus, shows his
joy thereat.   He continues with those accompanying
him; (3.) Corelli drinks at the fountain of Hippocrene,
his company continue; (4.) Enthusiasm of Corelli caused
by the waters of Hippocrene; (5.) Corelli, after his
enthusiasm, falls asleep, and his companions play the
following slumber music very softly; (6.) The Muses
awake Corelli, and place him beside Apollo; and (7.)
Thanks of Corelli. Couperin's object in writing the
Apothéose de Lully was ' to do honour to the greatest man
in music whom the preceding century had produced,' and,
in doing so, to ' diminish the prejudice of those who know
his works only by reputation.'   Here is the programme :—
(1.) Lully in the Elysian Fields concerting with
the lyrical shades; (2.) Air for the same (*les mêmes*);
(3.) The flight of Mercury to the Elysian Fields to
announce the descent of Apollo; (4.) Descent of Apollo,
who comes to offer to Lully his violin and his place
on Parnassus; (5.) Subterranean noise caused by the
contemporaries of Lully; (6.) Complaints of the same,
for flutes and violins very subdued; (7.) The carrying off of
Lully to Parnassus; (8.) Reception *entre-doux et hagard,*
given to Lully by Corelli and the Italian Muses; (9.)
Thanks of Lully to Apollo; (10.) Apollo persuades Lully
and Corelli that the union of the French and the Italian
taste ought to make music perfect; (11.) Lully playing

the principal part and Corelli accompanying; (12.)
Corelli playing in his turn the principal part, while
Lully accompanies ; (13.) The peace of Parnassus made
on the remonstrance of the French Muses, subject to
the condition that in future when their language was
spoken there, *sonade* and *cantade* should be said, just as
as one says *ballade, serenade,* &c.; (14.) Sally [*Saillie*].

That these programmes deal with matters craving for
musical expression is not likely to be asserted. Indeed,
subjects like Corelli asking to be received among the
Muses and drinking at the fountain of Hippocrene,
the flight of Mercury, Apollo's descent, his offer to
Lully of a violin and a place on Parnassus, the
subterranean noise, &c., if not anti-musical, are
unmusical. Moreover, the treatment of some of them
—for instance, of the flight of Mercury and the
subterranean noise—is childish. But varied character
cannot be denied to the pieces, most of them are
even decidedly expressive. And, apart from their
quality as programme music, we must allow them to be
good and pleasing music. What makes them further
interesting is their style, which is different from that of
the *Pièces de Clavecin*—it is more contrapuntal and
sometimes more imitative, and clearly shows the influence
of Italy. Another difference is the much more sparing
use of grace-notes. The parts of the Apotheoses are
self-contained, except the first, which ends on the
dominant, and thus leads up to the second part. All
the pieces have not the same key-note. In the Corelli
Apotheosis there is D major besides B minor, and in
the Lully Apotheosis there are, besides G minor and
major, E flat and B flat major. The length of the pieces
varies greatly, especially in Lully. Most of them are

D

short, and some very short. In the latter work one has
no more than ten, another no more than sixteen bars.
Two pieces, however, are of considerable length. One
of these two, No. 10, the composer describes as an essay
in the form of an overture—in fact, it is a French, or
Lully overture, consisting of a slow, a quick, and a slow
movement; the other, No. 14, although not so described,
is an Italian, or Scarlatti overture, consisting of a quick,
slow, and quick movement. Interesting and admirable
as Couperin's concerted pieces are, we cannot but feel
that Couperin le Grand and his *chefs d'œuvres* are not
to be found there. His solo pieces for his own
instrument have a raciness and a perfection not possessed
by his other compositions. And it is also there that
he proves himself a greater master of programme
music. To the *Pièces de Clavecin* we must now once
more turn.

That Couperin really aimed at expression as well as
at a pleasing combination of sounds may be gathered
not only from the passage (in the preface to the first book)
already quoted, and the titles of the pieces, but also
from the indications frequently prefixed to the pieces,
such as : *Majestueusement; Gracieusement; Tendrement;
Gayement; Nonchalamment; Affectueusement; Dou-
loureusement; Voluptueusement.** It may be further
gathered from his insistence on the necessity of
correctly and expressively performing his compositions.
In the preface to the third book of harpsichord pieces,
he declares that his music will never fail to make an

---

* Speaking of *mesure* and *cadence*, the spirit and the soul of music,
Couperin says : ' The sonatas of the Italians are hardly susceptible of
this cadence. But all our violin airs, and clavecin, viol, and other pieces,
point to, and seem desirous to express, some sentiment. Hence words
such as *tendrement* and *vivement*.'

impression on persons of taste, if it is played with an
exact observation of the composer's markings. He does
not leave us in doubt as to the importance he attaches
to expression when he says : ' I greatly prefer what
touches me to what surprises me.' But it may be
asked : Is expression possible on the harpsichord ? Let
us hear the master on this point. ' The harpsichord is
perfect in compass and brilliant in itself ;* but as one
can neither swell nor diminish its tones, I should always
be obliged to those who, by an infinite art supported by
taste, are able to succeed in making this instrument
susceptible of expression. It is to this that my
ancestors applied themselves, independently of the
beautiful composition of the pieces. I myself have
endeavoured to perfect their discoveries.' (Preface to
Book I.) Those acquainted with the mechanism of the
instrument may suspect Couperin to have been under a
delusion. But to be convinced of the contrary, you
have only to hear so expert a player and so loyal an
interpreter as Madame Wanda Landowska. She seems
to have rediscovered the discoveries of the Couperins.
The rough-and-ready renderings of Couperin's music on
the harpsichord to which we are accustomed, and, what
is still worse, those on the pianoforte, cannot do justice
to the master, cannot make us realize the sentiment
and wit of his charming poetic conceptions. It would
be an exaggeration to say that Couperin's compositions in
all cases entirely fulfil what their titles seem to promise.
But there is no exaggeration whatever in saying that
unprejudiced hearers must be both struck and delighted

* In the *Avis* to *L'Apothéose de Lully*, the master claims for his
instrument *un brillant et netteté qu'on ne trouve guère dans les autres
instruments.*

by the exquisite touches of truthful expressiveness and
humorous descriptiveness with which the *Pièces de
Clavecin* abound.   Something, however, besides deficient
interpretation, militates against the adequate recognition
of Couperin.   Like Chopin, he is a victim of a mighty
prejudice, of the almost universally adopted standard of
judgment according to which greatness depends upon
bigness of size and noise.

It is a great and lamentable mistake to undervalue
Couperin and his music because he confines himself to
miniatures, because he never approaches the deeper and
stronger emotions, because he is always sprightly, tender,
and graceful—now sweetly melancholy, now playful.
These dainty, exquisite qualities are no less valuable
than the more vigorous and tumultuous ones.   Moreover,
we should not overlook that just in this lightness and
slightness lies much of the merit of Couperin's music
viewed from the standpoint of historical development.   We
may call him the first great modern of the composers for
keyboard instruments.   The creations of Couperin remind
us of the *naïveté* of his older contemporary, the poet
La Fontaine; they remind us also of the quaint grace
and coquetry of his younger contemporaries, the painters
Watteau, Lancret, and Pater, and of the humour and
sentiment of the still later Greuze.   Couperin, however,
has a complexion of his own: his sentiment was more
natural, and his humour more exuberant, than that of
his contemporaries and successors, and, what is
especially notable, his choice of subjects was more
popular — 'fêtes galantes' *à la* Watteau, &c., were not
much in his way.   With so strong an individuality the
nowadays obligatory reference to the character of his
time and country is only to a very limited extent

illustrative, in fact, hardly illustrative at all.   What has
Couperin in common with Corneille, Racine, and Bossuet,
who are nevertheless in the highest degree characteristic
of their time ?   No doubt, he has more in common with
La Fontaine, and with Watteau, Lancret, and Pater,
with considerable differences however.   But Couperin's
creations remind us not only of the above-mentioned
poet and painters of long ago, they remind us also of
composers much nearer our own time—of Schubert and
his short pianoforte pieces, sometimes of Mendelssohn
and his songs without words, and often of Schumann
and his playfully fantastic miniatures.   In short,
Couperin is one of the moderns, notwithstanding his
periwig, frills, trimmings, and other old-fashioned
ornaments, which to some extent hide the natural grace
and beauty of his melody and the purity of his harmony.
There can be no doubt that we have in François
Couperin a tone-poet of a most abounding, varied, and
delicate fancy, a composer of a perfect and exquisite
craftsmanship, and, although working in a little *genre,*
one of the greatest masters of the art.

Of the other members of the French Clavecin School,
by far the most important is the somewhat later JEAN
PHILIPPE RAMEAU (1683-1764), the contemporary of
J. S. Bach and Handel, whose fame rests chiefly on his
great achievements as a theorist and composer for the
stage.   His compositions for harpsichord are, however,
a very valuable contribution to the department to which
they belong.   The first book of harpsichord pieces,
consisting of a prelude and nine untitled dances, was
published by the as yet immature Rameau in 1706.
His next publication of harpsichord pieces did not take
place till 1724 (republished in 1731) : *Pièces de clavecin*

avec une méthode pour la mécanique des doigts. Among
its twenty-four pieces we meet with the following titled
ones : *Le Rappel des Oiseaux, Le Tambourin, La
Villageoise, Les tendres Plaintes, Les Niais de Sologne,
Les Soupirs, La Joyeuse, La Folette, L'Entretiens des
Muses, Les Tourbillons* (that is, as the composer explains
in a letter, whirls of dust, raised by violent winds),
Les Cyclopes, Le Lardon, and *La Boiteuse.* Several
years afterwards appeared the *Nouvelle Suite de Pièces
de Clavecin.* Besides dances, these twenty-three pieces
comprise *Fanfarinette, La Triomphante, Les Tricotets,
L'Indifférente, La Poule, Les Triolets, Les Sauvages,
L'Enharmonique, L'Egyptienne,* and *La Dauphine.* To
these solo pieces has to be added a collection of *Pièces
de Clavecin en Concert* with violin, or flute, and viol, or
a second violin (1741). Almost all of the sixteen pieces
bear titles : most of these are family names, such as
La Rameau, La Livri, La Poplinière, &c. ; some indicate
characters, such as *L'Agaçante, La Timide, L'Indiscrète,*
&c. ; and two are respectively called *La Pantomime*
and *Le Tambourin,* the latter an altogether different
composition from that of the same name in the earlier
collection. Five of the sixteen pieces were arranged by
Rameau for harpsichord alone.

Although a later composer, Rameau does not, in his
harpsichord pieces, go beyond Couperin either in form
or programme. Indeed, as regards programme music
for the harpsichord, Rameau is, both in quantity and
quality, inferior to Couperin. The younger master has
neither the wealth of subject nor the striking
characterization of the older master. This, however,
does not mean that Rameau has not among his
musically excellent and delightful *Pièces de Clavecin*

some programmatically first-rate specimens, both of the
emotional and imitative kind.   To this bear witness the
universally popular *Tambourin* and *La Poule*, in which
the Provençal fife (*galoubet*) and drum and the cackling of
the hen are treated in a most artistic manner.   Rameau's
harpsichord style differs greatly from Couperin's : it is
simpler, broader, and manlier.   The comparative
fewness of grace-notes is striking.   In the *Pièces de
Clavecin en Concert* the superior concerting quality of
the harpsichord cannot escape notice.*   Of Rameau's
programme music in another department something
will be said farther on.

LOUIS CLAUDE DAQUIN (1694-1772) and JEAN
FRANÇOIS DANDRIEU (1684-1740), composers on a
much lower level than Couperin and Rameau, deserve at
least passing notice.   Who does not know Daquin's
pretty *Le Coucou*, from his *Pièces de Clavecin* (1735)?
Whose curiosity is not raised by the title of Dandrieu's
first *Livre de pièces de Clavecin contenant plusieurs
divertissements dont les principaux sont les caractères de
la Guerre, ceux de la Chasse et la Fête de Village* (1724)?
The superficially pleasing Daquin treats us to trifles
with old and seemingly ever fresh themes, such as
Le Coucou, Le Tambourin, La Musette, La Joyeuse, and
La tendre Silvie, but also to rarer subjects, such as
L'Hirondelle, Les Vents en courroux, La Guitarre, and
even to a series of scenes, *Les Plaisirs de la Chasse:
L'appel des chasseurs, Marche, L'appel des chiens,
La prise du cerf, La curée,* and *Réjouissance des chasseurs.*
Dandrieu's *Fête de Village* consists of five rustic dances,
the programme of which lies in the rusticity of their

---

* The complete works of Rameau are in course of publication under
the direction of Saint-Saëns.   (Paris: A. Durand et Fils.)

character.   The *Chasse* consists of six pieces :—(1)
without special title, (2) *Première Fanfare*, (3) *Second Bruit
de Chasse*, (4) *Fanfare Rondeau*, (5) *Troisième Bruit de
Chasse*, and (6) *Fanfare*.   The horns are to the fore, and
there is no pause in the bustle and joyousness,
throughout set forth in 6/8 time.   *Les Caractères de la
Guerre* were originally published (in 1718) for trumpets,
bassoons, kettle-drums, violins, oboes, and fifes, with the
sub-title *Suite de Symphonies ajoutée á l'Opéra*.   The eight
characters of war are as follows : *Le Bouteselle, La
Marche, Première Fanfare, Seconde Fanfare, La Charge,
La Mêlée* (in the course of which occur : *Les Cris* and
Les Plaintes), *La Victoire* (*Rondeau*), *and Le Triomphe*.
This composition contains here and there some really
interesting touches of tone-painting, and is much
better music than battle symphonies and sonatas usually
are.   Nevertheless *Les Caractères de la Guerre* and
La Chasse are examples of the lower, material kind of
programme music.   This is especially the case in
La Charge and *La Mêlée* of the former work.   The higher
kind of programme music is to be found in the other
pieces, some of which are truly charming.   Among these
pieces we find interesting tone-painting in *Les Tourbillons,
Les Cascades,* and *La Cavalcade*.   The pieces named
after instruments imitate the characteristics of the tunes
written for them.   *La Gémissante* and others are of real
emotional expressiveness.   It is impossible to deny
Dandrieu's music prettiness, but it is extremely slight
as well as *mignonne*.

I must not omit to quote an interesting passage from
Dandrieu's preface to his *Livre de Pièces*.   After telling
the reader that the cannon reports occurring in
La Charge are indicated by a four-part common chord,

but that the player, in order to express better the noise of the cannon, might put the palm of the whole left hand on the lowest keys, the author proceeds thus : ' As to the names chosen by me, I have drawn them from the character of the pieces which they denote, so that they may determine their style and movement, and awaken simple ideas acquired by ordinary experience or common and natural sentiments. Perhaps I have not always succeeded.'

CHAPTER II.

FOURTH PERIOD (18TH CENTURY) : MORE GENERAL STRIVING
AFTER EXPRESSIVENESS IN INSTRUMENTAL MUSIC, AND
SPREADING OF THE CULTIVATION OF PROGRAMME MUSIC—
RAMEAU, HANDEL, J. S. BACH, DOMENICO SCARLATTI, TELEMANN,
VIVALDI, AND GEMINIANI, GREAT MASTERS OF THE FIRST HALF
OF THE 18TH CENTURY.

Unlike the third, which is simple, the fourth is a
complex period. We meet in it not only with miniature
genre and portrait-painting in the style of the French
Clavecin School, and isolated attempts at programme
music on a larger scale and of a more ambitious nature,
but we notice also a more general and more earnest
striving after expressiveness throughout the whole
domain of instrumental music, and a spreading of what,
for brevity's sake, we will call the programmatic tendency
in the narrow sense of the word. To study this aspect
in the history of music, we have to direct our attention
especially to three branches of the art : (*a.*) Overtures,
entr'actes, and incidental music to plays, operas,
oratorios, &c.; (*b.*) Melodrama (from 1770 onward); and
(*c.*) Sonata and symphony, especially the latter, and more
especially that with a programme, of the last quarter
of the 18th century. We have already seen that the
Italian opera composers of the 17th century used the
overture and incidental instrumental music for
illustrative (programmatic) purposes. Their successors,
ALESSANDRO SCARLATTI and others, followed them

in this as far as the decreasing dramatic character of
their works called for such illustration. LULLY, the
principal founder of the French opera, availed himself
to some slight extent of this means in the operas brought
out by him at Paris in the seventies and eighties of
the 17th century ; his successors MARAIS and
MONTÉCLAIR did so in a higher degree; and
J. PH. RAMEAU did so in a very high degree and most
striking manner. Not one of Rameau's predecessors
or contemporaries did as much as he did in the way of
characteristic, that is, picturesque and expressive,
instrumental music in opera.   This striving of the
composer's gave rise to the description of him as a
'distillateur d'accords baroques,' and the levelling at
him of the following amusing epigram :—

> ' Si le difficile est le beau,
> C'est un grand homme que Rameau ;
> Mais si le beau, par aventure,
> N'était que la simple nature,
> Quel petit homme que Rameau ! '

The accompaniments and *ritornelli* of the arias and
choruses of Rameau's operas are full of happy orchestral
illustrations, and the independent incidental instrumental
pieces are genuine programme music. Of the overture
to *Naïs* (1749), which paints the contest of the Titans
against Jove, Lavoix *fils* says that it was probably the
first overture worthy the name that had been written.
Notable instances of picturesque music are the sunrise,
the sleep of Endymion, and the storm in *Zaïs*. Besides
programmes of the highest order, we also find
programmes of the lowest. For instance, that of the
overture to *Acanthe et Céphise*, which reads : (1.) 'Vœu de
la nation ; (2.) Canon et feu ; (3.) Fanfare et Vive le Roi.'

Quite legitimate are the imitations of the croaking of frogs, the braying of the ass, and the screeching of birds in *Platée*, which is a comic ballet. Taking up *Dardanus*, one of the master's best operas, we find opening the first act, after the Prologue, a ' Ritournelle tendre' (for which the second edition substitutes a 'Prélude' of the same character); opening the second act, a ' Ritournelle vive' (the stage represents a solitude), followed in the course of the act by the sorcerer Isménor s incantation and a chorus of his ministers; in the fourth act, the lulling to sleep of Dardanus by a 'troupe de Songes,' and his dreams (the announcement of 'Le monstre sortant des flots'; the orchestral piece 'Le ravage du monstre'; the songs 'Ah! que votre sort est charmant,' with independent flute melodies; the instrumental 'Calme des sens,' and 'Air tendre'; the chorus 'La Gloire vous appelle'; the orchestral 'Triomphe'; the trio and chorus 'Il est temps de courir aux armes'), the awakening of Dardanus, more descriptive music relative to the dragon, the tempest, and the fight; after the fourth act, the orchestral piece 'Bruit de Guerre'; and, to mention one more of the innumerable interesting points, the sweet voluptuous 'Ariette gracieuse,' with the triplet runs in the accompaniment, which occurs in the third scene of the fifth act, when Venus and a 'troupe d'Amours et de Plaisirs' are on the stage. Enough, I think, has been said to justify Rameau's right to the place given him here.

It is strange that so powerful a composer and so voluminous a writer on music as Rameau has said so little on the subject of musical expression. Among the few things to be found in his writings is the following

fundamental statement from the sixteenth chapter of
the *Code de Musique Pratique*. 'One may say that
music—considered merely with regard to the different
inflexions of the voice, and leaving out of account gesture
—must have been our first language until terms for
expressing ourselves had been invented. This language
is born with us ; the child furnishes us with the proof.'
In the same chapter (*De l'Expression*) Rameau says
also : ' C'est à l'âme que la musique doit parler.'

Among the great composers who have written pure
instrumental music, it would be difficult to discover one
less open to the suspicion of being a writer of programme
music than HANDEL (1685-1759). His concertos,
suites, fugues, and overtures, for whatever instrument or
instruments, belong to the most absolute of absolute
music. These compositions have a beautiful sonority, a
pleasing harmoniousness, and a refreshing healthfulness;
but a deeper meaning they lack. Their most definite
expression, as a rule, is that of the generic feelings of
cheerfulness or sweet melancholy; their prevailing
expression that of the primary and most general feeling,
the joy in existence, the pleasure of the healthy in
action and in repose. That in these circumstances the
music not infrequently degenerates into a mere play
with sounds cannot surprise. Handel's overtures have
no reference to the works to which they are prefixed :
you may exchange them—at least you may exchange the
opera overtures, and you may exchange the oratorio
overtures—without doing any harm. Charles Jennens,
the compiler of the libretto of the *Messiah*, writes to a
friend : ' I have with great difficulty made him correct
some of the gravest faults in the composition, but he
retained his overture obstinately, in which there are

some passages far unworthy of Handel, but much more unworthy of the *Messiah.*' Yes, whatever its absolute musical value may be, the overture is unworthy (that is, not in keeping with, not up to the height of, the argument) of the *Messiah*, and consequently also unworthy of the composer. The overture to *Belshazzar* has been claimed as a programme overture, but the claim cannot be admitted. Even the utilization of a subject from the body of the work, as in *Joseph*, does not necessarily make an overture programmatic. Handel's incidental symphonies, though more closely connected with the works than the overtures, are nevertheless for the most part neutral, or nearly so, as far as expression goes, being mere harmonious combinations of sounds, spirited and stirring, but not particularly significant. At any rate, the character is not always obvious : it has to be ascertained by a careful consideration of the incidents and circumstances of the plot. Working on a large scale and in a large manner, he was often content to treat things conventionally, indicating his meaning, as it were, by a few quick, broad strokes and splashes of his brush. As instances of such neutral incidental music may be cited the symphonies in the second and third part of *Saul*, which bridge over gaps in the action, but do not depict the events that fill the gaps. The brisk symphony at the beginning of the third act of *Solomon* is, no doubt, meant to picture the brilliant reception of the Queen of Sheba. Descriptive of the intervening event as well as filling a gap in the bustling orchestral movement in *Belshazzar*, is the quaintly named ' Sinfonia Postillions ' (so in the score of the German Handel Society : perhaps the last ' s ' should be an ' e '), which follows the king's

words : ' Call all my wise men, sorcerers, Chaldeans,
astrologers,' &c.   Evidently a whole host of servants at
once go post-haste in search of the desired counsellors.
In *Samson*, preceding Manoah's recitative ' Heav'n !
What noise ! horribly loud,' there is a short symphony
slightly descriptive of the confusion in the Temple of the
Philistines.   *Saul* has a chime symphony, on the theme of
which is based the chorus ' Welcome, mighty king,' that
life-like realization of the joyous excitement of the
Israelites hailing the return of the victorious David.
An example of abstention from tone-painting is to be
found in *Joshua*.   The words ' Sound the shrill
trumpets, shout, and blow the horns,' are followed by a
march for an orchestra including two trumpets and two
horns, but about which there is nothing terrible
whatever.   Of course the Bible tells us only of ' seven
priests bearing trumpets of rams' horns.'   But what of
' the people shouted with a great shout ' ?   Our present-
day composers would have more convincingly shown
why the walls of Jericho fell.   They cannot but regard
Handel as totally blind to one of the most pregnant
opportunities of sensational tone-painting, and guilty of
one of the most flagrant sins of omission of a tone-
painter.   Exceptions, incidental pieces of a higher order,
are the Dead March in *Saul*, and the Pastoral Symphony
in the *Messiah*.

But to see Handel as a soul- and body-painter by
instrumental means, we must turn to the accompaniments
of the vocal parts of his works.   There the orchestra is
often picturesquely and emotionally illustrative, adding
to and reinforcing the expression of the voices.   As
a rule the picturesque body-painting is discreet as well as
effective.   Only the fascination of the feathered songsters

leads the composer sometimes to overstep the line of wise moderation. A famous imitation of the kind is in the sixth scene of the first act of the opera *Rinaldo* (1711). The stage direction runs: 'A delightful place with fountains, avenues, and an aviary in which birds are flying and singing.' Before the singer begins 'Augeletti, che cantate, Zefiretti, che spirate,' we hear a symphony of twenty-five bars in which two flutes and a flauto piccolo play the most important parts; and the piccolo, the representative of the nightingale, concludes the aria with a long warble. Read about this scene Addison's amusing paper in the *Spectator* (No. 5). Of course the reader remembers 'Hush, ye pretty warbling choir,' from *Acis and Galatea* (piccolo and violins), and, what is less certain, may know 'Hark! 'tis the linnet and the thrush,' from *Joshua* (solo violin and flute). Among other compositions of Handel's with ornithological music there is *L'Allegro, Il Pensieroso ed Il Moderato*, a work that is brimful of tone-painting of all sorts. The orchestra tells us of 'loathed melancholy,' of 'deluding joys,' of the spirit of Venus and Bacchus, of the sprightliness, quips, cranks, smiles, and laughter of the Nymphs, of the tripping on the fantastic toe, of the devout, pure, sober, steadfast nun, of Mirth and her crew, of the sweet, musical, melancholy nightingale (flute), of the curfew bell, of the cricket on the hearth, of the running, murmuring brooks and rivers, of the towers and battlements among high-tufted trees, of the merry chimes and the jocund rebecks, of the whispering winds, &c., &c., &c. Turning to *Israel in Egypt* we meet with illustrations of jumping frogs, buzzing midges and flies, the rushing and crashing of hail, darkness, the waters overwhelming the enemy, &c. Very striking tone-painting is to be found in Juno's

recitative in *Semele*, 'Awake, Saturnia,' in connection
with the words: 'And down, down, to the flood of
Acheron, let her fall, fall, fall! rolling down the depths
of night,' where the composer revels in the falling and
rolling,—but the cursing and trembling, too, get their
share of his attention. The mention of the illustration
of falling and rolling reminds one of many questionable
illustrations to be met with in Handel's works. Like
other composers of his time, and earlier times, he could
not easily pass words such as 'ascend' and 'descend'
'high' and 'low,' 'round' and 'rugged' 'flow' and 'roll,'
'bound' and 'walk' 'joy' and 'glory,' &c. If the illustration is in proportion to the importance of the word, there
can be no objection to the proceeding, but sometimes
Handel accentuates and dwells on the subordinate and
inessential. In fact, we find in his works examples as
bad or nearly as bad as those censured in connection with
Purcell's works. In *Joshua*, in the chorus 'Glory to
God,' the words 'The nations tremble' are artistically
illustrated in the instrumental accompaniment, and
inartistically in the vocal parts, where repercussion is
employed, the first syllable of 'tremble' getting five
monotone quavers and the second syllable one. 'And
lovely life with pleasure steals away,' in *Judas Maccabæus*,
ends with a long trailing *coloratura* on the last syllable of
the last word. 'Compassed *round*,' in *Samson*, and the
swift roll and *flow* of Jordan's stream in *Saul* and elsewhere receive insistent and persistent picturing. In these
and other similar illustrations *coloratura* plays a chief
part. Now, there is legitimate and illegitimate *coloratura*.
It is legitimate if it is appropriately expressive, and
illegitimate if it is inappropriately expressive or merely
intended for the display of *bravura*. It is extremely

E

instructive to examine the choral and solo *coloratura* in the *Messiah*. The italicized words are the bearers and inspirers of the *coloratura*. 'And he shall *purify*' (expressive of continual labour); 'For unto us *a Child is born*' (implied *joy*); 'His yoke is *easy*'; 'All we like sheep have gone *astray*'; we have *turned* ev'ry one to his own way'; 'He trusted in God that He would deliver Him if He *delight* in Him'; 'He is the King of *Glory*'; '*Great* was his *company*'; 'Let us break their bonds asunder, and cast *away* their yokes from us'; 'Every valley shall be *exalted*'; 'He shall *shake* them'; 'He is like a *refiner's fire*'; '*Rejoice* greatly'; 'Why do the nations *rage*'; and 'This mortal must put on *immortal*.'

To return to Handel's illustrative accompaniments, the following examples are noteworthy :—' Why does the God of Israel sleep?' in *Samson*, where the orchestra with its scales, trills, and rolling figures paints the excitement of the speaker and illustrates words and phrases such as these : ' Arise with dreadful sound,— thy thunder deep,—the trumpet of the wrath now raise,—in whirlwinds them pursue'; ' Let there be light,' in the same oratorio, where, after the unaccompanied voices, the orchestra strikes in *forte* with brilliant figures ; the Witch of Endor's conjuration and the appearance of Samuel, in *Saul*, where an eerie effect is produced both by the drawing and the colouring (the employment of the bassoons should be specially noticed) ; Joseph's interpretation of Pharaoh's dream, in *Joseph*, with dream-like interludes ; and the chorus ' Scenes of horror, scenes of woe,' in *Jephthah*. Not to be wearisome, I shall add only a few familiar, but beautiful and striking examples from the *Messiah*, a masterpiece, familiarity with which prevents us from appreciating its superlative qualities :

the accompaniments to 'Why do the nations so furiously rage together,' 'All they that see Him, laugh Him to scorn'; 'Thou shalt break them'; 'O thou that tellest glad tidings to Zion'; 'Surely He hath borne our griefs' (expressive of heavy weight); 'And lo! the Angel of the Lord came upon them'; and 'And suddenly there was with the Angel a multitude of the heavenly host.' The last two are given to show how much can be done by a few slight touches—here to suggest the celestial brightness and serenity.

It is to be hoped that the reader is as conscious as the writer of the fact that little has been said of the illustration of the emotional accents and rhythms by the orchestra, and of Handel's most potent means of tone-painting, the voice, which after all is the first of musical instruments. Moreover, whatever critical thoughts may sometimes arise in our minds with regard to Handel's works—about the predominance in them of generic over specific feelings and the limited sympathies of sturdy strength, their conventionalism, and even mannerism, and the lack of inventiveness of instrumental figures—we have to confess that in the master's presence we are silenced by the authoritativeness of his imposing personality, whose every act, word, and tone seems to be exactly what it ought to be if seen from his point of view. Let us, then, turn our backs on criticism, and reverently pay due homage to the man of power, the great genius, and the consummate artist.

J. S. BACH (1685-1750) was in his instrumental music, even in his most recondite fugues, more intent on specific expression, and less easily content with conventionalism, than Handel. A comparison of Bach's and Handel's instrumental compositions brings out a great contrast. You will look in the latter's works in vain for anything that could be placed by the side of the Fantasia and Fugue in G minor for the organ, the Chromatic Fantasia for the clavier, the Chaconne for the violin, and the Air for stringed instruments in the D major orchestral suite. I mention only a few things that every one knows, but I might have continued the enumeration *ad infinitum.* For instance, to how many romantic slow movements in concertos, sonatas, &c., might I not have pointed? Bach's instrumental music displays, on the one hand, emotional intensity and finely differentiated characterization, and, on the other hand, a wealth of artistic inventiveness and ingenuity immeasurably superior to Handel's. What would not Bach have accomplished in the nature of expression if the fugal form and the close contrapuntal texture had not restrained him! For although this form and this texture are favourable to the expression of some states and ideas, they are unfavourable to a much greater number of others. They hamper the freedom of movement even in one who, like Bach, plays with the greatest contrapuntal difficulties. Was not J. S. Bach a clandestine cultivator of programme music? Such a suspicion might easily be justified by strikingly speaking instances from his purely instrumental works, but it could still more easily be justified by the instrumental portions of his vocal works—the overtures; incidental symphonies; preludes, interludes, and postludes; and the accompaniments. What more speaking than the wailing introductory symphony of the opening chorus, 'Come, ye daughters, weep with me,' of the *Passion according to St. Matthew;* than the clanging, warbling, and whirring of the trumpets, flutes, oboes, bassoon, and stringed instruments in the symphonies and accompaniments of the first chorus in the *Christmas Oratorio*, ‘Jauchzet, frohlocket! auf, preiset die Tage’; than the independent orchestral piece, that exquisite and true pastoral symphony, preceding the words ‘Und es waren Hirten in derselben Gegend,’ in the second part of the same work; than the instrumental accompaniments to the chorus in the third part, ‘Lasset uns nun gehen gen Bethlehem,’ in which the impatience of the shepherds to see for themselves what has happened at Bethlehem is well described, especially by the semiquavers of the violins; than the *Sinfonia* of two movements that opens the *Easter Oratorio;* than the *Sinfonia* (*Adagio assai*) prefixed to the Cantata ‘Ich hatte viel Bekümmerniss’; than the long introductory symphony to the first chorus of the *Magnificat!* Returning to the *Passion according to St. Matthew*, let me remind the reader of three excellent examples of programme music : (1.) The rending of the veil of the Temple in the recitative, ‘And behold the veil of the Temple was rent in twain from top unto the bottom’; (2.) The symphonies and accompaniments to the chorus, ‘O man, thy many sins lament’; and (3.) The symphonies and accompaniments to the aria (with violin solo) ‘Have mercy upon me, O Lord.’

But J. S. Bach has left us also an acknowledged example of programme music in the narrow sense of the word. It is the *jeu d'esprit* entitled *Capriccio sopra la lontananza del suo fratello dilettissimo* (*Capriccio* on the departure of his very dear brother), composed at the age of nineteen (1704), with the impression of the recently published Bible Sonatas of Kuhnau fresh in his mind. The superscriptions of the several parts are : (1.) *Arioso, Adagio,* ‘Cajolery by his friends to dissuade him from his journey'; (2.) 'Representation of the different accidents which might befall him in foreign parts'; (3.) *Adagiosissimo,* 'General lament of his friends'; (4.) 'Here his friends, seeing that it cannot be otherwise, take leave of him'; (5.) *Poco Allegro,* 'Air of the Postillion'; and (6.) 'Fugue in imitation of the Postillion's horn.' Delightful and amusing as this *jeu d'esprit* is, it will be readily admitted that an immense deal of the master's instrumental music without published programmes has more significance, is, in short, of a higher order and of a more genuine kind of programme music, than this *capriccio.*

The admirable spirited pieces of DOMENICO SCARLATTI (1685-1757), the contemporary of J. S. Bach and Handel, often conjure up human faces and figures, smiling, laughing, and grimacing, dancing, capering, and frolicking. Nevertheless, the master was no doubt to some extent right when, in the preface to the thirty *Essercizi* published by him, he says : ' Reader, whether you be amateur or professional, do not expect in these compositions profound intention, but rather ingenious sport (*scherzo*) of the art, to perfect yourself in easy freedom (*per addestrarti alla franchezza*) on the harpsichord.' Only we must not accept his statement too literally.

It is one of the greatest mistakes to think that the history of the development of an art can be fully read in the achievements of the few outstanding geniuses whose names are in everybody's mouth. Often—I am not sure whether I ought not to say oftenest—the seeds and germs of progress are to be found in the less perfect works of the minor masters. This truth will be illustrated by some of the composers to whom the reader's attention will now be called.

A slight allusion suffices in the case of GOTTLIEB MUFFAT (1690-1770), and the pieces *La Hardiesse, La Coquette,* and *Menuet en Cornes de Chasse* in his *Componimenti* of 1739 ; a more emphatic allusion is due to CHRISTOPH GRAUPNER and his four clavier suites of 1733, entitled *The Four Seasons ;* and to J. J. FUX— to us best known as the author of the contrapuntal treatise *Gradus ad Parnassum*—and his orchestral suite consisting of an overture celebrating Spring, and move- ments superscribed *Pour Le Rosignol,* Menuet, Passepied, Air, Gigue, *Pour la Caille,* and *Pour le Coucou.*

I must dwell somewhat longer on GEORG PHILIPP TELEMANN (1681-1767), an extraordinarily prolific composer, and one of the most famous musicians of his time. Two orchestral suites of his, the acquaintance with which I owe to Dr. Hugo Riemann, engage our attention, for they are programme music, and the programmes are interesting. One of them is called *Wassermusik* (water music). It begins with an overture in which we cannot fail to recognize a calm, smooth sea in the *Grave* (mark the sustained notes of the oboes, and afterwards of the violins and viola), and a breeze and rippling waves in the *Allegro.* The movements that follow are entitled : (2.) The sleeping Thetis ; (3.) The wakening Thetis ; (4.) The amorous Neptune ; (5.) The playful Naiads ; (6.) The sportive Tritons ; (7.) The stormy Æolus ; (8.) The pleasant Zephyr ; (9.) Ebb and Flood ; and (10.) The merry Mariners. Of still greater interest is the other suite, that which bears the title *Don Quixote.* As the overture has no special title, it may be supposed to have a general character, in other words, to be an introduction to the whole conception of Cervantes. The titles of the remaining members run as follows:

(2.) *La réveille de Quichotte ;* (3.) *Son attaque des moulins à vent ;* (4.) *Les soupirs amoureux après la princesse d'Aline ;* (5.) *Sanche Panche berné* (blanketed) ; (6.) *Le galop de Rosinante ;* (7.) *Celui de l'âne de Sanche ;* and (8.) *Le coucher de Quichotte.* The fancifulness of the titles is here in most cases more striking than their significance. The latter, apart from the overtures, is most apparent in the frolicking No. 6, the boisterous No. 7, and the jolly No. 10 of the Water Music ; and in the bustling, determined No. 3, the sighing No. 4, the tossing and tumbling No. 5, the galloping Nos. 6 and 7 of *Don Quixote.* Telemann shows himself rather a ready and spirited writer than an original and profound one. The amusing externalities are better hit off than the weightier internalities. But one thing ought to be acknowledged, and that is the admirable craftsmanship of men like Telemann, Graupner, and other contemporaries of Bach and Handel. The wider one's acquaintance with their work, the higher they rise in one's esteem.

The spirited and inventive Venetian violinist and composer ANTONIO VIVALDI (*c.* 1680-1743) contributes some extremely interesting examples of programme music. The first three concertos of his Op. 10 have titles : (1.) *La Tempesta di Mare* (Storm on the Sea) ; (2.) *La Notte* (the Night) ; (3.) *Il Gardellino* (*i.e., Cardellino,* the Goldfinch). In addition to these headings, there occur two further superscriptions in the course of the second concerto—*Fantasmi* (Fantasms) over the second movement (*Presto*), and *Il Sonno* (Sleep) over the fifth (*Largo*). As to the tone-painting indicated by these titles, we may say that the somewhat stormy character of the first movement of the first concerto is more likely to have suggested the title, than the idea of a tempest the music.

The second concerto is of a more decidedly programmatic character. The sombreness of the first movement (Night), the eccentric figures of the second (Fantasms), and the softness and vagueness of the fifth, with its winding melodic lines and muted instruments (Sleep), are truly illustrative. Op. 8 is even more interesting than Op. 10. Let us note first the general title: *Il Cimento dell' Armonia e dell' Inventione* (The Trial of Harmony and Invention); and next the passage of the dedication in which the author says that he publishes the four concertos entitled *The Four Seasons* (the first four of the *Opus*) not only with four sonnets but also with a most distinct declaration of all the things set forth in them. Accordingly there follow four sonnets: (1.) *La Primavera* (Spring); (2.) *L'Estate* (Summer); (3.) *L'Autunno* (Autumn); (4.) *L'Inverno* (Winter). These sonnets are divided into lettered parts, and the lettered parts, preceded by a short summary, are placed above those passages of the music to which they apply. Briefly stated the content is as follows :—

Spring.—(*a.*) Spring is come; (*b.*) The festive birds salute it with their merry songs; (*c.*) The fountains run with a soft murmur under the breath of the zephyrs; (*d.*) The sky becomes overcast, and thunder and lightning ensue; (*e.*) When calm is restored, the birds recommence their singing; (*f.*) On the flowery meadow, amidst the rustling of leaves and plants, sleeps the goat-herd with his faithful dog by his side; (*g.*) Pastoral Dance to the sound of the rustic bagpipe.

Summer.—(*a.*) The heat of the sun makes man and flock languid; (*b.*) The cuckoo sings; (*c.*) The dove and the goldfinch; (*d.*) First zephyrs, then suddenly Boreas; (*e.*) Lament of the fearful villager; (*f.*) Fear of lightning and thunder and swarms of flies disturb his repose; (*g.*) The heavens thunder and lighten, and the hail destroys the ears of corn.

Autumn.—(*a.*) The villagers celebrate the harvest festival with dance and song; (*b.*) Bacchus seduces many; (*c.*) Sleep concludes their enjoyment; (*d.*) Dance and song cease and all are wrapped in sweet slumber; (*e.*) The hunters set out at dawn with horns, guns, and dogs; (*f.*) The fleeing quarry is followed; (*g.*) Stunned and tired by the noise of shots and barks, it is wounded; (*h.*) It dies fleeing.

Winter.—(*a.*) Shivering with cold; (*b.*) A terrible wind; (*c.*) Running and stamping from cold; (*d.*) The teeth chatter; (*e.*) Feeling quiet and contented by the fireside, while outside the rain pours down; (*f.*) Walking on the ice; (*g.*) Walking cautiously and timidly; (*h.*) Walking boldly, slipping, and falling; (*i.*) Running boldly on the ice; (*l.*) The ice breaks up and melts; (*m.*) The sirocco; (*n.*) Boreas and all the winds at war. [And farther on in the same section:] This is Spring, bringing with it joy.

In the external and internal tone-painting which Vivaldi seriously attempts in these compositions, he makes use of characteristic accents and figures, frequent *forte, piano,* and *pianissimo* indications, more than usual *legato* and *staccato* markings, and occasional muting of the strings. Compared with his contemporaries, Vivaldi shows himself in several respects in advance of his time.

Of another great violinist and composer for his instrument, FRANCESCO GEMINIANI (1680-1762), mention has to be made both on account of a theory and of a work. I shall quote Sir John Hawkins's account. He writes in his *History of Music* thus: 'About the

same time [about the year 1755] he published what
he called the *Enchanted Forest*, an instrumental
composition, grounded on a very singular notion, which
he had long entertained, namely, that between music
and the discursive faculty there is a near and natural
resemblance ; and this he was used to illustrate by a
comparison between those musical compositions in
which a certain point is assumed in one part and
answered in the other with frequent iterations, and the
form and manner of oral conversation.   With a view to
reduce this notion to practice, Geminiani has endeavoured
to represent to the imagination of his hearers the
succession of events in that beautiful episode contained
in the thirteenth canto of Tasso's " Jerusalem," where, by
the arts of Ismeno, a pagan magician, a forest is
enchanted, and each tree informed with a living spirit,
to prevent its being cut down for the purpose of making
battering-rams and other engines for carrying on the
siege of Jerusalem.'   Hawkins says that the publication
of *The Enchanted Forest* preceded that of the two
numbers of a work entitled *The Harmonical Miscellany*.
Fétis wrongly states that the work is contained in the
Miscellany; but until recently the composition itself
was lost sight of.   Now, however, we know of an
autograph copy at the Royal College of Music, and a
printed one newly acquired by the British Museum.
The   autograph   copy   bears   the   words   ' Gift   of
Francesco Geminiani, the author, to James Mathias,'
and is dated Dec. 7, 1761.   The Italian title runs thus :
La Selva Incantata del Tasso, composizione istrumentale.
The printed copy bears the title : *The Inchanted Forrest.*
An Instrumental Composition Expressive of the same Ideas
as the Poem of Tasso of that Title.   The part for the

horns has, however, the superscription : *La Foresta incantata.* There are parts for first and second violin, first and second *ripieno* violin, first and second viola, violoncello (figured), *basso ripieno* (figured), first and second flute, first and second horn, and trumpet (employed only in the second part). The work consists of two parts, each of which comprises a series of continuous movements—the first of twelve and the second of fourteen movements, varying in length from a few bars, or even one, to as many as over ninety. Apart from the title, there are no programmatic indications either in the way of preface or superscriptions. The music is fresh and pleasing as music ; and if the title were not there to suggest a programme, few would guess that the composer had one in his mind. Nevertheless it would be impossible not to be struck by the expressive qualities of the composition ; and here and there — by a more than usual amount of modulation, by dramatic touches, by passages where thought rather than sweetness seems to be aimed at— the attentive reader or hearer would be led to the conviction that the master is wrestling with expression. Some light may be thrown on Geminiani's views by a passage in his *The Art of Playing on the Violin* (1751). Treating of musical ornaments, he writes : ' This [the Beat] is proper to express several Passions ; as, for example, if it be performed with strength, and continued long, it expresses Fury, Anger, Resolution, &c. If it be play'd less strong and shorter, it expresses Mirth, Satisfaction, &c. But if you play it quite soft, and swell the Note, it may then denote Horror, Fear, Grief, Lamentation, &c. By making it short and swelling the Note, it may express Affection and Pleasure.'

CHAPTER III.

FOURTH PERIOD (18TH CENTURY) CONTINUED : MUSIC TO
PLAYS, PROGRAMMATIC MATTER IN ALL KINDS OF VOCAL AND
INSTRUMENTAL MUSIC AND MELODRAMA—SCHEIBE, AGRICOLA,
ETC., GLUCK, C. PH. E. BACH, HAYDN, AND MOZART,
ROUSSEAU, BENDA, ETC.

Programme music of a more serious kind than that
discussed at the end of the preceding chapter we have in
the music to plays—overtures and *entr'actes*—that began
to be written in the second quarter of the 18th century.
J. A. SCHEIBE (1708-1776) is said to have been the first
to cultivate this field, writing in 1738 music to Corneille's
Polyeucte and Racine's *Mithridate*. He tells us in the
Kritischer Musikus (No. 67, p. 617) that the opening
symphony must refer to the first act; the symphonies
between the acts partly to the close of the preceding and
partly to the beginning of the following act; and the
concluding symphony to the last act. This double
relation of the *entr'actes* has, however, not been
generally adopted by composers. For instance, the later
J. F. Agricola (1720-1774), in his music to Voltaire's
Semiramis, connects the *entr'actes* with the preceding act.
Lessing discusses Agricola's music and the whole subject
of music to plays in his *Hamburgische Dramaturgie* of
July 28, 1767. He condemns *entr'actes* related to the
following act because they anticipate and thereby weaken
the effects of the play. Lessing's view was that in plays
the orchestra takes the place of the antique chorus.
This author also informs us that connoisseurs had long

wished that music to plays should be more in keeping
with the contents. Of other composers who wrote music
to plays may be mentioned : Joh. Christ. Hertel (1726-
1789), with his music to Cronegk's *Olint und Sophronia;*
Michael Haydn (1737-1806), with his music to Voltaire's
Zaïre; Abbé Vogler (1749-1814), with his music to
Shakespeare's *Hamlet;* and Mozart, with his music to
Von Gebler's drama *Thamos, König in Egypten.*

More important and voluminous than the instrumental music to plays is that to operas. Here we meet
now CHRISTOPH WILLIBALD GLUCK (1714-1787),
the reformer, the hero among opera composers. The
utterances of the master that more especially characterize
his mature views on music are a passage in a letter
addressed to J. B. Suard, printed in the *Journal de Paris*
of October 21, 1777, and a passage in the preface to
Alceste, published in 1769. From the former we learn
that Gluck considered 'music not merely as the art
of amusing the ear, but as one of the grandest means of
moving the heart and of exciting the affections.' In the
latter he says : 'I thought that the overture ought to
prepare the spectators for the action about to be
represented, and to form, so to speak, its argument ; that
the instrumental accompaniments should be regulated
according to the interest and passion of the drama.'
Other utterances of his, however, throw additional light
on his views. To Corancez, a Paris acquaintance, Gluck
remarked in conversation : 'When composing, I strive
above all things to forget that I am a musician.' This
somewhat obscure saying may be elucidated by the
following observations from the preface to *Alceste:*
'Again, I have thought that my main task should be to
seek a noble simplicity, and I have avoided parading

difficulties at the cost of clearness. The discovery of any novelty I have considered precious only in so far as it was naturally called forth by the situation, and was in harmony with the expression. Lastly, there is no rule I have not thought it my duty to sacrifice willingly in order to secure an effect.' In another part of the same document Gluck seems to assign a rather low rôle to music : 'I endeavoured to reduce music to its true function, that of supporting the poetry by strengthening the expression of the sentiments and the interest of the situations without interrupting the action or weakening it by superfluous ornaments. It seemed to me that music should do for poetry what the vivacity of colours and the well-matched contrast of light and shade do for a correct and well-proportioned design, which serve to animate the figures without altering their contours.' Here the reformer escapes from the control of the philosopher. The comparison is bad, the balance not being fairly held between poetry and music. Gluck must have come to see this himself, for eight years later he wrote the first of the above quotations, the declaration which speaks of music as the grandest means of moving the heart, that is, speaks of music having immeasurably greater powers than he allowed it to have in the last quotation. Moreover, let us not overlook that the master himself says that he had not always this high idea of the powers of the art he cultivated. For a long time he was a traditionalist and time-server, and wrote conventional Italian operas and French operettas. It was not till the age of forty-eight that he brought out at Vienna his first reform opera, *Orfeo ed Euridice.*

Strange to say, notwithstanding his description of what an opera overture ought to be, only one of the

overtures of his reform operas corresponds with his
description.   The overture to *Orfeo* (1762) is a mere
lively curtain raiser, with no particular appropriateness
to the work to which it is prefixed ; indeed, it is more
appropriate to many another opera than to this.   The
desirableness of overtures essentially connected with
the contents of the operas, of significant premonitory
forewords, does not seem to have presented itself to his
mind until he undertook to write his second reform opera
Alceste, in the preface to which he records his newly-
obtained view of the matter.   But of *Alceste, Paride ed
Elena, Armide,* and *Iphigénie en Tauride,* it cannot be said
that they altogether conform to his prescription.   There
is a connection between the overtures and the operas, but
only to some extent and in some degree.   The overture
to *Alceste* (1767) may be said to picture the sadness of
Alcestis ; and that to *Paride ed Elena* (1769) the pomp
and passion of the Trojan lover, the doubts and regrets
of Helena, and the festive rejoicings.   Marx calls the latter
overture the first of Gluck's that is closely related to the
drama.   The overture to *Armide* (1777) had already
served twice—for *Telemacco* and for *Le Feste d'Apollo.*
The connection therefore can be only of a very general
nature.   As to the overture to *Iphigénie en Tauride*
(1779), a distinctly programmatic composition, it is an
introduction to the first act, not the argument of the
opera.   The programme is indicated by the composer by
means of superscriptions : a Calm, Storm at a distance,
Storm approaches nearer, Rain and Hail, and the Storm
ceases.

Not one of these five overtures, although they are not
without merit, is—what the often played and greatly
admired overture to *Iphigénie en Aulide* is in so eminent

a degree—a poetic conception of the first order, great in
truth, power, and beauty of expression. All of them are
absent from the concert *répertoire,* and nobody mentions
them nowadays even when the operas are discussed.
Altogether different is the overture to *Iphigénie en Aulide*
(1774).   In it Gluck comes before us as the first
composer of a meaningful opera overture.   If you
are in doubt as to the poetic basis of the master's
overture to *Iphigénie en Aulide,* read Richard Wagner's
enthusiastic interpretation of it in his essay *On the
Overture.*   There the later composer says that the earlier
master 'draws the principal thought of the drama in
mighty lines and with an almost obvious distinctness.'
In his *Gluck's Overture to ' Iphigenia in Aulis '* Wagner
describes the content as follows:—(1.) A motive of
Invocation from painful, gnawing heart-sorrow; (2.) A
motive of force, of an imperious, overwhelming
demand; (3.) A motive of grace and maidenly tenderness;
and (4.) A motive of painful, tormenting sympathy.' In
short, the overture is the distillation of the emotional
essence of the drama.

'Though Gluck studies simple nature in his *cantilena,*
or voice part,' says Burney, 'yet in his accompaniments
he is not only often learned, but elaborate, and in this
particular he is an excellent painter; his instruments
frequently delineate the situation of the actor, and give
a high colouring to passion.'   In speaking of 'learned'
and 'elaborate,' the historian is not felicitous in the
choice of his words; for Gluck's accompaniments were
as a rule extremely simple, sometimes even bald, never
learned, and hardly ever elaborate. But Burney was
right in the main : Gluck could on occasion be an
excellent painter.   A few examples of incidental

F

instrumental music and accompaniments from two of
his operas will prove it. In *Orphée* may be pointed
out the pantomime of the mourners at the tomb of
Euridice; the *ritornello* expressive of Orpheus's grief
after the words addressed to his friends, 'I would remain
alone with my sorrow'; the powerfully characteristic
dances of the Furies; the ballet music descriptive of
the peacefulness and blissfulness of the Elysian Fields;
the exquisitely conceived and scored accompaniments to
the quasi-recitative 'How pure the sky, how bright the
sun, how sweet the fluttering sounds of the beautiful
winged singers that are heard in the vale!—the
whispering of the air, the murmuring of the brooklet,
everything inviting here to eternal peace'; and, besides
other matters worthy of attention, the accompaniments
to the gruesome chorus of the Furies, in the second of
which occurs the famous howling of Cerberus, so much
admired by Berlioz. Again, in *Iphigénie* may be pointed
out the mysteriousness of the priest Calchas's
declaration of Diana's will; the plaintive cries of nature
(oboe and bassoon) in Agamemnon's aria 'Peuvent-ils
ordonner'; the quickly-changing thoughts in his
recitative 'Tu décides son sort'; the anger and
indignation in Clytemnestra's aria 'Armez-vous d'un
noble courage'; and the high-strung emotionalism of
her recitative and aria when Iphigenia is led to the
sacrifice, especially the former, which is worthy to be
placed beside Donna Anna's recitative in *Don Giovanni*
on discovering her dead father, and probably was the
inspirer and model of it: 'You hear the cries of a
furious people . . . Mighty gods, I invoke you.
No! no! no! I will not suffer it . . . plunge the knife
into the mother's breast . . . Ah, I faint beneath the

weight of sorrow . . . my daughter . . . I see her
under the inhuman knife . . . her barbarous father
sharpening the knife with his own hands! A priest
surrounded by a cruel crowd dares touch her with his
criminal hand. See, he mangles her breast, and with
his prying eye looks into the palpitating heart, consulting
the will of the gods. Hold your hand! Bloody monsters,
tremble! It is the pure blood of the sovereign of the
gods with which you dare to redden the earth'—
'Mighty Jove, cast forth thy lightning.'

Gluck produces often grand, sublime, and picturesque
effects. Nevertheless both his musical inventiveness
and craftsmanship were very limited. He could write
smoothly and pleasingly, could write naturally and with
ease. Greatness he achieved only by intellectual efforts,
by calculation. In this he differs *toto cœlo* from
his immediate successor, Mozart, distinguished
by unsurpassed spontaneous creativeness as well as by
supreme craftsmanship. One might say paradoxically,
if Gluck had been a greater composer of absolute
music, he would have been a greater composer of
programme music.

J. S. Bach's great, but now too little known and
appreciated son C. PH. E. BACH (1714-1788), one of the
chief propagators of the 'gallant' (elegant) style in
instrumental music (so called in contradistinction to the
grave, contrapuntal style), must, judging by the nature of
his genius and the character of his instrumental music,
have a considerable amount of programme music among
his sonatas and symphonies. Of revealed programmes
we find among his compositions comparatively few.
Among the shorter pieces we meet with titles like those
of the French school: musical portraits with Christian,

family, or characteristic names, such as *La Louise,
La Caroline*, and *La Philippine; La Gleim, La Pot*, and
La Stahl; and *La Journalière, La Sybille, La Complaisante,
La Capricieuse*, and *L'Irrésolue;* or picturings of moods
such as *Les Langueurs tendres*, &c. But he also published
a larger composition with a detailed programme, a trio for
two violins and bass, a Dialogue between a *Sanguinicus*
and a *Melancholicus*. These two dispute with, and
try to convert each other in the first and the second
movement, and the *Melancholicus* gives in at the end of
the latter. In the third movement, they remain at one,
although the *Melancholicus* has lapses into sadness.
The composer describes the course of the dialogue, and
mentions no fewer than forty-two points. C. Ph. E. Bach
does not give titles, still less programmes to his sonatas,
symphonies, and fantasias, but their expressiveness is
such as to make one suspect that there must often have
been something of the sort in the composer's mind.
Reichardt said of a Sonata in F minor presented to him by
the master that, 'thanks to his genius, it was more
speaking, more singing, more ravishing than anything I
can imagine.' The speaking nature of the music shows
itself in the melody generally, but in a particular way in
the recitative-like passages he sometimes introduces.
C. H. Bitter, C. Ph. E. Bach's biographer, found on an
old copy of the Sonata in F minor written in red pencil :
'The April day drawn from nature.' But the most curious
fact bearing on the speaking expression of that master's
music is that the poet H. W. von Gerstenberg wrote two
sets of words to a Fantasia of C. Ph. E. Bach's—'Socrates
drinking the poison cup,' and ' Hamlet's monologue'—and
derived the two differing vocal melodies for the words from
the florid right-hand clavier part. The original clavier

Fantasia appeared in 1753 in the volume of examples
(pp. 19-20) accompanying Bach's *Versuch über die wahre
Art das Clavier zu spielen*, and Gerstenberg's versions with
words in 1787 in C. F. Cramer's *Flora* (Kiel).   All this
can be conveniently studied in the *Vierteljahrsschrift für
Musikgeschichte* of 1891 (Part I., pp. 5-14).   Along with
this let us remember C. Ph. E. Bach's opinion that the
clavier player can, especially by improvisations if they
come from a good musical soul, produce a speaking
expression and quick emotional transitions better than
any other musical performer.   The Fantasia in question
he puts forward as a proof.   But he says also that
the musician to be able to move must himself be moved.
It may not be superfluous to point out the similarity
of the emotional substratum of the two texts, and the
unlikelihood that any sensible person should pretend that
the music expresses the entire contents of the words,
intellectual and emotional. Gerstenberg's example,
however, cannot be recommended for imitation.   It
would not often be possible to find such favourable
conditions and obtain such happy results as he found
and obtained.

Every one, if he has not actually heard, has at
least heard of the tone-painting in *The Creation* and
The Seasons of JOSEPH HAYDN (1732-1809).   In these
works for solo voices, chorus, and orchestra, we find
grand pictures, slight sketches, and descriptive touches ;
and these pictures, sketches, and touches are of all sorts.
The Creation begins with an instrumental introduction
representing Chaos ; and the four parts of *The Seasons*
open with introductions representing respectively
' Transition from Winter to Spring,' ' Dawn,' ' The
peasants' joyous feelings at the rich harvest,' and

'The thick mist with which Winter begins.' Apart from
the innumerable imitations of the expression of the
emotions—the most valuable imitations—we have in
The Creation the picturing of light ('Let there be *light*');
of the throng of hell's black spirits sinking to the deep
abyss; of lightning, thunder, rain, and wind; of
the billowing sea, the flowing river, and the gliding
purling brook; of the roaring lion, the flexible tiger,
and the noble steed; of the peaceful herds and flocks;
of the eagle soaring on mighty pens, the cooing dove,
the merry lark, and the tuneful nightingale; of the
flashing shoal of fish and the immense leviathan; of
the buzzing host of insects; of the sinuous serpent, &c.
In *The Seasons* we have the picturing of fleeing winter
and his howling ruffian winds, the torrents of melting
snow, the tepid air of spring and zephyr's breath; of
the morning light on the mountain tops, the rising sun,
dusky night, and gloomy caves; of the whispering
foliage and murmuring streamlet; of thrilling nerves;
of the ill-omened lich-owl, shrill-voiced cock, bounding
lambkins, sporting fish, twittering birds, chirping cricket,
croaking frogs, bright-coloured insects, and barking
dogs; of the whirring spinning-wheel; of the shepherd's
pipe, the merry fife and drum, the loud hunting horns,
the spaniel roving in search of scent, the fleeing
stag, and the pursuing men, horses, and dogs. Of
the many scenes conjured up vividly before the reader,
I will yet mention the thunderstorm in *The Seasons*
and the moods of nature and man that precede and
follow it. Haydn has been often blamed for his
childlike delight and ready indulgence in the painting
of material things; but it should be acknowledged that
his painting of material things is, far from being

crude, almost always genuinely artistic as well as
sufficiently suggestive, and—although often superfluous
and sometimes unduly prominent—for the most part
discreet, *i.e.*, in subordination to the painting of the
emotions.

But among Haydn's compositions there is a purely
instrumental work that is undoubted programme music
—namely, *The Seven last Words of our Saviour on the
Cross*, which he wrote in 1785 for use in the cathedral of
Cadiz on Good Friday. Originally written for orchestra,*
the master arranged it immediately afterwards for string
quartet, and fifteen years later transformed it into a
cantata. The work consists of seven *Adagios* illustrating
the seven sentences spoken by Christ from the Cross:
'Father, forgive them; for they know not what they do.'
'Verily I say unto thee, to-day shalt thou be with me in
Paradise.' 'Woman, behold thy son; and thou, behold
thy mother.' 'My God, my God, why hast thou
forsaken me.' 'I thirst.' 'It is finished.' 'Father,
into thy hands I commend my spirit.' The conclusion
is formed by a *Presto*, entitled 'The earthquake'; for
does not St. Matthew say: 'The earth did quake, and the
rocks rent'? Haydn, in a letter to the publisher Forster,
writes: 'The last words of the Saviour are expressed in
such a manner by instrumental music that the deepest
impression must be awakened in the most inexperienced.'

After this the question will be asked: 'How about
the sonatas, trios, quartets, and symphonies?' Well,
none of them have explicit programmes, and only a few
of the symphonies have titles. Some of these titles,
however, do not indicate a programme; nor are we able

---

* The composer produced it in London under the title of *Passione
instrumentale.*

to tell which were given by the composer and which by others. The *Maria Theresa* Symphony is so called because it was played before that Empress ; *La Reine de France*, no doubt, because it pleased Queen Marie Antoinette ; and the *Oxford* because it was performed there on the occasion of the composer's receiving the honorary degree of doctor of music. The *Surprise* Symphony owes its title to the kettledrum effect in the *Andante ;* The *Clock* Symphony to the tic-tac in the *Andante ;* the *Roxelane* Symphony to the utilization of the French romance of the same name in the *Andante ; L'Ours* and *La Chasse* to the character of the last movement ; and the *Military* Symphony to the character of the second movement. Why another symphony bears the title *La Poule* is not known. The *Farewell* Symphony was a musical petition to Prince Esterhazy not to keep the band any longer at his palace in Hungary, and away from Vienna and their families. The programme music is in the last two movements, during the latter of which the members of the band one by one depart, till at last only two violinists are left. Noteworthy are the three early symphonies *Le Midi, Le Matin*, and *Le Soir.* As to the programmes of the symphonies with the following titles, they are unknown : *Laudon, The Schoolmaster, Lamentations, Il Distratto, The Philosopher*, &c. It is of course impossible to gather from titles to what extent Haydn was a programme composer. His biographers, however, throw some light on this subject.

Griesinger (see his *Biographische Notizen über Haydn*, 1810) was told by Haydn : ' I sit down to the pianoforte, and begin to extemporize, sadly or joyously, gravely or playfully, as my mood happens to be. When I have

laid hold of an idea my whole endeavour aims at
elaborating and sustaining it in accordance with the rules
of the art.'   But the master also told his biographer
that he had often depicted moral characters in his
symphonies ; and that in one of the oldest of them the
ruling idea was how God spoke with a hardened sinner,
and begged him to mend his ways, but without making
any impression. The poet Giuseppe Carpani, another
biographer, relates (in *Le Haydine ovvero Lettere sulla
vita e le opere del celebre maestro Giuseppe Haydn*, 1812
and 1823) that Haydn, after washing and dressing
as if he were going out, began his work by
' weaving a kind of romance or programme on which to
hang the musical ideas and colours.'   In this way he both
stimulated his imagination and directed it into a given
channel. On one occasion the composer imagined a friend,
rich in a large family and poor in worldly goods, setting
out for America to improve his circumstances, succeeding
in his project, and returning in safety. The principal
vicissitudes of this enterprise formed the subject of the
symphony: Embarcation of the adventurer ; departure
of the vessel with a favourable wind, and the lamentation
of the family and the good wishes of the friends on shore ;
a prosperous voyage; arrival in strange lands; barbarous
sounds, dances, and voices are heard (about the middle
of the symphony) ; after an advantageous exchange of
merchandise the homeward voyage is entered upon ;
propitious winds blow (return of the first motive of
the symphony), then a terrible storm supervenes
(a confusion of tones and chords) ; cries of the passengers,
roaring of the sea, whistling of the wind (the melody
passes from the chromatic to the pathetic); fear and
anxiety of the wretched voyagers (augmented and

diminished chords, and semitone modulations); the elements become calm again; the wished-for country is reached; joyful reception by family and friends; general happiness. Although Haydn had pointed it out to him, and Pichl had cited it, Carpani did not remember what symphony this was. In another symphony, which the biographer likewise failed to identify, Haydn is said to have given a dialogue between God and an obstinate sinner, 'shadowing forth in it the parable of the prodigal son.' 'And,' adds Carpani, 'in this way were produced other symphonies, to which, without saying why, Haydn assigned names that without the explanation now given would appear unintelligible and ridiculous.' Of the titles indicative of the little romances on which the composer worked, Carpani quotes the following: *The beautiful Circassian Girl, Roxelane, Grecian Helena, The Solitary, The Schoolmaster, Persiana, The Poltroon, The Queen,* and *Laudon*.

The conclusion to be drawn from Haydn's works and the testimony of his biographers is that, apart from the obvious tone-painting, there must be a not inconsiderable portion of his compositions that cannot be called absolute music in the strict sense of the word, that is, in the sense of being unconnected with and uninfluenced by anything definite outside the tones themselves.

WOLFGANG AMADEUS MOZART (1756-1791), who came into the world twenty-four years after Haydn and left it eighteen years before him, has given to it no symphonies, sonatas, or other instrumental compositions with titles, and only one account has come down to us of his having at any time had a programme in his mind. Still, Mozart was a composer of programme music— in the overtures to his operas, in the *entr'actes* to

T. Ph. von Gebler's drama *Thamos, König in Egypten*,
and in the melodramatic pieces in his opera *Zaïde*. His
overture to *Don Giovanni* has impelled many to attempt
a programmatic exposition, among others E. T. A.
Hoffmann in No. 4 of the *Phantasiestücke*. The sub-title
of Beaumarchais's comedy *Le mariage de Figaro*, which
supplied the subject for Mozart's *Le Nozze di Figaro*,
suggests the programme of the overture to that opera—
La folle Journée. In the overture to *Die Zauberflöte* we
cannot fail to recognize its connection with the opera at
least in the solemn calls of the trombones, but the
connection by no means stops there. Richard Wagner,
in his essay *On the Overture*, makes the following
striking remarks : 'After Gluck it was Mozart that gave
the Overture its true significance. Without toiling to
express what music neither can nor should express, the
details and entanglements of the plot itself—which the
earlier Prologue had endeavoured to set forth—he
grasped the leading thought of the drama with the eye
of a veritable poet, stripped it of all the inessential and
accidental of the factual occurrence, and reproduced it in
the transfiguring light of music as a passion personified
in tones, a counterpart both justifying that thought
and intelligibly explaining the dramatic action to the
hearer's feeling.' The superscriptions of the *entr'actes*
to *Thamos* testify to the correctness of the above
classification, as they point to the last scene of the
preceding act and its content. Moreover, there are among
Mozart's purely instrumental compositions others than
those already mentioned whose spiritual consistency and
speaking expressiveness make one suspect inspiration by
something definite, at least by a definite and perhaps
also conscious mood or series of moods, and not

improbably sometimes even by a conscious train of thoughts or impressions. I may mention as particularly striking instances of such compositions the G minor Symphony, and the C minor Fantasia and A minor Rondo for pianoforte. But we have at least one instance of unquestionable programme music in Mozart's instrumental works—and an extremely interesting and significant one, a case of portraiture. In the latter part of 1777 he writes from Mannheim to his father that he had composed a sonata for Cannabich's daughter Rosa, a beautiful and amiable girl of fifteen;* and that on being asked by someone, after finishing the first movement, how he would write the *Andante,* he had replied: 'I shall compose it after the *caractère* of Mlle. Rose.' He was himself thoroughly pleased with the result, for he said : 'She is exactly like the *Andante.*' What she was like we may see still more clearly from the following words of the composer: 'She has a staid manner and a great deal of sense for her age ; she does not speak much, but what she says is said with grace and sweetness.' The sonata is supposed to be that in C major with a *Rondo* as its last movement (Köchel, 309).† But in spite of all it has to be admitted that, generally speaking, Mozart's instrumental music is more absolute than that of any of his peers since the middle of the 18th century. None of them gave freer play to tonal beauty for tonal beauty's

---

* Otto Jahn says 'thirteen.'

† The sonata in question was composed in the first half of November, 1777, but we cannot be sure which one it is. For the C major Sonata speak excellent authorities; J. S. Shedlock, on the other hand, mentions the A minor Sonata (Köchel, 310). The only and insufficient hints we get from Mozart are that the *Andante* is full of expression, and that the last movement is a *Rondo.*

sake, and submitted more fully to the supremacy of form. Nevertheless it is equally true that he was at no time a cold formalist, but always infused into his formally wonderfully varied compositions at the very least a gentle warmth of sentiment, of tenderness, melancholy, or gaiety. As a programme composer Mozart shines most brilliantly in opera. Note here how he takes up and improves upon every hint of the librettist; but note also how, unlike Haydn, he does not readily indulge in the imitation of external material things. Where, however, Mozart imitates, he only indicates slightly, as, for instance, in the greatest of his operas, in the fight of the Commandant and Don Giovanni (the flashing of the swords and the fall), and in the second finale the heavy step of the Guest and his knocking at the door. The imitation of the beating of the heart in Zerlina's aria ' Vedrai carino,' here playfully introduced, brings us to the imitation of the physical phenomena that accompany the emotions, which Mozart, the subtle psychologist, does not neglect. *Le Nozze di Figaro* is full of illustrative, suggestive, and expository tone-painting. I shall mention only a humorous example, Basilio's aria of the ass's skin. To show you the master as a composer of programme music in all his sublimity I point to Donna Anna's accompanied recitative in the first act of *Don Giovanni,* when she finds her dead father, ' Ma qual mai s' offre, oh Dei, spettacolo funesto agli occhi miei ' (What is this I behold ?), and the following duet. This one composition is indeed a more eloquent and convincing proof of the expressive power of music than can be furnished by a hundred volumes of excellent reasoning. Who would not agree with the concluding words of the remarks which Mozart made when on November 8, 1777, he was going to congratulate his father on his birthday! 'I cannot write poetry : I am not a poet. I cannot artfully group phrases so as to give light and shade : I am not a painter. I cannot even express my thoughts and sentiments by signs and pantomime : I am not a dancer. But I can do so by tones : I am a musician.'

We have now to consider a species of music which has played a significant and stimulating part in the history of programme music and the development of musical expression—namely, Melodrama, in the sense of music accompanying the spoken word. JEAN JACQUES ROUSSEAU, the Geneva philosopher, prose poet, and musician, wrote in the sixties of the 18th century *Pygmalion*, a lyric scene in prose intended to be recited and acted on the stage, with instrumental music accompanying not the words, but the actor's pantomime during the pauses between the words. Here are a few indications of the music asked for by the poet. 'The first piece, like the overture with which it is connected, depicts the dejection, uneasiness, vexation, and despondency of Pygmalion.' When he begins to speak, the orchestra remains silent until, after some sentences, he throws down his tools in disgust, walks up and down, with his arms crossed, dreaming. 'The music expresses with rapidity the first of these movements, slackens gradually, and ends with dull tones thrown out at intervals.' In other places the author asks for : 'Some bars which depict a tender melancholy'; 'Perplexity and incertitude are expressed by some measures interrupted by silences'; 'This pantomime (the unveiling of the statue of Galatea) commences in silence : a single stroke of the bow marks the moment when the veil falls from the hands of Pygmalion'; and 'the music assumes [when, the statue having become animated, Galatea steps from the pedestal towards Pygmalion] a livelier character, is interrupted by some silences, expresses the timid desire, the emotion of Galatea, the ardour, the intoxication of Pygmalion, and does not cease until he presses the hand of Galatea to his heart.'

The first performance of this work took place at Lyons in 1770. The music employed on that occasion was by the Lyons amateur Horace Coignet, if that gentleman's account may be trusted. His music certainly was used when *Pygmalion* was produced in Paris in 1775. Two pieces in it were, however, by Rousseau. The originator of this new species justifies his invention by saying that the French language, being entirely without accents, is unsuitable for music, and especially for recitative, and that consequently he contrived a kind of drama in which words and music, instead of going together, follow each other, and the spoken phrase is, in a way, indicated and prepared by the musical phrase. Rousseau was not blind to one great drawback of such a combination— namely, the disagreeable contrast between the *speech* of the actor and the *music* of the accompanying orchestra, a contrast which, however, should and could be mitigated by approximating the declamation to music, that is, by heightening its accents and varying its tones. A drawback not mentioned by Rousseau is that the music of a melodrama consists of a series of snatches, which cannot by any possibility be moulded into a continuous and harmonious whole. No doubt, as a rule the music in melodrama does not, as Rousseau demands, altogether cease during the speaking ; but what goes on during the speaking is rarely more than a sustained chord or two, the really important and descriptive matter being reserved for the breaks in the recitation. However, the evils of fragmentariness and disconnectedness can be greatly mitigated by judicious and ingenious management. Coignet's music, though popular in Paris, was of no artistic value. In 1780 Antoine Laurence Baudron wrote new music to Rousseau's words, and Ch. H. Plantade did so again in 1822. German translations of *Pygmalion* came out as early as 1771, and German composers were not slow in writing new music— Aspelmeier in Vienna in 1772, and Anton Schweitzer and Georg Benda in Middle Germany respectively in 1777 and 1780. The above-mentioned Baudron wrote also music to Larive's melodrama *Pyrame et Thisbé* (1781).

But it was in Germany that the *genre* was most popular and most successfully cultivated. *Facile princeps* of the melodramatic composers was GEORG BENDA (1722-1795), who in 1775 wrote music to Brandes's *Ariadne auf Naxos* (after a poem of Gerstenberg's), and subsequently to Gotter's *Medea*, and to *Almansor und Nadine*, a mixed composition including arias and choruses. His setting of *Pygmalion* has already been mentioned. J. F. Reichardt treated melodramatically Ramler's *Ino*, and *Cephalus und Procris;* Neefe, Meissner's *Sophonisbe;* Franz Danzi, a *Cleopatra;* Abbé Vogler, Lichtenberg's *Lampedo;* C. Eberwein, Goethe's *Proserpina;* Fr. W. Rust, Schink's *Ynkle und Yariko;* Zumsteeg, Klopstock's *Frühlingsfeier;* and later on Reissiger, *Yelva;* and Lintpaintner, *Hero and Leander.*

On hearing a melodrama for the first time, MOZART tells his father in a letter of November 12, 1778:

'Nothing ever surprised me so much . . . it is music like *recitativo obbligato* . . . Sometimes the speaking goes on during the music, which produces a magnificent effect. I love the two works [Benda's *Ariadne* and *Medea*] so much that I always carry them about with me . . . Do you know what my opinion is? Most recitatives in opera should be treated thus.' Mozart occupied himself with the composition of a melodrama, *Semiramis*, and may have finished it; but nothing further is now known of it. The only specimens of Mozart we have in this *genre* are to be found in the serious operetta *Zaïde* (1780-1781). As he did not again make use of this form, the composer must have changed his opinion. While the cultivation of the melodrama as an independent form was of short duration, its introduction into operas and plays by the great composers—Beethoven, Weber, Marschner, Mendelssohn, Schumann, &c.— saved it from oblivion. Later on in the 19th century it reappeared, however, as an independent form, more especially as a pianoforte accompaniment to poems—Schumann, Liszt, Mackenzie, Richard Strauss, among others, cultivating the *genre*.

G

CHAPTER IV.

More important than the history of the melodrama, and at least equally interesting, is that of the programme symphony. There are still people who believe that Berlioz was the founder of serious programme music and the first writer of programme symphonies. What Beethoven and others after him did in this respect they look upon as merely tentative and half-hearted. In this they are wrong. But they are still further from the truth in imagining that nothing of the sort was thought of in the ante-Beethoven times. We have already examined Haydn's position. FRANÇOIS JOSEPH GOSSEC (1734-1829), who published his first symphony in 1754 (five years before Haydn produced his first), wrote (about 1770) a symphony entitled *La Chasse*, which soon became and long remained popular. The first and the last movement are in *Tempo di Caccia*, and three of the four movements, the first, second, and fourth, are in 6/8 time. A quarter of a century later ÉTIENNE NICOLAS MÉHUL (1763-1817) modelled his famous Hunting Overture to the opera *Le jeune Henri* (1797) to a certain extent on the last movement of Gossec's symphony. Whilst the good republicans hissed the opera off the stage, on account of the presence of a king among the *dramatis personæ*, they encored the overture. Hunting symphonies were very numerous in the second half of the 18th century. Besides Gossec, Leopold Mozart, Stamitz, Roessler, P. Maschek, Wranitzky, Hofmeister, Sterkel, and others, supplied this article for which there was so great a demand. Equally numerous or nearly so were the battle symphonies. I shall mention only one—Franz Christian Neubauer's Grand Symphony, Op. 11, *La Bataille de Martinestie, à la Gloire de S. A. Msgr. le Prince de Saxe Cobourg* (1794), generally called simply *La Bataille*, and sometimes referred to as Coburg's victory over the Turks (*i.e.*, in 1780). Battle symphonies naturally lead to peace symphonies. Paul Wranitzky (1756-1808)—whom I have already mentioned as the composer of a hunting symphony — produced, besides two Coronation Symphonies, a *Characteristic Symphony for the Peace with the [French] Republic* (1797), scored for twenty-one instruments, with an explicit printed programme.

It cannot be difficult to find subjects of greater interest for us than hunts, battles, and peace celebrations. The titles of a series of nine and of a series of three symphonies by WENCESLAS PICHL (1741-1805), respectively called *Les neuf Muses* and *Les trois Graces*, seem to be fancy names rather than indications of programmes. It is otherwise with three of FRANZ ANTON HOFMEISTER'S six symphonies published in 1791,—*La Primavera* (Spring), *La Chasse*, and *La Festa della Pace* (the celebration of Peace); and especially with two works by FRANZ ANTON ROESSLER, or ROSETTI (1750-1792), who, besides *La Chasse* already alluded to, wrote a grand Imitative Symphony, *Calypso et Télémaque*, performed at Paris

in 1791, and another, entitled *La Chute de Phaéton.*
Further, mention may be made of a symphony in
E flat major by IGNAZ HOLZBAUER (1711-1783),
the last movement of which is entitled *La Tempesta
del Mare.*

A higher degree of the climax of my enumeration is
formed by the symphonies of CARL DITTERS VON
DITTERSDORF (1739-1799), the subjects of which he
took from Ovid's *Metamorphoses.* They are, as far as
our present knowledge goes, the best and most interesting
programme music in the symphonic form that was
written in the ante-Beethoven time. Their time of
production is supposed to be 1783-1785. In his autobiography *(Carl von Dittersdorf's Lebensbeschreibung)*—
dictated to his son, and edited by J. C. Gottlieb Spazier*
—the composer says: ' Three years ago I hit upon
the idea of writing some characteristic symphonies on
subjects from Ovid's *Metamorphoses,* and on my arrival
at Vienna [1786] I had twelve of the kind ready.' He
went to Vienna, as we learn from the same source, for
the purpose of producing his new oratorio *Job,* but had
also performed the first six of his Ovid symphonies at a
concert in the Augarten, and the other six a week
later at the theatre. The available information is
rather confusing, and not always so easily cleared up
as the following point : Did Dittersdorf compose
twelve or fifteen Ovid symphonies ? In Gerber's *Lexikon*
(1790) we read that Probst Hermes wrote in a press
notice : 'His 15 symphonies, which contain what he
felt in reading those poems.' No doubt ' fifteen ' is a
misprint, and should have been ' twelve '; for Hermes

---

* There is an English translation of this work by A. D. Coleridge :
The Autobiography of Karl von Dittersdorf.

wrote an analysis of twelve symphonies. The same *Lexikon* informs us also that 'Dittersdorf not only brought his symphonies to a hearing at Vienna in 1785 [1786] with extraordinary applause from connoisseurs and non-connoisseurs, from high and low, but that he himself saw to their publication, which was generally desired.' As to the publication of these works, we know this: Hermes's *Analysis*, dated 1786, is said to have been issued with the first-published part of the symphonies. The author states in it that the composer had sold them to a publisher, and that their publication was secured by subscribers. The Vienna publisher Artaria engraved three, and three more were for sale in manuscript. The Berlin publisher Torcelli printed the first three about the end of the 18th century; the second three were discovered in manuscript at the Dresden Royal Library in 1898; the Gebrüder Reinecke of Leipzig published the first six, edited by Josef Liebeskind, in 1899; and the other six (VII.-XII.) are lost. The subjects of the lost ones we learn from Hermes's *Analysis.** They are:

VII. *Jason carries off the Golden Fleece.*
VIII. *The Siege of Megara.*
IX. *Hercules is translated to Olympus among the gods.*
X. *Orpheus and Euridice.*
XI. *Midas as judge between Pan and Apollo.*
XII. *Ajax and Ulysses contend for the armour of Achilles.*

---

* Johann Timotheus Hermes, a clergyman at Breslau, author of the novel *Sophiens Reise von Memel nach Sachsen* (1769-1773), and a friend of Dittersdorf's, wrote the *Analyse de XII. Metamorphoses Tirées d'Ovide, et mise en musique par Mr. Charles-Ditters de Dittersdorf* in French. In 1899 Georg Thouret published a German translation of it, preceded by a sketch of the composer's life and works.

The subjects of the six republished symphonies are :

I. *The four Ages of the World.*

II. *The Fall of Phaeton.*

III. *The Transformation of Actæon into a Stag.*

IV. *The Rescue of Andromeda.*

V. *The Lycian Peasants transformed into frogs.*

VI. *The turning into stone of Phineus and his friends.*

The structure and texture of these symphonies of Dittersdorf's are those of the classical form of the Haydn-Mozart period. By this is meant that with regard to periodicity, distribution of keys, disposition of subjects, grouping of parts, and thematic development, he worked on the same principles, not that he always adhered to the orthodox cut of the sonata, rondo, and lesser forms, and the orthodox sequence of the movements. All the symphonies consist of four movements, or rather divisions; and each has one movement in regular first-movement sonata form. But the movement in sonata form is not always the first division; in the first and the fourth Symphony the opening division is an independent slow movement not in first-movement sonata form. The forms of the slow movements and the minuets are the usual ones. Excepting that of the third Symphony, all the *finales* consist of two or more movements loosely joined together. They differ from each other, and do not belong to any of the named types of form. They may be said to be in free form, or, better, in forms dictated more or less by the poetic contents. In some cases, however, the concluding movement of the *finale* seems to be outside the programme, put there for the purpose of providing a cheerful ending.

In nearly all cases the several divisions have prefixed to them a few words from Ovid's *Metamorphoses*, with the number of book and line.   These superscriptions are not so much mottoes as indications of the places where the programmes may be found.   There is a great deal of tone-painting, and really excellent tone-painting, in these symphonies, but extremely little of what is popularly so-called, namely, imitation of sounds in nature.   The objects of the composer's painting are moods and feelings, and scenes and actions in their brightness or darkness, their rest or movement, their swiftness or slowness, their precipitance or reluctance, their vigour or languor, their roughness or smoothness, &c., &c.   In the first Symphony, Dittersdorf characterizes *The four Ages of the World*—the golden, the silver, the brazen, and the iron — and succeeds especially in depicting the innocence and eternal spring of the first and the hardness of the last.   A more ambitious theme is that of the second Symphony, *The Fall of Phaeton*. Whilst in the first we have solely painting of character, we have here a great deal of description and action, more especially in the first and the last division.   In the former he brings out in a masterly manner the brilliancy and grandeur of ' the Palace of the Sun raised on stately columns,' and in the latter the rush, tumult, and confusion of ' Jupiter, thundering aloud, and darting the poised lightning from the right ear against the charioteer, at the same time depriving him of his life and his seat, and by his ruthless fire restraining the flames.'   *The Transformation of Actæon into a Stag* presents us with four exquisitely painted pictures : First, Actæon and his companions wandering along the lonely haunts ; then, Diana bathing ; next, Actæon entering the grove where Diana is bathing; and, lastly, Actæon hunted and torn by his own dogs. Everything is as vivid as it is charming. The imitation of the barking and tearing of the dogs will be noticed, but not disapproved. It is one of the few imitations of the material kind. In the two slow movements of *The Rescue of Andromeda,* the composer pictures, no doubt, first her grace and sweetness, and afterwards her anguish; in the other two he certainly pictures Perseus 'cleaving the liquid air with his winged ankles' and his fight with the sea-monster (first half of the *finale*), and reception by the parents of Andromeda. The contents of *The Transformation of the Lycian Peasants into frogs* may be indicated thus : (1.) The gathering of bulrushes by the peasants ; (2.) A dialogue between Latona asking for water to slake her thirst and the rude peasants refusing it ; (3.) Probably the beseeching of Latona and the jeers and laughter of the peasants; and (4.) The transformation of the peasants, preceded by Latona's prayer to Jove, and ending with a *coda* in which the croaking of the frogs is heard. The four divisions of *The Turning into stone of Phineus and his friends* are concerned with the wedding of Perseus and Andromeda ; the dying Lycabas looking around for Athin ; Iapetides singing to the lyre ; and the fight, finished by Perseus holding up the Gorgon's head. The movement that concludes the *finale* is one of the cheerful endings outside the programme.

Besides the six Ovid symphonies the Gebrüder Reinecke have published another example of Dittersdorf's programme music, namely, a *Divertimento,* a suite of pieces, entitled *Il Combattimento dell' umane Passione,* the eight numbers of which bear the superscriptions

Il Superbo (the proud one), *L'Umile* (the humble one),
Il Matto (the mad one), *Il Dolce* (the gentle one),
Il Contento (the contented one), *Il Costante* (the constant
one), and *Il Vivace* (the lively one)—all very
characteristic and pleasing, but, of course, less interesting
than the symphonies.

To analyse, describe, and appraise Dittersdorf's six
programme symphonies would be a pleasing task and
one worth doing, but space cannot be found for it here.
A few general remarks on the music and the composer
must suffice. The 'Actæon' Symphony seems to me the
most perfect. Next to it I place the 'Lycian' and the
'Phaeton' Symphonies. But all are full of beauties and
points of interest. They well deserved to be reprinted,
and well deserve to be read and played. I am sure that
if presented in a proper manner and in suitable
surroundings, they will not fail to be heard with pleasure.
In fact, I had proof of this at the Edinburgh University
Historical Concerts, where two of them were performed
under my direction by a small orchestra in a moderately-
sized hall, and were not preceded and followed by
compositions of the modern sensational type. The style
of the symphonies is that of a facile, but not of a careless
or insipid writer. Dittersdorf had not the powerful genius
and the pronounced originality of a Haydn, a Mozart, or
a Beethoven, but the freshness and abundance of his ideas
and his dexterous handling of the form, prove that he was
more than a mere man of talent; that, in fact, he too
was a genius, only much less exalted than the three
sublimities. What is especially noteworthy about his
programme music is the entire absence of straining after
effects, although piquant, touching, and powerful effects
are not wanting; and, further, that however descriptive

the music is, it never ceases to be good music from the absolute point of view. Dittersdorf is one of those composers who are over-estimated in their lifetime, and under-estimated, if remembered at all, afterwards. To be looked upon as a rival of Mozart, and to have his music more highly valued than Mozart's by many, the Emperor Joseph included, and then to fall well-nigh into complete oblivion, is a sad fate. Who knows nowadays anything of Dittersdorf's oratorios and operas? Only in Germany they still remember one of the latter, the humorous *Doctor und Apotheker*. Of late, however, we hear occasionally one of his numerous string quartets. But that was all that seemed to remain of him, until, in the last year of the 19th century, a hundred years after his death, the compositions above discussed and a few more were published. Some of Dittersdorf's works, as indeed also those of many forgotten composers, are worthy of a revival. We really stand sorely in need of simple, joyous, and wholesome music. But even if we have no inclination to revive much of his work, we ought to revive the memory of the jovial master who gave to many so much pleasure.

The highest degree of the climax is reached on coming to a work the programme of which is almost identical with that of Beethoven's Pastoral Symphony—I mean the grand symphony of JUSTIN HEINRICH KNECHT (1752-1817), entitled *Portrait musical de la Nature*, and published in 1784.* One can hardly believe one's eyes in reading the following words, in which the composer sets forth his intentions :—

'(1.) A beautiful country, where the sun shines, gentle zephyrs frolic, brooks cross the valley, birds twitter, a

* A copy of the work is in the Library of the Royal College of Music.

torrent falls from the mountain, the shepherd pipes, the lambs gambol, and the sweet-voiced shepherdess sings.

' (2.) Suddenly the sky darkens, an oppressive closeness pervades the air, black clouds gather, the wind rises, distant thunder is heard, and the storm slowly approaches.

' (3.) The tempest bursts in all its fury, the wind howls and the rain beats, the trees groan, and the streams rush furiously.

' (4.) The storm gradually passes, the clouds disperse, and the sky clears.

' (5.) Nature raises her joyful voice to heaven in songs of gratitude to the Creator.'

Knecht published (in 1794) also *The shepherds' merry-making interrupted by a thunder storm, a musical picture for the organ ;* and from Gerber's *Lexikon* we learn that he composed two symphonies the subjects of which were *Don Quixote* and *the Death of Prince Leopold of Brunswick*, and one of several pianoforte pieces on stanzas from Wieland's *Oberon.* Knecht—who published theoretical books as well as vocal and instrumental works, and had the reputation of being an excellent organist, pianist, violinist, and a second Kirnberger in learning, and more than that in practical composition— lived as organist and musical conductor in the free-town of Biberach, now a part of Würtemberg. It is a notable fact with regard to him that he founded an orchestral society whose concerts, which were still going on in 1790, differed in three particulars from the customs of the day : firstly, the programmes consisted only of three compositions—a symphony, an *intermezzo,* and another symphony ; secondly, the compositions played at the concerts were carefully rehearsed on the preceding day ;

and, thirdly, printed information was given about these compositions. This last point will be noted by those who take an interest in the history of the annotated programme.

I spoke of Knecht's *Le Portrait de la Nature* as the highest degree of the climax of my enumeration of programme symphonies, but I did so simply because of the nature of the programme and the stimulating effect it may have had, and I think it really had, on Beethoven. As to the composition, it is poor as music and poor as description. We need not hesitate in declaring Knecht's originality to be *nil*, his inventiveness extremely limited, his melody and harmony jejune, his developing obvious, and his form monotonous and pithless. He was a well-trained, intelligent, industrious, and worthy craftsman, but decidedly not a composer by the grace of God. The work comprises, in accordance with the programme, five divisions of unequal length. Not one of its movements is in first-movement sonata form, although the first and the third of the first division could, by a stretch of the imagination, be regarded as respectively the exposition and the abbreviated recapitulation of the exposition of that form. The first and most satisfactory division consists of five continuous movements, which we will distinguish by the first five letters of the alphabet. Here is a short summary of the composition :—

I.—(*a*) *Allegretto*, 4/4, beginning in G and ending in D major. We cannot fail to recognize the serenity of nature, the calls of the cuckoo and quail, the twittering of other birds, and the murmuring of brooks.

(*b*) *Andante pastorale*, 3/8, in D major. Gambols of the lambs, and piping of the shepherd.

(c) *Allegretto*, 4/4, G major, with modulation to C. The same subject-matter as in (a).

(d) *Villanella graziosa, un poco Adagio*, 2/2, C major. The song of the shepherdess.

(e) *Allegretto*, 4/4, G major.   The same subject-matter as in (a).

From this analysis the reader will understand that the musical as well as the poetical subject-matter are the same in (a), (c), (e), although there are, of course, modifications and variations.

II.—A single movement: *Tempo medesimo*, 4/4, G major, modulating finally to the dominant of D major. The music hardly illustrates what the programme promises.

III.—*Allegro molto*, 4/4, D major. This contains a most unconvincing thunderstorm.

IV.—*Tempo medesimo*, 4/4, D major. Even duller than any of the preceding parts, and not more expressive.

V.—*L'Inno con variazioni: Andantino*, 4/4, G major. *Coro: Allegro con brio*, 3/4, D major; and *Andantino*, 4/4, G major. The only thing interesting about this is the title ' Hymn.'

There can be no comparison between Knecht's and Beethoven's Pastoral Symphony, because the former is nothing and the latter everything. But apart from the resemblance of the programmes one cannot but be struck by the similarity of the moods and even by other similarities ; for instance, the relationship of the opening *ranz des vaches* motive of Knecht's first and Beethoven's last movement; the introduction of the cuckoo and quail; and the title of the last movement and the use of variation made in it. Enough of Knecht and his *Portrait de la Nature* for the present ! We may recur to them in connection with Beethoven's Pastoral Symphony.

We have seen symphony composers inspired by hunting, by war, by public ceremonials, and by the ancient classics. To these sources we have to add Shakespeare, for among the subjects treated by them we find *King Lear*. It would be a mistake to omit the mention of a work of a sacred character, one that reminds us of Haydn's *The seven last Words of our Saviour on the Cross*, and probably was suggested by it—namely, the compositions on the *Lord's Prayer*, consisting of seven characteristic sonatas with an introduction for nine-part orchestra, published in 1794 by the amateur musician Baron von Kospoth.

CHAPTER V.

FOURTH PERIOD (18TH CENTURY) CONTINUED : CURIOSITIES,
FATUITIES, AND NOTABILITIES—LESUEUR, A THEORIZING
COMPOSER; LACÉPÈDE, A COMPOSING THEORIST; CLEMENTI,
DUSSEK, STEIBELT, WOLF, VOGLER, TARTINI, AND BOCCHERINI.

Striking testimony to the programmatic tendency of
the age is borne by two Frenchmen. The first of these
witnesses is J. F. LESUEUR (1760-1837), the master—
note this—of Berlioz. He published in 1787 a book with
this title: *Exposé d'une musique une, imitative, et
particulière à chaque solennité.* The object of music, he
says, must always be imitation. If poetry and painting
are in many cases more expressive than music, music
is in other circumstances more expressive than poetry
and painting. If music cannot invest poetry with a
meaning which it has not, it can at least reinforce it, and
in a thousand ways modify, nay, even divert and change it.
'Music can imitate all the inflections of nature. All the
sentiments are also within its domain.' What the
principle adopted by the master mainly aimed at was
un ensemble dramatique. I need not repeat here what
I have quoted already. But I must exemplify Lesueur's
notions of what music should do by some extracts from
his plans for a kind of oratorio music suitable to the
Mass on the several high festivals, such as Christmas,
Easter, &c. In doing so, I shall preserve to some
extent his strange and awkward phraseology. Speaking
of the overture of the music suitable to the Christmas
Day Mass, he writes : 'At the beginning of the overture

the intention of the composer will be to recall several prophecies regarding the birth of the Messiah. For this purpose an imposing passage will be executed by all the stringed and wind instruments, with which mingle the sombre inflections of the trombones, the sounds of which, if various writers may be believed, resemble the religious trumpets of the ancient high-priests. Soon after, the trombones detach themselves from the rest of the orchestra in order to make an imposing announcement, to which succeed strains of grave, sombre harmony which cannot but inspire a certain sacred horror.' After a noble and imposing short march there will be expressed ' the ardent desires of the Prophets for the coming of the Messiah.' In the prelude to the *Gloria in excelsis* the composer ' will endeavour to induce the idea of the calm of the night during which the shepherds were watching their flocks near Bethlehem. To accomplish this, the orchestra must endeavour to diffuse a calm, a freshness, resembling that of night, by peaceful music, in which movement makes itself only faintly felt. . . . . Afterwards has to be attempted the painting of the vivid light that shines about the throne of the Eternal, and which, suddenly piercing the darkness of the night, casts terror among the shepherds.' In the music for Whitsunday ' the musician's task in the overture will be to awaken the idea of thunder, of lightning, and of the imposing display which accompanies the descent of the Eternal.'

Examining Lesueur's *Super flumina*, psalm for grand chorus and orchestra, we meet with characteristic music and remarks. Accompanying the opening instrumental bars we read : ' The chorus of the Hebrews recalling their captivity at Babylon, when they mingled their

tears with the murmuring of Euphrates.' A little
farther on appears above the music the following note :
'The particular character and colour of the musical
execution of this *historical* psalm should furnish not
only the imitation of Euphrates, but also the imitative
image of the dull noise of the contrary winds and the
distant roaring of the cataracts of the river, which
seemed coming to join the lamentations of the Hebrews,
their dolorous chants, and the plaintive accents of the
musical instruments with which they accompanied their
chorus.' The murmuring is expressed by various forms
of a repeated turning figure and the device of repercussion
combined with vibrato. These means are employed by
the strings. The wind, on the other hand, is full of
sighs, expressed by a two-note figure consisting (in
4/4 time) of a syncopated crotchet followed by a falling
quaver. In another movement of the psalm we find
the composer's intentions indicated by words and phrases
like *fieramente et avec élan, con sentimento,* and *misterioso.*
And in still another part of the psalm we come on this
remark : 'Ensemble piece. Chorus that sings the vision
of the Prophet Ezekiel hearing, in spirit, the chariot of
the Ancient of days, or God, the joyous accents of
the cherubim, seraphim, archangels, and seeing
prophetically the Son of man, or the Saviour.'

Here surely was a tone-poet with high aspirations
and a belief in the expressive power of music. Lesueur,
however, has left us only stage and church music, no
independent orchestral compositions.*

---

* For further information about the interesting, though eccentric
and nebulous, Lesueur *see* Octave Fouque's *Les Révolutionnaires de
la Musique* (Paris, 1882), and Adolphe Boschot's *La Jeunesse d'un
Romantique, Hector Berlioz* (Paris, 1906). The author of the latter book
has made use of Lesueur's voluminous unpublished literary manuscripts.

H'

The other witness I wish to call is COMTE DE LACÉPÈDE (1756-1825), a scientist and amateur musician, who composed operas, a requiem, and instrumental compositions, and wrote a book entitled *Poétique de la Musique* (1785). His views of instrumental music, which he endeavoured to realize in a suite of movements descriptive of scenes from Fénélon's *Télémaque*, Lacépède sets forth in the chapter *Des Symphonies, des Concerto,* &c., vol. ii., pp. 329-341. After pointing out, on the one hand, the great resources of instrumental music, and, on the other hand, the vagueness of its images, owing to its inability to communicate the circumstances of the passions it interprets, he continues (I shall quote only the main statements of our loquacious and somewhat obscure author) as follows : 'A symphony consists usually of three pieces of music . . . The composer ought to consider them as three grand acts of a theatrical piece, and imagine himself to be working at a tragedy, a comedy, or a pastoral . . . These three acts, as we call them, have to be distributed into several scenes . . . In order to distinguish the different interlocutors, one chooses in the orchestra the more prominent instruments the nature of which is most in keeping with the characters represented. Thus by the use of single instruments and combinations of instruments, monologues, dialogues, scenes with several persons and choruses may be introduced . . . The musician must skilfully observe the succession and the natural increase and decrease of the human passions ; and, in designing such a drama, and forming it of a sequence of sentiments that develop, interpenetrate, and grow from each other, he must take care not to assign to the passions another order than

that of nature . . . But in producing pieces of this kind,
whether the subject be drawn from some known event or
be entirely imagined, the composer should never introduce
into the scenes anything that cannot be represented by
music ; he should offer nothing but emotions or pictures.
It is like designing a pantomimic ballet and afterwards
setting it to music. The work is divided into three grand
portions formed by the three pieces of a symphony. To
these may be left almost their ordinary characters ; with
one difference, however—namely, that there will be
lacking the resources of the spectacle, the scenery, and
the action of the dancers.' The author, later on, asks :
'Even if the composer were not to succeed in making
his intentions known, would he not always say enough
to secure being listened to with more interest, to
captivate the attention more fully, to engage uninter-
ruptedly both mind and heart, to cause the hearer to
seek what is not pointed out, to induce him to exert
himself to divine the word of the enigma, to know the
exact place of the scene, the causes of the events, the
names and the characters of the personages represented,
in short, all the objects which it was the aim to show,
and of which at every moment a part was unveiled ?
Moreover, is this not the only way in which the musician
can give to the passions which he represents, and to
their picturing, their true order ? And could we have
indicated to him a more powerful means of producing
more animated, varied, and contrasting images, of
being more penetrated by the subject in composing,
and more influenced by the passions whose fire he
wishes to spread ? ' The truth of the last idea
expressed by Lacépède—whatever we may think of
the rest—seems to me indisputable. Even though

the hearer does not understand it in its entirety, he is the better off for the programme in the mind of the composer, who thereby is enabled to be more impressive and logical, more of a tone-poet than a mere tone-artificer.

From the domain of the pianoforte sonata there is not so much to report in the way of programmatic music as from that of the symphony. And, as we shall see, this holds good also during the following two periods. Of pianoforte pieces of the inferior orders there is even less to report. The battle programme is the only kind largely represented. The warlike time from 1789 to 1815 naturally inspired warlike music, or at least created a taste and demand for it. One of the most famous compositions of this kind was the *Battle of Prague* for pianoforte, violin, and violoncello, by the Bohemian composer FRANZ KOTZWARA (who died by his own hand in London in 1791). Notwithstanding its fame, the composition has not any music in it worth speaking of. Indeed, the battle programme is the lowest of all programmes. And why? Because it is the most unmusical, the most grossly materialistic. It appeals by noise and rhythmically strongly marked popular tunes rather to the nerves and muscles than to the mind. Not a single work of the kind ever created has high artistic value, not even Beethoven's battle, and extremely few have as much as a modicum of value. Battle-pieces afford to the musician hardly anything but matter for disgust and amusement—disgust at their inartistic aims and means, and amusement at their naive intentions and execution. On the whole, the naiveness is rather on the side of the purchasers than of the manufacturers.

MUZIO CLEMENTI (1752-1832), who composed so many sonatas, has given titles to two only—Op. 17, in D major, *La Chasse*, published in 1787, and Op. 50, in G minor, *Didone abbandonata*, published in 1820-1821. The former, however, is not very characteristic; and the latter, a fine example of a sonata and of programme music, belongs to the next, the Beethoven period. The suave and nobly sentimental JOH. LUDWIG DUSSEK (1760-1812) provides more material for our study, but the titles of his sonatas and shorter pieces indicate for the most part rather moods than stories—for instance, these sonatas: Op. 44, *Les Adieux de Clementi;* Op 61, *Élégie harmonique sur la mort du Prince Louis Ferdinand de Prusse, en forme de Sonate;* Op. 70, *Le Retour à Paris;* Op. 77, *L'Invocation.* To these sonatas may be added his Military Concerto, Op. 40, and the piece in rondo form, *La Consolation*, dedicated to the memory of Prince Louis Ferdinand, his patron, a good pianist and composer as well as a brave soldier, who fell at Salfeld in 1806.

Dussek worked also after programmes of a very different nature, and in doing so produced music quite unworthy of himself. One would like to suggest as an excuse that he wrote the stuff to help his father-in-law, the well-known musician and Edinburgh music publisher, Domenico Corri. Unfortunately, this suggestion does not bear examination. Corri did not publish all these pieces; and, moreover, Dussek himself was interested in the publishing concern. Of this unholy class of programme music are the following: *Combat naval,* sonata for pianoforte, violin, violoncello, and *grand tambour, ad lib. The naval Battle and total Defeat of the Dutch Fleet by Admiral Duncan*, October 11, 1797;

A complete and exact Delineation of the Ceremony from St. James's to St. Paul's, on Tuesday, the 19*th December* 1797, *on which day their Majesties, together with both Houses of Parliament, went in solemn Procession to return thanks for the several Naval Victories obtained by the British Fleet over those of France, Spain, and Holland;* and *The Sufferings of the Queen of France: A musical composition, expressing the feelings of the unfortunate Marie Antoinette during her Imprisonment, Trial, &c.,* Op. 23. A very few words regarding the last two pieces will be more than sufficient. The only detailed indications of the programme of *A complete and exact Delineation of the Ceremony* are: ' Cannons; Trumpets; Horses prancing; The Procession began; The acclamations of the people; The Procession arrives at St. Paul's.' None but expressions permissible neither in parliament nor in polite society would be applicable to this, if one did not prefer silence. *The Sufferings of the Queen of France* must likewise be denounced, and can only be described as scrappy, uninspired, and not in the least convincing as regards painting and expression. Here is the detailed programme: ' 1. The Queen's Imprisonment; 2. She reflects on her former greatness; 3. They separate her from her children—the farewell of her children; 4. They pronounce the sentence; 5. Her Resignation to her fate; 6. The situation and reflections on the night before her execution—The Guards come to conduct her to the place of Execution; 7. March; 8. The savage tumult of the rabble; 9. The Queen's invocation to the Almighty just before her death—The Guillotine drops [crashing chord with quickly descending diatonic scale] ; 10. Apotheosis.' What a waste of subject! And what a desecration of the sacredness of misery for filthy lucre's sake !

More numerous are the contributions to programme music of the talented, but vain and unprincipled DANIEL STEIBELT (1765-1823), one of the most popular composers of his day. In his overweening conceit Steibelt once had the foolhardiness to challenge Beethoven as an improviser, but only once. The last movement of his famous third pianoforte Concerto, in E major, is entitled *L'Orage précédé d'un Rondeau pastorale*, and was one of the greatest popular successes of the time. Other concertos of his with titles are: the fifth, *À la Chasse;* the sixth, *Voyage au Mont Saint Bernard;* and the seventh, *Grand Concert militaire.* Among his sonatas we find *L'Amante disperata*, a military sonata, a *Défaite des Espagnols par l'armée française*, and a martial sonata. Then there are fantasias and pieces of various sorts: *La Fête de Napoléon, La Bataille de Gemappe et Neerwinden, The Threatening and Deliverance of Vienna, The Destruction of Moscow, La Journée d'Ulm, Britannia, or Admiral Duncan's Victory* (1797), *Le Rappel de l'Armée, Le Combat naval, St. Paul's Procession, The Christening of the Neva*, and the rondos *Les Papillons* and *Le Berger et son troupeau.* The warlike exceeds unmistakably and largely the idyllic, and the material the spiritual. Even without looking at the music we must come to the conclusion that composition was with Steibelt for the most part a catchpenny affair; that he was oftener bent on catching money and applause, than on catching souls. However we will look at a few of them.

The *Battle of Neerwinden* consists of military signals and tunes, ringing of alarm bells, rifle and cannon shots (the latter interpreted by bringing the palms of the hands down on the key-board), groans of the wounded, and rejoicings over the victory. It is the same with *La Journée d'Ulm* and *Britannia*, denominated ' an Allegorical Overture in Commemoration of the signal Naval Victory obtained by Admiral Duncan over the Dutch Fleet, the 11th of October, 1797.' More interesting, because less common, is the programme of the *Public Christening on the Neva at St. Petersburg*, ' a Characteristic Fantasia,' a concoction somewhat of the nature of Dussek's *A complete and exact Delineation of the Ceremony from St. James's to St. Paul's*, but longer and more elaborate and pretentious. The music and the painting are less than worthless—in fact, they are non-existent. The foolishness of the programme is such that I cannot resist quoting it. ' The Bells announce the ceremony. Firing the Guns. The joy of the People. The Emperor sets out from the Palace. The throng of the People. Chorus in *Iphigenia* by Gluck. March of the troops. Acclamation of the People. His Majesty's arrival at the place where the Ceremony is performed. The Divine Service. Te Deum. Chorus. "Let us pray," sung by the Patriarch. Departure of his Majesty. The joy of the People. Firing of the Guns. The People thronging from the place. Air in *Alceste* with three variations.' And such stuff was bought, played, and, alas! enjoyed. Let us look at two more *musical* works of Steibelt's. Whilst the famous *Pastoral Rondo* of the 3rd Concerto is undeniably pretty, the *Storm*, happily of short duration, has neither musical nor descriptive qualities to recommend it. A note to the 6th Concerto informs us that the composer's intention was to depict in the first movement the terrors of the St. Bernard— the dismal, wild, imposing aspect, the glaciers, hurricanes, roaring of the torrents, thunder of the avalanches, crash of the cracking ice, &c., with the contrasting bell of the hospice and the chants of the monks heard from time to time by the traveller ; and in the second movement, a Rondo, the descent from the summit to the Piedmontese valley. The realization, however, falls very far short of the intentions—neither the grandeurs nor the terrors find adequate expression. What merits the composition has, it derives from the pleasing qualities of absolute music.

Steibelt has been called a man of genius. Unless we are very lavish in the use of the word, the right attribution in this case must be denied. But he was a composer of a luxuriant imagination, who wrote melodiously, brilliantly, and with great facility.

Among the compositions of the less famous composers we may note *A Sonatina and four emotional* [*affectvolle*] *Sonatas with an explanatory introduction* (1785) by E. W. WOLF. And that remarkable composer FRIEDR. WILH. RUST (1739-1796), who points so emphatically to Beethoven, produced in 1775 a *Sonata Eroica*, and in 1794 a Sonata in D major, the second movement of which is superscribed *Wehklage* (Lamentation) and the last movement *Schwermuth und Frohmuth* (Melancholy and Mirth). With regard to the *Wehklage*, J. S. Shedlock, in his book *The Pianoforte Sonata*, writes : 'Rust's eldest son, a talented youth, who was studying at Halle University, was drowned in the river Saale, 23rd March, 1794. Matthisson, the "Adelaide" poet, sent to the disconsolate father a poem entitled *Todtenkranz für ein Kind*, to which Rust sketched music, and on that sketch is based this pathetic movement, which sounds like some tone-poem of the 19th century.'

It would be unpardonable to pass over ABBÉ G. J. VOGLER (1749-1814), the teacher of Weber and Meyerbeer, a remarkable composer, theorist, and *virtuoso* on the organ, the same after whom Robert Browning named one of his poems.* Well, Abbé Vogler, the restless contriver and schemer, composed a characteristic sonata for pianoforte and string quartet, entitled *The Matrimonial Quarrel* (in German, *Der eheliche Zwist;* in French, *Brouillerie entre mari et femme*), and startled the world with his improvisations on the organ, depicting storms and other sensational displays, including the Fall of the walls of Jericho. Here are a few specimens of the programmes that have come down to us :—

Naval Battle.—1. Beating of the drums. 2. Martial music and marches. 3. Movement of the ships. 4. Crossing of the waves. 5. Cannon shots. 6. Cries of the wounded. 7. Shouts of victory of the triumphant fleet.

Musical imitation of Rubens's Last Judgment.— 1. Magnificent introduction. 2. The trumpet resounds through the graves ; they open. 3. The wrathful Judge pronounces the terrible judgment on the reprobates; their fall into the abyss ; wailing and gnashing of teeth. 4. The Just are received by God into eternal blessedness ; their bliss. 5. The voices of the blessed unite with the choirs of angels.

Death of Prince Leopold of Brunswick.—1. The quiet course of the river ; the winds that chase it into greater rapidity ; the gradual rise of the water ; the complete inundation. 2. The general terror and lamentation of the unfortunate who foresee their misery ; their

---

* Not that the poet's presentment has anything to do with the real man. The same remark applies to Browning's other musical poems.

shuddering, complaints, tears, and sobs. 3. The arrival of the Prince, who resolves to help them; the representations and prayers of his officers, who wish to keep him back; his voice in opposition to them, which at last stifles all lamentation. 4. The boat sets out; its reeling through the waves; the howling of the wind; the boat capsizes; the Prince sinks. 5. A touching piece with the feeling that suits the occasion.

The joyous life of the shepherds, interrupted by a thunderstorm, which, however, passes by, and then the naive and loud rejoicing on that account.

Concerning Italian composers little has as yet been said in connection with the fourth period, and little need be said. Many readers on turning their attention to Italy will think of *Il trillo del diavolo.* In this excellent violin sonata of the illustrious GIUSEPPE TARTINI (1692-1770), however, the title points to the genesis, not to the programme of the composition, the master having endeavoured to write down on awakening what, in a dream, he had heard the devil play. On the other hand, several pieces of information that have come down to us lay Tartini under the gravest suspicion of being a composer of programme music, a composer who sought inspiration in poetry and illustrated his effects by poetry. Algarotti relates that before beginning to compose, Tartini read one of Petrarch's sonnets in order that, starting from a definite subject, he might not lose himself in empty phantasies. To explain how Tartini performed his music, one of his pupils gave Lipinski a poem, and told him to read it and then play a Tartini Adagio. We know also that the master wrote in cipher over the movements mottoes such as, ' Ombra cara ' (Dear shade), ' Volgete il riso in pianto ' (Turn your laughter into tears), &c.,—and lines of the poets under portions of them. One of his best sonatas, Op. 1, No. 10, in G minor, used to be called *Didone abbandonata.* If we remember his beautiful expressive adagios, and the words often addressed by him to violinists who played to him— 'That is beautiful! That is difficult! But here (pointing to his heart) it has told me nothing '—we cannot but feel inclined to number him with the band of composers of programme music.

LUIGI BOCCHERINI (1743-1805), the charming composer of string quintets and quartets, symphonies, and much else, who, on account of his greater sweetness than energy, has been called the wife of Haydn, wrote a quintet for two violins, viola, and two violoncelli, entitled *L'Uccelliera* (the Aviary), in which, as his biographer, L. Picquot, says, he 'intended to depict a rural scene, where the song of birds unites with the sound of the hunting horn, the shepherd's bagpipe (*musette*), and the dance of the villagers.'

A few words in addition to those of Picquot, who regards the work as a picture of the most exquisite originality, are desirable. The quintet in question is the last of the six quintets Op. 13. The first movement (*Allegro giusto*, preceded by an *Adagio assai*), superscribed *L'Uccelliera,* is full of birds' voices; the second movement (*Allegro*), superscribed *I Pastori e li Cacciatori,* alternates between the pastoral and the venatorial; the third movement (*Tempo di menuetto*) bears no superscription; and the fourth movement contains, after twenty-nine introductory bars, a repetition of the third division, the recapitulation of the exposition, of the first *Allegro*, and thus the birds end as well as begin the delightful composition.

BOOK III.

FULFILMENTS.

CHAPTER I.

FIFTH PERIOD (FROM THE CLOSE OF THE 18TH CENTURY):
PROGRAMME MUSIC IN THE LARGER CLASSICAL FORMS AND
VITALIZATION OF THE LESSER FORMS.—BEETHOVEN.

After the prophecies and preparations of the preceding
period, we come now to the fulfilment and consummation.
The masters that dominate this period are Beethoven,
the first in time and quality, Weber, Schubert, Spohr,
Mendelssohn, and Schumann. Although I pointed out
programme music in the larger classical forms as the
most distinguishing feature, this period is also remarkable
for the substantialization, revivification, poetization, and
spiritualization (*venia sit verbis*) of the smaller forms,
a fact sufficiently proved by the mention of the
names of Schubert, Mendelssohn, Chopin, Schumann,
and Henselt.

It required a master mind, a tone-poet of the highest
potency, to accredit programme music at once and
legitimize and justify it for all time to come. That
mind and that poet was LUDWIG VAN BEETHOVEN
(1770-1827). If the declarations accompanying his
compositions marked the limits of Beethoven's activity
as a composer of programme music, we should be
obliged to say that his contributions to this class of

music were not numerous, but some of them of the greatest importance. Let us see which works of Beethoven have declared programmes. Among his thirty-two sonatas there are two with titles—Op. 13, the *Sonate Pathétique*, and Op. 81, the Sonata in E flat major, the three divisions of which are respectively superscribed, Farewell, Absence, and Return (*Wiedersehen*). There are also two titled works among the nine symphonies—Op. 55, the Heroic Symphony, and Op. 68, the Pastoral Symphony. Further, we have a Battle Symphony, *Wellingtons Sieg oder die Schlacht bei Vittoria*, Op. 91, four overtures to his opera *Fidelio* (*Leonore*), an overture to *Coriolanus*, overtures and incidental music to *Egmont, King Stephen*, and *The Ruins of Athens*, the ballet *Prometheus*, and the independent overtures *Zur Namensfeier*, Op. 124, and *Die Weihe des Hauses*, Op. 138. To these may yet be added the movement in the string quartet, Op. 132, superscribed 'Thanksgiving song in the Lydian mode, offered to the Divinity by a convalescent,' the concluding division of the string quartet, Op. 135, superscribed *Der schwergefasste Entschluss*, and the posthumously published *Rondo a capriccio*, Op. 129, which in the original manuscript bore the title *Fury over the lost penny, vented in a capriccio.* Of the sum total of the master's works the compositions here enumerated form but a small portion. Moreover, this small portion has to be sifted before we get the really noble and notable examples.*

* The epithets 'Pastorale' and 'Appassionata,' contained in the titles respectively of the Sonata Op. 28, in D major, and the Sonata Op. 57, in F minor, do not derive from the composer, nor did they appear on the title-page of the first edition : they are, in fact, inventions of later publishers. Equally unauthorized is the name *Moonlight Sonata*

We have first of all to set aside the Battle Symphony, which is indeed important among battle pieces, but not among Beethoven's works. When Tomaschek, a great admirer of the master, heard it, he was greatly pained to find 'Beethoven, whom Providence had probably appointed to the highest throne in the realm of tones, among the grossest materialists.' According to the same authority Beethoven himself declared the symphony to be 'eine Dummheit' (a tomfoolery). Nevertheless there are some interesting programmatic points in it, and even some beauties. The composition consists of two parts: (1) The Battle; and (2) The Triumphal Symphony (*Sieges-Symphonie*). The advance of the English is announced first by their drums and trumpets and then by 'Rule, Britannia' as a march; immediately afterwards appear on the field the French, whose advance is announced first by their drums and trumpets, and then by 'Malbrough s'en va-t-en Guerre' as a march. Next are heard the challenge and counter-challenge, which lead to the battle proper—first a tremendous tussle, then a storming march, and at last the defeat of the French, indicated by a few bars of 'Malbrough' in minor, with a

popularly given to the Sonata Op. 27, No. 2, in C sharp minor, dedicated to the master's beloved and loving pupil the Countess Giulietta Guicciardi. The Viennese called this sonata also the *Laubensonate*, imagining that the *Adagio* was composed in an arboured walk of the beautiful countess's garden. Another fancy title is that of *Geistertrio* for the Trio Op. 70, No. 1, in D major. The name was given to it on account of the character of the *Largo assai ed espressivo*. Lenz, however, saw in it not 'ghosts, but shadows cast by a darkened soul-mood.' Sir George Grove connected with the *Adagio* of the fourth Symphony, in B flat major, and the first movement of the fifth, in C minor, Beethoven's 'immortal love' (*unsterbliche Geliebte*), now by many supposed to have been the Countess Theresa von Brunswick; but this love affair is still involved in obscurity, and the correctness of the assumption cannot be proved by anything more substantial than contemporaneity.

tremulous ending. Of the second part I need not say more than that it consists of several continuous movements from which 'God save the King' is not absent.

The other works that may be excluded from our consideration are the music to *King Stephen* and to *The Ruins of Athens*, plays which Kotzebue wrote for the opening of the new German Theatre at Pesth in 1812. Kotzebue's poetry was not of the sort that could inspire Beethoven, who, moreover, was not a master of occasional compositions. He needed a grand theme, and time to think it out. As he had neither, these works are among his least valuable ones. Best known of all the music to these plays is the characteristic Turkish March from *The Ruins of Athens*.

The *Rondo a capriccio* is, of course, not seriously-meant programme music. On the other hand all the remaining works of those I have enumerated must interest us from our present point of view. The title of Op. 13, the *Sonate Pathétique*, points out only the general character of the work, not a particular programme. But there is a speaking expressiveness and an unmistakable depicting of moods in every one of the three movements—in the first, of storm and stress; in the second, of devout contemplation and a trustful upward looking; and in the third, of agitation and sweet melancholy. Beethoven's oracular utterance about two principles in the middle movement is not intelligible. In Op. 81, on the other hand, we are not troubled by any mystery. The superscriptions clearly indicate the intention of the composer and the music bears out fully what the superscriptions indicate. In the first division, *Farewell*, is expressed the tender regret and emotional perturbation

of parting; in the second, *Absence*, the affectionate
remembrance of and longing for the absent one; and in
the third, *Return*, the elation, joy, and contentment on
meeting again.   I said there is no mystery about Op. 81.
This, however, is not the case in every respect.   At least
one puzzling question confronts us.   Who is the parting,
absent, and returning one ?   After the sketches for the
first movement of the work, one of the composer's note-
books contains the following entry : ' The Farewell—on
the 4th May—dedicated to, and written from the heart
for, His Imperial Highness.'   But was the master's
pupil, the Archduke Rudolph, really so dear to him that
his going, staying away, and coming back, could move
Beethoven to the extent we find him moved in this
sonata ?   The feelings expressed seem to suggest rather
a lady-love than a male scholar.   No doubt the Archduke
had a great affection for his master, and was his
benefactor.   It may also be noted that he left Vienna on
account of the approach of the French, and did not
return till nine months afterwards.   Still, the amount
and quality of feeling seems excessive.   If the Archduke
was really and solely the subject, idealization must have
played a great part in the composition.   This, indeed,
was necessarily the case, as the sketches for the second
and third movements were written before the Archduke's
return.   Another solution of the riddle is conceivable—
namely, that the honoured patron received a compliment
that was called forth by another person or by an
imaginary occurrence.

About the origin of the superscription of the last
division of the string quartet, Op. 135—'A resolution
formed with difficulty,' followed by two musical motives
with the question and answer: ' Must it be ? ' ' Yes, it

I

must be ! '—there are two stories told respectively by
Schindler and Lenz (informed by Holz). In the one the
master's cook asks for housekeeping money, and in the
other an outwitted wealthy Viennese amateur plays a
part. Now, I cannot believe that Beethoven, to whom
his art was sacred, would in a serious work introduce a
motto originating in a comical incident. It is more
easily conceivable that he would evade a tiresome
question by a jocular reply. As to the *Canzona di
ringraziamento offerta alla divinità da un guarito, in modo
lidico*, in the string quartet, Op. 132, it was written by
Beethoven on his recovery from a severe illness.

The music to the ballet *Prometheus* does not belong to
the master's great and strong works, but it contains
besides much charming music some notable music
illustrative of the pantomimic scenes. Lenz goes so far
as to describe it as a mine of dramatic instrumental
music. At any rate, on hearing and reading it, one is
here and there reminded of a Frenchman's saying of the
ballets of a later time—'they are veritable *symphonies
dansées.*'

Some may think that the independent overtures *Zur
Namensfeier* (for the name-day of Emperor Francis II.),
Op. 115, and *Die Weihe des Hauses* (for the opening of
the Vienna Josephstadt theatre), Op. 124, cannot be
included in programme music. Well, though they are
not in the midst of it, they are at least on the border-
land. For they are not merely finely constructed tone-
edifices, but also highly characteristic and expressive
tone-poems. They have both a festive ring, and
surround us with stirring life and brilliant light; both
are joyous, but the one sparklingly and the other
majestically.

Beethoven wrote altogether four overtures to his opera *Fidelio;* three of them are called *Leonore,* but that is only another name for *Fidelio.* To prevent confusion I shall place the three *Leonore* overtures in the order in which they were for a time thought to have been written, and add in parentheses the years in which they were really written: Op. 138 (1807-1808); Op. 72*a* (1805); and Op. 72*a* (1806). We need not dwell on the first of these overtures, which is quite overshadowed by its two sisters; nor on the finer *Fidelio* overture, Op. 72*b*, composed in 1814, which differs from the three *Leonore* overtures in not being connected with the opera by musical motives. As to the two remaining overtures, it will suffice to consider only the later, the familiar *Leonore* overture, as it is not a new work, but merely a more perfect and more grandly developed version of the earlier. But what shall I say of this composition? It is a *résumé,* it is the essence, of the music-drama for which it is written. It focuses the devotion, sufferings, struggles, and victory of Eleonore and Florestan. It is the most powerful and colossal work of its kind—as grand in thought as in form, as pure and noble as it is passionate and stirring. It is, as Wagner has said, not an overture to a drama, but itself a drama, and presents the contents more completely and strikingly than the following action.

Two other powerful and poetical conceptions are the overtures to *Coriolanus* and to *Egmont.* The former, Op. 62, Beethoven wrote to von Collin's tragedy *Coriolan,* but his recollection of Plutarch and Shakespeare may have helped to inspire him. Who can fail to recognize Coriolanus's haughty, contemptuous defiance, Volumnia's and Virgilia's deprecation, and the hero's struggle with himself and the world, and final ruin? Or, as Wagner puts it: 'The tragic-idea of the powerful work lies entirely in the personal fate of the hero. An irreconcilable pride, an all-overtopping ultra-vigorous and ultra-overweening nature can engage our sympathy only by its downfall: to let us feel the coming of it, and, at last, see the consummation, that was the master's intention. . . . Beethoven seized upon a single scene, but that the most decisive, in order to focus in it the true, the purely human emotional content of the whole extensive subject-matter, and transmit it again to the purely human feeling.'

We now come to the third of Beethoven's three pre-eminent tone-poems in the overture form—namely, the overture to *Egmont*, Op. 84. In Goethe's play, the love of Egmont and Clara is but an episode. In Beethoven's overture, the composer ignores altogether the intimate drama enacted in the burgher house, and concentrates his thoughts on the grand historical drama. It would be a great mistake to regard the overture as a conventional introduction to a play, for in reality it is itself a drama—a symphonic poem, if ever there was one. The three movements of which it consists tell us of oppression, conflict, and victory. We have in it—firstly, the stern command of iron-willed tyranny, and the wails and plaints of the downtrodden; secondly, the timid murmurs rising to bold discontent, the angry agitation growing into open revolt, and a persistent struggle that becomes fiercer and fiercer as it goes on; and, lastly, the high-spirited, loud-voiced triumph of liberty.

Beethoven's music to *Egmont* is one of the finest examples of such music. I would use the superlative absolute, were I not convinced of the wrongness of using it in art. The first *entr'acte* looks backward and forward ; it tells us of Brackenburg's broken-heartedness (*Andante*), and the disturbed state of the citizens (*Allegro con brio*). It continues for twelve bars after the rising of the curtain, and closes on the dominant. The second *entr'acte* (*Larghetto*), which begins immediately after the falling of the curtain, refers to the preceding interview between Egmont and Orange. No sooner are the last words of Clara spoken than the orchestra strikes in with the third *entr'acte*, before the curtain has fallen, and it continues for more than twenty bars after the curtain has again been raised. The first half (*Allegro* and *Allegretto*) is a love transport (the meeting of Clara and Egmont), the second half (*Marcia vivace*) brings on the scene the stern Spanish soldiery, and dies away into a passage that depicts the fear of the citizens. The fourth *entr'acte*, too, begins before the fall and continues after the rise of the curtain, and points backwards and forwards. The first half (three bars *Poco Sostenuto e resoluto*, and *Larghetto*) refers to the arrest of Egmont ; and the second half (*Andante agitato*) to the anxiety of Clara. Very beautiful and significant is a piece of music in the fifth act, superscribed 'Indicating Clara's death.' The stage remains empty ; the lamp on the table flickers yet a few times, and then dies out. In the same act is a short melodrama, followed by music descriptive of Egmont's dream, in which he has a vision of Clara, who bids him be of good cheer, tells him that his death will procure victory for his country, and presents a laurel wreath to him. At the end of the play the orchestra strikes up a *Siegessymphonie* (triumphal symphony).

In the opera *Fidelio* the orchestra is symphonic
and the music throughout programme music, often
indeed of the most striking, intense, and penetrating
kind. Take, for instance, the introduction to the
second act, Florestan's recitative and aria, and the
melodrama, one of the most impressive that have been
written.

Next we have to examine the symphonies with
declared programmes. To speak of a declared
programme in connection with the third symphony, the
Sinfonia eroica, Op. 55 (1804), is saying rather too much.
But we know that Beethoven in writing this work had
in his mind Napoleon Bonaparte, the young general and
consul, for whom and for republicanism he had a great
admiration. In fact, the original title ran 'Sinfonia
grande, written on Bonaparte.' It was Beethoven's
anger at Napoleon's betrayal of republicanism by his
acceptance of the Imperial crown that made him adopt
the present title : 'Heroic Symphony [I translate from
the Italian], composed for the celebration of a Great
man.' Although this is the only information the
composer ever vouchsafed—if we except one remark,
which I shall presently quote—it is neither impertinent
nor too daring to say that the contents of the several
movements may be indicated thus : (1) Character and life
of the hero; (2) Funeral ceremony; (3) Scene in the camp;
(4) Apotheosis, or celebration of the memory of the
hero. Beethoven's remark above alluded to is that made
by him on hearing of Napoleon's death : 'I have already
composed the proper music for that catastrophe,' that is,
the second movement, the *Marcia funebre.*

Unlike his proceeding in the *Heroic* Symphony and
in every other case, Beethoven supplies a pretty full

and detailed programme in the sixth, the Pastoral
Symphony, Op. 68, first performed on December 22,
1808. We have here frankly acknowledged programme
music in the fullest sense of the word. The superscriptions of the five movements, the last three of which
are continuous, are in their final form as follows:
'(1) The cheerful impressions excited on arriving in the
country; (2) By the brook; (3) Peasants' merrymaking
(more literally : merry meeting of country folk); (4)
Thunderstorm; and (5) Shepherds' hymn; gratitude
and thanksgiving after the storm.' Of what kind
Beethoven's programme is may be gathered from the
subtitle on the back of the title-page of the first violin
part (whilst the parts were published as early as 1809,
the score was not published till 1826): 'Pastoral
Symphony or Recollection of country-life (expressive of
feeling rather than painting).' Certain remarks in the
master's sketch-books make his position clearer still.
There he wrote : 'All painting in instrumental music, if
pushed too far, is a failure.' But he was sure he had
not gone too far, for he wrote also: 'Anyone who has
an idea of country-life can make out for himself the
intentions of the author without many titles.' These
intentions, however, he struggled hard to reveal. One
of his attempts resulted in the following explanation :
'Pastoral Symphony: not a picture, but something in
which are expressed the emotions aroused in men by
the pleasure of the country (or), in which some feelings
of country-life are set forth.'

But although Beethoven was mainly concerned with
the inner impressions that outward things had made
upon him, he by no means altogether abstained from
painting those outward things. Only, this painting was

kept subordinate to the expression of the inner man.
Hence the master's explanation is quite correct:
'expression of feeling rather than painting.' This
uymphony makes us realize Beethoven's love of nature.
He said of himself,—'no man on earth loves the country
more.   Woods, trees, and rocks give the response which
man requires.   .   .   .   Every tree seems to say:
"Holy, holy." '

Beethoven was right in saying that 'anyone who has
an idea of country-life can make out for himself the
intentions of the author without many titles.'   I should
say, even without any titles at all.   Who could be in
doubt about the meaning of the first movement?   The
superscription, 'The cheerful impressions excited on
arriving in the country,' seems to be superfluous.   The
open-air feeling of freshness and brightness is unmistakable.   So are the serenity and joyousness inspired by
the rural sights, odours, and sounds.   What light-
heartedness, what high spirits!   What smiles, laughter,
and singing!   What tripping, skipping, and running!
In short, what innocent joy, what perfect happiness!
Of whatever age, we feel ourselves young again,—feel
spring in our veins and hearts.

The slow movement of the *Pastoral* Symphony, 'By
the Brook,' is full of the sounds of nature—of the
murmuring of the brook, and the twittering of the birds.
But whilst this is to be found in the accompaniment, the
melody furnishes the human element—the leisureliness,
the *dolce far niente*, the dreaminess, the comfort, the
contented self-abandonment to the moment that come
over us on a sunny summer day in such surroundings.
The form, like the mood, is vague, is, as it were, an
aimless wandering, a lingering and lounging.

The third movement, 'The merry gathering of country-people,' is a delightful specimen of Beethoven's humour. You see the peasants capering and wheeling about; you hear the village orchestra with its peculiarities and deficiencies; and at one time you get the hobnailed rustics at their roughest and noisiest. There is nothing vague about the form this time. The rustic strains and rhythms are as plain as possible.

Suddenly a thunderstorm breaks out, and puts an end to the merrymaking. Instead of a loud tonic chord of F major, we hear a *pianissimo* roll on a kettle-drum tuned in *d* flat. Here, in this fourth movement, Beethoven is a painter of outward things more than in any other movement—thunder, lightning, gusts of wind, and showers of rain are depicted—but the human element is not absent. The *staccato* quaver figure, first heard in the third and following bars, tells us of the timid flight of the peasants; the wailing crotchets of bars 5 and 6 are unmistakable. And besides this the composer depicts not only the noises of the storm, but also the awe with which the sublime spectacle, grand as well as terrible, inspires the spectator. Everything is expressive and descriptive, both the matter and the form. A thunderstorm in rondo or sonata form could not but have a tame and artificial effect. The wild anarchy of keys and motives is more appropriate. The anarchy, however, is apparent rather than real—it is an ordered disorder. At any rate, Beethoven has succeeded in producing in this movement the most magnificent picture of a storm, whether colour- or tone-picture, that so far has been given to the world.

Whilst in the fourth movement all is uproar and strife among the elements, and fear and awe among men, in the fifth all is serenity and peace, all joy and gratitude.

Some critics have found the last movement too long, considering its contents, and some have even hinted that the whole symphony and especially the last movement was on a lower level than that on which Beethoven usually moves in his symphonies. These people forget that the master's intention was to write a *pastoral* symphony and to depict certain things which he clearly indicated by words. Now, as this was his intention, he had necessarily to write something that was totally different from the *Heroic* and other symphonies. Was the subject chosen unworthy of the artist? Surely, it was not. Was the treatment of the subject unworthy of him? Again, surely, it was not. Indeed, in the *Pastoral* Symphony the composer was as great as in the grandest of his other symphonies, and nothing could be more beautiful. That Beethoven knew how to be idyllic as well as heroic proves him so much the greater an artist. Why not be for once content with perfect serenity and pure beauty, without stress and strain?

A question of greater pertinence and importance in connection with the *Pastoral* Symphony is the legitimacy of the material tone-painting to be found there. The master has been greatly blamed for writing programme music, and still more for certain features of it, and most of all for the introduction of the nightingale, quail, and cuckoo, towards the end of the slow movement. This was not to be wondered at ninety years ago. But it is strange that even at the present day there are people who think it necessary to make excuses for Beethoven, or are so kind as to make allowances for his eccentricities. Two tests decide the legitimacy of material tone-painting. Is it subordinate to the spiritual? Is it of an artistic nature? The unprejudiced cannot but admit that the passage in question stands the application of these tests. The imitation of the bird voices occupies only a few bars of the long movement; and both the imitation and the manner of introduction are in the highest degree artistic. I have not the least hesitation in asserting that the effect of the last eleven bars of the scene 'By the Brook' is truly poetical.

Some instruction on this point may be got from the master's sketch books. Among his notes for the *Pastoral* Symphony there is one superscribed, 'Thunder,' which, however, was not in any way utilized. Then in an earlier note-book, years before he began to write the symphony, he had twice jotted down the tones and rhythms he had heard in the murmuring of brooks; the second version being a fifth lower and accompanied by the remark, 'the larger the brook, the deeper the tone.' These notes, or the experiences that suggested them, were not forgotten when he wrote the scene 'By the Brook'; but he remembered them as an artist who allows nature to suggest, not to dictate. Beethoven's attitude towards materialistic tone-painting is, as my interpretation has shown, well illustrated by the scene 'By the Brook' and by the thunderstorm, where he combines with an idealistic imitation of the sounds of nature, the expression of human emotions.

Did the composer of the *Sinfonie Pastorale* owe anything to the composer of the *Portrait musical de la Nature?* The opinion has been hazarded that Beethoven was unlikely to have been acquainted with Knecht's work. But if certain circumstances are taken into account, the likelihood of his having known it is much greater than the unlikelihood.   The striking similarity of the programmes speaks of course strongly in favour of the assumption that Beethoven knew the earlier composition.   The circumstances alluded to are, however, these.   Bossler, of Spire, who in 1784 published Knecht's symphony, also published in 1783 and 1784 the boy Beethoven's first compositions, three sonatas and two songs.   Knecht was a widely known musical respectability, both as a writer of and on music.   His portrait appeared in 1791 in the musical periodical *Musikalische Korrespondenz der deutschen Filarmonischen Gesellschaft* (Bossler, Spire), and may have been seen by Beethoven; his works were reviewed in, and he wrote articles for, the *Allgemeine musikalische Zeitung* (Breitkopf & Härtel, Leipzig; 1798, &c.), an influential periodical which Beethoven no doubt read; and his life and works were described in Gerber's *Lexicon*, which Beethoven possessed.   From these data it is not rash to conclude that Beethoven did know Knecht's symphony, and that he was inspired by it; but only by the programme, not by the music, or at least not otherwise by the music than with the desire of doing well what had been done badly.

There is one work of Beethoven's which, though it has not an explicit programme, may be said to have an implicit one,—I mean the *Choral* Symphony.   The programme is hinted at by the stanzas from Schiller's *Ode to Joy*, on which the last division of the work is founded, and by Beethoven's own words which connect this division with what precedes.   The contents of the symphony, as I understand it, are briefly this : The first movement spreads out before us a world dark, void, and without form.   The solitary individual, confronted by stern unbending necessity, looking into a joyless,

hopeless, merciless mysterious infinitude, is filled with
indescribable despair.   No grander, gloomier, and more
awe-inspiring picture has ever been painted by brush or
pen.   It is a dread revelation of infinite Nature to finite
Man.   In the second movement, the *Scherzo*, with its
wild capricious sportiveness, there is a desperate gaiety,
with   mad   pranks   and   boisterous   outbreaks.   It
represents   diversion,   not   happiness.   The   third
movement, an *Adagio*, is a vision of all that is sweet and
beautiful.   Nothing could be more enrapturing.   But it
is only a vision, only a dream—as the dire dissonances
with which the next division opens prove only too
conclusively.   After fierce cries and volleys of wild
ejaculations, as of one seized by sudden pain, after sullen
recitatives by the double-basses, after reminiscences of the
Scherzo and the *Adagio*, after the presentment of a new
and comforting thought and another fierce cry and volley
of wild ejaculations, a human voice strikes in with the
words : 'O Friends, not these tones, let us sing more
pleasing ones.'   And now begins Schiller's *Hymn to Joy*.
How the composer revels in the expression of the poet's
themes all know who have heard the work.   What indeed
could be more congenial to the master than sentiments
such as these :—

> 'Embrace, ye millions—let this kiss,
>   Brothers, embrace the earth below !
>   Yon starry worlds that shine on this,
>   One common father know.'

In short, the *Choral* Symphony is a musical exposition of
Beethoven's philosophy.*

* Compare with the above Wagner's different but not incongruous
exposition in his *Report on the Performance of the Ninth Symphony of
Beethoven.*

We have now exhausted Beethoven's works and parts of works with superscriptions. These, however, are not the master's only programmatic compositions. He had for years, from 1816 onwards, the intention of bringing out a new complete edition of his sonatas, one of the moving reasons being his desire to indicate the poetic ideas on which many of these works were based, and thus to facilitate the comprehension and determine the reading of them. We owe this information to Schindler, Beethoven's friend and biographer, who tells us also that in later years the master spoke of the *Largo* of the Sonata Op. 10, in D major, as depicting the mood of a melancholy person with all the varied *nuances* of light and shade in the picture of melancholy and its phases; of the two Sonatas Op. 14, as the contention of two principles (the entreating and the resisting), or a dialogue between two persons, a husband and wife, or a lover and sweetheart, the dialogue and its meaning being more pregnantly expressed and the opposition of the two persons more palpable in the second sonata; and (in a conversation of 1823) of the *Sonate Pathétique*, Op. 13, as also containing in the middle movement two principles. When Schindler asked Beethoven what was the poetic idea of the Sonata Op. 31, No. 2, in D minor, and the Sonata Op. 57, in F minor, the master replied: ' Read Shakespeare's *Tempest*.' A very interesting story is told by Schindler of the Sonata Op. 90, in E minor, dedicated to Count Moritz Lichnowsky. ' When Count Lichnowsky received this sonata,' he writes, ' it seemed to him that his friend Beethoven had wished to express a definite idea in the two movements of which it consists. He did not fail to ask the master. As the latter never kept back what was

in his mind, he had no hesitation in replying now.
Laughing loudly, he at once remarked that he had
intended to picture in his music the love-story of the
Count and his wife ; adding that if a superscription was
required, that of the first movement might be " Struggle
between head and heart," and that of the second,
" Conversation with the beloved one." ' These
superscriptions fit the music very well.   As to the
Count's love-story, it is briefly told as follows.   He fell
in love with an opera singer of talent and exemplary
character.   His relations opposed a *mésalliance*.   But after
the death of his elder brother, Prince Carl, Count Moritz
followed the dictates of his heart, and married the amiable
lady.   One more of Beethoven's indications has to be
mentioned.   Regarding the first five bars of the C minor
Symphony, he remarked to Schindler, with impetuous
enthusiasm : ' Thus does Fate knock at the door.'

But can we trust Schindler ?   I believe we can.
Moreover, his communications are corroborated by other
witnesses.   Ferdinand Ries says of his master :
' Beethoven often thought of a definite subject in his
compositions.'   And Carl Czerny, who saw much of
Beethoven, and had his help in studying his works, writes :
' It is certain that many of Beethoven's finest works were
inspired by similar visions and pictures drawn from
reading and his own imagination ; and that if it were
possible to obtain a sure knowledge of these circumstances, we should have the key to his compositions
and their rendering.'   To these general statements may
be added a particular one.   Beethoven told his friend
Amenda— who informed Lenz—that when composing the
Adagio of the String Quartet in F major, Op. 18, No. 1,
he thought of Romeo and Juliet in the tomb scene.

But even if Schindler's, Ries's, and Czerny's reports were unknown to us, our knowledge of Beethoven's character would make us guess as much. One with so intensive a soul-life could not but infuse it into his art-work. And one with so sublime a conception of art could not wish the two, the soul-life and the art-work, apart. In fact, his lofty mind could not but despise mere ingeniously contrived structures of meaningless tone combinations, however sensuously beautiful. We must be careful not to measure Beethoven by the common standard. To understand him, read his will, the letters to his 'immortal love,' his apostrophes to Fate, and his exaltation of music. 'Music is the mediation between the spiritual and the sensuous life.' 'Art and science alone point out to us and let us hope a higher life.' 'Music is a higher revelation than all wisdom and philosophy.' 'All that is called life shall be sacrificed to the sublime one (music), and be a sanctuary of art.' These are a few of the many striking sayings to be found in the master's letters and note-books. They distinctly point to the fact that Beethoven was a moral as well as an æsthetical force. And this brings me to the last and most powerful proof, the impressions produced by Beethoven's music on the hearer. Does he not feel that there is in it more than a clever display of beautiful and piquant tone combinations, that there is in it meaning, and meaning of profound and noble import, and not merely something vague but something definite, although perhaps the definite be not easily translatable into words? When Mendelssohn played (on the pianoforte) the first movement of Beethoven's C minor Symphony to Goethe, the latter was strangely affected by the music. At first he said: 'That does not move one at all; it only

astonishes; it is grandiose.' After a long time, he
resumed: ' That is very grand, quite mad, it makes one
almost afraid the house will come down; and when it is
played by all the people [the full orchestra] !' And so
much was the musically untrained and really unmusical
Goethe stirred by what he had heard that later in the day
he once more returned to the subject. It is interesting
to compare the experience of the poet Goethe with a
reflection of Julian Schmidt, the literary historian. ' In
connection with Beethoven's symphonies we have the
feeling that they are concerned with something very
different from the usual alternation of joy and sorrow, in
which music without words is wont to move and have its
being. We divine the mysterious abyss of a spiritual
world, and torment ourselves to fathom it. We wish to
know what has driven the tone-poet to this boundless
despair and to this extravagant jubilation. The need
makes itself the more felt, the deeper music penetrates
into the inner world, as in Beethoven's last period.'

To the testimony of untrained music lovers let us
add that of some professional musicians. Wagner's
Programmatic Explanations of the Sinfonia Eroica and
the Coriolanus overture, his *Report and Programme* of
the ninth Symphony, and his remarks on the great
Leonore overture in the essay *On the Overture*, are
unsurpassable masterpieces. His writings, moreover,
are full of light-giving *obiter dicta* concerning the great
master's works. In fact, Wagner's *dicta* on this subject
are always excellent except where theorizings inspired
by his own practice lead him to misinterpret his
predecessor, as, for instance, in the characterization of
the seventh, the A major Symphony (see *Art-work of the
Future*). Marx, who in his *Life and Works of Beethoven*

K

analyzes many of the master's compositions, suggests here and there programmes, and always accentuates the fact of an ideal content. Parenthetically I will mention the amateur Lenz's *Critical Catalogue of Beethoven's Works,* in which are to be met with, besides numberless idle conceits, not a few happy hints. Tchaikovsky, who is one of the many musicians who have expressed regret that Beethoven has not himself provided programmes, asks in one of his letters the question : 'Has Beethoven's fifth Symphony a programme ?' And he answers it thus : 'It not only has a programme, but there cannot be the slightest difference of opinion as to what the symphony purports to express.' He further confesses that his own fourth Symphony has the same programme.* Rubinstein saw even in the early works besides the æsthetical, the ethical element ; saw that Beethoven's instrumental music could express the dramatic and even the tragic ; saw that his humour rises to irony. 'He is incredibly great in his adagios— his utterances reach from the most beautiful lyrical to the metaphysical and mystical. But quite incomprehensibly great he is in his scherzos. Some of them I feel inclined to compare with the Fool in *King Lear.* One hears in them smiling, laughing, bantering, not unfrequently bitterness, irony, anger—in short, a world of psychological expression. It seems to come not from a man, but, as it were, from an invisible Titan, who now rejoices over humanity, now is vexed at it, now makes fun of it, now weeps over it. In one word, Beethoven is wholly incommensurable.' Among the best and truest words that have been said on the same subject are the following ones of Edward Dannreuther :

* See this in the account of Tchaikovsky, Book V., Chapter III.

' While listening to such works as the overture to *Leonora*,
the *Sinfonia Eroica*, or the ninth Symphony, we feel
that we are in the presence of something far wider and
higher than the mere development of musical themes.
The execution in detail of each movement and each
succeeding work is modified more and more by the
prevailing poetic sentiment. A religious passion and
elevation are present in the utterances. The mental
and moral horizon of the music grows upon us with
each renewed hearing. The different movements—like
the different particles of each movement—have as close
a connection with one another as the acts of a tragedy,
and a characteristic significance to be understood only
in relation to the whole ; each work is in the full sense
of the word a revelation. Beethoven speaks a language
no one has spoken before, and treats of things no one
has dreamt of before. . . . The warmth and depth of
his ethical sentiment is now felt all the world over, and
it will ere long be universally recognized that he has
leavened and widened the sphere of men's emotions in a
manner akin to that in which the conceptions of great
philosophers and poets have widened the sphere of men's
intellectual activity.'

After reading the foregoing pages many will no doubt
admit that Beethoven was a composer of programme
music to a much larger extent than they had thought.
Some of them, however, will add that he differs from
composers of the Berlioz and Liszt types in that he
subordinated the programme to the form.   Is that true?
No ! So far is this from being true that one is perfectly
justified in saying that the widening and strengthening
of the instrumental forms which we owe to Beethoven is
the offspring of his poetic ideas, of his programmes.   To

be sure, his form is always classical, that is, lucid and beautiful, and satisfactory considered by itself; but it is not invariably traditional, conventional, both the structure and number of the movements being dictated by the underlying poetic ideas, by the programme in his mind. Of course, among Beethoven's compositions there are many which deviate not at all or only very little from the traditional Haydn-Mozart form, and many are not based on programmes or are based on programmes of a more or less shadowy kind. Nevertheless my proposition remains unaffected. Schindler says: 'It is well known that Beethoven did not confine himself to writing in the traditional forms, but often avoided them because the idea by which he allowed himself to be prompted demanded another treatment, or, more correctly, a new vesture. Hence the sometimes heard remark: "Beethoven's sonatas are operas in disguise."' Let me give a few familiar examples. The episodes of the first movement of the *Heroic* Symphony have their justification in the programme. The third movement of the overture to *Egmont* is not merely a brilliant *coda* to the preceding movement, but the expression of a new idea. Again, it was the programme that in the *Pastoral* Symphony called for five instead of four movements, and caused the form of the slow movement to be vague, that of the Storm to be non-architectural, and that of the others to be more or less deviating from the traditional. Whoever has studied the great *Leonore* overture knows that the form of this work is largely influenced by the poetic contents.* The same holds good with regard to the *Choral* Symphony. It is difficult to be so blind as

---

* We must concede this even if we agree with Wagner in thinking that the recapitulation of the first after the middle division is a weakness.

not to see this in the first movement of this work; it is impossible not to see it in what immediately precedes the vocal portion. We need not go for confirmation of my proposition to the master's last string quartets, in which he so widely departs from the sonata form; we find it in many and many of his works in which the traditional form is to a more or less extent adhered to. In short, the traditional forms did not mould Beethoven's ideas, but the ideas moulded the forms and sometimes even broke them. This, at any rate, was the state of matters with Beethoven at his best.

It is important that we should form a clear and correct notion of Beethoven's position with regard to programme music, and this could only be arrived at by a sober statement of the facts of the case. Having such a statement before him, the reader, I think, will be as firmly convinced as I am myself that not only were the master's tendency and practice in this respect less limited in extent than is mostly supposed, but also that the time cannot be far off when he will be regarded as the chief founder and the greatest cultivator of programme music.

CHAPTER II.

Beethoven's younger contemporary, CARL MARIA VON WEBER (1786-1826), plays a much more important part in the development of programme music than he is credited with. Indeed, those who have no eyes but for the obvious do not so much as dream of him as a composer of programme music. Leaving for the present the overtures out of account, only one of Weber's purely instrumental compositions—the *Momento capriccioso* need not be considered—bears a title hinting at a programme, namely Op. 65, *Aufforderung zum Tanz* (Invitation to the Dance); and not a few musicians look upon this title as a mere fancy title, attractive but meaningless. An indisputable authority, however, the composer's wife, has corrected this view. When Weber had finished the piece in 1819 (it was not published till 1821), he played it to her, and accompanied the performance with the following commentary : 'First approach of the dancer (bars 1-5) ; the lady's evasive reply (5-9) ; his pressing invitation (9-13—the short *appoggiatura c* and the *appoggiatura a♭* are very significant) ; her consent (13-16) ; they enter into conversation—he begins (17-19), she replies (19-21), he speaks with greater warmth (21-23), she sympathetically agrees (23-25). Now for the dance ! He addresses her with regard to it (25-27), her answer (27-29), they draw together (29-31), take their places, are waiting for the

commencement of the dance (31-35).—The dance.—
Conclusion : his thanks, her reply, their retirement.
Silence.' The commentary leaves us in the lurch as
to the main part of the composition, the dance.
Nevertheless it would be a mistake to conclude from this
gap in the story that Weber's waltz is no more than a
rhythmic and melodic accompaniment of the motions of
the dancers. So far is this from being the case that it
has been described by someone as the poetic idea of the
dance, and by someone else as the expression of all that
the German dance contains of poetry, chivalry,
tenderness, and grace. In fact, we may read in it a
whole story of youthful joyousness, coquetry, courtship,
and love. The piece made quite a sensation among
musicians as well as among the general public. Men
like Liszt and Berlioz, on making its acquaintance, were
enthusiastic about it ; the latter, in after years, scoring
it for the orchestra. Recently Felix Weingartner, too,
scored it, with additions of his own. It has also been
arranged for two pianofortes, and for all sorts of
instruments ; Tausig transmogrified it even into a
bravura concert piece.

Fresh, spirited, and delightful as the *Aufforderung
zum Tanz* is, Op. 79, the *Concertstück* (Concert
Piece) for pianoforte and orchestra must be admitted
to be a more serious and weighty contribution to
programme music. This is the Concerto in F minor
mentioned in a letter addressed to Rochlitz, where
Weber speaks about his conceiving a story extending
over the whole of the work, and his fear of being
numbered with the charlatans. His fear getting the
better of him, he concealed the programme from the
public. Fortunately, it was fully revealed to his

wife and Julius Benedict, his pupil, to whom the happy
composer played the *Concertstück* immediately after
finishing it, at Berlin, on the 18th of June, 1821, the
day of the first performance of *Der Freischütz.* Weber's
commentary ran thus : ' The lady sits in her tower : she
gazes sadly into the distance. Her knight has been for
years in the Holy Land : shall she never see him again ?
Battles have been fought ; but there is no news of
him who is so dear to her. In vain have been
her prayers and her longing. A dreadful vision rises
in her mind :—her knight is lying on the battlefield, deserted by his companions ; his heart's blood is
ebbing fast away. Could she but be by his side !—could
she but die with him ! She falls down exhausted and
senseless. But hark ! What is that distant sound ?
What glimmers in the sunlight from the wood ? What
are those forms approaching ? Knights and squires with
the cross of the Crusaders, banners waving, acclamations
of the people ; and there !—it is he ! She sinks into
his arms. What a commotion of love ! What an
infinite, indescribable happiness ! The very woods and
waves sing the song of true love ; a thousand voices
proclaim its victory.' *

The programme is undoubtedly poetical and romantic.
But does the music realize it ? Yes, certainly ! It
realizes vividly its spirit, sentiments, and colour.
Weber asserted no more than the truth when he wrote
to Rochlitz that the parts of the composition follow each

* The above-mentioned letter to Rochlitz is of March 14, 1815. The
composer indicates the programme of his projected F minor Concerto
briefly thus : ' *Allegro*, Separation ; *Adagio*, Lament ; *Finale*, Profoundest
sorrow, consolation, meeting again, and jubilation.' He adds that he
hates titled tone-pictures, but that the idea irresistibly obtrudes itself
upon him, and endeavours to convince him of its effectiveness.

other in accordance with the story, and receive their character from it in a detailed and dramatic manner. Especially noteworthy is that the story determined the form of the work. Hence Weber's denomination of the composition—not concerto, but *Concertstück.*

Although we do not hear of any other programmes in connection with the master's pianoforte compositions, one cannot listen to works like the A flat major Sonata, and the E flat and the E major Polonaise—to mention only the most striking examples—without suspecting that there is something more in them than the general characteristics of Weber's romanticism—namely, the chivalrous, the supernatural, and the naively sentimental. Weber's bibliographer, F. W. Jähns, looked upon each of the sonatas, 'those four extraordinary works,' as mirroring a particular character-picture with the rarest distinctness; and the composer's son and biographer remarks significantly of his father's chamber works and songs that they are 'so many reflexes of the dramatic tendency of his genius, preparatory studies for his dramatic works.'

Whatever may be the extent and quality of the programmatic in Weber's purely instrumental compositions, the master is more eminent as a composer of programme music in his stage than in his concert and chamber works. On having his attention drawn in this direction, the reader's first thought will be of the Wolf's Glen scene in *Der Freischütz.* The gruesome horrors of this scene are indeed musically drawn with wonderful originality and immense force. But whilst fully admitting the originality and powerfulness of the tone-painting in this case, one may yet hold that the depicting of the Satanic influence in the first act of the same opera, of the fairy world in *Oberon*, and of the ghostly vision of Emma and the pomp and circumstance of chivalry in *Euryanthe*, is no less original and powerful, although less violently striking. These are only a few remarkable examples of that admirable tone-painting, of things internal and external, in which Weber's operas abound. At least two or three more may yet be specified for reference—Max's aria in the first act of *Der Freischütz*, to which I have already alluded, Agathe's aria in the second act of the same opera, and Rezia's aria in *Oberon*, ' Ocean! thou mighty monster.'

Of programme music apart from words and action, Weber's operas furnish us with brilliant examples in the overtures, especially *Der Freischütz, Euryanthe,* and *Oberon*. They summarize the contents of the operas, not, however, the incidents of the plot, but the emotional substrata and the atmosphere and the colouring. It would be an egregious mistake to look upon these overtures as a kind of *potpourri* because they contain motives from the operas. These musical motives are at the same time fundamental emotional or otherwise characteristic motives. Let me indicate in a few words the programmes of the compositions in question.

The essence of the *Freischütz* overture is this: The peace and innocence of forest life, broken in upon by the powers of darkness; struggle between good and evil; victory of the former. The main part of the introductory movement (*Adagio*) depicts the sweet peacefulness; later on, the inimical intrusion makes itself felt by the fear-inspiring motive characteristic of Samiel, the evil spirit. The further course may be traced by means of the following analysis of the *Allegro*. In the first subject are incorporated a motive from Max's aria (' What evil pow'r

is closing round me '), and another from the Wolf's Glen
scene, when a thunder-storm accompanied by hail
breaks out, and flames start from the earth ; in the second
subject, another motive from Max's aria ('No ray will
shine upon my darkness '), and the jubilant one from
Agathe's aria ('How every pulse is flying, and my heart
beats loud and fast, we shall meet in joy at last').
This last is the redeeming motive, which, after the
struggle between the good and evil influence that goes on
through the rest of the tone-poem, finally triumphs.

Chivalry is the predominant note of the *Euryanthe*
overture. After a brilliant, dashing period follows the
knightly motive from Adolar's aria (' I trust in God and
my Euryanth '). In the second subject we notice a love-
laden motive from another aria of Adolar (' O, bliss ! I
do not fathom thee '). Between the exposition and the
development occurs an episode (*Largo*), the ghostly
apparition of Emma, with which is connected the cause
of the troubles depicted in the middle division. Chivalry
and love, however, gain the day at last, as the ending of
the third division, the modified recapitulation with *coda*,
shows.

In the *Oberon* overture the temptation to suspect a
potpourri or mosaic of motives is greater than in the
other two. For here we meet in the introduction with
a magic horn motive, a fairy motive, and a Charlemagne
motive (from the march at the end of the opera) ; and in
the *Allegro con fuoco*, a travel, or adventure motive
(from the quartet ' On board then '), and the motives of
devotion and jubilation (Huon's thoughts of love and the
beloved, in the aria ' From boyhood trained in battlefield,'
and Rezia's rejoicing at the supposed approach of
deliverance, in the Ocean aria). Nevertheless the

overture is a whole, and, moreover, enables one to realize something of the spirit and colour of the opera without knowing it. The tones of the magic horn at the beginning transport us at once into a strange and beautiful world on which we gaze spell-bound. Ambros sees in the opening *Adagio* a moon-lit magic night full of floating rose perfumes from the wondrous gardens of the East, and thinks that he who has Heine's sound-picturing talent must feel in this overture as if he saw passing before him shining cupolas, fantastic minarets, palm woods, lovely women, Saracen and occidental knights in combat and sport, and all the strange wonders of the Orient in a dazzling *Fata morgana*. This is an enthusiastic and poetic, but hardly a legitimate interpretation. The excellent Ambros—who, by-the-way, was not a favourer of programme music — proves, however, by his eloquent words his conviction that Weber really painted a tone-picture. My account of Weber as a composer of programme music would be incomplete without some reference to his incidental use of melodrama. In *Der Freischütz* it is notable for its characteristically effective alternation with song, in *Preciosa* for the rhythmical notation of the recitation.

Whoever knows the songs of FRANZ SCHUBERT (1797-1828) knows too that in them the greatest song composer is also a great composer of programme music. The adding of a fitting musical accompaniment to verses did not seem to him a task worthy of a tone-poet. He felt impelled to re-create the word-poet's creations. In fact, the poems he set to music were to him but programmes for the realization of which he had to have recourse to the pianoforte as well as to the voice. It would be impertinent on my part to offer examples proving my assertion. Nobody's memory will fail to supply some, and any volume of the master's songs will furnish a multitude more.

But was Schubert in purely instrumental works a composer of programme music? Not a confessed one. Was he, then, an unconfessed one? The question is difficult to answer; at least cannot be answered with a bold unqualified 'yes' or 'no.' Not one of his independent purely instrumental compositions has an explicit programme, and only two hint at a programme—namely, the fourth Symphony, entitled 'Tragic Symphony,' and one of the pianoforte duets, entitled *Lebensstürme* (Storms of life). No accounts or rumours of concealed programmes have been transmitted to us by the composer's friends and biographers. All this, however, does not dispose of the possibility, or even of the probability, that Schubert may after all have been a composer of purely instrumental programme music. I have no doubt that some will advance as an objection that Schubert was a dreamer, not a thinker, and that his music is a spinning-out of notes 'with many a winding bout of linked sweetness long drawn out.' There is some truth in this. He was a dreamer of dreams: but for the most part he was a wide-awake dreamer of most vivid dreams. His songs are unimpeachable witnesses to his clear-eyed penetrating vision as well as to the luminousness of his imagination. His smaller pianoforte pieces—the *Impromptus, Moments musicals,* &c. —testify to the same qualities, if only we listen to them attentively. Some of them are song-like, and all have speaking expressiveness and pronounced character. Without forgetting Beethoven's *Bagatelles,* we may say that Schubert was the originator of the vitalized pianoforte literature in the lesser forms of the 19th century. Who would confidently assert that these strikingly expressive and characteristic little tone-poems were all the offspring of vague moods and a fertile formative musical genius; that none were engendered by anything more definite than vague moods—none by conscious emotions, sentimental complications, interesting occurrences, literary productions, and landscapes? And again, if you listen, listen attentively, to works like the D minor and the A minor Quartet, the two Trios, the C major Symphony, and the unfinished B minor Symphony—to mention only a few of many: are you not here, too, struck, and even more forcibly, by the fact that inasmuch as there is dreaming in them, it is dreaming of the most vivid kind, and that not a little of what is offered us seems to be real life in its intensest forms?

Let us see what Schumann says of Schubert, whom he partly discovered, and whose genius he first fully recognized. He calls him on one occasion a 'romantic painter.' On another occasion he speaks of 'the bright, blooming romantic life' in the master's C major Symphony. Again, he says: 'Schubert has tones for the finest feelings, thoughts, and even events and circumstances.' Note the concluding words of this sentence; and note also the following remarks: 'Schubert will always remain the favourite of the young; he shows them what they want—an overflowing heart, daring thoughts, and quick deeds; relates to them what they like best—romantic stories of knights, maids, and adventures, with which he mingles also wit and humour, but not so much that the gentle fundamental mood is thereby dimmed.'

Schumann omits to mention Schubert's love of Nature
—of fields and woods, of flowers and trees, of lakes and
rivers, of clouds, of sun, moon, and stars. There is
little of it in his letters, but his music is full of it.
Ambros points out a very true and interesting distinction
between Beethoven and Schubert. The meaning of his
words is as follows : ' Beethoven in his flight keeps his
eyes turned upward to the eternal stars, the infinite
depths of the heavens; Schubert in *his* flight never
loses sight of the beautiful earth, looking smilingly down
on it and its flower gardens, cornfields, and vineyards.'

It will be for the reader to decide to what extent
Schubert, when composing, had distinct extra-musical
subjects in his mind, was possessed by definite ideas,
impressions, and feelings. I will give an impulse to the
inquiry by asking a few questions. Do you not hear in
the introductory *Andante* of the C major Symphony a
serene hymn of praise to God, who is all love and
goodness? Do not the rapids of imagination in the
following *Allegro* shoot you along with giddy swiftness
through a sunny, laughing world, in which sorrowing and
praying are heard only like far-off sounds from another
sphere ? Do you not perceive the stream of fluctuating
moods in the *Andante con moto*—the melodic complaint,
the rapt contemplation that loses itself in the twilight of
a beautiful dreaming vision, &c. ? Do you not wish to
join in the boisterous sport and graceful dance of the
Scherzo, and the hearty chorus of the *Trio* ? Do you not
feel yourself carried away in the *Finale* by the high-
spirited joyousness and the irresistible onward movement,
which suggested to one commentator ' Magyar heroes
riding past brandishing their sabres ' ? And, lastly, do you
not share Schumann's opinion that in this work there is

significance everywhere, and that it leads you into regions where you cannot remember to have been before ? Or, turning to the unfinished B minor Symphony, does not the second movement, the *Andante con moto*, conjure up in your mind a picture of peace, contentment, and happiness somewhat like this ?—Smooth pasturage, with sleek cattle quietly grazing ; well-cultivated fields bordered along the country lanes by green hedges ; not far off a limpid brook gliding, now silently, now gently whispering, over its shallow bed ; the whole scene illuminated by the subdued light of the setting sun, for it is late in the afternoon, and in an hour or two the sun will disappear behind those mountains which form the dark background to this pleasing picture. The mild loveliness and suavity of the scene soothe and lull the beholder into a dreamy state of semi-wakefulness. Momentarily he is startled by forebodings, dark and indefinite as that gloomy mountain side. But the future is soon dispelled by the present, the distant by the near, and once more he is bewitched by the play of colours, by the songs of the birds, and by the numerous other elements of which such a scene is composed.

The discussion of Schubert as a composer of programme music may be fitly concluded with a remark made by Schumann in his Heidelberg student days (1829) : 'What a diary in which they enter their momentary feelings is to others, the music paper to which he confided all his humours was to Schubert. His out-and-out musical soul wrote notes where others employ words.'

LOUIS SPOHR (1784-1859) cannot be omitted from the history of programme music, although he is of much less importance than Weber and Schubert. An initial difficulty presents itself as to where to place him ; for he outlived not only these two composers and Beethoven, but also Mendelssohn, Schumann, and Chopin. The three works that concern us especially are *Die Weihe der Töne* (The Consecration of Sound), *Irdisches und Göttliches im Menschenleben* (The Earthly and the Divine in human life), and *Die Jahreszeiten* (The Seasons), composed respectively in 1832, 1841, and 1850.

After a first reading of the poem which furnished the subject, or rather subjects, of the earliest of these three works, Spohr thought of treating it as a cantata, but afterwards came to the conclusion that it did not lend itself to such treatment. The composer himself wrote on October 9, 1832 : 'Recently I finished another great instrumental composition—a fourth symphony, which in form deviates greatly from the preceding ones. It is a tone-picture after a poem by Karl Pfeiffer, *Die Weihe der Töne*, which must be printed and distributed or recited aloud before the performance. In the first division it was my task to form out of the sounds of Nature a harmonious whole. This and the entire work was a difficult, but highly attractive task.'

The opening of the poem runs, in bald English prose, and without improvement of the sense, as follows : ' The earth was lying solitary in the flowery splendour of spring. Amidst the silent forms man walked in darkness, following only wild instinct, not the gentle promptings of the heart. Love had no tones, Nature no speech. Eternal Goodness determined to manifest itself, and breathed into the human breast sound, and caused love to find a language that penetrated blissfully to the heart.' After alluding to various sounds in Nature, the poet dwells

L

feelingly on the employment of music on different occasions.

Spohr sets forth the contents of his Symphony thus:

First Division.

Largo : The unbroken silence of Nature before the generation of sound.

Allegro : Subsequent active life.   Sounds of Nature. Uproar of the Elements.

Second Division.

Cradle Song.   Dance.   Serenade.

Third Division.

Martial Music.   Departure for the battle.   The feelings of those remaining behind.   Return of the victors. Thanksgiving.

Fourth Division.

Funeral music.   Comfort in tears.

It may not be superfluous to point out that although previous to 1832 Berlioz had composed and brought to a hearing in Paris his overtures *Waverley* and *Francs-Juges,* the *Huit Scènes de Faust,* and the first version of the *Symphonie fantastique,* there is not the slightest likelihood that Spohr knew at that time any of the young Frenchman's compositions, and very little likelihood that his attention had been attracted to their tendencies. Fétis's concert accounts in the *Revue musicale* might have done so; but everybody knows how languid people's interest is in the doings of nameless *débutants.* Moreover, the internal evidence alone justifies us in saying that Spohr as a composer of programme music was neither then nor subsequently influenced by Berlioz. Both the programmes and the form

show this. Spohr, in the passage from a letter quoted
by me, states that the form of his fourth Symphony
deviates from that of the preceding ones. That is true.
But, in spite of deviations from the usual structure of
symphony movements, the form is classical. The work
has not one but a series of programmes, between which
there is no connection. Objections to it on account of
its being programme music ought, however, to be
confined to the first division; for, after all, the other
divisions are simply characteristic pieces. As to the
first division, the objection made to the *Largo* is that
the composer depicts silence by sound. A poor objection.
What he depicts is numbness and desolateness.
Moreover, Félicien David has depicted silence very
effectively by sound. And has not Haydn depicted
chaos by harmony? The objection made to the *Allegro*
is, that the composer indulges in material tone-painting
—in the warbling and twittering of birds, the murmuring
of brooks, and the rustling of trees (second subject), and
in the uproar of the elements (the middle section that
occupies the place of the development). This may be
met by the statement that the imitation is idealized,
and the whole treatment artistic.

If Spohr fails to fully satisfy us as a composer of
programme music in this his best work of the kind, and
fails still more in the others, it is not because of the
defects of the *genre*, but because of the character and
narrowness of his individuality. His was an out-and-out
elegiac nature, whose element was a transcendental
sentimentality of feminine tenderness and aristocratic
exquisiteness. His musical style matched his nature,
being smooth and harmonious, and hence also
excessively chromatic. The successful composer of

programme music requires a wider emotional range, and a more virile and less monotonous style. In short, he requires a greater adaptability than Spohr could boast of. The desire to get out of his natural and habitual sphere of feeling may be at least one of the causes of his having recourse to programmes and opera libretti.

My remarks on the other works need not be long. Spohr's *The Earthly and the Divine in Human Life* is a symphony for two orchestras : a small orchestra of eleven solo string instruments represents the divine, and a full orchestra represents the earthly. There are three divisions : the first depicts childhood ; the second, the time of the passions ; and the third the final victory of the divine. A beautiful and novel idea! Moritz Hauptmann—who never could resist the temptation of uttering a *malice* at his dear master's cost—said of this composition that its contents were interesting harmonic progressions. Of course, the remark was more pungent than just. The symphony which Spohr entitled *The Seasons* falls into two divisions : the first depicts Winter, transition to Spring, and Spring ; and the second, Summer, transition to Autumn, and Autumn. To these works may yet be added his overtures, notably that to the opera *Faust,* to which are prefixed the following lines of Goethe :—

> " The God that in my breast is owned
>   Can deeply stir the inner sources ;
>   The God, above my powers enthroned,
>   He cannot change eternal forces.
>   So, by the burden of my days oppressed,
>   Death is desired, and Life a thing unblest ! "

Nor should the eighth Concerto, in the form of a vocal scena, be passed over in silence. On the other hand, the *Historical Symphony*, No. 6, Op. 116, which consists of imitations of different styles, and the *Concertino Sonst und Jetzt* (Past and Present), Op. 110, do not come within the scope of the present inquiry. But I must still mention the Fantasia on Raupach's *Die Tochter der Luft*, in the form of a concert overture, Op. 99 (used as the first movement in his fifth Symphony, in C minor, Op. 102); the *Duo concertante* for pianoforte and violin, Op. 96, entitled 'Echoes of a Journey to Dresden and Saxon Switzerland' (also called 'Travel Sonata'); and the Duettinos for pianoforte and violin, Op. 127, 'Elegiac and Humorous' (Songs without Words).

CHAPTER III.

FIFTH PERIOD CONTINUED : A MISCELLANY OF COMPOSERS BORN BEFORE THE END OF THE 18TH CENTURY—BOIELDIEU, AUBER, ROSSINI, KALKBRENNER, MOSCHELES, LÖWE, AND MEYERBEER.

Before proceeding to the generation of composers that arose about the year 1810, I must set down a few notes regarding some more of the earlier masters. BOIELDIEU (1775-1834), in the overture to *Le petit Chaperon rouge* (1818), endeavours to tell part of the story of that opera, and places the programme under the music phrase by phrase. A more honourable mention is due to AUBER (1782-1871) for the clever orchestral interpretation of the dumb Fenella's thoughts and gestures in *La Muette de Portici*, in England called *Masaniello* (1828). In mentioning this detail I am reminded of a remark by Wagner, who was an enthusiastic admirer of the opera—namely, that the music seemed to him to be real music-pictures. ROSSINI (1792-1868) had a liking for all sorts of tone-painting, but especially for storms. Everybody must remember that in the third act of *Il Barbiere di Siviglia*. In *Guillaume Tell* there are two, one in the fourth act (Tempesta), and a finer one in the overture. GEORGE ONSLOW (1784 - 1852), a Frenchman of British descent on his father's side, famous as a composer of chamber music, depicts in his fifteenth Quintet the pain, the irregular beating of the pulse, and the gratitude on recovery, felt by him after an accident at a wolf hunt, when a spent ball hit him in the face.

Among the compositions of the illustrious pianist FREDERIC W. M. KALKBRENNER (1788-1849) we meet with the following promising titles :—*La femme du Marin, Pensée fugitive ; Le Rêve, Grande Fantaisie,* Op. 113 ; *Le Fou, Scène dramatique,* Op. 136 ; *L'Ange déchu, Grande Fantaisie,* Op. 144 ; and *La Brigantine ou Le Voyage sur Mer,* Op. 103.* The programme of *Le Fou* resembles somewhat that of Berlioz's *Symphonie fantastique.* It runs thus : ' A young pianist deceived in his first affections becomes mad. He expresses on his pianoforte the various sensations he experiences.' Mendelssohn, who heard the second of the above works at a concert of the Paris Conservatoire in 1832, writes : ' Kalkbrenner played at the end of the first part his *Rêve :* that is, a new pianoforte concerto, in which he has gone over to romanticism. He previously explains that he begins with vague dreams, that after that comes despair, then a declaration of love, and in conclusion a military march.'† Mendelssohn adds : ' Scarcely had HENRI HERZ heard this when he likewise quickly composed a romantic pianoforte piece, and likewise prefixed an explanation to it ; there is first a dialogue between a shepherd and a shepherdess, then a thunderstorm ; next a prayer with evening bells, and, lastly, a military march. You will not believe it, but it is really so.' The piece alluded to is no doubt

---

* Did Lamartine's poem *La Chute d'un ange* inspire or suggest Kalkbrenner's *L'Ange déchu ?*

† The curious who wish to study the first four of the above-mentioned productions can easily procure them at a small outlay. (Kalkbrenner-Album : Litolff Edition.)

La Fête pastorale, Grande Fantaisie, Op. 65. CZERNY (1791-1857), the most prolific and least inspired of composers, wrote not only a piece illustrative of a conflagration, and a contemplation of the ruins of a conflagration, but also four *Fantaisies à quatre mains, inspirées des romans de Walter Scott.*

Enough of this pseudo-romanticism and pseudo-programme music. The more musical IGNAZ MOSCHELES (1794-1870)—at least more musical after the vanities and temptations of his early *virtuoso* period—produced, besides a *Sonate caractéristique*, a *Sonate mélancholique*, a *Concert fantastique*, a *Concert pathétique*, and a *Concert pastorale*, and three *Allegri di bravura* (*La Forza, La Leggerezza*, and *Il Capriccio*), the following more distinctly programmatic compositions : an overture for orchestra to Schiller's *Maid of Orleans*, a characteristic piece after the same poet's *Der Tanz*, two fantasias after *Die Erwartung* and *Sehnsucht*, likewise by Schiller, and the twelve Characteristic Studies, Op. 95 (composed about 1836-1837), truly characteristic compositions respectively called Anger, Reconciliation, Contradiction, Juno, Fairy Tale for Children, Bacchanal, Tenderness, Popular Festival Scenes, Moonlight on the Seashore, Terpsichore, Dream, and Fear ; also, the two studies, Op. 98 (*L'Ambition* and *L'Enjouement*), and the four studies, Op. 111 (*Rêverie et Allegresse, Le Carillon, Tendresse et Exaltation*, and *La Fougue*).* In this connection should be read a passage from a letter

---

* The Studies Op. 70 ought to be mentioned, although they are to a larger extent more technical than those enumerated above ; for not only does the composer call them 'twenty-four characteristic compositions,' and say that it was not so much his intention 'to cultivate mechanical perfection as to address himself to the imagination of the performer,' but he also proposes to himself in the last study a 'Conflict of Daemons.'

written by Moscheles in 1859 to his daughter, then studying in Paris : ' In your attempts at composition I advise you to express always a definite feeling, grave or gay, contented or anxious, &c. If you then succeed in little pieces, you may venture on larger ones, in which the feelings as it were dramatically change. Always think of a scene from actual life, and disdain mechanical means for the mere purpose of producing effect.' Here we have, no doubt, a revelation of the master's own practice.

A more interesting phenomenon in the history of programme music than any of those mentioned after Spohr is J. K. G. LÖWE (1796-1869) — interesting, though little regarded in this respect. As Schubert, the greatest song composer, proves himself in his songs a great composer of programme music, so does Löwe, the greatest ballad composer, in his ballads. Without pointing out examples in this branch of composition, I shall proceed to his purely instrumental works, only remarking by the way that even in his oratorios Löwe shows a predilection for the picturesque. His instrumental compositions consist of works with and without programmes, but the former are the more successful. Schumann asserted that in Löwe's compositions without programmes one suspects something behind the music, and wishes to discover it. In fact, it is clear that Löwe was one of those composers who require an impulse from without if they are to do their best, or indeed anything at all. The tasks Löwe set himself are so interesting that I am sure the reader will not complain of my quoting some of the titles, and adding here and there a few words of further elucidation.

Abendfantasie (Evening Fantasia), Op. 11.

Mazeppa, a tone-poem after Byron, Op. 27. One movement, *Allegro feroce*, 6-8 time. A postscript gives the detailed programme: The Ride of Mazeppa bound by an outraged husband to a wild horse—their aimless course, under a burning sun, over fields and heaths and through woods, then across a broad river, and, thus refreshed, again through woods, now followed by packs of hungry wolves, and meeting other wild horses, which the strange sight puts to flight—the breakdown of the horse, vultures circling in the air ready to swoop on their prey, Mazeppa trying to scare them by moving his fingers—at last, deliverance by men who untie his fetters.

Der Barmherzige Bruder (The Brother of Charity), a tone-poem, Op. 28.

Der Frühling (Spring), a tone-poem in sonata form, Op. 47, called Pastoral Sonata. In addition to the main title, there are superscriptions of the several movements and other indications. (1) *Der erwachende Morgen* (Dawning Day). Under the first bars of the slow Introduction are printed the first two stanzas of Uhland's Morning Song (from the *Wanderlieder*): 'As yet the sun's light is hardly perceptible, the morning bells in the dark valley have not yet sounded. How quiet the wide expanse of the wood! The birds are only twittering in their dreams, not yet singing.' At the beginning of the *Allegro* we read *Morgenfeier* (Morning Celebration), and in the course of it occur the words *con espressione religioso*. (2) *Allegretto con commodezza*. *Naturleben* (Life in Nature). *Grand Jour* (Broad Daylight). (3) *Scherzo*. *Gang zu Ländlichen Gruppen* (Walk to Rustic Groups). *Vie Champêtre*.

One part of the movement is superscribed 'From the Village,' another 'From the Town.' (4) *Allegro assai. Tagesneigen* (Waning Day).

Alpenfantasie (Alpine Fantasia), Op. 53.

Biblische Bilder (Biblical Pictures), Op. 96. They are: Bethesda, The Walk to Emmaus, and Martha and Mary.

Zigeuner Sonate (Gipsy Sonata), Op. 107. The five movements of this work bear the following super-scriptions: (1) *Waldscene* (Scene in the Wood); (2) *Indisches Märchen* (Indian Tale); (3) *Tanz* (Dance), comprising 'Corps de Ballet,' 'Torch Dance of the Men,' 'Women dancing round the Wood Wreath,' and 'Egg Dance of the Children'; (4) *Abend-Cultus* (Evening Worship), with the additional information, 'They await the rising of the moon, which they adore as the reflection of the Indian Temple of the Sun.' (5) *Aujbruch am Morgen* (Departure in the Morning).

Vier Fantasien (Four Fantasias), Op. 137, respectively entitled: The Emigrant's Farewell to the Fatherland, The Emigrant's Sea Voyage, The Prairie, and The Emigrant's new Home.

To the above compositions for pianoforte alone has to be added the *Schottische Bilder* (Scottish Pictures), Op. 112, for pianoforte and clarinet.

It is almost incomprehensible how a composer who distinguished himself so greatly in one branch of the art, could fall so far below that level as Löwe did in his instrumental music; and it is quite incomprehensible how a trained and poetically gifted musician could publish compositions so insipid and even childish, so lacking in imaginative power, and even in mere inventiveness as most of those I have enumerated. In

the *Evening* and the *Alpine* Fantasia Löwe is at his
worst; they are without the slightest musical and
programmatic interest. In the Four Fantasias the
master is not much better, although more ambitious.
The *Brother of Charity* has at least a modest, mildly
pleasing air about it. In the *Spring* Sonata the programme interests, but the execution disappoints. What
a distance from this Pastoral Sonata to Beethoven's
Pastoral Symphony! *Mazeppa* shows the composer in
closer grip with the programme than in any other of his
compositions; and on that account it deserves attention,
notwithstanding the slightness of the musical outcome.
A comparison with Liszt's Study (No. 4 of the *Études
d'exécution transcendante*) and Symphonic Poem of the
same name would not turn out to the advantage of the
older composer. Löwe is at his best, musically and
programmatically, in the *Gipsy* Sonata. However, in
saying that he is musically at his best, I do not mean
that he is as good as in his ballads, or that, by this
sonata, he has added a masterpiece to the treasury of
the art, but only that he is at his best in the matter of
instrumental music. To resuscitate unjustly forgotten
works is almost as meritorious as to produce new
ones. It is impossible to perform that pleasing task
in the case of Löwe's instrumental compositions.
If, however, one of them deserves resuscitation it is
the *Gipsy* Sonata.

If the reader considers not only the year of birth, but
also the year of death of the composers mentioned in
this chapter, and, further, the nature of the music they
produced, he may wonder whether some might not have
been more appropriately placed in a later chapter.
Kalkbrenner would not have written his *Le Fou* without

Berlioz's previously written *Episode de la vie d'un artiste* (*Symphonie fantastique*). But *his* modernity was merely an assumed dress, the man himself really belonged to an earlier generation. In the long-lived mouldable Moscheles we have a different case. He, too, is rooted in an earlier generation, but able actually to assimilate much of the spirit of the new age, the spirit of Mendelssohn and Schumann, and in part that of other contemporary masters. Yet another case is presented by the composer I shall now introduce, one whose place here is solely determined by his nativity.

GIACOMO MEYERBEER (1791-1864) began his career as a German composer with scanty success, continued it as an Italian composer with considerable success, and completed it as a cosmopolitan composer with a phenomenally brilliant success. The light of this new sun burst upon the world in 1831, when at Paris his *Robert le Diable* was produced. *Les Huguenots* followed in 1836, *Le Prophète* in 1849, *L'Etoile du Nord* in 1854 (a new version of *Des Feldlager in Schlesien*, produced at Berlin in 1844), *Le Pardon de Ploërmel* (*Dinorah*) in 1859, and *L'Africaine* in 1865. Schumann and Wagner lavished upon him abuse and contempt, and the later generations of musicians subserviently and unthinkingly echoed these. But the judgment, which the opinion of the public has ignored or annulled, needs revision. It is of course undeniable that Meyerbeer was an eclectic, and that his was an unblended, a kaleidoscopic eclecticism. But this drawback, and also that other drawback, his eagerness for effect at any price, while destructive of the highest artistic quality, unity and chasteness of style, did not nullify his many and great virtues, nor justify his excommunication from the realm of art. Meyerbeer, though not an exclusive individual personality and an artist of immaculately pure ideals, was a musician of genius, possessed of a complete mastery of all the resources of the art, of a wonderful inventiveness, and of a power of expression extending from the lightest gaiety to the most sublime and powerful pathos, and ranging through the whole scale of the characteristic and the picturesque. In short, he has to be numbered with Mendelssohn, Schumann, Chopin, Berlioz, Wagner, and Liszt, that is, as one of the masters who were the chief shapers of music from the fourth decade of the 18th century onward. His contributions to the development of the art have not yet been sufficiently acknowledged. They are certainly not confined to the department of instrumentation, where, of course, there are innumerable records of the miracles performed by him. The programme music of Meyerbeer's operas is too voluminous to admit of enumeration and too obvious to require it. The inquirer has only to dive into the master's scores, and wherever he looks he will discover examples of all sorts and conditions of expressing and picturing the inward and outward. To indicate a few places : in *Robert le Diable*, the sweetness of peaceful nature contrasted with the terrors of the din of hell, the resurrection of nuns in the midnight cloisters; in *Les Huguenots*, the severity and rudeness of the martial Calvinist Marcel, popular life in amity and strife, the plotting and fanaticism of the conspirators, the passionate dialogue of the lovers whilst the tocsin is booming, the sombre solitary marriage service amidst the horrors of St. Bartholomew's night, the bloodthirsty cruelty of the inhuman murderers, &c.

It is worth noting that Meyerbeer's early Italian opera *Il Crociato in Egitto* (The Crusader in Egypt) opens with what the composer calls a *pantomima*, that is, with dumb-show on the stage accompanied by descriptive music in the orchestra. A jailor unlocks the doors of a prison, the prisoners come out, embrace each other sadly, and begin their labours, dragging heavy weights from the harbour and raising stones for building; the blows of the masons' hammers and chisels are heard; some sentimental incidents enacted. But Meyerbeer has given us also an example of programmatic orchestral music apart from his operas—namely, his music to his brother Michael Beer's tragedy *Struensee* (1844), which, though it is the least known of his works, excellent judges agree in pronouncing the finest.

CHAPTER IV.

Like Beethoven, MENDELSSOHN (1809-1847) cannot but be regarded by the opponents of programme music as an extremely inconvenient fact. Both are classicists and producers of unexceptionable absolute music (or what is supposed to be such), and yet have not recoiled from touching the unclean thing. Indeed, by what they have done these great masters have conclusively testified to the legitimacy of programme music. Mendelssohn is even a more inconvenient fact than Beethoven. For we have of him not only many pieces of acknowledged programme music, but we have also authoritative information about unacknowledged programmes, and various utterances by himself defining clearly his attitude towards the question. With regard to the last point, it should be noted that, although he disliked and shunned æsthetical discussions, he had considéred the problems of his art, and knew how to express on occasion the conclusions he had come to. But what were these utterances? First of all we have his remark that since Beethoven had taken the step he took in the Pastoral Symphony, it was impossible for composers to keep clear of programme music. Then we have his reply to the question of a correspondent who wanted to know what some of the *Songs without Words* meant. The composer declined to give the desired information; and he did so, not because of the indefiniteness of music, but because of the indefiniteness of words. 'A piece of music that I love expresses to me,' he writes on October 15, 1842, to Marc André Souchay, 'thoughts not too indefinite to be put into words, but too definite. Hence I find in all attempts to express these thoughts something true, but at the same time something insufficient ; and this is my feeling with regard to yours also. This, however, is not your fault, but the fault of the words, which cannot do better. If you ask me what were my thoughts when composing the *Songs without Words,* I say, " Just the songs as they stand." And though in one or the other I had in my mind a definite word or definite words, yet I do not like to communicate them to anyone, because words have not the same meaning for one as they have for another, since only the song can say the same thing to one that it says to another, and awaken the same feeling in one as in another,—a feeling, however, which cannot be expressed by the same words. Resignation, melancholy, praise of God, the hunt,—these words do not call up the same thoughts in everybody; to one resignation is what melancholy is to another; and a third is unable to form a vivid idea of either. Nay, to him who is by nature a keen hunter, the hunt and the praise of God might come pretty much to the same thing, and for him the sound of horns would really and truly be also the right praise of God. We should hear in it nothing but the hunt, and however much we disputed the matter with him, we should never get further. The word remains ambiguous, and yet we should both of us understand the music aright.' That Mendelssohn expresses here a settled belief, not a passing conceit, may be gathered from a passage in a letter addressed to Madame von Pereira (July, 1831).

M

She had asked him to set to music Zedlitz's ballad *Die nächtliche Heerschau*, and he excuses himself for failing to do so. 'I am inclined to take music very seriously, and do not consider it permissible to compose anything I do not thoroughly feel. It would be like telling a lie. For *have not notes as distinct a meaning as words—perhaps even a still more distinct meaning?* Well, it seems to me impossible to compose a descriptive poem.' The discussion of the position of music with regard to narrative poetry generally and to the poem in question particularly is extremely interesting for the musician, but it must not detain us now. The quotation was made on account of the italicized words.

Further light is thrown on Mendelssohn as a composer of programme music, and on his *Songs without Words* as programme music, by another letter of his, one of June 14, 1830, addressed to his sister Fanny. (In passing I may mention that the first of his *Songs without Words* was composed in 1828.) 'To-day I received your letter of the 5th, and from it I see that you are still unwell. I should like to be with you, and see you, and talk to you. As this is impossible, I have written you a song to let you know what I wish and mean. In doing so I thought of you, and this moved me very much. There is, I suppose, almost nothing new in it. But you know me, and know what I am. I am still the same, and so you may laugh and be glad at it. I could tell and wish you something different, but nothing better. Nothing else shall be in the letter. That I am yours you know—and so may God give what I hope and pray for.' And then follows the *Song without Words* that was to express what he felt,—not one of those published. Mendelssohn sent home Songs without Words on other similar occasions, for instance, one to Fanny on June 26, 1830, the first version of the eighth published one, in B flat minor, Op. 30, No. 2; saying : 'I felt thus when I received your [his people's] half anxious and half cheerful letter.'

In our present inquiry the following extracts from Lobe's Conversations with Felix Mendelssohn (in *Consonanzen und Dissonanzen* p. 360) are of the greatest interest :—

Mendelssohn : 'What has Beethoven done in his overtures ? He has painted the content of his pieces in tone-pictures. I have done the same.'

Lobe : 'You ascribe, then, the originality of the invention to the definite subject you had in your mind ?'

Mendelssohn : 'Certainly.'

Lobe : 'According to your theory, Mr. A., Mr. B., Mr. C., &c., would have written your *Midsummer Night's Dream* overture if they had undertaken to paint in tones the content of the piece.'

Mendelssohn : 'If they had undertaken it with the same seriousness, if they had transported themselves with the same zeal into the piece, they would all have produced nobler and more important works than are achievable without this procedure.'

Lobe : 'I remember very well what an excitement your *Midsummer Night's Dream* overture produced by its originality and truth of expression, and that from that moment you rose high in the estimation of musicians and music lovers.'

Mendelssohn : 'I, too, believe that, and this shows that one should trust a little to luck.'

Lobe : 'Luck ? I should think such an overture is created not by luck, but by the genius of the artist.'

Mendelssohn : 'Of course, it requires talent. But I call it luck to have been inspired with such a subject, a subject that was capable of furnishing me with such musical ideas and forms as generally appealed to the larger public. What I could do as a composer, I could do before writing the overture. But I had not yet had before my imagination such a subject. That was an inspiration, and the inspiration was a lucky one.'

Lobe does not profess to report the *ipsissima verba.* On the contrary, he states that he gives merely the gist of what was said, and briefly noted down by him immediately after the conversations.

In our inquiry we have to take into account Mendelssohn's keen, open-eyed perceptivity and sympathetic, enthusiastic receptivity. Beauty appealed to him in all its forms of manifestation, and fertilized his creative power. He found music in scenes of nature (the Campagna he heard singing and ringing on all sides), in immortal works of art (which seized him with a joyful thrill), even in the capital of a column; and he confesses that he owes most of his music not to musical works, but to ruins, pictures, and the serenity of nature (November 20, 1830).

The above are not the only utterances of Mendelssohn that bear on programme music. Various *obiter dicta* of his shall be noticed in the course of our review of some of his works. From what has already been laid before the reader, he may gather that Mendelssohn thought music expressive and capable of expressing some things better and more definitely than other media can ; that he had sometimes programmes in his mind ; that this seemed to him advantageous to the composer if the programmes were of the right sort, and that he regarded

programme music as a legitimate kind of music. It is
noteworthy about Mendelssohn that his most poetic and
original works are programme music, and were either
wholly composed or at least planned and partly written
from 1826 to 1833. I am speaking of the four concert
overtures, the *First Walpurgis Night*, and the *Scotch* and
the *Italian* Symphonies. The two oratorios, the psalms,
and most of the other works composed from 1834
onward, however noble, however estimable, and however
admirable in many ways, have much more of homeliness
and less of imaginative iridescence about them than
the earlier works already indicated. Even Wagner,
to whom Mendelssohn was so antipathetic, could
not resist the charm of some of those earlier works.
In a conversation with Dannreuther he remarked,
'Mendelssohn was a landscape painter of the first
order, and *The Hebrides* overture is his masterpiece.
Wonderful imagination and delicate feeling are here
presented with consummate art. Note the extraordinary
beauty of the passage where the oboes rise above the
other instruments with a plaintive wail like sea winds
over the sea. *Calm Sea and Prosperous Voyage* also is
beautiful; but I am fond of the first movement of the
Scotch Symphony. . . . . As regards the overture
to *A Midsummer Night's Dream*, it must be taken
into account that he wrote it at seventeen. And yet
how finished the form!' Mendelssohn's most original
instrumental composition is undoubtedly the *Midsummer
Night's Dream* overture — it was his most beautiful
dream, his first and highest flight as Schumann calls
it — and his most original vocal-instrumental composition
is the *First Walpurgis Night*. *The Hebrides* overture, on
the other hand, must be declared the most perfect of

his compositions, if we take into account all the qualities and the degrees of all the qualities that go to the making of a great work—the poetic, formal, and technical. And now let us examine the compositions already mentioned, and one or two more.

The first piece of programme music of which information has come down to us is the *Scherzo* of the string octet, Op. 20, of 1825. To his sister Fanny alone, Mendelssohn confided that in composing it he had in his mind the last four lines of the *Walpurgis Night Dream, or Oberon and Titania's Golden Wedding*, in the first part of Goethe's *Faust :*—

> ' Cloud and trailing mist o'erhead
> Are now illuminated :
> Air in leaves, and wind in reed,
> And all is dissipated.'

Fanny writes : 'Everything is new, strange, and yet so pleasing, so friendly. One feels oneself so near the spirit world, so lightly lifted into the air. One would like even to take a broom-stick oneself, to follow the airy company. At the end, the first violin flutters upward as lightly as a feather—and all has vanished into thin air.'

The next piece of programme music is *A Midsummer Night's Dream* overture of 1826. But not to interrupt my account of the most important compositions, I shall first take up the string Quartet in A minor, Op. 13, and the *Trois Caprices* for pianoforte, Op. 16. The former work I shall mention in passing, merely pointing out that the composer prefixes to it his song, ' Ist es wahr ? ' which forms the emotional as well as the musical motive of the composition : ' What I feel she alone comprehends who feels it with me, and who remains true to me for ever and for ever.' The *Trois Caprices*, dedicated severally to the three Misses Taylor, were composed in 1829, when he was staying at their father's house at Coed-du, near Holywell, North Wales. The eldest sister (Miss Anne Taylor), to whom No. 1 is dedicated, relates (*vide* Grove's *Dictionary*) that Mendelssohn entered deeply into the beauty of the hills and the woods. 'His way of representing them was not with the pencil; but in the evenings his improvised music would show what he had observed or felt in the past day. The piece called *The Rivulet* [No. 3 of Op. 16], which he wrote at that time for my sister Susan, will show what I mean; it was a recollection of a real actual rivulet. We observed how natural objects seemed to suggest music to him. There was in my sister Honora's garden a pretty creeping plant [*Eccremocarpus*], new at that time, covered with little trumpet-like flowers. He was struck with it, and played for her the music which (he said) the fairies might play on these trumpets. When he wrote out the piece (called a *Capriccio* in E minor [*Scherzo* No. 2 of Op. 16]) he drew a branch of that flower all up the margin of the paper. The piece (an *Andante* and *Allegro* [No. 1 of Op. 16]) which Mr. Mendelssohn wrote for me, was suggested by the sight of a bunch of carnations and roses. The carnations that year were very fine with us. He liked them best of all the flowers, would have one often in his button-hole. We found he intended the *arpeggio* passages in that composition as a reminder of the sweet scent of the flower rising up.'

It is fortunate for the writer of these lines that Mendelssohn wrote a letter which confirms her statements, otherwise they would have met with much scepticism. The letter in question—of September 10,

1829—contains the following passage : ' I have to thank
them [the three Misses Taylor] for three of my best
pianoforte pieces.   When the two younger sisters saw
that I was in earnest about the carnations and the rose
[given him by the eldest] and began to compose (of
course in Susan's summer house), the youngest came up
with yellow, open little bells in her hair, assuring me
they were trumpets, and asking me whether I would
introduce them into the orchestra, as I had mentioned
I required new instruments ; and when in the evening
we danced to the miners' music and the trumpets were
rather shrill, she gave it as her opinion that her trumpets
would do better to dance to ; so I wrote a dance for her
in which the yellow trumpet-bells supplied the music.
And to the other sister I gave *The Rivulet,* which had
pleased us so much during our ride that we dismounted
and sat down by it (I think I wrote to you about it).
This last piece, I believe, is the best of the kind I have
as yet done : it is so slowly flowing and quiet, while a
little tediously simple, that I have played it to myself
every day, and have got quite sentimental over it.'

And now to the great masterpieces.

' To-day or to-morrow,' wrote Mendelssohn on July 7,
1826, ' I shall begin to dream the *Midsummer Night's
Dream* '; and by August 6 of the same year the young
man of seventeen had dreamt the dream, and in dreaming
it had performed a miracle.   What constitutes the chief
originality of the overture is the musical creation of the
moonlit fairy world with its nimble, delicate, and
beautiful population.   Before our mind's eye are called
up Oberon and Titania as they meet in ' grove or green
by fountain clear or spangled starlight sheen '; the
elves, who, when their king and queen quarrel, creep

into acorn cups; their coats, made of the leathern wings of rere-mice; Peaseblossom, Cobweb, Moth, and Mustardseed; the knavish sprite Puck, alias Robin Goodfellow, who delights in playing merry pranks; and the scene following Oberon and Titania's command to their subjects:

OBERON.—' Through the house give glimmering light,
By the dead and drowsy fire :
Every elf and fairy sprite
Hop as light as bird from brier ;
And this ditty, after me,
Sing, and dance it trippingly.'

TITANIA.—' First, rehearse your song by rote,
To each word a warbling note :
Hand in hand, with fairy grace,
Will we sing, and bless this place.'

But there are other things in the overture than fairies. There are Duke Theseus and his betrothed, Queen Hippolyta, and their train; the two pairs of lovers— Lysander and Hermia, Demetrius and Helena; and those hempen homespuns, the Athenian tradesmen—Quince, Snug, Bottom, Flute, Snout, and Starveling. In short, Mendelssohn comprehended Shakespeare's fancy, romance, and humour so well, and made them so thoroughly his own, that he could give a faithful musical reflection of them. But let us see where the different *dramatis personæ* are to be found in the overture.

The sustained chords of the wind instruments are the magic formula that opens to us the realm of fairyland. The busy tripping part of the first subject tells us of the fairies; the broader and dignified part of Duke Theseus and his following; the passionate first part of the second subject, of the romantic lovers; and the clownish second part, of the tradesmen, the braying reminding us of Bottom's transformation into an ass. The development is full of the vivacious bustle and play and fun of the elves. The beginning of the recapitulation too is full of fun; and the *pianissimo* passage towards the end, with the opening motive of the Theseus music, signifies the elves' blessing on the house of the Duke. In conclusion we have once more the magic formula, which now dissolves the dream it had before conjured up.

And how do we know that these were really Mendelssohn's ideas? First, because he expressed them so clearly and unmistakably; and secondly, because he wrote in 1843 a commentary on the overture—namely, in his other music to the play. There we find all the motives of the overture connected with Shakespeare's words, characters, and scenes, with one exception, the lovers' theme, which appears only in the overture. But the *entr'actes* and incidental music contain also programmatic matter not in the composer's original dream. Not to speak of the uniquely festive Wedding March and the mock-pathetic Funeral March, there are pieces and snatches of airy fairy music; a charming *Intermezzo*, 'Hermia seeks Lysander, and loses herself in the wood,' with its mocking echoes and impression of breathless anxiety; and the lovely *Notturno*—the lovers, to whose cross purposes fatigue has put an end, lie asleep, the wood is wrapt in silence, through the foliage and down on the clearings the moon and stars of a cloudless midsummer night's sky send their pale, peaceful rays. It would be delightful to dwell longer on these lovely conceptions, but we must tear ourselves away and turn to others.

Mendelssohn conceived the overture entitled *The Hebrides, or Fingal's Cave,** when he visited Scotland in 1829. His friend Klingemann, who accompanied him, writes in a letter dated Glasgow, August 10 : ' Staffa, with its strange basalt pillars and caverns, is in all picture-books. We were put out in boats, and climbed, the hissing sea close beside us, over the pillar stumps to the celebrated Fingal's Cave. A greener roar of waves surely never rushed into a stranger cavern—comparable, on account of the many pillars, to the inside of an immense organ, black and resounding, lying there absolutely purposeless in its utter loneliness, the wide grey sea within and without. . . . We returned in the little boat to our steamer, to that unpleasant steam-smell. When the second boat arrived I could see with what truth they represent at the theatre the rising and falling of a boat, when the hero rescues the heroine from some trouble.'

Mendelssohn himself writes from one of the Hebrides on August 7, 1829, as follows : ' In order to make you understand how extraordinarily the Hebrides affected me, the following came into my mind there.' Then follow ten bars and a-half of *The Hebrides* overture, here written as twenty-one bars, the notes being of double the present length. Continuing the above letter, he writes from Glasgow on August 11, 1829 : ' How much lies betwixt then and now ! The most fearful sickness, Staffa, scenery, travels, people—Klingemann has described it all, and you will excuse a short note, the more as what I can best tell you is contained in the above music.' From London on September 10, 1829, Mendelssohn makes the announcement : ' *The Hebrides* story builds

* In his letters the composer calls it also *The Solitary Island.*

itself up gradually.' And from Paris he writes on January 21, 1832 : 'I cannot bring *The Hebrides* to a hearing here because I do not consider it finished as I originally wrote it. The middle section in D major is very stupid, and the whole so-called development smells more of counterpoint than of blubber, gulls, and salted cod.' The first performance of the work took place at a concert of the London Philharmonic Society on May 14, 1832.

As to the music of *The Hebrides*, you have only to abandon yourself to its influences, and the sensations, thoughts, and feelings that engendered it will rise up in your imagination—you will think of yourself in a ship, gliding along over rocking waves, about you a vast expanse of sea and sky, light breezes blowing, the romantic stories of the past colouring the sights seen.

The first we hear of Mendelssohn's third concert overture is contained in a letter of the composer's sister Fanny, of June 18, 1828. 'Felix,' we read there, 'is writing a great instrumental piece after Goethe's *Meeresstille und glückliche Fahrt* (Calm Sea and Prosperous Voyage). It will be thoroughly worthy of him. He wished to avoid an overture and introduction, and has formed the whole into two pictures standing side by side.' From this we gather that the original conception differed from the final version. In fact, in a letter of August 6, 1834, he tells a friend that he has completely re-written the overture and thinks it thirty times better. Mendelssohn, whom a stay on the shores of the Baltic in 1824 had made acquainted with the varied phases of the sea, translates into the musical idiom the contents of Goethe's poem. He illustrates

first a fear-inspiring, deathlike stillness and the
motionlessness of the sea and air, of an immense
expanse of smooth surface; and then (in the *Molto
Allegro e vivace*) the parting of the mist, the clearing of
the sky, the ship dividing the waves, the approaching
distance, and the appearance of land.

We now come to the fourth of Mendelssohn's concert
overtures, that *To the Legend of the lovely Melusina*.
The reader may be credited with some knowledge of the
legend of the fair being fated to be on certain days half
fish and half woman, and to forsake human society if
seen in that state; and of her husband's broken promise
to leave her alone on those days, and the consequent
catastrophe. Writing from Düsseldorf on October 26,
1833, Mendelssohn says: 'I think the overture to
Melusine will be the best which I have made.' He
remained in this mind, for the work pleased him when
he heard it at a private rehearsal got up by himself at
Düsseldorf on August 4, 1834; and in a letter of
January 30, 1836, he remarks: 'Many people believe
that *Melusine* is the best of my overtures; it is certainly
the most inward [*innerlichste*]. But what the *Musikalische Zeitung* [he meant, no doubt, Schumann's article
in the *Neue Zeitschrift für Musik*] says about red corals,
green marine animals, magic castles, and deep seas, is
astounding.' About the origin of this overture and the
composer's intention we find extremely interesting
information in a letter addressed by the master to his
sister Fanny on April 7, 1834. 'You ask me which
legend you are to read. How many, then, are there?
And how many, then, do I know? And do you not
know the story of the beautiful Melusine? And ought
one not to wrap oneself up and hide oneself in all

possible instrumental music without titles, if even one's
sister (you unnatural sister !) does not like the title ? Or
have you really never heard of the beautiful fish ? . . .
I have written this overture to an opera by Conradin
Kreutzer [*Melusine*], which I heard last year about
this time at the Königstädter Theatre [Berlin]. The
overture (that of Kreutzer) was encored, and displeased
me quite particularly ; afterwards also the whole opera ;
but not Hähnel [the *prima donna*], on the contrary, she
was very charming, especially in one scene where she
presents herself as a pike and dresses her hair ; it was
then that the desire was excited in me also to compose
an overture, one which people would not *encore*, but
which should have more inwardness ; and I took what
pleased me of the subject (and that is exactly what
coincides with the legend). In short, the overture came
into the world, and that is its family history.'

The overture does not tell a story. It illustrates
certain features of it : the loveliness and the loving
nature of Melusina ; the hardness of her fate and the
anxiety caused by it. The waving motion is indicative
of her grace, and at the same time reminds us of the
element with which she was connected. In the twice-
repeated A flat—F (accompanied by the chord of the
diminished seventh), before the return of F major, near
the end, we may recognise her cries on being discovered
by her husband. The rest is like the vanishing of a
beautiful reality into a beautiful memory.

We must not leave these poetic musical master-pieces
without taking note of a remark made by Hans von
Bülow, who, in his earlier years one of the chief
propagandists of Berlioz and Liszt, wrote in 1884 : ' I
now revere in Mendelssohn's Overtures to *The Hebrides*,

Melusine, and *Calm Sea and Prosperous Voyage*, the more perfect ideal of the " symphonic poem." '

The two best symphonies of Mendelssohn, the 3rd, in A minor, Op. 56, and the 4th, in A major, Op. 90, do not bear titles; but the composer always referred in his letters to the former as the *Scotch* Symphony, and to the latter as the *Italian* Symphony. That these epithets do not indicate merely the country in which they were written or begun may be proved, at least as regards the A minor Symphony, by remarks in the master's letters. After describing a visit in profound twilight to Holyrood Palace, where Queen Mary lived and loved, and Rizzio was murdered, and to the adjoining chapel, roofless, grown over with grass and ivy, at the broken altar of which Mary was crowned Queen of Scotland,* he writes in a letter, dated Edinburgh, July 30, 1829 : 'All is dilapidated and decayed there, and the serene heavens shine into it. I believe I have found there to-day the beginning of my *Scotch* Symphony.' Note also two more remarks. The first of them occurs in a letter dated London, September 10, 1829 : 'The *Scotch* Symphony, as well as the *Hebrides* story, is gradually being built up': and the second, in a letter dated Rome, March 29, 1831 : 'From April 15 to May 15 is the finest season in Italy. Who can blame me for not being able to transport myself into the Scotch mist mood,' *i.e.*, that he cannot work at his *Scotch* Symphony. Although far advanced before he left Italy in the summer of 1831, the work was not finished till January 20, 1842. Of the other symphony Mendelssohn writes from Naples on April 27, 1831 : 'If I go on as I

---

* Of course, Mendelssohn was mistaken, Queen Mary was not crowned there.

have done, I shall finish the "*Italian* Symphony" in Italy.' That expectation was not realized, but the work was finished on March 13, 1833, although not published till after the composer's death. Briefly, then, Mendelssohn's remarks and especially his music must convince us that the contents of the symphonies were intended to be respectively *Scotch* and *Italian*, and to communicate to the hearers some of the impressions received by the composer from the atmospheres of the countries, the characters of their landscapes and peoples, and the scenes really or imaginatively seen. The difference of atmosphere and character of the two works is most striking. The sunlight mood of the *Italian* Symphony is as unmistakable as the mist mood of the romantic *Scotch* Symphony. The first movement of the former calls up Mendelssohn's enthusiastic delight on entering the southern country. 'This is Italy! and what I have thought of as the greatest joy of my life since I began to think, has now commenced, and I do enjoy it.' On January 22, 1831, he writes from Rome to his sister Fanny: 'It [the *Italian* Symphony] will be the gayest thing I have yet done, especially the last movement.' He will not finish the work before he has seen Naples, and puts off the composition of the slow movement until then. This movement is generally known as the Pilgrims' March, a name justified by the nature of the piece, but not by anything the composer has said. The last movement, the *Saltarello*, may have been inspired by the Roman carnival, which the composer looked forward to eagerly, and enjoyed immensely.

In Mendelssohn's setting of Goethe's *First Walpurgis Night* there is a great deal of tone-painting, and of the most picturesque kind. When the master was occupied with the composition, he wrote with the greatest glee and delight of the effect which especially certain portions of it would produce. ' At the beginning there are Spring songs and the like in plenty; then, when the watchmen make a noise with pitch-forks, spears, and owls, there comes the witches' spook (*Hexenspuk*), for which, as you know, I have an especial *faible;* then the sacrificing Druids in C major with trombones; then again the watchmen, who are afraid, on which occasion I shall introduce a tripping eerie chorus; and finally the full sacrificial song ' (Rome, February 22, 1831). In the next year the composer finished the overture, which, he says, represents 'bad weather,' and the introduction, 'in which it thaws and becomes Spring.' And accordingly we find in the score the first part of the overture (*Allegro con fuoco*) superscribed *Das schlechte Wetter* (Bad Weather), and the second part (*Allegro vivace non troppo*) *Der Uebergang zum Frühling* (Transition to Spring). Berlioz, not a warm admirer of Mendelssohn, was filled with the greatest enthusiasm when he heard the *First Walpurgis Night.* 'The vocal instrumental effects cross each other in all senses, oppose each other, clash with each other, with an apparent disorder that is the height of art. I shall mention especially as magnificent things in two *genres*, the mysterious placing of the watchmen, and the final chorus, where the voice of the priest rises now and then calmly above the infernal din of the troop of counterfeit demons and sorcerers.' Unquestionably the *First Walpurgis Night* is a most brilliant, original, and powerful example of tone-painting.

Many other works of Mendelssohn's would furnish matter for comment; for instance, the overtures to his

N

vocal works; but the discussion of his most important instrumental works and the *First Walpurgis Night* suffices. A few words about the *Ruy Blas* overture may, however, be added. It is worth noting why, although full of *verve*, it is so much less poetical than the four concert overtures. This work was written to a German translation of Victor Hugo's play, which Mendelssohn thought execrable; and was written in haste, in a few days, to please the Leipzig musicians who wished it for a performance in aid of the orchestral pension fund.

After the foregoing presentation of the facts of the case, the question : Whether Mendelssohn was really a composer of programme music? cannot be regarded as an open question; nor can we be in doubt as to his reticence in revealing his programmes.

CHAPTER V.

FIFTH PERIOD CONTINUED : SCHUMANN.

ROBERT SCHUMANN (1810-1856) proves himself in his musical works, and confesses himself in his critical writings and letters, a composer of programme music. The proposition may be startling to many ; for expressions of his are sometimes quoted to show that he disapproved of programmes, and described his titles as afterthoughts. Nevertheless the proposition is quite true. No doubt, Schumann is on some occasions vague and self-contradictory on the subject, but the aggregate of his statements confirms the above proposition. The cause of the occasional vagueness and self-contradictoriness is his anxiety to protest against a too materialistic view and use of programmes. As Schumann's sayings throw much light on the question, and not only do that, but also give us a deep insight into his own creative processes, I shall not apologize to the reader for drawing largely from the master's criticisms and correspondence. Indeed I have not the least fear of complaints on that account, as Schumann is too delightful a writer, and his artistic self-revelation positively unique. My method will be to quote chronologically his principal declarations on programmes and titles from his *Collected Writings on Music and Musicians*, interjecting a note of my own here and there, and adding a particularly interesting passage from one of his letters ; and then to illustrate the nature of his works for the most part by remarks derived from his correspondence.

The first excerpts are of the year 1835.

In reviewing a sonata of Löwe's, Schumann writes: ' Yet another thing I scent in Löwe's compositions, namely, that when he has finished, one still wishes to know something more. Unfortunately it has often seemed to myself silly when somebody asked me what I was thinking of in writing my own extravagant out-pourings. Therefore I do not want an answer. Still, I maintain that in Löwe's case there is something behind it.'

Spohr's *Consecration of Sound* gives rise to the following reflection: ' Beethoven very well understood the risk he ran in writing the Pastoral Symphony. In the few words, " expression of the emotions rather than painting," which he prefixes, there lies a whole system of æsthetics for composers.'

The longest discussion of the subject is called forth by Berlioz's *Symphonie fantastique.* After giving the French master's programme of that work, Schumann writes: ' So much for the programme. Germany makes him a present of it: such sign-posts have always something unworthy and charlatan-like about them. At any rate, the five superscriptions would have been sufficient; the particular circumstances—which, on account of the personality of the composer, who has himself lived the symphony, must of course interest us—would have been transmitted by oral tradition from generation to generation. In one word, the sensitive German, more averse to the personal, objects to having his thoughts so obviously directed. Even in the Pastoral Symphony he felt offended that Beethoven did not trust him to divine the character without his help. Man stands in awe of the workshop of genius; he does not wish to know anything of the causes, tools, and secrets of creation. Nature, too, manifests a certain delicacy in covering its roots with earth. Let the artist therefore shut himself up with his throes of travail; we should learn terrible things if we could see down to the bottom of the origin of every work.'

Schumann overlooks that it is a question as to the intention of the composer, not as to the throes of labour. The delicacy of the German nature, its disinclination to be grossly led, the advantage of oral tradition over black and white, and the shyness of humanity with regard to the working of genius, are arguments fanciful rather than convincing. Further on, he says : ' If the eye is once directed to a certain point, the ear no longer judges independently.' But if the eye is rightly directed, there can be no illegitimate interference with the ear's independence, only interference with the ear's going wrong. After this Schumann continues :

' If you ask whether music can really do what Berlioz demands in his symphony, you should try to substitute other pictures, pictures of a contrary character. At first the programme spoiled also my enjoyment, all free outlook. But when it retired more and more into the background, and my own imagination began to create, I found not only everything, but much more, and almost everywhere a living, warm tone.'

The critic is evidently struggling with a prejudice. We find him more enlightened and enlightening in the following remarks :

' As regards the difficult question, how far instrumental music may go in the representation of thoughts and occurrences, many are far too timid. People are certainly mistaken if they believe that composers prepare pen and paper with the miserable intention of expressing, describing, and painting this and that. But chance influences and impressions from without should not be under-estimated. Along with the musical imagination an idea is unconsciously operative; along with the ear, the eye; and this, the ever active organ, in the midst of the sounds and tones, then holds fast certain outlines, which, with the advancing music, may condense and develop into distinct figures [*Gestalten*]. The more elements akin to music the thoughts and forms [*Gebilde*] engendered by the tones bear in them, the more poetic and plastic the expression of the composition will be; and the more fantastically and acutely the musician conceives, the more the work will elevate and move. Why should not Beethoven in the midst of his fantasies be seized by the thought of immortality? Why should not the memory of a great fallen hero inspire him with a work? Why should another not be inspired by the remembrance of a happy time? Or do we intend to be ungrateful to Shakespeare for having evoked from the breast of a young tone-poet a work worthy of him—ungrateful to Nature, and deny that we borrowed of her beauty and sublimity for our works? Italy, the Alps, the picture of the sea, a spring twilight—has music told us nothing of all this? Nay, even to smaller, more special pictures music can give such a charming, definite character, that one is surprised at her being able to express such traits. Thus a composer told me that, while composing, the picture of a butterfly, drifting on a leaf down a brook, incessantly obtruded itself. This had given the little piece all the delicacy and naïveness which the picture possesses in reality. In this fine *genre* painting Schubert especially was a master, and I cannot omit to mention out of my own experience how, during one of Schubert's marches, the friend with whom I was playing, replied to my question whether he did not see quite peculiar figures : " Truly, I found myself in Seville, but more than a hundred years ago, in the midst of dons and donas, with long-trained dresses, pointed shoes, and rapiers, &c." Strange to say we were at one in our visions, except as to the town. Let no reader strike out this trifling example.'

On another occasion Schumann writes : ' The less cultured people are inclined to hear in music without words only sadness or only joy, or (what lies midway between the two) melancholy, but are not able to distinguish the finer shadings of passion, as for instance, in the former, anger, repentance, &c., and in the latter, ease, comfortableness, &c. Consequently they find it so difficult to understand masters like Beethoven and Franz Schubert, who could translate into tone-speech every state of life.'

We shall now proceed to the year 1838, when the *Studies*, Op. 95, of Moscheles suggest the following reflections :—

' The superscriptions on pieces of music, which in recent times have again become frequent, have here and there been censured, on the ground that " good music does not stand in need of such directions." But it as certainly loses nothing thereby, and by this means the composer most surely obviates misunderstanding. If poets do it, if they endeavour to wrap up the meaning of a whole poem in a superscription, why should not musicians ? Such a hint should, however, be given with judgment and taste ; and just in this the culture of a musician will be recognizable. Thus we have in the

Studies before us twelve characteristic pictures, whose significance rather gains by the superscriptions.'

It will be convenient to insert here two more utterances on titles respectively of the years 1841 and 1839, the former in connection with *Songs without Words* by Julius Schaeffer, and the latter in connection with the *Etudes de Salon*, Op. 5, by Henselt.

'These *Songs without Words*, too, have superscriptions. We think it would have been better to omit them. There are hidden states of the soul where a verbal hint by the composer can lead to a quicker comprehension, and must be thankfully received. Our composer, however, gives known ones for which indications such as "Calm Sea," "Do I dream? No, I am awake," and "Melancholy" seem too affected; the second we regard even as insipid.'

'One cannot but conceive an affection for the *Ave Maria*. Here we have an example of how a well-chosen superscription may enhance the effect of the music. Without that superscription, the piece would have been played by most pianists like a study of Cramer's, to one of which it has much resemblance. In an *Ave Maria* even the most prosaic person thinks something, and makes an effort.'

Returning once more to 1838, we find charming remarks on Sterndale Bennett's *Three Sketches :* The Lake, The Mill-stream, and The Fountain.

'They seem to me to surpass in delicacy and naïveness of presentation all I know of musical *genre* painting; the composer, as a true tone-poet, having indeed observed Nature in some of her most musical scenes Or can it be that you have never heard music that would call you across the lake at evening? Never the angry, tumultuous music that drives the wheels so that the sparks fly? In what way the *Sketches* have come into existence, whether from within outward, or the reverse, is of no consequence and difficult to decide. For the most part, composers do not know that themselves : one piece is made in one way, another in another. Often an outside picture leads further ; again, often a tone-series calls forth a picture. If only there remain music and independent melody, do not rack your brains, but enjoy.'

In 1839, Schumann again dealt with the subject of programmes *à propos* Berlioz's *Waverley* overture. Note the last two sentences contradicting the preceding ones :—

'People will ask, to which chapter, to which scene [of Scott's novel], why, and to what purpose did Berlioz write his music ? For critics always wish to know what the composers themselves cannot tell them ; and often critics understand hardly the tenth part of what they discuss. Heavens, will the time ever come when we are no longer asked what we intended by our divine compositions ? Hunt for consecutive fifths, and let us alone. Some explanation, however, is on this occasion given by the motto on the title-page of the overture :—

> Dreams of love and lady's charms
> Give place to honour and to arms.

This brings us somewhat nearer the track.'

Schubert's C major Symphony inspired Schumann in 1840 with the following enthusiastic words :—

'That the outside world, as it shines to-day and darkens to-morrow, often influences the inner world of the poet and musician, you may confidently believe ; and that in this symphony there lies hidden more than mere beautiful melody, more than mere sorrow and joy such as music has uttered already in a hundred ways, yea, that it leads us into regions where we cannot remember to have ever been. To grant this you have only to hear such a symphony. Here is, besides masterly musical technique of composition, life in every fibre, colouring down to the finest shading. Significance everywhere, the clearest expression in the details; and, lastly, diffused throughout, a romanticism such as we have become acquainted with in other compositions of Schubert.'

Spohr's *Irdisches und Göttliches* prompts in 1843 the following characteristic utterances :—

' We confess we have a prejudice against this kind of creation [namely, with a programme], and share this perhaps with a hundred learned heads, who, it is true, have often strange notions of composing, and refer always to Mozart, who is supposed never to have thought of anything in composing. As I said, not a few may have that prejudice; and if a composer holds up a programme to us, before the music, I say: "First of all let us hear that you make beautiful music, afterwards we shall be glad of your programme." . . . Indeed, the philosophers may think the matter worse than it is; certainly they are mistaken if they believe that a composer who works after an idea, sits down like a preacher on Saturday afternoon and arranges his text in accordance with the usual three heads, and develops it thoroughly; certainly they are mistaken. The creation of the musician is quite another thing; and if a picture, an idea, hovers before him, he will feel happy only if it comes towards him in beautiful melodies, borne by the same invisible hands as the "golden buckets" of which Goethe speaks somewhere. Therefore keep your prejudice ; but at the same time examine, and do not make the masters suffer for the bungling of the pupils.'

Schumann's most important utterance on programme music and most complete self-revelation as a creative artist is to be found in a letter of April 13, 1838, addressed to his beloved Clara ; and with it I shall close this series of somewhat bewildering extracts. After saying in an early part of this long epistle that he would give to his fantasias which were about to be published the name of ' poems ' [*Dichtungen*], a word for which he had long sought, and which seemed to him noble, and significant for musical compositions, he writes further on as follows :—

' Behold your old Robert—is he not still the silly, the teller of spook-stories, the terrifier ? Now, however, I can also be very serious, sometimes for days—and that need not alarm you—these are for the most part the incidents of my soul-life, thoughts on music and compositions. Everything that goes on in the world affects me—politics, literature, men ; in my own way I meditate on every-thing, and afterwards it vents itself in music. Thus many of my compositions are difficult to understand because they are connected with distant interests ; often, too, they are significant because every remarkable passing event affects me, and I must then express it musically. Hence few recent compositions give me satisfaction because, apart from the defects of crafts-manship, they deal in musical sentiments of the lowest kind, in commonplace lyrical exclamations. The highest that is there achieved does not reach up to the beginning of the art of my music. The former may be a flower, the latter the so much more spiritual poem.

The former an impulse of crude nature, the latter a work of poetic consciousness. I, too, do not know all this at the time of composing, it comes afterwards.'

What is said in the last paragraph will be further explained and illustrated by Schumann's remarks about his own compositions, which reveals his practice much better than his theorizings and criticisms of other masters' compositions.

Schumann's musical productions comprise programme music of all kinds, qualities, and degrees. Beginning his career in a spirit of sportive fancifulness (as exemplified in the *Papillons* and *Carnaval*), the composer, on becoming an ardent lover, developed an earnest imaginativeness (as exemplified in the *Davidsbündler*, Sonatas, *Fantasiestücke*, *Fantasie*, *Kreisleriana*, *Novelletten*, and other pianoforte pieces), and this earnest imaginativeness broadened, deepened, and solidified on his reaching mature manhood and the goal of marriage (as exemplified in the larger compositions of 1841 and later years). Schumann was as verbally reticent in the orchestral and concerted chamber works as he was communicative in the short pianoforte pieces. In fact, if we except the overtures, none of the orchestral and none of the chamber works has as much as a title, and of few of them has any programmatic information come down to us. Now it will be said that this shows that as he grew older the composer abandoned the giddy romantic ways of his youth and turned to a romanticism sobered by classicism. There is some truth in this; but it does not settle the matter, for Schumann up to the last years of his life continued to compose acknowledged programme music—overtures and short pianoforte pieces. If he had written in later years letters as intimate as he

wrote to Clara before his marriage, we should know
more about the conception and meaning of the works of
those years.

The *Papillons*, Op. 2, composed partly in 1829 and
partly in 1831, is a young *Carnaval.* 'When you have
a minute to spare,' he writes to his friend Henriette
Voigt, 'I beg of you to read the last chapter of the
Flegeljahre, where all is to be found in black and white.
. . . I may also mention that I set the words to
the music and not the music to the words—the opposite
seems to me a foolish proceeding.' He also advises his
relatives to read as soon as possible the closing scene of
Jean Paul Richter's *Flegeljahre*, informing them that the
Papillons are intended to translate this masked ball into
tones, and asking them if something in the *Papillons* does
not reflect Wina's angelic love, Walt's poetic soul, and
Vult's sharp-flashing mind. To the famous Berlin critic
Rellstab, the composer writes : ' You remember the last
scene in the *Flegeljahre*,—the masked ball, Walt, Vult,
masks, confessions, anger, revelations, hasty departure,
concluding scene, and then the departing brother. Often
I turned over the last page : for the end seemed to
me a new beginning—almost unconsciously I was
at the pianoforte, and thus came into existence one
papillon after another.' The *Papillons* are strikingly
characteristic and even dramatic. You cannot hear
them without feeling that ' there is something behind'
these charming tone-combinations. They suggest
characters, scenes, and situations—the stir and brilliance
of the ballroom, particular masks and their manners,
the spirit of the dances and the feelings of the dancers,
the *tête-à-tête* of the favoured and the unfavoured lover,
Walt and Vult, and the beloved one, the incomparable

Wina. Schumann may not have thought of the last
scene but one of J. P. Richter's *Flegeljahre* when he
wrote in 1829 Nos. 1, 3, 4, 6, and 8, but I have not the
slightest doubt that those of 1831 were inspired by the
masked ball there depicted. As we have seen, Schumann
writes that he set the words to the music, not the music
to the words; but he writes also that in the *Flegeljahre*
everything is to be found in black and white, that the
Papillons translate the masked ball into tones. The
Finale is a curious conception. It pictures the last scene
of the ball and the dying away of the noise of the
carnival. Towards the end of the movement we read,
printed above the music: 'The noise of the carnival
dies away. The church clock strikes six.' The
conclusion of the ball is indicated by the old and old-
fashioned Grandfather's Dance, danced at the end of balls
and especially at the end of weddings. This is followed
by the reappearance of the first slow waltz. Then the
two are contrapuntally combined, and gradually die
away.

Of the *Carnaval, Scènes mignonnes*, Op. 9, composed in
1834 and 1835, Schumann writes to Moscheles: 'The
Carnaval came into existence incidentally, and is built
for the most part on the notes A S C H [*h* is the German
name for *b*], the name of a little Bohemian town,
where I have a musical lady-friend, but which, strange
to say, are also the only musical letters in my name.
The superscriptions I placed over them afterwards.
Is not music itself always enough and sufficiently
expressive? *Estrella* is a name such as is placed
under portraits to fix the picture better in one's
memory; *Reconnaissance*, a scene of recognition: *Aveu*,
an avowal of love; *Promenade*, a walk, such as one

takes at a German ball arm-in-arm with one's partner.
The whole has no artistic value whatever; the manifold
states of the soul alone seem to me to be interesting.'
It is impossible to agree with the depreciatory remark
contained in the first half of the last sentence. The
Carnaval is a higher kind of *Papillons*. Somebody
called it 'a glorification of the ballroom, of its noisy
rejoicings, its motley masquerade, and its secret
whisperings of love.' Schumann himself refers to it as
a *Maskentanz*, a masked ball, and before adopting the
present title thought of *Burlesques* and of *Frolics on Four
Notes*. The *Carnaval* is not one comprehensive view,
but rather a series of glimpses. In comparing it with
the *Papillons* we find that the young master's drawing
shows greater firmness of line and more forcibleness of
characterization. In short, both as a man and as an
artist Schumann proves himself maturer. The *Carnaval*
comprises twenty-one pieces, each having a superscription.
Some of these have already been explained in Schumann's
letter. Of the others, the greater number do not stand
in need of explanation—such as *Préambule*, *Valse
allemande*, and *Valse noble*; *Pierrot*, *Arlequin*, and
Pantalon et Colombine; *Coquette*; and *Chopin* and
Paganini. *Florestan* and *Eusebius* are the representatives
of Schumann's dual nature—*Eusebius* is tender and mild,
an enthusiastic dreamer; *Florestan* is wild, impetuous,
and fantastic. The *Réplique* is no doubt a mocking
reply to the *Coquette*. The *Papillon* on this occasion
means a real butterfly. *Chiarina* is Clara Wieck, and
Estrella Ernestine von Fricken, a rival attraction.
As to the town Asch, there lived the same Ernestine, to
whom the composer at that time was engaged. The
last piece but one is entitled *Pause*. During the *Pause*

a great bustle is going on; there is a hurrying to and fro, everyone hastens to join his standard and prepare for the fight. And then begins the 'Marche des Davidsbündler contre les Philistins,' the march of the champions of progress and idealism against the upholders of tradition and commonplace. It is the climax of the piece. Exuberance of youth, and faith in their good cause animate the valiant band of the *Davidsbündler.* The Philistines, represented by the old-fashioned Grandfather's Dance, show pluck, but in the end are completely routed.

There are hardly any particulars to record of the Sonata in F sharp minor, Op. 11 (1833 and 1835). But it is so full of storm and stress, of fire and intensity of passion, of tenderness and fantastic imagery, that we may well believe that there is of the composer's heart's blood in it, that it tells us of the actualities of his soul-life—of strong emotions, brave endeavours, and high aspirations. We obtain the certainty of this from two allusions in Schumann's letters. In one of them he states that the sonata is one of the works almost entirely occasioned by Clara Wieck; and in the other he indignantly exclaims : ' Your father calls me phlegmatic ? —the *Carnaval* phlegmatic !—the F sharp minor Sonata phlegmatic ! '

The eighteen *Characteristic Pieces for Pianoforte,* Op. 6, composed in 1837, entitled *Die Davidsbündler* (The David Leaguers), originally *Davidsbündler Tänze* (Dances of the David Leaguers) are, Schumann informs Clara, quite different from the *Carnaval,* the former, compared with the latter, being like faces compared with masks. In a letter of his to Henselt we read: 'Just now I have finished eighteen *Davidsbündler Tänze*—in

the midst of a sadly stirring life.' This is an allusion
to his struggles for Clara. Passages in two letters to
his beloved one reveal much of what he put into this
composition. ' In the dances are many wedding thoughts
—they arose in the most beautiful excitement that I can
remember to have experienced. Some day I shall
explain them to you.' 'What I have put into these
dances will be discovered by my Clara, to whom they
are dedicated, more than anything else of mine. The
story is a whole wedding eve [*Polterabend*]. You can
picture to yourself beginning and end. If I was ever
happy at the pianoforte it was when I composed them.'
Of the *Davidsbund* (David League) Schumann says:
' The society was more than a secret one, since it
existed only in the head of the founder.' And again:
' The *Davidsbund* is a spiritual, romantic one, as you have
long perceived. Mozart was as great a *Bündler* as
Berlioz is now, as you are [Dorn], without nomination
by diploma.' The composition is headed by an old
rhyme, which says that at all times joy and sorrow are
connected, and gives the advice to remain godly in joy
and have courage ready in sorrow. The musical motto
by Clara Wieck (two bars) with which the composition
opens is like the sign of the prompter, after which the
curtain rises and lays open to us the scene of action—
the poet's soul. The eighteen scenes of which the
performance consists are full of interest and surprising
variety. The *dramatis personæ*, Eusebius and Florestan,
in their monologues and dialogues unfold themselves
more and more. Of these eighteen numbers some are
signed by Eusebius, some by Florestan, others by both.

Schumann's Op. 12, the *Fantasiestücke* of 1837, consists
of eight titled pieces,—*Des Abends* (in the Evening), full

o

of quiet twilight dreaminess; the impassioned and impatient *Aufschwung* (Soaring); the questioning and longing *Warum* (Why); the delightfully humorous *Grillen* (Whims); the grandly and stirringly emotional *In der Nacht* (In the Night); the chatty *Fabel* (Fable); the dizzy *Traumeswirren* (Dream Visions—literally *Wirren* = confusion, entanglements); and lastly, the joyous *Ende vom Liede* (End of the Song). Schumann writes : ' When I had finished the work I found in *Die Nacht* the story of Hero and Leander. I suppose you know it. Every night Leander swims across the sea to his beloved, who is waiting for him on the tower with flaming torch to show him the way. It is an old, beautiful, romantic legend. When I play the *Night* I cannot forget the picture—how he plunges into the sea, she calls, he answers, struggling through the waves reaches the shore safely, then the *cantilena* when they are in each other's arms, then he must leave and cannot separate from her, and at last the night envelopes everything in darkness. With regard to the concluding number the composer wrote to Clara: ' I must praise you for having thought of Zumsteeg [the famous composer of ballads] in connection with the *End of the Song*. Yes, it is true, my thought was, a merry wedding is going to be the end of it after all; but at the last the sorrow about you returned, and so it sounds like the intermingling of marriage and funeral bells.'

The naming of the *Fantasie*, Op. 17, composed in 1836-1838 went through various transformations. Before the last was reached there were discarded the titles *Grande Sonate* and *Fantasien*, the sub-title *Dichtungen* (Poems), and superscriptions of the three movements— Ruins, Trophies, Palms; or Ruins, Triumphal Arch,

Crown of Stars ; or Ruin, Triumphal Arch, Constellation.
Also the motto, four lines by Friedrich von Schlegel, was
an afterthought. It may be literally rendered thus :
' Through all the tones that sound in Earth's much-
mingled dream, a gentle tone is heard by him who harks
with quiet heed.'   The inwardness of the history of
Op. 17 is, however, to be found in Schumann's letters to
his Clara.   ' I have finished a *Fantasie* in three movements, which I sketched down to the details in June,
1836.   I do not think I ever wrote anything more
impassioned than the first movement; it is a profound
lament about you.   The others are weaker, but need not
be ashamed of themselves' (March 17, 1838). ' The
Fantasie you can understand only if you transport
yourself back to the unhappy Summer of 1836, when I
resigned you.   Now I have no reason to compose in so
miserable and melancholy a way ' (May 19, 1839).
' Tell me what you think in hearing the first piece of the
Fantasie ?   Does it not call up pictures in you ? . . .
Don't you think the " tone " in the motto is you ?   I
almost believe it ' (June 9, 1839).   Clara replies to this
on June 16 : ' Many pictures rise before me, too, when I
play your Fantasia—they are sure to be very much in
agreement with yours.   The March makes upon me the
impression of a triumphal march of warriors returning
from battle ; and at the A flat major I always think of
young village girls, all clad in white, each with a wreath
in her hand, crowning the kneeling warriors, and a great
deal more that you know already.'

Of his pianoforte compositions, Schumann liked best
the *Fantasiestücke*, the *Kreisleriana*, the *Novelletten*, and
the three *Romanzen*, of which again he liked best the
Kreisleriana, Op. 16, composed in 1838.   The title is

derived from E. T. A. Hoffmann, the author of fantastic tales, who also was a lawyer, musician, painter, &c. Schumann describes Johannes Kreisler, Hoffmann's creation, as 'an eccentric, wild, and *geistreicher* [clever, intellectual, &c., &c.] *Capellmeister*. 'No one acquainted with Schumann's work can for a moment doubt that he describes here his own and not Kreisler's joys and sorrows. In fact, Schumanniana would be a more correct title than *Kreisleriana*. However, we are not left to guessing. To Dorn, the composer writes : ' Of the Concerto, the Sonata, the *Davidsbündler*, the *Kreisleriana* and the *Novelletten*, she [that is, Clara] is almost the sole cause' (September 5, 1839). He is more outspoken to Clara herself : ' Oh, this music in me ! And always such beautiful melodies ! Imagine, since my last letter I have finished again a whole book of new things. "Kreisleriana" I will call them, in which you and a thought of you play the principal *rôle*, and I will dedicate it to you,—yes, to you and to no one else. How sweetly you will smile when you recognize yourself. My music seems to me now so wonderfully involved [*verschlungen*] notwithstanding all its simplicity, so eloquent from the heart ; . . . When shall you be standing beside me, while I sit at the pianoforte—ah ! then we two shall weep like children—that I know, it will overwhelm me' (April 13, 1838). 'Do play sometimes my *Kreisleriana !* In some parts of it there lies a veritable wild love, and your life and mine, and many a look of yours (August 3, 1838).

Of the *Novelletten*, Op. 21, likewise composed in 1838, Schumann speaks as ' larger connected romantic stories ' (*abenteuerliche Geschichten*—Stories of Adventure). On February 6, 1838, he writes to his Clara : ' I do not

know who could prevent me from writing as much again
to you as you have written to me. I should like best to
do it in music—for that is the friend who best brings out
everything that is within.   So I have composed an appalling amount for you during the last few weeks—drolleries,
Egmont stories, family scenes with fathers, a wedding, in
short, charming things. The whole I call *Novelletten,*
because your name is Clara, and Wiecketten would not
sound well.' This last sentence contains a playful allusion
to Clara Novello. A little more than a year later, in a
letter of June 30, 1839, he says : ' Four books of *Novellettes*
by me have just been published. They are intimately
connected, and were written with great gusto. They are
for the most part cheerful and superficial, except for
something here and there where I touch the bottom.'
Perhaps we may say—the *Kreisleriana* are intimate
revelations, outpourings from the depth of the soul;
the eight *Novelletten,* on the other hand, deal, for the
most part, with feelings that lie on or near the surface,
or at least may be openly shown to all the world.   The
above extracts are from letters to mere male acquaint-
ances. A more intimate peep into the true nature of
the work is afforded by the following words addressed by
the composer to his beloved one, ' Bride, in the *Novelletten*
you appear in all possible situations and positions and
other irresistible things about you. Yes, do look at me !
I assert that *Novelletten* could only be written by one
who knows such eyes as yours and has touched such lips
as yours. In short, one may make better things, but
not similar ones ' (June 30, 1839).

About the *Nachtstücke* (Night Pieces)—the title is again
derived from E. T. A. Hoffmann—Op. 23, composed in
1839, we get from Schumann some exceedingly interesting

information. ' I wrote to you [Clara] of a presentiment. I had it during the days from the 24th to the 27th of March while occupied with my new composition. There is a passage in it to which I continually returned; it is as if some one sighed with a very heavy heart: "Oh, God!" While occupied with the composition I always saw funeral processions, coffins, unhappy, despairing people; and when I had finished, and for a long time was seeking for a title, I always fell upon *Leichenphantasie* (Funeral Fantasia). Is that not remarkable? While composing I was often moved to tears and did not know why, and had no cause for it. Then came Theresa's letter and everything was clear to me.' The letter announced that his brother Eduard was dying. In another letter to Clara the composer says: ' I have put the *Night Pieces* in order. What would you think of my naming them: (1) *Trauerzug* (Funeral Procession); (2) *Kuriose Gesellschaft* (Strange Company); (3) *Nächtliches Gelage* (Nocturnal Orgies); (4) *Rundgesang mit Solostimmen* (Roundelay with solo voices)?' These titles for the individual pieces were, however, omitted.

The *Scenes of Childhood*, Op. 15, of 1839, consist of thirteen pieces with superscriptions: Of Foreign Lands and People, Curious Story, Catch me if you can, Entreating Child, Happiness enough, Important Event, Dreaming, At the Fireside, The Knight of the Hobby Horse, Almost too Serious, Frightening, Child falling asleep, and The Poet Speaks. When the work came before the Berlin critic Rellstab, he asked whether the composer was in earnest or joking, and remarked: ' When we see a piece of music superscribed " Of foreign lands and people," we feel our pulse to find out if we are not in fever dreams. To where has Art strayed through some false fundamental principles? To what irrational solutions do these irrational roots and equations lead?' This annoyed Schumann not a little. 'Anything more inept and narrow-minded than what Rellstab has written about my *Scenes of Childhood* I have never met with. He seems to think that I place a crying child before me, and then seek for tones to imitate it. The reverse is the case. However, I do not deny that while composing some children's heads were hovering before me; but of course the superscriptions came into existence afterwards, and are indeed nothing else but more delicate directions for the rendering and comprehension of the music.' What Schumann says here about the superscriptions of the *Scenes of Childhood,* and in another place (letter of March 8, 1839) about the superscriptions of all his compositions having come into existence subsequently, may be true, but it is nevertheless misleading. His remark about some children's heads hovering before him shows this. It is shown more strikingly by many other remarks about the contents of his compositions, among others by the comparison of the *Scenes of Childhood* with the *Album for the Young,* Op. 68, of 1848, forty-three pieces with superscriptions. ' These *Scenes of Childhood,*' Schumann writes, ' are reminiscences of an older person for older ones, whilst the *Christmas Album* [the *Album für die Jugend*] contains rather foreshadowings, presentiments, future states, for younger ones.' With regard to the *Album,* he writes in the same letter : ' The first piece I wrote for my eldest child on her birthday, and thus one after the other was added. It seemed to me as if I once more began composing anew. You will trace some of the old humour here and there.' Very interesting are Clara's remarks on the *Scenes of Childhood.* ' Just now occurs to me *Fürchtenmachen* [Frightening]. You understand that so well . . . Your whole inwardness reveals itself in these scenes : for instance, the touching simplicity of the *Bittendes Kind* [Entreating child]—one sees it with folded hands; and the *Kind im Einschlafen* [Child falling asleep]—it is impossible to close the eyes more beautifully. . . . The *Curiose Geschichte* [Strange story] I like much. And the *Haschemann* [Catch me if you can]—that is funny, quite wonderfully depicted . . . *Träumerei* [Dreaming] is a beautiful dream ; the *Kamin* a German, not a French fireside . . . When you have time write to me something about these scenes—tell me how you wish them to be played, and what were your thoughts in composing them, whether they were my thoughts.'

Speaking of pieces for children reminds me of the *Twelve Pianoforte Pieces* for four hands, Op. 85, of 1849, the superscriptions of which are similar to those of the *Album for the Young.* One day, when Schumann and his wife were playing No. 2, the Bear Dance, he imitated the heavy, awkward movements of the bear. He composed No. 9, the Fountain (*Am Springbrunnen*) while staying in the country, where, in the garden in front of the house, a fountain was playing. This piece may be called a soundpicture—the gushing and dripping of the fountain, with the *crescendos* and *decrescendos* produced by the play of the breeze with the water, no one can fail to recognize. But, of course, there is more in the music than the imitation of the sounds of the fountain. Clara writes : ' *At the Fountain* is extremely original in its loveliness and dreaminess. One is transported to the fountain, and sees in it all sorts of wonderful things—the ball which twists about most curiously, and yet finally returns to its first position. In short, unconsciously one joins in the dream, until the end of the piece, when each smiles contentedly at the other. So it is with us when we play it together.'

In the *Ball Scenes*, Op. 109, and the *Children's Ball*, Op. 130, both for four hands, the composer returns to scenes which in earlier years had a great charm for him. To the former work he refers as 'a masked ball.' The *Préambule* opens a view of a scene full of joyous excitement—brilliantly lighted rooms, a throng of finely-dressed people, a general appearance of festivity, beaming faces, &c. It is not difficult to recognize the passages to which Schumann alluded when, playing these pieces with his wife, he playfully interpreted, saying, 'Here the waiters are still rushing about with the dishes among the company'; and, further on, 'Now the grown-up people begin to mingle with the little ones, and things are becoming more serious.'

To find nobler themes we have only to turn to the *Bilder aus dem Osten* (Pictures from the East), Op. 66, of 1848. In a prefatory note, Schumann says: 'The composer of the following pieces thinks that with a view to a better understanding of them he ought not to leave unmentioned that they owe their existence to a special suggestion. The pieces were written while the composer was reading Rückert's *Makamen* (Tales after the Arabic of Hariri); and while composing he could not forget the strange hero of the book, Abu Seid—who could be compared to the German Eulenspiegel, except that the former has more poetry and nobility about him—and also the figure of his honest friend Hareth. This

explains the foreign character of some of the pieces.
The first five are not based on definite situations; only
the last might perhaps be regarded as an echo of the last
Makame, in which we see the hero concluding his merry
life in repentance and penance. May this attempt to
give some expression in our art to the Oriental
manner of poetry and thought, as has already often
been done in German poetry, find a favourable reception
among sympathizers.'

Before leaving the pianoforte compositions and taking
up the orchestral ones, I must quote at least the
superscriptions of the *Forest Scenes*, Op. 82, of 1848
and 1849 : Entry, Hunter in Ambush, Solitary Flowers,
The ill-reputed Spot (followed by eight lines by
F. Hebbel), Pleasing Landscape, Wayside Inn, The Bird
as Prophet, Hunting Song, and Farewell. Further
information about these pieces, and information—at
least of any importance—about the contents of the
compositions not mentioned, is looked for in vain in
the correspondence.

None of Schumann's symphonies has a title, still
less an explicit programme ; but that two of them had a
programmatic basis we learn from the master's letters
and from other sources. 'It is quite impossible for
me to give my thoughts to the journal,' he writes
in February, 1841. 'During the last few days* I
finished a work (at least in outline) over which I have
been quite blissful, but which has also thoroughly
exhausted me. Imagine a whole symphony—and,
moreover, a Spring Symphony—I can hardly believe
myself that it is finished. But the scoring has still

* He actually sketched the work in four days.—January 23-26,
1841.

to be done.' Truly, the B flat major Symphony,
Op. 38, 'was born in a fiery hour,' as the composer
remarked. 'I wrote the symphony,' he says in a letter
to Spohr on November 23, 1842, 'at the end of the
winter of 1841, if I may say so, in that flush of spring
(*Frühlingsdrang*) which carries man away even in his old
age, and comes over him anew every year. Description
and painting were not part of my intention; but I
believe that the time at which it came into existence
may have influenced its shape and made it what it is.'
Schumann gives a more explicit commentary in a letter
to the conductor and composer Taubert, of January 10,
1843: 'Try to inspire the orchestra with some of the
spring longing which chiefly possessed me when I wrote
the symphony in February, 1841. At the very beginning
I should like the trumpet entry to sound like a call to
waken. In what follows of the Introduction there might
be a suggestion of the growing green of everything,
even of a butterfly flying up; and, in the *Allegro*, of the
gradual assembling of all the constituents of spring.
But these are fancies which presented themselves
to me after the completion of the work. Only of
the last movement I will tell you that I like to think of
it as Spring's Farewell, and that therefore I should not
like it to be rendered frivolously.' The first impulse to
the work was given by a poem of Adolf Böttger. This
poem, which is of a melancholy cast, concludes as
follows: 'Thou Spirit of the cloud, dim and dank, why
hast thou scared away all my happiness? Turn, O turn
thy course! In the valley rises spring.' To the truth
of my statement we have the best testimony—
Schumann's own. In October, 1842, he presented
Böttger with his portrait, and on it he wrote the opening

notes of Op. 38, and below them: 'Beginning of a symphony prompted by a poem of Adolf Böttger; to the poet as a souvenir from R. Schumann.' The composer begins where the poet ends. The last line of the latter might have been taken by the former as the motto of the first movement: 'In the valley rises spring.' From the authentic information given in Litzmann's *Clara Schumann* we learn that the four movements were originally entitled: *Frühlingsbeginn* (Commencement of Spring), *Abend* (Evening), *Frohe Gespielen* (Merry companions), and *Voller Frühling* (Full Spring).

The programmatic nature of the last of Schumann's symphonies (the third in the order of publication), the one in E flat major, Op. 97, of 1850, is likewise ascertainable. The composer himself says of this work in one of his letters that there was probably 'here and there a piece of life in it.' Wasielewski tells us that Schumann remarked in conversation that the sight of Cologne Cathedral gave the first impulse to the work; and the original superscription of the fourth of the five movements—'in the character of the accompaniment to a solemn ceremony'—points, no doubt, to the influence exercised on the composer by the ceremony of the installation of a new archbishop of Cologne, which took place while he was at work on the symphony. Thus we see that the epithet 'Rhenish' given to Op. 97 is justified by facts, if not authorized by the master. The rescinding of the above-mentioned superscription and his remarks on it are very characteristic of Schumann's position with regard to programme music. 'One should not,' he said, 'show people one's heart—a general impression of an art-work does them more good; at least, they make then no perverse comparisons.'

Schumann's overtures, with one exception, have all titles and a poetic basis. His best is that to Byron's *Manfred*, to which dramatic poem the composer wrote also other programme music (melodramatic matter, an *entr'acte*, &c.) ; his second best, the overture to his opera *Genoveva ;* the third best, that to Schiller's *Bride of Messina ;* and after them follow the less valuable ones to Shakespeare's *Julius Cæsar*, to Goethe's *Faust*, and Goethe's poem *Hermann and Dorothea*. The 'Festival overture' with the 'Rhine Wine Song,' Op. 123, stands by itself. Of the close connection between poem and music even in the case of the less valuable overtures we cannot have the slightest doubt. To Richard Pohl, who had proposed Schiller's play as the subject of an opera libretto, Schumann writes : 'After reading *The Bride of Messina* several times, to realize the tragedy quite clearly, there came thoughts of an overture, which I then finished.' In the same way, Moritz Horn's proposal of *Hermann and Dorothea* as the subject of a concert oratorio seems to have suggested the overture to that poem, which the composer wrote in five hours, and for which he had a great affection. The greatest achievement of Schumann as a composer of programme music, and indeed as a composer generally, is the overture to *Manfred*. It is one of the most original and grandest orchestral compositions ever conceived, one of the most powerful, but at the same time one of the most sombre soul-portraits ever painted. The sombreness is nowhere relieved, although contrast to the dark brooding and the surging agitation of despair is obtained by the tender, longing, regretful recollection of Astarte, the destroyed beloved one. And when at last life ebbs away, we are reminded of Manfred's dying words to the Abbot;

> ' 'Tis over—my dull eyes can fix thee not ;
> But all things swim around me, and the earth
> Heaves as it were beneath me.   .   .   .
>
> .   .   .   .
>
> Old man ! 'tis not so difficult to die.'

We need not trace Schumann's tone-painting in his accompanied vocal music; the words indicate it sufficiently. Moreover, the greater importance of Schumann's pianoforte accompaniments to his songs, as compared with those of his predecessors, is one of the commonplaces of musical history. Indeed, the pianoforte is sometimes even more important than the voice in the interpretation of the words. Before my task is done, I have to refer to three compositions which not only are patent programme music, but initiated the recultivation of an interesting subordinate department of that kind of instrumental music. Melodrama, although employed in operas and plays, had for some time been neglected as an independent form. Schumann's example soon found imitators, one of the first being Liszt, and now the writing of pianoforte accompaniments to recitations, especially of ballads, has become a pretty common practice. The contributions of Schumann to this *genre* are Op. 106, *Schön Hedwig*, ballad by F. Hebbel (composed 1849, published 1853) ; Op. 122, No 1, *Ballade vom Haideknaben*, by F. Hebbel; and Op. 122, No. 2, *Die Flüchtlinge* (The Fugitives), ballad by Shelley (composed 1852, published 1853). With this not unimportant piece of evidence of Schumann as a composer of programme music, I take leave of ' the most romantic of the romanticists.'

CHAPTER VI.

FIFTH PERIOD CONTINUED: THREE PIANIST COMPOSERS—
CHOPIN, HENSELT, AND HELLER.

What is the position of the superlatively poetical and emotional CHOPIN (1809-1849), with regard to the subject under discussion? Not a single one of his compositions has a programme prefixed to it, or bears a title indicative of one; and a search, with a view to unrevealed programmes, among his letters and his friends' accounts of him yields but an extremely poor outcome. 'Whilst my thoughts were with her' [his love, Constantia Gladkowska], Chopin writes on October 3, 1829, 'I composed the *Adagio* of my Concerto' [in F minor, Op. 21]. On August 21, 1830, he writes : 'The *Adagio* [of the E minor Concerto, Op. 11] is in E major, and of a romantic, calm, and partly melancholy character. It is intended to convey the impression which one receives when the eye rests on a beloved landscape that calls up in one's soul beautiful memories—for instance, on a fine moonlight night.' There is only one other epistolary remark of Chopin's of this kind, and that is jocular rather than serious. Writing in 1839 to Fontana about the B flat minor Sonata, that with the Funeral March, he says of the short *Finale* : 'The left and the right hand *unisono* are gossiping after the march.' The information to be gathered elsewhere is not much more abundant. First we learn that the news of the capture of Warsaw by the Russians on September 8, 1831, inspired Chopin, then at Munich, with the Etude, Op. 10, No. 12, full of fuming rage and passionate ejaculations. Next, George Sand writes with her magic pen in her *Histoire de ma Vie* about the *Préludes*. Describing her and Chopin's stay in Majorca (1838-1839), at the deserted monastery of Valdemosa, she relates that to him the monastery was full of terrors and phantoms ; that on returning with her children from her nocturnal explorations among the ruins, she found him at the pianoforte, pale, with haggard eyes and hair standing on end, unable to recognize them at once ; and that after an effort to smile, he played to them sublime things he had composed, or rather terrible and heart-rending ideas that had taken possession of him, as it were unconsciously, in this hour of solitude, sadness, and terror. ' Several present to the mind visions of deceased monks and the sounds of funeral chants which beset his imagination ; others are melancholy and sweet—they occurred to him in the hours of sunshine and of health, with the noise of the children's laughter under the window, the distant sounds of guitars, the warbling of the birds among the humid foliage, and the sight of the pale, little, full-blown roses on the snow. Others, again, are of a mournful sadness, and, while charming the ear, rend the heart.' About one of the latter, one which occurred to him on a dismal rainy evening, and which produces a terrible mental depression, George Sand has a long story. She and her son Maurice had gone to Palma and were overtaken by tempestuous weather. Chopin's anxiety for them became a kind of calm despair, in which, bathed in tears, he played the prelude in question. On their return, he exclaimed with a wild look and in a strange tone : ' Ah ! I knew well that you were dead.' Afterwards he confessed to her that he had seen in a dream all she experienced, and that no longer distinguishing this dream from reality, he had grown calm and been lulled to sleep while playing the pianoforte, believing that he was dead himself. 'He saw himself drowned in a lake, heavy, ice-cold drops of water fell at regular intervals upon his breast, and when I drew his attention to those drops of water which were actually falling at regular intervals upon the roof, he denied having heard them. He was even vexed at what I translated by the term Imitative Harmony. He protested with all his might, and he was right, against the puerility of these imitations for the ear. His genius was full of mysterious harmonies of nature, translated by sublime equivalents into his musical thought, and not by a servile repetition of external sounds. His composition of this evening was indeed full of the drops of rain which resounded on the sonorous tiles of the monastery, but they were transformed in his imagination and his music into tears falling from heaven on his heart.' This account is very interesting; but it would be more valuable than it is if George Sand were not known to have loved poetry more than truth.

Then there is a story told by Louis Enault. One evening, when George Sand had been speaking of the peacefulness of country life and unfolding a picture of rural harmonies, Chopin remarked: 'How admirably you have spoken!' To which the reply was: 'Well, then, set me to music!' Whereupon, we are told, the master improvised a veritable pastoral symphony. Another anecdote tells us that George Sand had a little dog which was in the habit of turning round and round in the endeavour to catch its tail. One evening when it was thus engaged she said to Chopin: 'If I had your

P

talent, I would compose a pianoforte piece for this dog.'
And Chopin at once sat down at the pianoforte, and
improvised the charming waltz in D flat (Op. 64), which
has obtained the name of *Valse du petit chien.* I do not
bring forward these pieces of information as weighty
evidence, but rather to show how little can be gathered
bearing on the subject. Somewhat more important than
the two preceding stories is the following. One night,
when Chopin was playing a polonaise immediately after
having finished composing it, he saw the door open, and a
long train of Polish knights and ladies dressed in antique
costumes, enter through it and file past him. The vision
filled the composer with such terror that he fled through
the opposite door, and dared not return to the room the
whole night. The Polish artist Kwiatkowski, a friend
of the composer's, who painted a water-colour and
two sketches in oils of this scene 'according to
Chopin's indication,' entitling it *Le Rêve de Chopin,*
told me that the polonaise was the one in A major,
Op. 40, No. 1.

Now, have we to conclude from the absence of titles
and programmes, and the dearth of other information,
that Chopin was a composer of the most absolute of
absolute music, that he never thought of anything but
the beauty and piquancy of the tonal combinations, and
that there is nothing whatever behind these combinations?
If we remember Balzac's saying that Chopin was less a
musician than a soul *qui se rend sensible ;* if we remember
Liszt's remark that Chopin summed up in his imagination
a poetic sentiment inherent in his nation ; if, more
especially, we remember the impressions received from
Chopin's works, it is impossible to come to such a
conclusion. As Chopin was a pre-eminently subjective,

a pre-eminently lyrical composer, it may well be that in many, perhaps even in the majority of cases his compositions were exhalations of his moods, and in not a few cases unconscious exhalations. The character of some of his compositions, more especially his Nocturnes, favours this view; but the character of others leads us to suspect something very different. It often seems to us that we follow trains of thought, hear passionate monologues, and witness sympathetically realized scenes. The strongest impressions of passionate monologues we receive from the Scherzi. And in them as well as in the Ballades, although not in those alone, we cannot fail to perceive the trains of thought. The Ballades are also notable for a certain narrative tone. Then think of the ideas, moods, pictures, and apparitions called up by the inimitably exquisite Preludes. In the Polonaises Chopin becomes epic and dramatic: they are historical and political—grand in their threnodies and in their pæans; in their memories of misfortunes and their visions of triumphs. In them the composer transcends the limits of his subjectivity—his individual egoism expands into national egoism. It is not without reason that Rubinstein called Chopin the pianoforte bard, rhapsodist, mind, and soul; found in his compositions the tragic, the romantic, the lyric, the dramatic, the fantastic, the psychic, the hearty, the dreamy, the brilliant, the grand, the simple, and every kind of expression; saw in the A major Polonaise a picture of Poland's greatness, and in the C minor Polonaise a picture of her fall; described the B flat minor Sonata as a complete drama, and heard in the last movement 'the nocturnal whizzing of the wind over the graves in the churchyard'; and says of the Études that they were without titles and programmes, but bore in themselves a world of psychic content.

Subjectivity is the beginning and end of Chopin. Happily he not only subjectivates the objective, but also objectivates the subjective. With Chopin music was a passioscope. To fit the art for this function, its materials had to be subtilized and sensitized. He who has studied the texture of the music of the great masters knows what that means, and knows also how much Chopin did for the development of music as an emotional language. We may say of the Polish master that by the extension of its vocabulary and phraseology he enabled the language of music to express an infinitude of things that before had been inexpressible. Chopin was a soul-painter, chiefly and almost solely. The strictest investigation yields little of body-painting, and that little is for the most part not direct imitation (sound by sound), but imitation by analogy, and, moreover, idealized. The only traces discoverable are the rocking in the Berceuse and Barcarolle, the dance rhythms in the Mazurkas, Polonaises, Valses, &c., and if our imagination is sufficiently alert, the clinking of spurs, the rattling of sabres, and the tramping of horses in the Mazurkas and Polonaises. The imitation of the graceful motions of the dancers is not only an idealization of the material actual, but also a symbolization of spiritual qualities. As a soul-painter Chopin is in several respects unique. What subtle shades in the incalculable variety of states of the mind, whether serene or moody, calm or agitated, depressed or elated, languid or ebullient! If we fully realize the distinctness of the impressions we receive from Chopin's compositions and at the same time realize the difficulty of describing what

we feel, Mendelssohn's remark as to the definiteness of
music and the indefiniteness of words may occur to us.
No one denies that Chopin was a tone-poet.   But how
could he be that unless he had something to communicate, unless he had the power of moving souls as
well as of tickling ears ?   What inevitably follows is this.
Being a tone-poet, and as such having something to
communicate, Chopin must be in one way or another a
composer of programme music.   Not, however, in the
way of Berlioz and Liszt, which he abhorred, nor in the
way of Schumann, whose warm sympathy he by no
means reciprocated.   Chopin's   way   was   his   own
supremely individual and original way—the way of the
delicate, passionate *âme qui se rend sensible.**

Before proceeding to the sixth period of the history of
programme music, I must say a few words about two
other composers, one of whom is ADOLPH HENSELT
(1814-1889), the great pianist.   Although not of the
rank of Mendelssohn, Schumann, and Chopin, and,
moreover, the very reverse of voluminous in his
productivity, he may claim a place here as a prominent
and refined writer of small titled and truly characteristic
tone-poems.   Hence I point out, not his Concerto and
Trio, but his *Frühlingslied* (Spring Song), *Wiegenlied*
(Cradle Song), *Poème d'amour*, *La Gondola*, among
other pieces, and especially his Studies, Op. 2 and 5,
each book containing twelve.   The Studies of Op. 2 bear
French superscriptions : ' Orage tu ne sauras m'abattre,'
' Pensez un peu à moi,' ' Exauce mes voeux,' ' Repos
d'amour,' ' Vie orageuse,' ' Si oiseau j'étais à toi je

---

* The curious will find in my *Life of Chopin* numerous attempts at
interpretations.   Here we have to deal with patent facts, not with
conjectures.

volerais,' 'C'est la jeunesse qui a des ailes dorées,' 'Tu m'attires, m'entraines,' 'Jeunesse d'amour, plaisir céleste,' 'Comme le ruisseau dans la mer se répand,' 'Dors-tu ma vie ?' and 'Plein de soupirs, de souvenirs.' Of the Studies, Op. 5, ten have titles : *Eroica, Hexentanz* (Witches' Dance), *Ave Maria, Lost Home, Thanksgiving Song after Storm, Elfenreigen* (Dance of the Fairies), *Romance with Choral Refrain, Vanished Happiness, Love Song,* and *Nocturnal Procession of Ghosts.* We have unfortunately no means of learning what were Henselt's processes of composition ; but we may confidently affirm that his titles and compositions cover each other. The former may, however, have been excogitated subsequently. The superscriptions of Op. 2 certainly make one suspect that there may be fancy as well as fact in the titles.

STEPHEN HELLER (*c.* 1813-1888), said Schumann, lacks the delightful euphony of Henselt, but he has more *Geist* (genius, *esprit*), and, he might have added, a more distinct and original individuality. It is impossible not to mention Schumann when speaking of Heller. They were congenial spirits. Both were under the spell of Jean Paul Richter, living in his world of sentiment, poetry, and humour. Schumann recognized this congeniality at once after reading one or two of Heller's letters and compositions. Indeed, so impressed was he by them, that he forthwith enrolled him, under the name of Jeanquirit, as a *Davidsbündler,* a slayer of the Philistines. The dedication of Heller's Op. 7 to Liane von Froulay, a female character in the German prose-poet's novel *Der Titan,* pleased Schumann greatly, and reminded him of the intention of dedicating one of his own compositions to Wina, another fascinating young

lady, in *Die Flegeljahre*. It is truly wonderful how
correctly Schumann gauged the capacities of Heller at
the very beginning of his career. He found him a
genuine artist-nature, full of invention, imagination,
wit, and humour, and a romanticist, but not of the
nihilistic and materialistic sort; on the contrary, natural
in feeling and clear in expression. Looking at him from
our (the programmatic) point of view, Schumann notices
that there is something behind the notes, something in
the background—namely, ' a peculiar attractive twilight,
rather dawnlike, which makes the really firm figures
appear in a strange light.' And he notices too that
while Heller's execution is fine and careful, his forms
are new, fantastic, and free. Yes, there is something
behind the tones. But what is it? Without further
information than is supplied in the foregoing chapter on
Schumann, we must be aware that the variety of
programmes is very great, that there are programmes
of all degrees of consciousness, and of all degrees of
spirituality and materiality, programmes adopted before
and after the act of composition. Of material tone-
painting there is hardly anything in Heller's music, but
its speaking nature must convince us that there is
meaning in it. Moreover, I had from the composer's
own mouth the information that in his compositions he
was incited and influenced by his reading and experiences.
In this connection it is worth repeating another remark
he made to me. He said : I have spent more time in
reading than in playing and composing. Heller has
been called the La Fontaine of music. It is an excellent
parallel as far as it goes, but it is decidedly partial. We
may compare Heller with La Fontaine the author of
the *Fables,* but not with La Fontaine the author of the

Contes. We may compare Heller with the easy-going, careless La Fontaine, who was content to *doucement laisser couler sa vie,* but not with La Fontaine the sybarite and parasite. Heller was a dreamer, not a man of action ; a recluse, not a man of society. Independence was his *magnum bonum,* and literature, art, and nature the darling resources of his life.

None of Heller's compositions have what can rightly be called a programme expressed in words. The large majority of them have not even titles, and the titles we meet with are at best of a general nature, some of them indeed being merely non-connotative names. Several of his titles show his affinity to Schumann : *Arabesques, Novellette, Scènes d'enfant, Album à la jeunesse,* &c., &c. His love of nature reveals itself in titles like these : *Scènes Pastorales, Eclogues, Bergeries, Dans les Bois.* The most famous titles are *Promenades d'un Solitaire* of the three series of pieces Op. 78, 80, and 89 ; *Rêveries du Promeneur,* Op. 101 ; *Nuits blanches,* of eighteen pieces, Op. 82 ; and lastly, *Dans les Bois,* of the three series Op. 86, 128, and 136. The first two are derived from *Les Rêveries du Promeneur solitaire* of J. J. Rousseau, who calls the several chapters of this supplement of his *Confessions* first, second, &c., Promenade. Of these several series of pictures only the second and third of the *Dans le Bois* have individual titles—those of the second book hint at Schumann's *Forest Scenes (Entrance, Forest-whispers, Hunter's Delight, Solitary Flower, Forest-Legend, Chased Squirrel,* and *Wandering homeward*), and those of the third point to Weber's *Freischütz (Max, Agathe, Caspar's Strophe, Aennchen* and *Agathe,* and *Wild Flowers*). Of peculiar interest is Op. 126, three overtures for pianoforte, respectively to a drama, a pastoral, and a comic opera. The most detailed programme occurs in connection with the *Étude*, Op. 29, originally written for the *Méthode des Méthodes*.* It runs thus: '*La meute est déchainée—les fanfares éclatent—Messire le roi Philippe sur son ardent coursier s'efforce à dissiper le chagrin que lui cause le trépas de sa mie, Agnès de Méranie . . .*' Quite the reverse as to definiteness and explicitness is the title of Op. 140, *Voyage autour de ma chambre*, conveyed by the composer from Xavier de Maistre's well-known charming book. Heller is especially famous for his *Études* and *Préludes*, which could with equal propriety be called *Poésies*. In conclusion: Is Heller a composer of Programme Music? Gentle reader, the reply depends entirely on your definition of the term.

The account of the fifth period of the history of Programme Music has now to be interrupted; but it is not yet concluded. As has already been explained, the fifth period continues its course side by side with the sixth, to which for a while we have to give our attention.

* By Moscheles and Fétis, published in 1840.

BOOK IV.

OTHER FULFILMENTS.

CHAPTER I.

SIXTH PERIOD (FROM ABOUT THE FOURTH DECADE OF THE 19TH CENTURY): DEPARTURE FROM THE CLASSICAL FORMS AND WIDER SCOPE OF SUBJECTS.

BERLIOZ.

The inspiring geniuses of the last period, which opens about the fourth decade of the 19th century, were BERLIOZ (1803-1869), LISZT (1811-1886), and RICHARD WAGNER (1813-1883). Radically unlike each other in their natures, diverse in their aims and in their action on the development of the art, they were nevertheless at one in their influence on programme music, which through them became the predominant *genre* of instrumental composition, indeed so predominant that even most of what was subsequently presented as absolute music was in reality but concealed programme music. This they accomplished by the extension of the expressive power of the art—by the increase of the harmonic, rhythmical, and colouristic means, by the freer treatment of form, and by the widening of the scope of subjects. Nothing discloses so strikingly the dissimilarity of nature and diversity of aim of these musical protagonists of the 19th century as their opinions of each other. Wagner thought meanly of Berlioz, Berlioz of Wagner, and both of Liszt, who alone

could go his own way and yet appreciate the ways of his
compeers.* As the personalities of these three men are
so important, influential, and extremely interesting, a
full and careful consideration is called for. Let us begin
with BERLIOZ, who is not only the first born of them,
but also the one who first made himself known as a
composer, and as a revolutionary composer too.

The preceding chapters must have convinced the
reader that programme music does not begin with
Berlioz, that composers before him cultivated it, and not
only occasionally and lightly, but even extensively and
seriously. This simplifies our inquiry, but does not solve
the problem with which we have to deal. The question
of the position of the French master with regard to
programme music is surrounded by prejudices of all
sorts; and I am quite sure that the remark which I
made as to the reader's conviction will be met by the
interjection: 'But was not Berlioz the first who used
explicit programmes?' The reply to this is, that he
was neither the inventor, nor, with one exception, a
user of explicit programmes. Nay, even in the exceptional case, the *Symphonie fantastique*, he attaches no
importance to the programme, and has no objection to its
being disregarded. Other prejudices afloat about Berlioz
are that his music is formless, or at least has a form
wholly different in kind from the classical; and that he
was the originator and proclaimer of a new system of composition opposed to the classical. A careful examination
of these points leads to an extremely curious result.

Let us first inquire into Berlioz's opinions as to tone-
painting and the expressive powers of music. They are
likely to prove positively startling to those imbued with

* What is here said applies to them only as composers.

the popular notions about the master. In his essay *De l'imitation musicale*, which appeared in the *Revue et Gazette musicale de Paris* of January 1 and 8, 1837, he handles the subject with a severity that could not be surpassed by an opponent of programme music. The articles in question are not remarkable for literary or philosophical excellence, but cannot fail to interest us as a confession of the master's faith. His main authority is Giuseppe Carpani, the biographer of Haydn, who, however, is no authority at all on æsthetics. Lacépède also is alluded to. With Carpani, Berlioz distinguishes physical (material) and sentimental (emotional) imitation. The latter he regards as by far the more important imitation, in fact as the only really important imitation; and in it music is superior to painting and poetry. As to material imitation, Berlioz held that in its employment there were four conditions to be observed. (1) It may be a means, but hardly ever an end—in other words, it may be a complement, but not the musical idea itself; (2) it should not be employed except on subjects worthy of the hearer's attention, at least in serious compositions; (3) it is admissible as a suggestion sufficiently faithful to be understood, but not as a literal transcript, not as substitution of nature for art; and (4) it must not arrogate to itself the place of emotional imitation, nor display its descriptive futilities when passion alone ought to speak. Berlioz is troubled by the question of how the soundless is to be expressed by tones. The proposed solution that soundless things—for instance, the denseness of a wood, the freshness of a prairie, &c.—may be expressed by expressing the emotional impressions they make, does not quite satisfy him. The freshness and obscurity of a wood makes, he remarks, different

impressions on the lover remembering happy or bitter
hours spent in it, on the hunter intent on the pleasures
of the chase, on the timid young girl approaching it, on
the brigand lying in ambush or dragging himself away
wounded. Berlioz is getting mixed in his reasoning.
But we must not tarry to discuss the problem. What
concerns us now is Berlioz's opinions.

In the very much more valuable essay in which
Berlioz treats of the Alcestis of several poets and composers (see his *A travers Chant*), he controverts several
of Gluck's positions. Berlioz maintains that expression
is not the sole object of dramatic music, that it would
be both maladroit and pedantic to disdain the purely
sensuous pleasure which we find in certain effects of
melody, harmony, rhythm, or instrumentation,
independently of their connection with the painting of
the sentiments and passions of the drama. The claims
here made for the purely sensuous hold good of course
with programme music as well as with the drama. No
doubt, the reader remembers Gluck's remark about opera
overtures—that they ought to prepare the spectator for
the action about to be represented, and to form, so to
speak, its argument. In representing Gluck to have said
' l'ouverture doit indiquer le *sujet*,' Berlioz hardly states
the case quite fairly. However, be this as it may,
Berlioz argues thus : ' Musical expression cannot go so
far as that. It certainly can express (*reproduire*) joy,
sorrow, gravity, playfulness ; it can mark a striking
difference between a queen's grief and a village girl's
vexation, between calm, serious meditation and the
ardent reveries that precede an outburst of passion.
Again, borrowing from different nations the musical
style that is proper to them, it can make a distinction

between the serenade of a brigand of the Abruzzi and that of a Tyrolese or Scotch hunter, between the evening march of pilgrims impregnated with mysticism and that of a troop of cattle dealers returning from the fair; it can contrast extreme brutality, triviality, and the grotesque, with angelic purity, nobility and candour.   But if it tries to overstep the bounds of this immense circle, music must necessarily have recourse to words—sung, recited, or read—to fill up the gaps left by its expressional means in a work that addresses itself at the same time to the intellect and to the imagination.   Thus the overture to *Alceste* will announce scenes of desolation and of tenderness, but it cannot inform us either of the object of the tenderness or of the cause of the desolation, it will never tell the spectator that the husband of Alcestis is a King of Thessaly condemned by the gods to die unless some one gives his life to him; yet this is the *subject* of the piece.   Berlioz anticipated that many readers would be astonished at finding the author of the article imbued with such principles, and explains that he had to thank for this astonishment certain people who believed or pretended to believe that in his opinions on the expressive powers of music he exceeded the truth as much as they came short of it, and consequently had generously bestowed on him their own full share of ridicule.

No one who has studied Berlioz's instrumental compositions can have the least doubt that as regards form the master followed in the main the lines of the classics, that where he deviated from these lines he still adhered to the principles that guided those who laid them down, and that, far from ever being formless, he never failed in securing clear structure, logical development, and internal connection, which is sure to be present where external connection is absent. Some of Berlioz's Overtures are closely modelled on the classical form, and only in one of them are we unable to distinguish the orthodox constituents—the first and second subject in the usual key-relation, the working-out section, the recapitulation, and the *coda*. Strange to say, the one exception, *Le Carnaval Romain*, is the most popular and most highly and universally appreciated of the overtures. If the deviations—such as a short working-out section, a greatly extended *coda*, the introduction of episodes, and the placing of the second subject before the first in the recapitulation (*Benvenuto Cellini*)—stood in need of justification, it would be easy to justify them by the quotation of classical examples. As authority for the precedence of the second subject even the pre-eminent classic Mozart may be cited. The first division of the *Symphonie fantastique* and in a less degree that of *Harold en Italie* have more or less pronouncedly some of the principal structural features of the traditional form. When a contributor to the *Neue Zeitschrift für Musik* accused Berlioz of formlessness, Schumann, the editor, added to the article a footnote to this effect : ' I have not been able to discover so much formlessness in Berlioz's music ; on the contrary, too often form without content.' And this was the opinion of the Schumann of 1844, that is, the mature Schumann, who had already composed the B flat major symphony, the string quartets, the pianoforte quintet and quartet, and *Paradise and the Peri*. Views similar to Schumann's have been expressed by other notable musicians—J. C. Lobe, W. Ambros, F. Weingartner, and F. Dräseke. It is also noteworthy that the conservative critic Hanslick, famous as one of the most uncompromising opponents of Liszt and Wagner, was an admirer of Berlioz. Lobe, who, although a perfervid supporter of the progressists of his time, was a follower of the classics as a composer and teacher of composition, went so far as to describe Berlioz's form as grand, bold, swinging, varied, spiritually always appropriate, and technically as regular and harmonious (*einheitlich*) as Beethoven's, and to say that he is clearer in the structure of periods than many a modern composer.

But what made people think and speak of formlessness if there was none? Berlioz's compositions had much about their structure and texture that was novel, and not a little that was uncouth : it was these things that misled the cursory hearers, including nearly all his critics. Perhaps the chief stumbling block in the way of just appreciation was the greater rhythmical freedom in the construction of phrases and periods, in which symmetricalness was no longer supreme, and after-phrase and after-period did not invariably correspond in rhythm and number of bars to the fore-phrase and fore-period. Be it noted that in the foregoing defence of Berlioz nothing has been said of *beauty* of form. Indeed, in this respect the French romanticist may have often fallen short of his classical predecessors. Schumann, who, in his criticism of the *Symphonie fantastique* (*Neue Zeitschrift für Musik*, 1835),*—the only thorough technical and æsthetical examination of any of the master's works ever attempted—defends Berlioz against so many accusations hurled against him, pointing out the good qualities of his form, the pithiness of his harmony, and his sobriety

---

* I say this with a full knowledge and appreciation of Liszt's in many respects excellent essay on the *Harold* Symphony.

in the employment of modulation, is not blind to the frequent sharp projecting corners in the form, and the awkwardness, crabbedness, vulgarity, distortedness, ugliness, and painfulness in his harmonies.

We now come to the third prejudice, that of regarding Berlioz as the originator and proclaimer of a new system. The master himself, however, nowhere pretends to have discovered new forms; and brilliant and voluminous writer though he was, he never published a manifesto. If you scan his writings in search of his system, theory, method, or doctrine, you will be disappointed. Berlioz claims for himself nothing, prides himself on nothing, but the grandeur, intensity, picturesqueness, and novelty of his ideas, and the forcible way in which he expresses them. This aspect of the case deserves to be looked at a little more closely. In studying it we find that the master had an absolute aversion to entering into a discussion of his views on and position in the art.

In 1884, the Paris *Ménestrel* published a letter of Berlioz's, dated Leipzig, November, 1853,* which had then changed hands at a public sale of autographs. As the content showed, it was a reply to one from the editor of the *Feuilles volantes,* who wished Berlioz to contribute to this journal a summary of his opinions on the musical art, on its present state, and on its future. A little reflection and research evinced that the editor in question was J. C. Lobe, and the journal, *Fliegende Blätter für Musik* (1855-1857). In the *Flying Leaves,* vol. i., p. 296 (1855), we find the letter in the original French and in a German translation, superscribed *Mein Glaubensbekenntniss* (My Confession of Faith). It is amusing to see the efforts which Berlioz makes to write

* That was the date given in the paper.

Q

something without saying anything. A few extracts giving the gist of the letter will suffice for our purpose.

' . . . . What you call upon me to publish is simply an authentic profession of faith. . . . . Is not my profession of faith in all I have had the misfortune to write, in what I have done and in what I have not done. . . . . Music is the most poetic, the most powerful, the most living of all the arts. It ought to be also the most free; still, it is not so as yet. Hence our griefs as artists, our obscure devotions, our lassitudes, our despairs, our aspirations unto death. . . . . Modern music, *music* (I do not speak of the courtesan of this name that one meets with everywhere), in some respects, is the antique Andromeda, divinely beautiful and nude, whose glances of flame are decomposed in multi-coloured rays in passing through the prism of her tears. Enchained on a rock on the shore of the vast sea, whose waves come beating and covering her beautiful feet with slime, she awaits the victorious Perseus, who is to break her chain and dash to pieces the Chimera called Routine, whose jaws menace her while shooting forth clouds of poisonous vapour.'

More informing are certain passages of a letter printed in the Postscriptum of the *Mémoires de Hector Berlioz*, and originally addressed to a gentleman who intended to write the composer's biography. ' I notice I have not yet said anything technical about my manner of writing, and perhaps you wish some details on that subject. Generally my style is bold, but it has not the least tendency to destroy anything whatever of the constitutive elements of the art. On the contrary, I endeavour to increase the number of these elements. I never dreamt, as people in France foolishly pretended, of composing music without melody. This school exists now in Germany, and I abhor it. . . . . The dominant qualities of my music are passionate expression, inward ardour, rhythmical animation, unexpectedness (*l'imprévu*). When I say passionate expression, I mean expression intent on reproducing the intimate sense of the subject, even where the subject is the contrary of passion, and where soft, tender sentiments and the utmost calm have to be expressed. . . . . It may be well to point out to you an order of ideas into which no modern composer except myself has penetrated, and of which the ancients did not foresee the extent. I mean those enormous compositions which certain critics designated by the name of architectural or monumental music. These are : my *Symphonie funèbre et triomphale*, for two orchestras and chorus; the *Te Deum*, of which the finale (" Judex crederis ") is without doubt my greatest production; the cantata for two choruses, *L'Impériale*, executed at the concerts of the Palais de l'Industrie in 1855 ; and especially the *Requiem.*' Berlioz remarks that those works in which he has made use of extraordinary means are exceptional; but the exceptions are many and of vast extent if we take into consideration the number and length of his compositions. However, let us allow Berlioz to state his case without interruption. ' In my *Requiem*, for example, there are four orchestras of brass instruments, separated one from the other, and dialoguing at a distance, placed around the grand orchestra and the mass of the voices. In the *Te Deum* it is the organ which from one end of the church converses with the orchestra of two choirs placed at the other end, and with a third very numerous choir in unison, representing in the *ensemble* the congregation that takes part from time to time in the vast sacred concert. But it is especially the form of these pieces, the largeness of the style, and the formidable slowness of certain progressions, whose final aim is not divined, that give to these works their strangely gigantic physiognomy, their colossal aspect. The enormous size of this form is another reason why people either understand nothing at all, or are overwhelmed by a terrible emotion.'

'As to my compositions conceived in the ordinary proportions, and for which I had recourse to no exceptional means, it is precisely their internal ardour, their expression, and their rhythmical originality which have done them the most harm, because of the execution which they demand. In order to render them well, the executants, and especially the conductor, must *feel* like me. An extreme precision, united with an irresistible *verve*, a regulated fire, a dreamy sensibility, a distempered melancholy, so to speak, are required, without which *traits de mes figures* are altered or completely effaced.'

An earlier passage in the same letter, too, is noteworthy. 'I have against me the professors of the Conservatoire, instigated by Cherubini and Fétis, whose self-love has been violently hurt and whose faith has been shocked by my heterodoxy in the matter of harmonic and rhythmic theories. I am an infidel in music, or, rather, I am of the religion of Beethoven, Weber, Gluck, and Spontini, who believe, profess, and prove by their works, that *everything is good* or *everything is bad;* the effect produced by certain combinations deciding alone whether they are to be condemned or absolved.'

On one occasion, however, Berlioz comes very near revealing what he regarded as being his position in music, indeed very near what might be called a manifesto; and this occasion was his criticism of the concerts given by Wagner in Paris in 1860 (see his article on ' Concerts de Richard Wagner : La musique de l'avenir,' in his book *A travers Chants*). Here the profound conservatism of the reputed revolutionist Berlioz manifests itself unmistakably. Whilst proclaiming Beethoven the greatest composer of modern times, he deplores the unfortunate tendencies of Wagner's system. He allows Wagner the possession of the rare intensity of feeling, the inward ardour, the will power, and the faith that move and carry away; but holds that these qualities would have greater *éclat* if they were joined to more invention, less far-fetchedness, and a juster appreciation of certain constitutive elements of the art. He reproaches Wagner and his School with not taking account of sensation, with seeing only the poetic or dramatic idea to be expressed, without troubling themselves as to whether the expression of this idea obliges the composer to overstep the musical conditions. But Berlioz had a personal complaint to make. Opinions had been attributed to him in Germany which were not his, and he had been the object of praises which he thought he could not but regard as insults. He protests against his inclusion in the School of the Music of the Future. He declares that he agrees with that School if its code says that the music of to-day is emancipated, free ; that many old rules, formulated by careless observers and followers of routine, are no longer binding; that various forms are too hackneyed to be still admissible; that everything is good or bad according to the use that is made of it, and the reason that leads to its use ; that in the union of tones and words the music should be in keeping with the feeling expressed and the personage expressing it; that the idea is higher than the sound, and the sentiment and passion higher than the idea. On the other hand, he does not agree with the School if its code says that you must do the contrary of what the rules teach; that people are tired of melody, of melodic design, of arias, duets, trios, and pieces with a regularly developed theme, of consonant harmonies, simple dissonances, prepared and resolved, of natural modulation artistically managed; that one has only to take into account the idea and not to pay the slightest attention to the sensation; that the ear should be despised and brutalized in order to subdue it, the object of music being by no means to be agreeable; that no respect should be paid to the art of singing, nor thought given to its nature and exigencies; that in opera the composer must confine himself to noting the declamation, even should he have to employ the most unsingable, absurd, and ugly intervals; that, in fact, the witches in *Macbeth* are right: 'Fair is foul, and foul is fair.'

The declaration of which I have given an abbreviated and condensed report cannot but be startling to those under the sway of the traditional popular opinion, which sees in Berlioz the subverter of all he found established and respected in his art. Who, indeed, could help being in the highest degree astonished at his denunciation of the very things of which he had himself been accused? After reading the excerpts just quoted we see Berlioz standing before us a thorough conservative,—a follower of Beethoven, Weber, Gluck, and Spontini; an opponent of the progressive party, of Wagner and Liszt and their following; the advocate of euphony and simplicity of melody, of self-contained, regularly developed forms, the enemy of all that is awkward, unnatural, and ugly, the respecter of rules, except those that are the outcome of shortsightedness.

But do Berlioz's declarations make his position clear? Not at all. They rather make confusion worse confounded. For his *dicta* contradict his *acta ;* and his *acta* contradict each other. In short, Berlioz was not only paradoxical, but, as Saint-Saëns says, *un paradox fait homme.* Whatever were his beliefs and principles, his works certainly differed greatly from those of the classics, as indeed from those of any other composer. Undoubtedly a man of genius, he certainly was not a classic. The causes of his defects were four in number,—his character as a man, the nature of his musical disposition, his training and opportunities, and the tendencies of the French romanticism of his time.

To take up first the third of the causes. Berlioz had no musical opportunities until at the age of eighteen, towards the end of 1821, he left his small native town of La Côte-Saint-André and went to Paris for the study of medicine. His musical training as a composer, or indeed as a musician, began later still; and when it began, it was, on the one hand, unmethodical, as he disliked the school-work of harmony, and especially that of counterpoint and fugue; and, on the other hand, was influenced by his favourite master, Lesueur, a disparager of fugues, whose bent and predilection, as we have already seen, was for the expressive, imitative, and picturesque in music. By the way, Octave Fouque, in his *Les Révolutionnaires de la Musique*, amusingly characterizes the relationship between master and disciple by two epigrams : ' Berlioz is nothing else but a successful Lesueur, and Lesueur an ineffectual Berlioz

(Berlioz manqué).' . . 'If Berlioz is God, Lesueur was assuredly his prophet.' Berlioz's models among the great composers were Beethoven, Weber, Gluck, and Spontini. They were, however, models which he but very partially imitated. He made the acquaintance of some of their works soon after he came to Paris, was profoundly impressed by them, and conceived for their authors a passionate admiration that passed into worship. These masters were his gods. For Palestrina, Bach, and Handel he had no understanding ; of Haydn and Mozart he speaks rarely ; and none of his contemporaries gained his sympathies, although he regarded the craftsmanship of Mendelssohn with respect. The consequence of his not going through a regular course of studies and of not mastering the traditional style before gradually evolving a style of his own, was that his music had almost always something angular in its structure and texture. One day Gounod exclaimed : 'Quel homme élégant que Berlioz !' And Saint-Saëns, to whom the remark was made, calls it profound. It certainly is not obvious. Saint-Saëns explains it by saying : 'The elegance of Berlioz does not appear at first sight in his clumsy and awkward style of writing ; it is hidden in the woof, one might say in the flesh itself, of his work ; it exists, in a latent state, in his prodigious nature, which could not injure any other by comparison, as no other could be compared to it.' If this explanation does not justify Gounod's remark, it at least supports mine.

As to the second cause, Berlioz's musical disposition was reflective rather than spontaneous, declamatory (even in its melodiousness) and descriptive rather than lyrical, and rhythmical and especially colouristic rather than harmonic. Genius though he was, the talent given him differs from that given to Mendelssohn and in a still higher degree to Mozart. These two composers were specifically musical,—music flowed from them as a brook from its source; it was their mother tongue, which they spoke without the least effort. With Berlioz the case was different. It needed a strong, external stimulus to make him conceive and bring forth, to make him evolve musical thoughts and tones for their expression. Certain words spoken by Wagner would seem to me even more appropriate in the mouth of the French than in the mouth of the German composer: 'Unless the subject absorbs me, I cannot produce twenty bars worth listening to.'

The principal cause, however, was the character of the man, which not only was the prompter and moulder of his artistic productions, but also influenced his training and the nature of his musical disposition. 'What an unhappy organization I have!' Berlioz exclaims, 'I am a real barometer, now high, now low, subject to the variations of the brilliant or sombre atmosphere of my devouring thoughts.' And again: 'One day well, calm, poetizing, and dreaming; another day suffering from my nerves, bored, feeling like a mangy dog, peevish, as mischievous as a thousand devils, vomiting life, and ready to put an end to it for nothing, if I had not always a delirious happiness in the nearest prospect—a bizarre destiny to accomplish, true friends, music, and lastly curiosity. My life is a romance that interests me much' (June 12, 1833). Indeed, his was not a normal healthy nature, but an eccentric morbid one. He had fierce and uncontrollable passions, and an unbalanced, unbridled mind, was mad rather than sane. No epithet characterizes him better than the word 'volcanic.' His words and acts as a man were volcanic, and so were also his achievements as an artist; in fact, the history of his life consists of a series of eruptions. Innumerable passages of his letters prove this strikingly and conclusively, but even a few extracts enable us to form an idea of the character of the man.

'Shakespeare falling upon me unexpectedly struck me like a thunderbolt; his lightning, in opening the heaven of art with a sublime crash, illuminated to me the most distant profundities. I recognized true grandeur, true beauty, true dramatic truth. I saw, comprehended, felt, that I was alive, and must rise and march.'

'My heart is the centre of a horrible conflagration; it is a virgin forest which lightning has set on fire; from time to time the fire seems lulled, then a gust of wind, . . . another outburst, . . . the cry of the trees breaking down in the flame reveal the terrible power of the devastating scourge.'

He writes of the 'infinitude' of his love, of his 'infernal passion' for Miss Henrietta Smithson, of whom more will be said presently (February 6, 1830).

'She reproached me with not loving her. Thereupon, tired of all this, I answered her by poisoning myself before her eyes. Terrible cries of Henrietta. Sublime despair! Atrocious laughter on my part. Desire to revive on seeing her terrible protestations of love. Emetic! . . . ' (August 30, 1833).

Quite in accordance with the man, we find the artist Berlioz frantically intense, bent on the picturesque, grandiose, colossal, terrible, in short sensational. 'Terrible' and 'frightful' are favourite words of his in describing the effect of his works. Of a descriptive symphony of *Faust* fermenting in his head he says:

'I want it to terrify the musical world'; of the overture to *Les Francs-Juges* he asserts: 'Nothing is so terribly frightful. . . . the fire of hell dictated it'; of the 'Tuba mirum' and other parts of the *Requiem* he mentions the 'terrible cataclysms,' the *foudroyant* effect, and the 'horrible grandeur.'

One characteristic of Berlioz has yet to be pointed out, for it plays as notable a part in his art as in his life,— namely, his love of attitudinizing and striving after effect. I still think that what I once wrote in regard to this matter is not in any way exaggerated. Berlioz does not for a moment forget that he is in the presence of an audience, though the audience may be his most intimate friend. His supreme endeavour is always to make himself interesting, and to set the world agape. To effect this he unhesitatingly sacrifices truth, friendship, the sanctities of love, and all that is noble and beautiful.

There remains still the fourth cause, the tendencies of the French romanticism of his time. This was not one of the most powerful factors in the moulding of Berlioz the artist, but it was a notable one. It certainly reinforced certain natural tendencies of the man. He belongs, however, not to the early generation of French romanticism, that of Chateaubriand and Madame de Staël, but to the later generation, that which arose in the third decade of the 18th century and of which Victor Hugo was the most characteristic, powerful, and glorious representative. Indeed, Berlioz used to be called, at least in his younger days, the Victor Hugo of music, and to become the Victor Hugo of music was certainly one of the ambitions of his youth. In the prefaces to some of the poet's dramas he must have found much that was entirely to his mind. For instance, the passage in that to *Cromwell* (1827), where Victor Hugo asks for liberty in matters of thought as in other matters. 'Let us bring down the hammer,' he writes, ' on theories, poetics, and systems. Let us tear down the old lath and plaster that masks the façade of art.' And how the author of the last division of the *Symphonie fantastique* (the Dream of a Witches' Sabbath) and the author to be of the last division of *Harold en Italie* (the Orgy of the Brigands), and certain portions of the *Damnation de Faust*, must have rejoiced over Victor Hugo's rehabilitation of the ugly—of physical deformity in *Le Roi s'amuse* (1832), and of moral deformity in *Lucrezia Borgia* (1833). A love of the picturesque, the fantastic, and the intense, in the most exaggerated degrees and forms, Berlioz had in common with the contemporary French literary and artistic romanticists. And it was these qualities alone that attracted him and them to the plays of Shakespeare, to the *Faust* of Goethe, and to the works of some minor deities of his.*

* The most important documents for the study of Berlioz's character are his *Mémoires* and his letters, especially the *Lettres intimes*, the *Correspondance inédite*, and *Lettres à la Princesse Carolyne Sayn-Wittgenstein*. Edmond Hippeau's *Berlioz intime* (new edition, 1889) tries to sift Berlioz's contradictory data. Adolphe Jullien has furnished a fair minded biography. The latest writers are hero-worshippers: Julien Tiersot in his *Hector Berlioz et la Société de son Temps* (1904) and Adolphe Boschot in his *La Jeunnesse d'un Romantique* (1906). Tiersot looks upon the *Mémoires* as perfectly faithful documents, holds that the predominant quality of Berlioz as a man and as an artist was sincerity, and sees in the many glaring contradictions of the *Mémoires* and letters only apparent contradictions. It may be true that Berlioz never made an intentional misrepresentation; but, as Tiersot states himself, Berlioz was often the victim of his imagination, which was the mistress of his acts and got the better of his reason—his passionate, fiery temperament exaggerates everything—his enthusiasms, ironies, loves, and hatreds vibrate in his writings.

Having made ourselves acquainted with the character of the man and artist, we are at last in a position to examine his works profitably. The *Requiem, L'Enfance du Christ, Le Cinq Mai*, the operas, and other vocal compositions do not concern us here, with two exceptions, however—*Roméo et Juliette*, in which the symphonic element predominates, and *La Damnation de Faust*, in which it is of considerable importance. Although disregarding so much, I do not undervalue the powerfully expressive and descriptive character of the instrumental accompaniments of the vocal works. There remain then for consideration only eight overtures, the *Symphonie fantastique*, with its sequel the monodrama *Lélio*, the symphony *Harold en Italie*, the dramatic symphony *Roméo et Juliette*, and the dramatic legend *La Damnation de Faust*. Another work that may perhaps be added is the *Symphonie funèbre et triomphale*, a ceremonial rather than a programmatic composition. And we must at least mention No. 3 of *Les Tristes (Tristia), La Marche funèbre pour la dernière scène d'Hamlet* (Paris, September 22, 1848), a little known composition, which Tiersot describes as full of sobs, panting, and heart-rending.

Of the eight overtures, four are written to operas, and the others derive their titles respectively from two novels by Scott, a verse-romance by Byron, and a tragedy by Shakespeare. These compositions have no other programme than that indicated by their titles; consequently the programme, if we may speak of one, can neither be called explicit nor definite. On turning from the titles to the contents, we discover that Berlioz nowhere attempts to tell the story, nor, as a rule, lays himself out to depict scenes and to enter into particulars, but usually confines himself to the rendering of general impressions and to the painting of characters. In fact, the overtures of Beethoven and Mendelssohn are just as much programme music as those of Berlioz; nay, we may even say that the former composers (for instance, in *Egmont* and the great *Leonore*, in the *Midsummer Night's Dream, Calm Sea and Prosperous Voyage*, and *Hebrides*) went considerably farther than the French master.

I said that the overtures had no other programmes than those indicated by the titles. In one case, however, this is not quite correct, for the *Ouverture de Waverley*, Op. 2, composed in 1827-1828 and first performed in 1828, has a motto as well as a title; but, as you will see, it is of a very general nature :—

'[While] dreams of love and lady's charms
Give place to honour and to arms.'

These are the concluding lines of the hero's poem 'Mirkwood Mere,' in the fifth chapter of Walter Scott's *Waverley*. The first line indicates the contents of the slow introduction, the second that of the *Allegro*. The overture reflects the chivalry of Weber. Form, rhythm, and harmony are simple; the musical ideas for the most part without distinction and even downright commonplace.

In the *Ouverture des Francs-Juges*, Op. 3, composed in 1827-1828, performed in 1828, we have a more important and characteristic work. It is unquestionably powerful, out also youthful and crude. Schumann appropriately described it as ' uncouthly Polyphemish.' Although this overture has much more of Berlioz about it than *Waverley*, the composer still keeps in touch with his predecessors, no less in melody and rhythm than in form. So much so indeed that it is difficult to understand now why the contemporaries objected to it so strongly and were so shocked by it. Remarks in Berlioz's letters throw some light on the intentions he had in writing this overture, which was to open an opera (never finished) for which his bosom friend Humbert Ferrand had furnished the libretto. 'Nothing is so terribly frightful as my overture *Les Francs-Juges* . . . It is a hymn to despair, but the most desperate despair, the most desperate despair imaginable, horrible and tender . . . In short, it is frightful ! All that the human heart can contain of rage and tenderness is in the overture.' The composer gives an amusing account of the convulsive impression produced on him and others by a performance. Forgetting that it was his own work, he exclaimed : ' How monstrous, colossal, and horrible it is !' Be it understood, these were words of admiration. Lobe interprets the introductory slow movement as follows. (I condense his remarks.) An accused, with his eyes bound, is led before the *Francs-Juges* (judges of the Vehmic Tribunal, *Vehmrichter*). He stands there in anguish, hardly daring to breathe (bars 1-6). On the removal of the bandage from his eyes, dismay seizes him at the horrible sight (7-12). He trembles (violins 8-12), considers himself lost (13-19). His self-commiseration in his unmerited position. The terrible accusations of the judges in a mighty chorus. Between them the appeals for mercy by the prisoner, always interrupted by the thundering ' no ' of the chorus, until finally he breaks down, timidly resigned, exhausted, and terrified by his fruitless attempts.

We need not dwell at great length on the *Ouverture du Corsaire*, inspired by Byron's verse-romance *The Corsair*. It is one of Berlioz's less successful works, and hardly

ever played. The master must have felt this himself;
for although the work was written in 1831, it was not
heard until, after being retouched, it was performed in
April, 1855.   In connection with this overture we must
remember what Berlioz relates of how during the hot
weather at Rome he enjoyed ensconcing himself in one
of the confessionals of St. Peter's with a volume of Byron
in his pocket.   ' I devoured at leisure this ardent poetry;
I followed through the waves the daring course of the
Corsair; I profoundly admired this character, at the
same time inexorable and tender, pitiless and generous,
a strange compound of two opposed sentiments, hatred
of the species and love of a woman.'

The next overture, the *Ouverture du Roi Lear* (composed
in 1831, performed and published in 1840), Op. 4, is
again a work that arrests our attention, a poetic
conception that cannot fail to stir the imagination of the
hearer mightily.   Hanslick remarks that it ' captivates
by a trait of grandeur and pathos which now and then
reminds one of Beethoven.   Low, touching complaints
and shrill cries of despair speak here to the hearer with
striking truth.'   But he adds also: ' Nevertheless the
whole has rather a strange and disturbing effect than an
æsthetically gratifying and edifying one.   As in most of
his works, especially the earlier ones, there lies in *Lear*
the forced, the hollow, and even the trivial close beside the
most powerful impulses.   A passionately stirred inner life
leads here to violently moving exclamations, but to no
connected speech.'   Interpretations by intelligent, sober-
minded, and competent men, although we may not look
upon them as authoritative, are always interesting.
The excellent composer Felix Dräseke sees in the introductory slow movement, which he regards as the best

part, the opening scene between Lear and his daughters, and sees it represented with such distinctness that it would be difficult to give to the music any other inter-pretation. He hears in the double-bass motive the voice of the king, in the higher repetitions of the motive the flattering hypocritical voices of Goneril and Regan, in the later peculiar melody of a tender maidenly character, the voice of Cordelia; and in the following outbreak of the orchestra the anger of Lear. In Berlioz's writings no hint is to be found as to the meaning of the overture, but in one of his letters (Nice, May 6, 1831) there is a passage which tells us of its origin. On his way from Rome, shortly before, he had been detained by a sore throat at Florence : 'On the banks of the Arno, in a delightful wood a mile from the town, I passed whole days in reading Shakespeare. It was there I read for the first time *King Lear*, and this work of genius made me utter exclamations of admira-tion ; I thought I should burst with enthusiasm, I rolled about in the grass, rolled about convulsively to satisfy my transports . . . I have almost finished the overture of *King Lear;* only the instrumentation remains to be completed.'

The *Ouverture de Rob-Roy*, composed in 1831, described by Berlioz as long and diffuse, once performed, badly received by the audience, and burnt by him on the same day, need not detain us ;* and the same may be said of the last of the master's overtures, that to his comic opera *Béatrice et Bénédict* (the libretto after Shakespeare's *Much Ado about Nothing*), which is one of the less important. But we must tarry for a while over the

* The composer's burning of the overture was not a thorough per-formance, for the work has in recent years been both published and played. Elsewhere he calls the music of *Rob-Roy* bad.

R

two overtures to the semi-serious opera *Benvenuto Cellini*, the second of which, entitled *Le Carnaval Romain*, was first performed in 1844, six years after the first performance of the opera. When the latter was brought to a hearing in London, the *Carnaval* was played before the second act. Both overtures rank with the best of the master's works.

There are excellent judges who value more highly the original *Cellini* overture than the later, but for all that it is rarely performed, whereas the *Carnaval* enjoys universal favour. As comparisons of dissimilar things are idle and even mischievous, I shall not imitate those who indulge in them. Speaking, however, absolutely, all will agree that *Le Carnaval Romain* is a wonderful composition, full of the most brilliant light and colours, full of the maddest gaiety and bustle. The principal movement, *Allegro vivace*, is based on the lively *Saltarello* danced in the Piazza Colonna in the second act of *Benvenuto Cellini*. A formal feature of these two and of two of the preceding overtures may deserve mention,—namely, two introductory movements, one quick and one slow. The former, which anticipates the first subject of the principal *Allegro*, is soon interrupted by the latter, a motive of which may reappear in the course of the main movement (*Corsaire*, and *Benvenuto Cellini*). Let us not overlook the finer workmanship, the more masterly form, the choicer content, and the unsurpassable instrumentation of the *Benvenuto Cellini* overture and the *Carnaval Romain*.

Thus far we have not discovered anything epoch-making in Berlioz as a composer of programme music. The state of matters is different in the works to which we have now to give our attention. Of these, the earliest no doubt produced the greatest sensation, and to it, rightly or wrongly, the composer is indebted for the popular beliefs about him. The work alluded to is the *Episode de la Vie d'un artiste, Symphonie fantastique* in five parts. The first conception, composition, and final revision covered a period of more than two years. It was conceived in June, 1829, composed in March-May, 1830, performed on December 5, 1830, retouched and partly re-written, especially the *Scène aux Champs*, during the next two years, performed again on December 9, 1832, published in a pianoforte arrangement by Liszt in 1834, and in score in 1846, and played under the composer's conductorship at Brussels and several German towns in 1842-1843. The reader will appreciate the importance of these dates : they are of real historical, not merely of biographical interest. To understand the nature and history of the work two love affairs have to be at least briefly alluded to. In September, 1827, a London company opened in Paris a season of English drama, with such success as to enable them to prolong it till the end of July, 1828. Among the members was the Irish actress Miss Harriet Smithson, who in the following years repeatedly returned to the French capital. The impression she made on the public by her impersonations of Ophelia, Juliet, Cordelia, &c., may without exaggeration be described as phenomenal. Her impression upon the poets, novelists, painters, and sculptors, more especially those of the romantic school, was even stronger and deeper than upon the general public. Berlioz, too, soon felt the power of her fascination—in short, he came, saw, and was conquered. No man was ever more in love with a woman than was Berlioz with Miss Smithson. He wrote letters to her and called at her house, but in vain. Not the least encouragement would she vouchsafe him. And yet he was fluctuating between hope and despair. Then, before leaving in spring, 1829, she left him this crushing message : ' There is nothing more impossible.' In a letter of August 21, 1829, he speaks of ' the new pangs of my despised love' (English), and of his heart being the focus of a horrible conflagration. And on February 6, 1830, he writes : '*Oh, malheureuse!* if she could but for a few moments conceive all the poetry, all the infinitude, of such a love, she would fly into my arms, even were she to die in my embrace. I was on the point of commencing my great symphony (*Episode de la Vie d'un artiste*), where the development of my infernal passion is to be depicted ; I have it completely in my head, but I cannot write anything . . . *attendons*.' A consolation, however, was at hand, for now intervened what he calls ' a violent distraction,' his love—this time a requited love—for Mlle. Camille Moke, whom the world learned to know as a pianist virtuosa under her marriage name. This Sylph, this Ariel, now became Berlioz's muse and the goddess of his boundless adoration. Towards the end of 1830, on his gaining the *prix de Rome*, the two lovers became engaged. But soon after his arrival in Rome Mme. Moke informed him of her daughter's marriage with Camille Pleyel, the musician and pianoforte maker. The rage and madness that followed may be easily imagined. The stirred-up volcano threatened murder and suicide. Time, however, brought balm with it also on this occasion. When on his return to Paris, in the latter part of 1832, Berlioz again saw Miss Smithson, the old passion got hold of him once more ; and after many struggles, caused by the opposition of the parents on both sides, and the vacillation of Harriet, they were married on October 3, 1833.

The programme of the *Symphonie fantastique,* an explicit one, and the only explicit one, underwent several changes, none of them, however, vital. There were at least three different versions. From the first of these versions we see that what is now the second was originally the third division, that is, the *Scène aux Champs* preceded the *Bal.* We find the first version in a letter of April 16, 1830, addressed to Humbert Ferrand: 'Here is how I have woven my romance, or rather my history, in which it will not be difficult for you to recognize the hero.

'An artist gifted with a lively imagination, finding himself in that psychical state which Chateaubriand has so admirably described in *René*, sees for the first time a woman who realizes the ideal beauty and loveliness his heart had long desired, and falls desperately in love with her. Strangely enough the image of her he loves never presents itself without the accompaniment of a musical thought in which he finds a character of grace and nobleness similar to that which he attributes to the loved object. This double *idée fixe* pursues him incessantly: this is the reason of the constant appearance, in all the divisions of the symphony, of the principal melody of the first *Allegro.*

'After a thousand agitations, he conceives some hope; he believes himself loved. Being one day alone in the country, he hears from afar two shepherds dialoguing a *ranz de vaches:* this pastoral plunges him into a delicious reverie. The melody reappears for a moment across the motives of the *Adagio.*

'He is present at a ball, the tumult of the fête cannot divert him; his *idée fixe* finds him out, and the cherished melody makes his heart beat during a brilliant waltz.

'In a fit of despair, he poisons himself with opium; but instead of killing him, the narcotic produces in him a horrible vision. Whilst it lasts he believes himself to have killed her whom he loves, to be condemned to death, and to be present at his own execution. March to the Execution; an immense procession of executioners, soldiers, and people. At the end the *melody* reappears again, like a last thought of love, interrupted by the fatal stroke.

'Next he sees himself surrounded by a hateful crowd of sorcerers and devils, gathered to celebrate the Witches' Sabbath. They call to each other in the distance. At last arrives the *melody*, which hitherto had appeared only in its graceful form, but which now has become a vulgar, ignoble tavern air; it is the beloved object who comes to the Witches' Sabbath to be present at the funeral of her victim. She is no better than a courtesan worthy to figure in such orgies. Then commences the ceremony. The bells ring, the infernal crew prostrate themselves, a choir sings the prose of the dead, the plain-chant *Dies irae;* two other choirs repeat it, parodying it in a burlesque manner. After that the round of the Witches' Sabbath whirls and whirls, and when it has reached the extreme degree of violence, combines with the *Dies irae*, and the vision ends.'

The two most noteworthy subsequent changes were made at the second performance (after the rekindling of his love for Miss Smithson), when the words 'she is no better than a courtesan worthy to figure in such orgies' disappeared, and in the programme prefixed to the printed score, where the lover is under the influence of the narcotic from the beginning. I had better give the opening paragraph of the last version in full.

'A young musician of a morbid sensibility and an ardent imagination poisons himself with opium. The dose of the narcotic, too weak to kill him, plunges him into a heavy sleep accompanied by strange visions, during which his sensations, sentiments, and recollections are translated in his sick mind into musical thoughts and pictures. The beloved woman, she herself, has become for him a melody, and, as it were, an *idée fixe*, which he finds and hears everywhere.'

With regard to the explicit programme, Berlioz says in the preface that if the *Symphonie fantastique* is performed by itself, without its sequel *Lélio*, it may, should it be thought desirable, be omitted, and only the titles of the five pieces indicated. Here are these titles, and after them, in square brackets, the short indications of character given in his letter to Ferrand :—

(1.) *Rêveries, Passions* [the wave of the passions (*le vague des passions*, a phrase borrowed from Chateaubriand) ; reveries without an object, delirious passion with fits of tenderness, jealousy, fury, fear, &c.].

(2.) *Un bal* [brilliant and animated (*entraînante*) music].

(3.) *Scène aux Champs* [thoughts of love and hope disturbed by dark presentiments].

(4.) *Marche au Supplice* [savage, pompous music].

(5.) *Songe d'une Nuit du Sabbat* (Dream of a Witches' Sabbath).

It must be obvious to every attentive reader of this programme that Berlioz did not in the first four divisions

attempt to express anything that is beyond the capacity
of music, or had been considered beyond the capacity of
the art by his predecessors. And even the almost
universal condemnation of the last division concerns
much less the question as to the limits of musical expressiveness than the question as to the limits of admissible
matter and treatment. I think the actual question
might, not unfairly, be formulated thus : Is the ugly
presented in an ugly form a suitable subject for music ?
The answer to this is generally in the negative, and
ingenuity and grotesque picturesqueness are not considered sufficiently mitigating circumstances. Whilst
.the last division is consequently the least satisfactory,
the third, the *Scène aux Champs,* is the most satisfactory
of them all, being indeed in every respect so beautiful
that it found favour in the eyes of Berlioz's severest
and most perverse critic, Wagner, who declared it to be
a perfect thing. The *Ball,* too, is full of grace and
charm, although not quite so perfect. In the March
the auditor cannot fail to be impressed by the powerful
characterization of the scene, attained chiefly by
rhythmic and colouristic means. The *Allegro* of the
first division is as notable for its great beauties as for
its crudities and awkwardnesses in texture and structure.
But judge the *Symphonie fantastique* ever so severely, and
say the very worst of it, you cannot evade the admission
that it is a work of great power and skill. As an
example of the worst that can be said, take Wagner's
adverse criticism. ' An immense inner wealth, a
heroically-vigorous imagination, forces out, as .from a
crater, a pool of passions; what we see are colossally-
formed smoke clouds, parted only by lightning and
streaks of fire, and modelled into fugitive shapes.

Everything is prodigious, daring, but infinitely painful.'
This and all Wagner's criticisms of Berlioz—which no
doubt contain grains of truth—are for the most part
enormous exaggerations, nay, more than that, they are
fantastic ravings which leave the actual thousands of
miles behind.   The *Symphonie fantastique* is not Berlioz's
best work, but it is one of the most representative,
exhibiting in the highest degree both his good and bad
qualities.   Gounod comes near the truth in saying that
this work was a real event in the musical world, the
importance of which might be gauged by the fanatical
admiration and the violent opposition it aroused.

   Before leaving the subject I must refer once more to,
and point out the importance of the *idée fixe*, the melody
representative of a person, which appears in all the
divisions, but in each in a different rhythmical form.

Berlioz was not the inventor of the *Leitmotiv* (leading,
guiding motive), but was the first who made use of it in
so prominent a manner and so developed a form.   From
Weber, for instance, we can gather earlier examples.   The
full developer of the device, however, was Wagner.   For
the transformation of such motives the happy designation
of dramatico-psychological variation has been found.
In conclusion I must point out Schumann's technical
and æsthetical analysis of the *Symphonie fantastique*
(*Neue Zeitschrift für Musik*, 1835), in which he turns
away with disgust from the last division, but acknowledges the many beauties of the others, especially of the
third, the proper proportions of the forms if measured

on a large scale, and the spiritual connection of the contents.

Lélio, ou le Retour à la Vie, lyrical melodrama for orchestra (including *piano à quatre mains*), and invisible chorus and solo voices, words and music by Berlioz, here calls for a few remarks only because the author describes it as the 'end and completion' ('superfluous addition' would have been a more correct description) of the *Symphonie fantastique,* which should precede *Lélio* when it is performed. Lélio, the hero of that symphony, who tried to poison himself, begins the miscellaneous proceedings by exclaiming: 'God! am I still alive . . !' This being unfortunately the case, there follows the rest of the spoken monologue which serves to string together six pieces of music composed at various times and not with a view to forming a whole, and does so in the most irresponsible, artificial, and inartistic manner imaginable. How a man of Berlioz's intellectual calibre and high artistic aims could concoct such an *olla podrida,* and write and, many years after, print such rigmarole made up of theatrical sentimental posturings and declamations, intermixed with diatribes against critics, editors, and the public (the enemies of genius), will always remain an unsolved problem. No wonder that the work has very rarely been performed, and that when it was revived in Paris in 1881, the monologue was not reproduced in its original form. Here are the six musical pieces: (1.) *Le Pêcheur* (the Fisher), ballade by Goethe; (2.) *Chœur des Ombres;* (3.) *Chanson de Brigands;* (4.) *Chant de Bonheur;* (5.) *La Harpe Eolienne—Souvenirs;* and (6.) *Fantaisie sur la Tempête de Shakespeare.*

We now come to the most perfect of Berlioz's larger instrumental works,—*Harold en Italie,* symphony in four parts, for orchestra and viola solo, composed in 1834, and performed on November 23 of the same year. There is no other programme than that suggested by the general title and the four sub-titles prefixed to the four divisions: (1.) *Harold in the mountains— Scenes of melancholy, happiness, and joy;* (2.) *March of Pilgrims singing the evening prayer;* (3.) *Serenade of a mountaineer of the Abbruzzi to his mistress;* and (4.) *Orgy of Brigands.* It was Paganini who gave the impulse to the composition of this work. Having an excellent viola, he wished to display its qualities in public, and therefore asked Berlioz to compose a piece in which that could be effectively done. The composer thought first of a piece descriptive of the last moments of Queen Mary Stuart, but afterwards decided in favour of Harold. 'My symphony with viola solo, entitled *Harold,*' he wrote on March 31, 1834, ' was finished two weeks ago. Paganini, I believe, will find that the viola has not been treated sufficiently in the concerto style. It is a symphony on a new plan and not a composition written with a view to letting an individual talent like his shine. Nevertheless I am obliged to him for having made me undertake the work.' Berlioz was right in his suspicion ; Paganini never played the part. Of course *Harold en Italie* was suggested by *Childe Harold's Pilgrimage.* But as the Harold of Byron's poem is Byron, so the Harold of Berlioz's symphony is Berlioz. Besides this difference we have to note that the scenes depicted in Berlioz's symphony are not to be found in the fourth canto of Byron's romaunt. 'The title clearly shows,' writes Liszt, 'that the composer wished to render the impressions which the magnificent nature of Italy, the impetuous and sensuously glowing and loving character of its inhabitants, could not but make on a soul languishing in sorrows, such as that of Harold in the monody of the symphony. We see here the wanderer in the lap of an enchanting environment full of that never to be calmed restlessness, of that disappointment of the mind, of that unhappy mood whose type in literature is still Byron, although [Chateaubriand's] René has disputed the exclusive right for other reasons than priority . . . . Only the sublime profundity of the sorrows, the elegiac tones which Childe Harold drew from René, have passed entirely into the musical Harold. Some of the characteristics of the British Harold, the conception of the tone-poet could not embrace.' The personality of Harold is represented by the viola solo part, called by Liszt the monody; and the leading characteristic of the hero by a theme which first appears in the *Introduction* :—

Afterwards it is heard in all the other movements, but in these not as a principal theme. To understand the rôle played by the viola, we have to note that Berlioz's Harold is for the most part an observer who comments on, and is only now and then an actor who joins and loses himself in the scenes in the midst of which he finds himself.

Whilst preserving the classical number of four divisions, Berlioz does not reproduce the classical internal

economy. The first division, consisting of an *Adagio*
and *Allegro*, is sufficiently characterized by the composer's superscription: ' *Harold in the Mountains—
Scenes of melancholy, happiness and joy.*' 'In the
Mountains' applies to all the divisions, but especially
to this *Allegro* in which Harold is face to face with
nature and under her influence. Liszt describes it
thus: ' On the background of magnificent natural
surroundings, a complex of suppressed discouragement
and exultant jubilation of the soul . . . Towards
the end, however, there appears the Harold motive in a
slow *tremolo*. The gloomy longing of the hero could
not be vanquished by the splendour of the external
world and its impressions.' As regards content and
form the first division is the most important and elevated
of the four. In motival development Berlioz follows
in the footsteps of his symphonic predecessors ; the
disposition of the parts (exposition of subjects,
working-out, recapitulation, &c.) shows his discipleship
much less distinctly.

The second division—*March of Pilgrims singing the
evening prayer*—was from the first the most popular
part of the work. We hear the procession approaching,
passing by, and losing itself in the distance, in a long
crescendo and *diminuendo*. At the eighth bar the March
melody is always interrupted by the mumbled chant of
the pilgrims. In the middle of the piece a *canto religioso*
intervenes. Harold's meditations mingle here and
there with the other sounds. The third division, which
brings in the *Serenade of a Mountaineer of the Abruzzi
to his mistress*, begins with a concert, a *ritornello* of the
pifferari (*Allegro assai*), then comes the lover's solo
(played on the Corno inglese.—*Allegretto*). after that

once more the *ritornello* of the *pifferari*, and lastly the sympathetic reflections of Harold, whose melancholy voice had already accompanied the music of the serenading mountaineer. At the end of the third division Berlioz is tired and sick of all this respectability. Like Mephistopheles after some edifying conversation with the student, he feels he must change the dry tone, and play the devil again. Berlioz says himself of the last division, the *Orgy of Brigands*, that it is somewhat violent. Wild bars of *Allegro frenetico* are at first again and again interrupted by reminiscences of the first wailing thought of the *Introduction*, the *March of Pilgrims*, the *Mountaineer's Serenade*, the principal subject of the first *Allegro*, and the Harold melody, but at last the *Allegro frenetico* takes its mad, headlong course, rushing wildly, furiously onward till near the conclusion, when during a short pause a faint reminiscence of the *March of the Pilgrims* and some dying wails of Harold are heard. This *Allegro frenetico*, although not so anti-æsthetical as the *Witches' Sabbath*, is bad enough to be only apologetically defended by Berlioz's friends. Liszt, for instance, says : ' It is not surprising that the *Orgy* is not received as the grandeur of the musical composition deserves it to be. It makes us participators in a monstrous banquet, reeking with brandy and crime, which so far exceeds the representations allowed by our manners and customs, that most of the hearers cannot form any idea of the howling and neighing in the scenes presented to them.'

In *Roméo et Juliette* Berlioz produced a work which shows his genius and craftsmanship at their highest pitch, but which as a whole is a monstrous jumble of

incongruities, a compound of all styles and *genres*, where
symphony and cantata, the narrative, the lyrical, the
dramatic, and the programmatic are intermixed in
defiance of taste and reason.   The five pieces that form
he predominating symphonic portion are of unequal
value—three of them belong to the composer's
very best achievements and most commendable
specimens of programme music, and two to his
least happy achievements and most doubtful specimens
of programme music.   The full title runs thus: *Roméo
et Juliette*, dramatic symphony with choruses, vocal solos,
and a prologue in choral recitative, composed after
Shakespeare's tragedy. Berlioz himself wrote the
libretto, but got Emile Deschamps to put his prose into
verse.   The subject had been long in his mind, since
1829, and when in 1838, thanks to the present of 20,000
francs he received from (or through) Paganini, the requisite
leisure for the composition of a grand work could be
secured, he took it up and worked at it for seven months.
He tells us in his *Mémoires* of the ardent life he lived
during that time, and of the vigour with which he was
swimming on this grand sea of poesy, caressed by the
playful breeze of the imagination, under the warm rays
of the sun of love lighted by Shakespeare, and believing
in his power to arrive at the marvellous island where
the temple of pure Art rises.   The first performance of
Roméo et Juliette took place on November 24, 1839; its
publication, after being retouched, in 1848.

The two unsuccessful symphonic pieces are the
Introduction, superscribed 'the Combats, Tumult, and
Intervention of the Prince,' and 'Romeo in the Tomb of
the Capulets—Invocation; Awaking of Juliet; Delirious
Joy, Despair, Last Anguish, and Death of the two

Lovers.' Here the musician failed in wisely choosing
and leaving the contents of his subject, and treating
what he had chosen in accordance with the nature of the
art. In the *Introduction*, the *Allegro fugato*, which
depicts the combats and tumult, may perhaps pass, but
decidedly objectionable are the preachings of the Prince in
the recitative style through the mouths of the trombones,
ophicleide, and other brass instruments. The most
objectionable parts of the other unsatisfactory piece are
the convulsions of the poisoned lovers' agony. In passing,
we may note that Berlioz makes use of Garrick's ending.
Weingartner says with regard to the last-mentioned
piece : 'Berlioz has here attempted to render the details
of the dramatic action by melodic fragments, accents,
chord-progressions, and expressive figuration with such
a distinctness as to incline one to believe in one's
capacity to follow in every bar the course of the action.
Nevertheless this piece is mostly left out at performances
of the work, because the impression, be the execution
ever so good, is a quite confusing and (I say it in spite
of my reverence for Berlioz) ridiculous one. The cause
lies in that music has here been charged with a task
which it cannot fulfil. If the title did not give an
indication of the course of action of the drama, we should
not know at all what we are hearing and should have the
effect of a senseless tone-complex. But the feeling of
senselessness is not removed when we know what we
have to imagine. We cannot help, however, being
astonished at the distinctness and clearness of even the
naked word of the title as compared to the music, which
at other times is able to give us much more powerful
impressions than even an excellent word-poem.
Something similar we experience at the commencement

of *Roméo et Juliette*, in the grand orchestral recitative,
which is meant to depict the intervention of the Prince.'

To the other three orchestral pieces nothing but praise
can be given—the first dreamy and then exceedingly
brilliant 'Romeo alone, Sadness, and Concert and Ball—
Grand Festival at the house of Capulet'; the enchanting
'Love Scene—a Serene Night, the silent and deserted
Garden of Capulet'; and the indescribable and inimitable
Scherzo, 'Queen Mab, or the Dream Fairy.'   Saint-Saëns
writes: 'The famous *Scherzo* is worth even more than
its reputation.   It is a miracle of lightness and
gracefulness.   Beside such delicacies and such
transparencies, the *finesses* of Mendelssohn in the
Midsummer Night's Dream seem heavy.   That is
because the unseizable and impalpable are not only in
the sonority but also in the style.   In this respect I
know only the chorus of the genii in *Oberon* that could
bear comparison.'   Berlioz preferred the Love Scene to
all his other compositions and thought that this was also
the opinion of most artists.   Wagner, however, although
he too regarded the *Scène d'amour*, at least in its main
motives as wonderfully touching, raises an objection to
it.   He says that in listening to it he lost the musical
thread and notwithstanding all his efforts could not
recover it.   He attributes this to Berlioz's following the
disposition of the dramatist, whereas the musician ought
to have gone about it in his own way, ought to have
ignored the accidents and details of common life, and
sublimated everything that underlies them in accordance
with their concrete emotional contents.   Is Berlioz really
guilty of the fault laid to his charge by Wagner?   Or is
this a case of delusion on the part of the latter, a delusion
born of a prejudice or an unreceptive mood?   At any

s

rate, other weighty judges who have expressed their
opinions on this composition do not seem to have been
struck by the supposed fault and disturbed in their
enjoyment of the fascinating loveliness of Berlioz's
tone-poem.

There remain now only two other pieces to be
noticed—namely the 'Ballet of Sylphs' and the
'Dance of Will-o'-the-Wisps' from the *Damnation de
Faust* (composed in 1846, first performed on December
6, 1846). Both of these, like the 'Queen Mab' *Scherzo*,
are fantastic conceptions of bewitching beauty, and like
it marvels of orchestration. I said there remain only
two other pieces to be noticed, but there is a third,
different in character and almost unknown, which must
not be passed over in silence—namely, Op. 15, the *Grande
Symphonie funèbre et triomphale* for military band (with
string orchestra and chorus *ad lib.*) in memory of those
fallen in the July Revolution. Of this Wagner declared
that he felt inclined to prefer it to all other compositions
of Berlioz's, that it is noble and grand from the first to
the last note, a high patriotic enthusiasm, which rises
from lamentation to the highest summit of apotheosis,
guarding it against morbid exaltation. Tiersot thinks
that this work occupies in music the same place
which is occupied in painting by Eugène Delacroix's
La Barricade, with its wild and energetic combatants.

The conclusions, then, to which the examination of
Berlioz's character, life, and works lead us are these.
Apart from the *Symphonie fantastique*, the master's
instrumental compositions have no explicit programmes,
and the subjects he chooses are as a rule unexceptionable,
the exceptions being the last movement of the *Symphonie
fantastique* and of *Harold*, and the *Introduction* to and

the Tomb scene of *Roméo et Juliette*.   In fine, the shortcomings of his works do not arise from any wrongness
in the *genre* of instrumental music he cultivated, but
from the defects of his musical endowment and training,
and more especially from the defects of his character
and aims, which manifest themselves in a too exclusive
devotion to the intense and picturesque, in a too great
desire to experience himself and to produce in his
audiences violent sensations.   But whatever may be the
just amount of adverse criticism to which his life-work
is open, there can be no doubt that Berlioz was a man
of genius, and not only an unsurpassed and unapproached
master of instrumentation and inventor of new orchestral
effects, but also a creator in a wider sense, one who has
left us works, some of them perfect works of their kind,
which on account of their originality and beauty deserve
to be treasured by this and future generations.   If the
vox populi were the *vox dei*, we should be obliged to
admit that Berlioz had been weighed and found wanting;
for he was neglected in his own time and nowhere more
than in his own country ; and in spite of the efforts of
the French after 1870 to make a national hero of him,
and the consequent temporarily increased interest taken
in him by other nations, the master still remains a
neglected composer.   Schumann remarks in a letter of
the year 1839 that Berlioz had too little sense of beauty.
But this opinion did not prevent him from advising
Breitkopf & Härtel to publish some of the French master's
works.   And why ?   Because he felt and declared that
there was much in Berlioz's compositions that was true
and even profound.   Moreover, it has to be further
noted that the sense of beauty was not totally lacking,
that in some respects it was even highly developed, and

although as a rule it was often under an eclipse, now and then it shone forth spotless with dazzling brilliance. The 'Romeo alone, and Ball,' the 'Queen Mab' *Scherzo*, and the 'Love Scene' from *Roméo et Juliette*, the 'Ballet of the Sylphs,' and the 'Dance of the Will-o'-the-Wisps' from *Damnation de Faust*, the 'March of Pilgrims' from *Harold en Italie*, the 'Scène aux Champs' from the *Symphonie fantastique*, and the overtures *Le Carnaval Romain* and *Benvenuto Cellini* are exquisite gems that ought to be considered ornaments of any orchestral programme. They are compositions for which no apology of any kind need be made. Then there is the complete *Harold en Italie*, which on the whole is a decidedly noble work, although we may wish some things in it different, and should not dream of putting it on a level with a Beethoven symphony. The *Symphonie fantastique* suffers from more and greater imperfections, but they are not such as to condemn it to eternal silence and the limbo of dusty library shelves. And there are one or two more overtures well worthy of occasional notice, first of all *King Lear*. No one will deny that in the case of Berlioz a selection has to be made; but that a selection has a strong claim on the attention, the interest, the admiration of musicians and the musical public is equally undeniable. Let us hope that Berlioz will before long come to his own.

CHAPTER II.

LISZT.

Important as Berlioz is in the development of programme music, LISZT is so far more. Indeed, he is the most important of all, and is this quite apart from the value of his productions as works of art. His importance lies chiefly and mainly in the impulses he gave—in the vistas he opened, the new problems he proposed, the solutions of old problems he attempted, in short, in the new ideas, methods, procedures, and means he suggested. Unlike Berlioz, Liszt had a system, and set it forth in unequivocal language. While in the quantity of his programme music and in the scope and variety of his programmes Liszt surpasses Berlioz, the latter must, I think, be allowed the possession of a larger amount of originality and creativeness. Of Berlioz I have already said that he was not one of the spontaneous composers, one of those whose souls are steeped in harmonious beauty, and whose natural language is music, in which their thoughts easily find adequate expression and perfect form. But although alike in being outside the blessed circle of the elect, they were nevertheless very different in many respects—in endowment, in training, in circumstances, in character, &c., &c. From the age of ten Liszt was trained by excellent masters and lived in artistic environment, first in Vienna and afterwards in Paris; Berlioz had no music teaching worth speaking of and lived in inartistic environment up to the age of eighteen, and not till some time after that had he the benefit of the advice of masters. Liszt became the greatest of the great pianoforte virtuosi, and had an opera of his performed in Paris at the age of fifteen; Berlioz was without skill on any instrument, except the guitar, and had his first composition, a Mass, performed at the age of twenty-one. Liszt sought the acquaintance of and sympathized with all kinds and styles of music of whatever period or country; Berlioz showed himself one of the most incurious and narrow-minded of musicians. And thus one could for a long while go on contrasting the two. It will be necessary to examine a little more closely Liszt's studies and career as a musician, more especially as a composer, for this is the way to discover his natural leanings and the encouragements and discouragements these met with.

Franz Liszt, the son of a Hungarian father and a German mother, was born at Raiding in Hungary on October 22, 1811. At the early age of nine he made his *debût* as a pianist. After some more public and private appearances several magnates combined in 1821 to provide him with an allowance of 600 florins for six years, so that his father might be in a position to take the boy abroad and procure for him a proper artistic training. They first went to Vienna. There Franz was placed under Czerny and Salieri, respectively for pianoforte playing and harmony and composition. The results of these studies were put to the proof at two concerts—on December 1, 1822, and April 13, 1823—at which he played, to the satisfaction and astonishment of all, Hummel's concertos in A minor and B minor and improvisations. Beethoven's kiss, given on the latter of the two occasions, testifies to the wonderful manner in which the young musician discharged his difficult tasks. In 1823 the Liszt family proceeded to Paris, Franz playing in several towns on the way. As, owing to his foreign birth, the boy could not get admission to the Conservatoire, he was left to his own resources as regards pianoforte playing. For counterpoint he had Reicha as a teacher, for composition Paër. Miss Ramann, Liszt's worshipping biographer, says that the boy practised to his master's satisfaction all the contrapuntal forms, double as well as single counterpoint, fugue as well as canon, and that half a year sufficed to reveal to him all the secrets of counterpoint. Perhaps the reader may consider this enthusiastic statement more astonishing than trustworthy. It took Bach, Handel, Haydn, Mozart, Beethoven, Mendelssohn, and others longer to reach that goal of perfection. Of the years 1824-1827, there are to be recorded his first public appearance in Paris, on March 8, 1824, his concert-tours in the French provinces and in England, the publication of his *Impromptu* in 1824, *Allegro di Bravura* in 1825 and *Etudes en douze Exercises* in 1827, and three performances at the Paris Opéra of his one-act *Don Sanche ou le Château d'amour*, described as an *opéra féerie*, in 1825. After the death of his father (in August, 1827), and on the termination of his allowance, Liszt settled down in the French capital as a teacher of pianoforte playing. Although he was now and then heard at Paris concerts—for instance in 1828 at an extra-concert in the Conservatoire in Beethoven's E flat major Concerto, a performance of which was then a deed and an event,*—the virtuoso in him remained for some time in abeyance. At any rate,

---

* I follow W. von Lenz's recollections of that time.

there was no thought of concert-touring for many years. Composition, too, seems to have been neglected. Between 1827 and 1835, Liszt published only the *Fantasie sur la Tirolienne de l'opéra ' La Fiancée'* (1829), transcriptions of parts of Berlioz's *Symphonie fantastique* (1833), and the *Grande Fantasie sur la ' Clochette' de Paganini*. The chronological list of the master's compositions contains also a very few unpublished works; indeed, only one original composition, or rather the sketch of one (*Symphonie révolutionnaire*, 1830), one semi-original (*Fantaisie symphonique* for pianoforte and orchestra on themes by Berlioz, 1834), and some transcriptions. Indeed, during at least three years of his residence in Paris (1827-1830), he was occupied with other things rather than with music. About Liszt's doing, thinking, and feeling at this period of his life we obtain invaluable revelations in his *Lettre d'un Bachelier ès Musique : à un poète voyageur* (the travelling poet was George Sand), dated Paris, January, 1837, and published in the Paris *Gazette Musicale*, on February 12, 1837.

' Two phases of my life have already been accomplished in Paris. First when my father's foresight snatched me from the Hungarian Steppes, where I grew up free and untamed among wild herds [not 'hordes,' as the traducing German translation has it], and threw me, poor child, into the midst of a brilliant society which applauded the *tours de force* of him whom they honoured with the glorious and withering stigma of "little prodigy." Then a premature melancholy began to weigh upon me, and I bore with an instinctive repugnance the ill-disguised degradation of the artistic servitude. Later, when, on returning alone to Paris after my father's death, I began to have a presentiment of what art might become and what artists ought to be, I was overwhelmed by the impossibilities rising up on all sides in the path which my thought had marked out. Moreover, finding nowhere a word of sympathy, neither among the men of the world, nor even among the artists, who dozed in comfortable indifference, I, altogether unconscious of myself, of what I ought to aim at, and of the capacities that were allotted to me, allowed myself to be invaded by a bitter disgust with art, reduced as I saw it to a more or less lucrative handicraft, to an amusement for the use of good society, and I should have preferred being anything else rather than a musician in the pay of the *grands seigneurs,* patronized and salaried by them like a juggler or like the clever dog Munito. Peace to his memory! . . .

'About this time I passed through a two-years' illness, at the end of which my imperious need of faith and devotion, finding no other issue, became absorbed in the austere exercises of catholicism. I bowed my burning forehead over the humid flags of St. Vincent-de-Paul, made my heart bleed, and prostrated my thought. A woman's image, chaste and pure as the alabaster of holy vessels, was the host which I offered with tears to the God of the Christians. Resignation of all that is earthly was the sole motive, the sole word of my life.

'But such an absolute isolation could not last for ever. Poverty, the old broker between man and evil, tore me from my contemplative solitude, and often brought me back before a public on whom my existence and that of my mother partly depended. Young and exuberant as I was then, I suffered painfully from the collision with the world without me, on which my calling as a

musician continually threw me, and which wounded so
intensely the mystic feeling of love and religion that
filled my heart.　Men of the world who have not
time to think of the sufferings of the man when they
come to hear the artist, and whose facile life is confined
between the two points of the compass called *convenance*
and *bienséance*, do not understand at all the contradictions and eccentricities unavoidably resulting from my
double life.　Tormented by a thousand confused instincts
and a need of unlimited expansion, too young to mistrust
myself, too *naïf* to concentrate myself within myself, I
gave myself up entirely to my impressions, admirations,
and repugnances.　I had the reputation of being an
actor because I did not know how to act in any way, and
because I let myself be seen as I really was, an
enthusiastic child, a sympathetic artist, an austere
devotee, in fact, everything one is at the age of eighteen,
when one loves God and man with an ardent passionate
soul not yet dulled by the cruel bruising of social
egoisms.'

The fervent piety spoken of in the above extracts was
not, however, a passing phase of the youth.　On the
contrary, it was a fundamental characteristic of the man.
As Berlioz may be instanced as the most irreligious
composer, Liszt may be instanced as the most religious.
More forcibly than by his receiving the ecclesiastical
minor orders, in 1865, this is borne in upon us by the
following passage from his testament, written at Weimar
on September 14, 1860.　'Yes, "Jesus at the Cross,"
the yearning desire for the Cross and the Elevation of
the Cross, that was always my true inner calling; I
have felt it in the depth of my heart since my seventeenth
year, when with tears in my eyes I humbly begged

permission to enter the Paris seminary. Then I hoped
I might be allowed to live the life of a saint and perhaps
even to die the death of a martyr. Unfortunately that
has not been my lot. But, in spite of the sins and errors
which I have committed, and for which I feel sincere
repentance and contrition, the divine light of the Cross
has never been wholly withheld from me. Sometimes
the splendour of this divine light has even flooded my
whole soul.'

It was only for a short time that religion absorbed Liszt
wholly. All through his subsequent life a remarkable
width of interest distinguished him — it comprised
philosophy and literature no less than art; painting,
sculpture, and architecture no less than music;
Germany, Italy, and England no less than France,
which was his first literary and philosophic nurse. 'He
is a man of an eccentric (*verschrobene*) but noble
character,' writes Heine, ' unselfish and without guile.
His intellectual tendencies are very remarkable. He has
great talent for speculation, and, even more than by the
concerns of his art, he is interested by the investigations
of the different schools that occupy themselves with the
solution of the great problem comprehending heaven
and earth. He was long enamoured of the beautiful
Saint-Simonian view of the world; subsequently the
spiritualistic, or rather vaporous thoughts of Ballanche
befogged him; now he raves about the republico-catholic
doctrines of Lamennais, who has planted a Jacobin cap
on the Cross . . . Heaven knows in what intellectual
stable he will find his next hobby. This indefatigable
thirst for light and godhead nevertheless remains
praiseworthy; it testifies to his sense of the holy, the
religious.' Heine further describes Liszt as a restless

head that is bewildered by all the troubles and doctrines of his time, who feels the need to concern himself with all the needs of humanity, and is fond of putting his nose in all the pots in which God cooks the future. George Sand, who in a letter to Liszt jocularly remarks that she would like ' to learn metaphysics as well as the celebrated M. Liszt, the pupil of Ballanche, Rodrigues [disciple of Saint-Simon], and Sénancour [author of the psychological romance *Obermann*],' depicts in a few lines the character of her friend better than anybody else has ever done, saying (in her *Lettres d'un Voyageur*) that he was ' full of humane heaven-scaling ideals, in his thirst for knowledge seizing every new idea.' As his open letter to Heine shows, Liszt was greatly irritated by some of the above-quoted remarks of the German poet, but they are nevertheless true in the main. We find the proof of this in George Sand's quip and description, and in a passage from another open letter of Liszt's, that addressed to Massart. In it he speaks of the life-period from fifteen to twenty-five, when the young man, stunned by the tumult of his own thoughts, does not live, but only aspires to live ; when all in him is curiosity, desire, restless aspiration, flux and reflux of contrary volitions; when he exhausts himself in the issueless labyrinth of his disordered passions ; when all that is simple, easy, and natural makes him smile with pity ; when he overshoots all his aims, is eager of all obstacles, disdains the good he could do, and the feelings that would make him happy; when he is mercilessly tormented by the sting of youth—in the time of ardent fever, of vainly spent strength, and of energetic and mad vitality. This is the picture not of any young man you please, but of the young man Liszt. And in noting the characteristics set forth in the foregoing pages, we may at once likewise note that the youth was the father of the man. Liszt never lost the religious and intellectual craving of his early days, and he never altogether reconciled the contradictions of his character. But as he grew older, he grew in self-restraint, charitableness, and nobility.

Having dwelled at some length on some of the qualities that are eminently characteristic of Liszt and strongly reflected in his works, we must now return to the examination of the incidents in his career and of his development as an artist. His mother used to say: *C'est le canon qui l'a guéri.* But other things contributed to his recovery from the two-years' illness. The sketch of the never-finished *Symphonie révolutionnaire* of 1830 is no doubt a significant fact. Of more importance, however, than the July Revolution, are Paganini's appearance in Paris in March, 1831, Chopin's arrival in the autumn of the same year, and the second performance of Berlioz's *Symphonie fantastique*, together with other compositions, on December 9, 1832. These three events roused Liszt from his lethargy and morbid brooding. The influence of Paganini showed itself in his attempt to transcribe the violinist's Caprices for the pianoforte (1832-1833); and Berlioz's influence, in his transcribing the symphonist's epoch-making orchestral work for the same instrument (1833). Chopin's influence was subtler and slower in taking effect, but for that none the less real. At any rate, the result of these combined influences was that Liszt created within a few years after the Revolution a new pianoforte style and made himself a man *sui generis.* Transcriptions were for many years his main output as a composer, but from 1834 he produced now and then original pianoforte compositions more or less of a programmatic kind.

Before 1830 a mutual affection between Liszt and a pupil, the Comtesse Caroline de Saint Criq, was nipped in the bud by the young lady's father. It was a youth's dream of love, to which he alludes in the words '*une image de femme chaste et pure comme l'albâtre des vases sacrés.*' Of another complexion and issue was his next great love. In 1834 began an acquaintance, which before long grew into a passion, between Liszt and the somewhat older Comtesse d'Agoult, who in literature became known as Daniel Stern. When, in 1835, he proposed to break the relation that existed between him and her, she left husband and children, and travelled with him, in Switzerland, France, and Italy, till November, 1839. A complete separation did not take place till 1844. The years 1836-1837 are notable for the contest with Thalberg. From 1839 up to the latter part of 1847 followed Liszt's triumphal concert-tours all over Europe. Then another influence was brought to bear upon him, a female influence that had a revolutionary effect on his career and development as an artist—ending his career as a virtuoso, and opening his career as a composer of symphonic and solo and choral vocal works. At Kiev, in February, 1847, he met the Princess Wittgenstein, saw her again at Odessa in the autumn, and in the winter passed several months at her country-seat Woronince, ' to execute commissions of compositions for her.' She believed in Liszt's creative genius, and fired his ambition ; and she not only fired it, but perseveringly fanned and stirred it when ablaze. In those months at Woronince the two came to an understanding, the outcome on her part being that she decided to get a divorce and marry Liszt. Not to expose herself to forcible detention and compulsion of any kind, she fled with her little daughter from Russia and settled in Weimar, where Liszt had become *Capellmeister.* Her efforts to free herself from the hateful matrimonial yoke failed again and again, but were not given up till 1861. And when in 1865 Prince Wittgenstein died, the Princess and Liszt did not take advantage of the circumstance, having probably drifted apart by living apart during the last five years. What she was to him may be best seen in the dedication he wrote on the autograph scores of his Symphonic Poems *Ce qu'on entend sur la Montagne* and *Hungaria,* which he presented to her on her birthday, February 8, 1855. ' To her who accomplished his faith by love, enlarged his hope through sorrows, edified his happiness by sacrifice. To her who remains the companion of my life, the firmament of my thought, the living prayer and the Heaven of my soul.'

One cannot but look upon it as a significant fact that after the early and lost compositions, the overture and sonata of 1825, the concerto of 1827, and the sketch of the *Symphonie révolutionnaire* of 1830, Liszt did not resume writing for the orchestra and in the larger forms until 1847-1848. His *Symphonic fantasia* on themes by Berlioz of 1834 and the Beethoven Festival Cantata of 1845 are not likely to be regarded as disproving the existence of the gap. Is it imaginable that an ambitious musician like Liszt, living in the midst of the leading literary, musical, and other artistic creators of a stirring time, would have remained so long silent if he had felt an inner call? His friends—as we learn from his open letter to Pictet (1837)—urged him to enter the wider field of dramatic and symphonic composition. But he declined to part with the pianoforte, which was to him what the ship is to the seaman, the steed to the Arab. The pianoforte was the confidant of all that moved his inmost being in the hot days of his youth; whose strings shook under his passions, and whose docile keys obeyed every humour. 'Can you,' he asks, 'wish that I should leave it in order to pursue more brilliant and noisy successes on the stage and in the orchestra? No! Even admitting that I were already ripe for such harmonies — which no doubt you admit too easily—even then it would remain my firm resolution not to give up the study and development of pianoforte playing until I shall have done all that is possible, or at least all that I can do for the present.' The explanation and argumentation will hardly seem to the reader as convincing as the author wished them to be. But be this as it may. If we survey the original compositions written by Liszt from 1834 to 1848, we find that, apart from songs (which he began to compose in 1841), they consist of programmatic pianoforte pieces. After this period there comes first a burst and flood of symphonic programme music, and then a great variety of all kinds of composition, large and small, among which grand choral works form an outstanding feature. Before examining Liszt's contributions to programme music, we must inquire into his views of this *genre* of the art.

The chief sources of information regarding this matter are Liszt's *Lettre d'un Bachelier ès Musique*, dated January, 1837, his review of Schumann's Op. 5, 11, 14, of the same year, likewise published in the *Revue et Gazette musicale*, and especially his essay *Berlioz and his Harold Symphony*, of 1855, the purpose of which was less to make propaganda for his French contemporary than to set forth his own ideas and justify his own practice.

Liszt combats the only too common, but in reality quite absurd notion that the composer of so-called picturesque music pretends to vie with the wielders of the brush, and like them strives to *paint* the aspect of woods, mountain crevices, the meandering of a brook through a meadow, &c. 'It is obvious that things in so far as they are objective are not at all within the department of music, and that the merest tyro in landscape painting can with one stroke of his pencil produce a scene more faithfully than a consummate musician with all the resources of the cleverest orchestra. But the same things, in so far as they in a certain way affect the soul, these things subjectivated (if I may so express myself) and become reverie, meditation, *élan*, have they not a singular affinity with music? And could not music translate them into its mysterious language? Supposing the imitation of the quail and cuckoo in the *Pastoral Symphony* to be chargeable with puerility, must we conclude from this fact that Beethoven was wrong in seeking to affect the soul as would the view of a smiling landscape, of a happy country, of a village festival suddenly interrupted by an unexpected thunderstorm? Does not Berlioz in the *Harold Symphony* strongly recall to the mind mountain scenes and the religious effects of bells that lose themselves in the windings of steep paths? In regard to poetical music, do you think that some stupid burden of a romance or some declamatory libretto is indispensable for the expression of the human passions—such as love, despair, and anger? . . . . Let me repeat once more

T

for the perfect satisfaction of *messieurs les feuilletonistes:*
Nobody thinks of writing music so ridiculous as that
which they call picturesque. What one thinks of, what
the strong men have thought of, and will always think
of, is to impress music more and more with poetry in
order to render it the organ of that part of the soul
which, if one may believe those who have felt, loved,
and suffered strongly, defies analysis and does not
admit of the settled and definite expression of the
human languages.'

Liszt holds that feeling becomes incarnate in pure
music, without—as in most arts, especially in the verbal
art—diffracting its rays on the thought. Other than
musical means of expression ' cannot immediately express
the full intensity of our feelings because they are obliged
to do it by pictures or comparisons. Music, on the
other hand, gives simultaneously the strength and
the expression of the feeling ; it is incorporated
apprehensible substance of the spirit. Perceptible by
our senses it penetrates them like an arrow, like dew,
like a spirit.'

Liszt differentiates clearly the composer of absolute
music from the composer of programme music, whom
he calls respectively the specific and the poetizing
symphonist. Of the former we are told that he
'transports his hearers with him to ideal regions, which
he leaves the imagination of every individual free to
conceive and adorn.' In such a case it is very dangerous
to wish to impose on our neighbour the same scenes and
series of thoughts to which our imagination feels itself
transported. Here everyone should be allowed to enjoy
silently his revelations and visions, for which there
is no name and no sign. The poetizing symphonist,

however, who sets himself the task of rendering with equal clearness a picture distinctly present to his mind, a series of psychical moods that unambiguously and definitely lie in his consciousness—why should he not endeavour to secure, with the help of a programme, a complete understanding?

Liszt labours hard to make his readers see what is a programme, and what is its object. He defines a programme as 'any foreword in intelligible language added to a piece of pure instrumental music, by which the composer intends to guard the hearer against an arbitrary poetical interpretation, and to direct his attention in advance to the poetical idea of the whole, to a particular point of it.' Again he says: 'The programme has no other object than to indicate preparatively the spiritual moments which impelled the composer to create his work, the thoughts which he endeavoured to incorporate in it.' In discussing the subject of programme music people often indulge in the most untenable arguments, arguments arising from their failure to distinguish what is distinct. No doubt, 'it would be childishly idle, indeed in most cases a mistake, subsequently to devise programmes and wish to explain the emotional content of an instrumental poem, as then the word must destroy the charm, desecrate the feelings, and tear the finest webs of the soul, which assumed just this form because it could not be put into words, pictures, and ideas.' This, although undoubtedly true, is true only if he who attempts it is another than the composer, or if the composer wrote without definite ideas and conscious moods. Therefore Liszt adds to the above: 'On the other hand, the master is master of his work; he can have created it under the influence of certain impressions,

of which he then would like to make the hearer fully
conscious.'

Of Schumann's pianoforte pieces he says that 'the
author has comprehended the significance of the programme more than anybody else, and has given the
most excellent examples for its employment. He has
most admirably succeeded in evoking in us musically the
effect which would have been produced upon us by the
reality of an object the representation of which he calls up
by the title. In conceiving the object from the poetic side
he attained the real end of the programme.' In short,
Liszt came to the' conclusion that instead of being a
symptom of exhaustion and degeneration, as many
formerly thought and not a few still think, the solution
of the problem of instrumental music contained in the
programme was the result of the development of his
time conditioned by the various still impending
advances of the art.

But there is another question implied in the problem
of programme music, not necessarily, but frequently,
namely, the question of form. In connection with the
symphonic programme music of Liszt, the discussion of
this question reaches the acute stage. It is therefore
advisable that we should mark his words carefully.

'In the so-called classical music the return and
thematic development of the themes are determined by
express rules, which are considered inviolable, although
the composers who originated them had no other precept
for them than their own imagination, and themselves
made the formal dispositions which people wish now to
set up as a law. In programme music, on the other
hand, the return, change, modification, and modulation
of the motives are conditioned by their relation to a

poetic idea. Here one theme does not, according to the
law, call forth a second theme; here the motives are
not the consequence of stereotyped approximations and
contrasts of tone-colours, and the colouring as such
does not condition the grouping of the ideas. All
exclusively musical considerations, though they should
not be neglected, have to be subordinated to the
action of the given subject. Consequently action
and subject of this kind of symphony demand a
higher interest than the technical treatment of the
musical material; and the indefinite impressions of
the soul are raised into definite impressions by an
expounded plan which is here taken in by the ear,
similarly as a cycle of pictures is taken in by the eye.
The artist who prefers this kind of art work enjoys the
advantage of connecting with a poetic idea all the
affections which the orchestra expresses with so much
power.

The position, the legitimate position, of the composer
of programme music is well stated in the above passage,
but the position of the composer of absolute music is
grossly misrepresented. We find the same mistaken
view still more forcibly and also still more offensively
formulated in one of Liszt's earlier pronouncements,
where we read of ' instrumental music as it was known
hitherto (Beethoven and Weber excepted), music laid
out squarely after a symmetrical plan that may be, so
to speak, measured by cubic feet.' The classics are not
the slavish formalists, the mechanical appliers of strict,
unbending rules, that Liszt and other moderns represent
them to have been. The variety they obtain within the
limits of the form is truly marvellous. Nevertheless it
is not to be wondered at, for the freedom is great, and

the restraint little. Indeed, it must be obvious to those who study the works of the classics with an unprejudiced as well as an observant eye that to these classics form was not a hard and fast framework, but a set of principles that could be realized in an infinitude of ways, and which it was permissible to modify and even depart from. All this might be proved from any of the great classics, the most classic of the classics, Mozart, not excepted. Of course the case is different, and Liszt right, if we consider, instead of the masterpieces of the original geniuses, their inferior productions or the works of imitators, of men of mere talent and no talent.

Hans von Bülow, in one of his criticisms, defines Liszt's school (which, he says, is not a school in the old sense of the word) as the artistic emancipation of individual content from schematism; and Liszt in a letter to his pupil thanks him for the definition and approves of it. But is it really a *defining* definition, one that distinguishes the case in question from every other case? It seems to me that, strictly speaking, it differentiates the works of the men of genius from those of the men of inferior gifts, and necessarily excludes schools. The appropriateness to Liszt in particular becomes apparent only after acquaintance with his views and the characteristics of his symphonies and symphonic poems.

As with Liszt the content is the determining factor, the form of every composition must differ from that of every other. Much positive information about the master's form can therefore not be supplied. We may indeed be voluble on what it is not, but must be taciturn on what it is. The new term Symphonic Poem (*Symphonische Dichtung*) was an invention of Liszt's, a happy one. The

same may be said of the thing itself, although it would
not be extravagant to assert that before him similar
things as poetical in content and as unconventional in
form had occasionally been produced. The symphonic
poem differs from the old symphony in that it consists
not of several separate pieces, but of one piece, in which,
however, there may be any number of changes of time
and measure and any number of themes. One of the
distinguishing features of the symphonic poem then is
continuity. In this respect Liszt's symphonic poems
differ also from his own two symphonies, which consist of
separate pieces, although not of the orthodox four, but
the one of three and the other of two. Of the formal
economy within the pieces no more need be said than
that it differs from that of the old overture and
symphony in the distribution of keys and subjects. But
no! A certain device plays so characteristic and
important a part in Liszt's symphonic works that it
would be unpardonable negligence not to discuss it—
namely, the metamorphosis of themes, that is, the
rhythmic, melodic, and harmonic modification, or rather
variation, of themes for the purpose of changing their
expression.

It was the example of Berlioz that gave the impulse
to the more extended use of *Leitmotive* by Liszt and
Wagner. But the use of the device by the three masters
differs in manner as well as in extent. The simple way
of Berlioz is only to a very limited extent followed by
Liszt and Wagner—Liszt favours complex processes.
Wagner at the height of his development revels in
infinite intricacies. Liszt's peculiar way is moreover
discriminated by the term 'metamorphosis of themes,'
which is not applied to the ways of Berlioz and Wagner,

although to some extent applicable also to them. But there is one difference between Berlioz on the one hand, and Liszt and Wagner on the other: With the first of the three masters the aim seems to me to have been purely poetical, purely expressional; with the two others, it was unquestionably also formal, structural. They used the device consciously as a means for securing unity, as a substitute for the abandoned old methods of design. But not only do we find great differences in the use of *Leitmotive* by these several masters, but we find also great differences in the use of them by Liszt in his several works. A glance at a few of these will suffice to prove the statement.

Liszt's way in the *Faust* Symphony is very like that of Berlioz in the *Symphonie fantastique* and *Harold en Italie*—the themes are representative of persons. But Liszt is not content with one theme. In the first division of the work he has quite a large number of special themes portraying the outstanding features of Faust's character—brooding inquiry (1), struggling aspiration (2), passionate appealing (3), love-longing (4), and triumphant enthusiasm (5). In the second division, where the Margaret themes are the principal, most of the Faust themes reappear as secondary themes, showing by their new guises the transformation which the sombre, solitary Faust experiences under the magic influence of love. In the third division, too, some of the Faust themes reappear, now in a caricaturing form, being intended to portray the sceptical, mocking Mephistopheles, the opposite of the noble, earnestly striving Faust. The following illustrations give only the principal Faust themes and their most important metamorphoses; or rather give only brief melodic indications of them, omitting the characteristic

accompaniments and instrumentation.   The numbers of
the themes in the several divisions correspond.

FIRST DIVISION.

SECOND DIVISION.

THIRD DIVISION.

In the *Faust* Symphony, then, the themes are representative of persons ; more generally, however, the
themes of Liszt's symphonic works are expressive of
moods and feelings unconnected with any particular
person.   This is the case, for instance, with the two works
to the formal aspect of which we will now direct our
attention.   The short and simple *Orpheus* is an improvi-
sation evolved from a single theme, the different phrases
of which are variously moulded and illuminated.   One
may therefore say that formally the composition had
more of the old than of the new *modus operandi*.   Quite
different is the state of matters, quite modern and
Lisztian, in *Die Ideale*.   To illustrate this way I shall
quote snatches of two of several themes on which the
composition is based, and follow up each of them by a
number of metamorphoses.   Mark that the composer
produces by metamorphosis not only music expressive of
shades of the same feeling, phases of the same mood,
but also music expressive of feelings of an altogether
different nature.

From the youthful aspiring exuberance of 1*a*, Liszt
evolves the disillusionment of 1*b*, the sad questioning of
1*c*, the activity of 1*d*, the stir of 1*e*, and the triumphant
pomp of 1*f*.

From the joy in germinating, growing Nature of 2*a*, Liszt evolves the disillusionment of 2*b*, friendship's sweet comfort of 2*c*, the joyous animation of 2*d*, and the victory proclaiming 2*e*.

Now let us leave these general discussions, and turn
our attention to the individual works. The numerous
programmatic pianoforte pieces are not important
enough to be examined in detail and at length. Only a
few of them possess that combination of charm of
content and perfection of form which constitutes a
successful art-work and gains the lasting affection of
the hearer. Most of them can only be regarded as
experiments and attempts—experiments in devising new
effects, attempts at expressing noble sentiments, moods,
and conceptions. Not unfrequently we are constrained
to admire the earnest endeavour, where the result is
unsatisfactory; but hardly less frequently our artistic
sense is outraged by extravagant futility or appalling
ugliness. Considering the greatness and capabilities of
the artist, these lapses into, these indulgences in, and
these coquettings with the unbeautiful must always
remain a difficult problem for the critic of the master's

works. The ugly, I think, has a greater space given to it in Liszt's than in any other composer's creations. This is not a prejudiced expression of opinion, but one slowly evolved and reluctantly adopted in the course of time. Moreover, there can be no doubt that Liszt and his disciples took delight in deviating from the customary, and in horrifying those whom they looked upon as Philistines by what Hans von Bülow calls *Ohrfeigen für feige Ohren* ('cuffs for cowardly ears'— an untranslatable play on the words *feige*, the noun differing in meaning from the adjective). The main object of the following review, however, will not be to gauge the excellence of the compositions, but to inquire into the nature of the programmes. As Liszt was in the habit of again and again rewriting his compositions, so that many of his early works were printed comparatively late in his life, and a considerable number were published in diverse versions, I shall, to save time and space, mention them regardless of chronology.

Liszt's *Harmonies poétiques et religieuses** derive their title from Lamartine's collection of poems thus named, and have also prefixed to them two paragraphs from the poet's *avertissement*. Two sentences of this *avertissement* suffice to characterize no less the musician's pieces than those of his admired poet's. 'There are meditative souls whom solitude and contemplation raises invincibly towards infinite ideas, that is towards religion; all their thoughts are converted into enthusiasm and prayer, their whole existence is a mute hymn to the Divinity and to hope. . . . . There are hearts broken by sorrow, trodden down by the world, who take refuge

* Published in 1853.

in the world of their thoughts, in the solitude of their soul, in order to weep, to await, or to adore.' The ten numbers of the musical collection are called: (1) *Invocation ;* (2) *Ave Maria ;* (3) *Bénédiction de Dieu dans la Solitude ;* (4) *Pensée des Morts ;* (5) *Pater noster ;* (6) *Hymne de l'Enfant à son réveil ;* (7) *Funérailles ;* (8) *Miserere ;* (9) *Andante lagrimoso ;* and (10) *Cantique d'amour.* Most of these pieces were directly inspired by Lamartine. The titles of Nos. 1, 3, 4, and 6 come from the *Harmonies,* and that of No. 10 comes from the poet's *Méditations poétiques* (Book II., No. 24). No. 9 is based on one of the *Harmonies,* entitled *Une Larme ou Consolation.* Nos. 1, 3, and 9 have some lines of the poet prefixed, and No 6. has the superscription ' composed on the text of Lamartine's *Harmonies.*' Of the others the *Miserere* ' after Palestrina,' and the *Pater noster,* with the words subscribed, a transcription of a four-part vocal composition of his own, hardly concern us here. The *Ave Maria* explains itself. Two of the remaining pieces, without more extended programmes than their titles, call for a few words of comment. The first edition of the *Pensée des Morts* was without this title, but had the indication ' avec un profond sentiment d'ennui.' By *ennui* is to be understood what Liszt described as *die Trübsal der armen Menschenkinder* (the sorrows of the poor children of men), and Bossuet as ' le fond de la vie humaine.' Liszt composed it when he was staying at La Chênaie with the famous cleric Lamennais. The *Funérailles* have reference to the political troubles of 1848-1850, in which perished his friends Felix Lichnowsky, Ludwig Batthyanyi, and Ladislas Teleki. To what has already been said about the *Cantique d'amour* may be added that

it is connected with the Princess Wittgenstein, on whose
estate it and the *Invocation* and *Bénédiction* were composed in 1847-1848.   To her Liszt dedicated the whole
collection—' à Jeanne Elisabeth Carolyne.'

A larger, more varied, and upon the whole more
interesting and valuable collection is that bearing the
title *Années de Pèlerinage.*   The three books of this
collection were published respectively in 1855, 1858, and
1883 ; but the compositions of the first book, which is
devoted to Switzerland, are of 1835-1836, those of the
second, which is devoted to Italy, of 1838-1839, and
those of the third, which is for the greater part devoted
to Italy, of much later times.   The nature of these
compositions is well characterized by the sub-title of the
first book of the earlier published *Album d'un Voyageur,*
which contained five of the Swiss pieces — namely,
Impressions et Poësies.   The subjects dealt with are
' Chapelle de Guillaume Tell,' ' Au Lac de Wallenstadt,'
' Pastorale,' ' Au bord d'une Source,' ' Orage,' ' Vallée
d'Obermann,' ' Eclogue,' ' Le Mal du Pays,' ' Les Cloches
de Genève.'   Of these nine pieces only two are accompanied by remarks in addition to the titles : the ' Vallée
d'Obermann ' is preceded by two short passages from
Sénancour's *Obermann* and nine lines from Byron's
Childe Harold ; and the ' Eclogue ' is followed by a long
passage and a note entitled ' De l'expression romantique
et du ranz-des-vaches.'   One may confidently point to
the serene *Lac de Wallenstadt* and the sparkling *Au bord
d'une Source* as the most happily inspired and finished
compositions.   While this first book contains nature
impressions, the second book contains art and literature
impressions : in (1) *Il Sposalizio,* Liszt expresses the
impression received from Raphael's work in the Milan

Brera ; in (2) *Il Penseroso*, the impression received from Michael Angelo's statue of Lorenzo de' Medici in the new sacristy of S. Lorenzo at Florence ; (3) *Canzonetta del Salvator Rosa*, is a setting of one of the Italian painter's poems, with the words under the music. Then follow the 47th, 104th, and 123rd Sonnets of Petrarch, the words being prefixed to the music : these pieces are transcriptions of vocal settings ; (7) the last number of the book is entitled 'After a reading of Dante, Fantasia quasi Sonata.' Let us not overlook that in the *Sposalizio* and *Penseroso* Liszt has no intention whatever to vie with the painter and sculptor ; he wishes to do no more than express in music the impression their works have produced on him, or, to be more exact, the moods engendered by them. These impressions are probably different from yours, I know they are different from mine, but that does not affect the legitimacy of the procedure. The third book, in which the composer's creative power shows less freshness and vigour,* contains, besides a transcription, 'Angelus ! Prière aux anges gardiens,' six original pianoforte pieces ; (2) and (3) both threnodies and bearing the same title *Aux Cyprès de la Villa d'Este* (at the Villa d'Este, Tivoli, the property of Cardinal Hohenlohe, Liszt often resided); (4) *Les jeux d'eaux à la Villa d'Este ;* (5) *Sunt lacrymæ rerum, en mode hongrois;* (6) *Marche funèbre* (in memory of Maximilian I., Emperor of Mexico, who died June 19. 1867) ; and (7) *Sursum Corda.* Before leaving the *Années de Pélerinage*, I must yet mention the piece *Lyon*, which opened the *Impressions et Poësies.* It bore the motto ' Vivre en travaillant ou mourir en combattant,'

---

* There is in it perhaps more ugliness, hollowness, and unmusicalness than in any other of the master's publications.

U

and referred to the insurrection of the workmen of Lyons in 1834, with its five-days' fighting in the streets.

Of the twelve *Grandes Etudes* (*Etudes d'exécution transcendante*) nine have significant titles : (3) *Paysage ;* (4) *Mazeppa ;* (5) *Feux follets ;* (6) *Vision ;* (7) *Eroica ;* (8). *Wilde Jagd ;* (9) *Ricordanza ;* (11) *Harmonies du Soir ;* (12) *Chasse-neige.* Without going beyond the titles, we can see that most of these have not the same importance as those of the pieces of the previously considered collections, that, in fact, they were fanciful after-thoughts. Along with the above studies ought to be enumerated the three *Etudes de Concert—Waldesrauschen, Gnomenreigen,* and *Ave Maria.*

Very notable among Liszt's pianoforte pieces are the two *Légendes—*' St. François d'Assise, La Prédiction aux Oiseaux,' and ' St. François de Paule marchant sur les flots.' The former may have been suggested by the sixteenth chapter of the famous *I Fioretti di San Francesco,* and the latter was no doubt suggested by Steinle's drawing which used to stand on Liszt's writing-table, ' St. Francis of Paula walks on the waves, his mantle spread out under his feet, holding a glowing coal in one of his hands, raising the other, either to conjure the storm or to bless the threatened sailors, looking heavenward, where in a glory appears the redeeming word "Charitas "' (from Liszt's testament). I cannot help seeing excellent programme music without revealed programmes in the *Consolations,* the master's least pretentious and sweetest tone-poems. Was it Sainte-Beuve's volume of poems that suggested the title ? Other compositions of interest in our inquiry are the unpublished six Hungarian portraits—Széchényi, Teleky, Eötvös, Deak, Vörösmarty, and Mosonyi ; the several

Mephisto Waltzes and the *Mephisto* Polka; Mosenyi's *Grabgeleite;* and some of the twelve pieces *Der Weihnachtsbaum* (the Christmas Tree); &c.

Between us and the discussion of the orchestral works there stand now only Liszt's melodramatic compositions —namely, the pianoforte accompaniments to Bürger's *Lenore* (1857 ?), Lenau's *Der traurige Mönch* (1860), Jokai's *Der todte Dichter* (1873), and Tolstoi's *Der blinde Sänger* (1860). Let us note the dates of at least the first of these compositions (written about 1857, and published in 1860); for Liszt was one of the first that followed the lead of Schumann, who had preceded him a few years (he wrote in 1849 and 1852, and published in 1853) in rehabilitating and bringing into vogue again the *genre* of musically accompanied declamation.

And now at last we come to Liszt's orchestral programme music, the twelve Symphonic Poems, the two Symphonies (Goethe's *Faust* and Dante's *Divina Commedia*), two Episodes from Lenau's *Faust*, and some compositions of less importance comprising a thirteenth Symphonic Poem, in short, the works by which the composer has challenged the world, and about which there has been so much controversy. I have already related that Liszt did not begin to compose these ambitious works till about the end of 1847, or rather did not begin to contemplate composing them till then, and did not actually begin their composition till two years later, at the age of thirty-eight. And I have also already related that it was the Princess Wittgenstein who induced him to abandon the career of a virtuoso and to grapple with the most difficult tasks a creative musician can set himself. Once on the path, he followed it with feverish eagerness. In April or May, 1854, he writes that seven of the twelve symphonic poems are entirely finished, and mentions the titles of two more. In 1854 follow the *Faust* Symphony, in 1855 the *Dante* Symphony; and in 1859 all the above-enumerated orchestral works, with the exception of the unimportant ones, were black on white. Sixteen symphonic works within ten years! And these were by no means the only compositions he wrote, nor was composition the only work he did. The publication of the works in question took place from 1856 to 1862. I shall begin my review with the symphonic poems in the printed order, although that is not the chronological order, then proceed to the symphonies, and conclude with some of the other works. The figures in parentheses after the titles are the years of composition and publication. Dante's *Divina Commedia* was the first subject that occupied Liszt, and the treatment originally contemplated by the composer and his inspiring muse was very different from the one ultimately chosen. Bonaventura Genelli's illustrations to Dante's great poem, and the success of Gropius's diorama shown at Berlin, suggested to them a combination of diorama and music. The Princess offered to provide the considerable capital for the outlay required for the realization of the idea. Lina Ramann says that the idea was given up because of the Princess's loss of fortune. May not the good sense of the projectors have had something to do with the abandonment of the scheme?

The first in the printed order of Liszt's twelve Symphonic Poems, *Ce qu'on entend sur la Montagne* (1849; 1857), is based on and named after No. 5 of Victor Hugo's *Les Feuilles d'automne*. The composer prefixes the whole poem to his score, and does not give any further information as to his intention. On a mountain

by the sea, the poet hears a vast, immense, confused
sound, vaguer than the wind in the thickly foliaged trees,
full of clanging chords, suave murmurs, soft as an
evening song, strong as the clash of arms, ineffable,
profound music. And in this world-enveloping symphony
he soon distinguishes two voices—the voice of Nature and
the voice of Humanity : the former, coming from the sea,
the voice of the waves, a song of glory, a hymn of
happiness ; the latter, coming from the land, full of
sadness, the murmur of man—the one magnificent,
joyous, peaceful, and triumphant; the other shrill, grating,
maledictory, and complaining. After listening and
meditating, the poet asks : Why are we here, what can
be the object of all this, what of the soul, is it
better to be or to live ? And why does God, who alone
reads in his book, mingle eternally in one fatal hymn the
song of nature with the cry of humanity ? This is a
brief indication of Victor Hugo's vision (if this word is
permissible in speaking of things audible) and the
questionings arising therefrom. It is obvious that music
cannot render the poet's meaning. It can only actualize
his imagery. In fact, Liszt's composition is pure
symbolism. We may even describe it as a gigantic
metaphor. This observation should be read as a
qualification of the work, not as a condemnation.
Symbolism is a legitimate form of art. What has to be
further noted in connection with this symphonic poem
is that Liszt does not follow Victor Hugo to the bitter
end. For the poet's pessimistic conclusion the composer
substitutes an optimistic one. After the confused sound
and the opposition and contention of the two voices, a
blissful reconciliation based on religious faith is
proposed, but not yet acquiesced in; the contention is

then renewed with even greater stress, and finally faith is the conqueror.

Although the centenary of Goethe's birthday and a performance of his *Tasso* gave the impulse to the composition of *Tasso: Lamento e trionfo* (1849; 1856), its chief inspirer was Byron's poem *The Lament of Tasso* rather than the German poet's drama for which Liszt was asked to write an overture. The title shows that the composer did not stop where the poet stopped. He contrasted with the miseries of the man's life the posthumous glory of the author of the *Gerusalemme liberata.* 'Tasso loved and suffered in Ferrara, he was revenged in Rome, and he lives still to-day in the folk-songs of Venice. These three moments are inseparable from his imperishable fame. To render them musically, we called up first his great shade as it still haunts the Venetian lagunes; we then saw his proud, sad face pass through the festivities of Ferrara, where he gave birth to his masterpieces; finally we followed him to Rome, the eternal city which in bestowing on him her crown, glorified in him the martyr and poet.' This quotation and the other information are from Liszt's preface, from which we learn also that the principal theme on which he based his composition is the melody to which he heard the Venetian gondoliers sing the opening stanzas of Tasso's epic.

Many years after the composition of the above work, Liszt added to it an epilogue, *Le Triomphe funèbre du Tasse* (1868; 1878). The preface consists of an extract from Serassi's biography of Tasso, in which the author relates how, after the poet's death at the monastery of S. Onofrio, on the Janiculum, his patron, Cardinal Cintio (Aldobrandino), prepared a magnificent funeral, and how the corpse, clad in a rich toga and crowned with laurel, was carried in great pomp, accompanied by the mighty and the learned to St. Peter's Place. But a much more interesting piece of information is furnished by the biographer of Liszt. One day the composer and a friend walked to S. Onofrio to view the sunset, following the route by which the corpse of Tasso returned from St. Peter's to the monastery; and so powerful was the impression Liszt received that on the same evening he had himself driven in a closed carriage over the same way. 'I imagined myself,' he remarked the next day, 'Tasso lying in his coffin, and I noted the feeling he was likely to have had, had he been conscious of the occurrence.'

Les Préludes (1854; 1856) were inspired by one of Lamartine's *Méditations poétiques.* The composer, who describes his work as *d'après Lamartine,* gives the following exposition of the content or rather of the underlying thought. 'What is our life but a series of preludes to that unknown song of which Death intones the first solemn note?—Love forms the enchanted aurora of every existence. But where is the destiny in which the first delights of happiness are not interrupted by some storm whose mortal breath dissipates its beautiful illusions, whose fatal lightning consumes its altar? And where is the cruelly wounded soul that after one of those tempests does not seek to soothe its memories in the sweet calm of country life? But man does not easily resign himself long to the enjoyment of the beneficent serenity in the bosom of nature which at first charmed him; and when the trumpet sounds the alarm, he hastens to the post of danger, whatever the war that calls him to the ranks, that he may

find again in the fight full consciousness of himself
and entire possession of his powers.' Here the composer
once more makes the inessential of the poem, the
similes, the essential of the music—the philosophic idea
was of course beyond the reach of the art. This,
however, does not prevent this symphonic poem from
being one of the most pleasing, popular, and effective
of the master's compositions.

In the preface to the fourth symphonic poem, *Orpheus*
(1854; 1856), Liszt tells us that once, while conducting
a rehearsal of Gluck's *Orpheus*, he could not help his
imagination straying from this touchingly and sublimely
simple point of view to that Orpheus who soars so
majestically and harmoniously above the most poetic
myths of Greece; and could not help having recalled to
his mind an Etruscan vase seen by him in the Louvre,
on which the ancient poet-musician is represented
draped in a starred robe, his forehead encircled with the
mystically royal band, his lips, from which flow divine
words and melodies, open, and his beautiful tapering
fingers energetically sounding the strings of his lyre.
Around this figure the composer imagined he perceived
the wild beasts of the forest enraptured, the brutal
instinct of man silenced, the rocks softened. 'To-day,
as of old and always,' remarks Liszt, 'Orpheus, that is
Art, should pour forth his melodious waves and vibrating
chords like a soft and irresistible light over the contrary
elements that tear each other and bleed in the soul of
every individual, as in the bowels of society. Orpheus
bewails Eurydice, that emblem of the ideal engulfed by
evil and pain, whom he is permitted to snatch from the
monsters of Erebus, to lead forth from the Cimmerian
darkness, but whom, alas! he cannot keep on this earth.'

Finally the composer formulates the thought in his mind thus : ' To render the serenely civilizing character of the melodies that radiate from every work of art; their suave energy, their august sway, their noble soul-encompassing sonorousness, . . . their diaphanous and azured ether enveloping the work and the whole universe as in an atmosphere, as in a transparent garment of ineffable and mysterious harmony.'

Liszt composed the fifth of his Symphonic Poems, *Prometheus* (1850; 1856), as an overture to Herder's dramatic scenes entitled *Der entfesselte Prometheus* (Prometheus unbound), which were performed at Weimar in 1850 on the occasion of the inauguration of a statue of that literary luminary. The composer remarks in the preface that the musician is concerned only with the sentiments that constitute the foundation of all the forms successively assumed by the myth. 'Audacity, suffering, endurance, and salvation : daring aspiration towards the highest destinies which the human mind can reach ; creative activity, need for expansion . . . expiatory pains giving up our vital organs to an incessant gnawing, without annihilating ourselves ; condemnation to a hard enchainment on the most arid shores of our nature ; cries of anguish and tears of blood . . . . but an inextinguishable consciousness of a native grandeur, of a future deliverance ; a tacit faith in a deliverer who will raise the long-tortured captive to the transmundane regions from which he stole the luminous spark . . . and, lastly, the accomplishment of the work of mercy when the great day has come. Unhappiness and glory ! Thus narrowed, the fundamental thought of this but too true fable lent itself only to a stormy, one may even say, fulgurant expression. A

desolation triumphant by the perseverance of a haughty
energy forms the musical character of these *data.*'

The subject of *Mazeppa* (1850 ; 1856) is the Mazeppa
of Victor Hugo's poem from *Les Orientales*. Liszt
prefixes the whole of that poem to the sixth of his
Symphonische Dichtungen, and does so without comment,
leaving it to the hearer to find out what the composer
chooses from it for interpretation, and what he is content
to ignore. The composition begins with a shrill cry
(*Un cri part*), and then the wild horse with Mazeppa
bound to it rushes away through valleys, rivers, steppes,
forests, and deserts, followed first by other wild horses,
then by birds of prey, till after a three-days' mad career
it falls dead. With it, still bound to it, lies the groaning
Mazeppa, naked, covered with blood, a living corpse;
but the time will come when this poor wretch shall rise
to be the ruler of the tribes of the Ukraine. Liszt's
Mazeppa is perhaps the most daring piece of tone-
painting in existence. It consists almost entirely of the
picturing of the outward. Nevertheless, the power
and genius displayed in it is such that the hearer
cannot but let himself be carried away by this restless,
breathless flight.

In the case of the seventh symphonic poem (1851 ;
1856) the whole programme vouchsafed by Liszt consists
in the title, *Festklänge* (Festal sounds). The composer's
biographer, however, makes a most interesting and
light-giving revelation concerning this work. The
Festklänge were to be his wedding music. In the
summer of 1851 it seemed as if the obstacles in the way
of his marriage with the Princess Wittgenstein would be
soon overcome. 'At this time arose the *Festklänge*—a
song of triumph over hostile machinations. In them

bitterness and pain were resolved into proud rejoicing, and the polonaise woven into them pictures the spiritual traits of the princely Polish lady who had made him her "soul-serf." Along with this there are woven into the work tender little episodes — festal sounds of the soul—pervaded by the poetic enchantment of personal experiences.'

Liszt has written a long, vague, and wordy preface to the *Héroide funèbre,* the eighth symphonic poem (1849-1850; 1856). Happily two or three of his sentences sum up his meaning. 'Everything can change in human societies—manners and cult, laws and ideas; sorrow remains always one and the same, it remains what it has been from the beginning of time. It is for art to throw its transfiguring veil over the tomb of the brave, to encircle with its golden halo the dead and the dying, in order that they may be envied by the living.' To enter still more fully into the intention of the composer, we have only to remember the nearness of the revolutionary movements of 1848, and to note that Liszt incorporated with this work a fragment from the *Symphonie révolutionnaire* sketched in 1830.

Of the *Hungaria,* the ninth symphonic poem (1854; 1857), I shall only say that it has no revealed programme, but indubitably is a historical and national picture of war, death, and triumph. *Hamlet,* the tenth symphonic poem (1858; 1861), which, too, has neither programme nor any kind of preface, is described on the original manuscript as a Prelude to Shakespeare's drama. It brings before the hearer the brooding prince—not the story of his life, not even his whole character, only a dominating feature. The indications 'very slow and sombre,' 'appassionato ed agitato assai,' 'this episode

in 3/2 time should be played extremely quietly, and
should sound like a shadow picture, pointing to Ophelia,'
'ironico, 'Moderato—lugubre,' show that allusions to
persons and circumstances affecting his mood are
not wanting. Also the *Hunnenschlacht* (Battle of the
Huns), the eleventh symphonic poem (1856-1857;
1861) has no programme prefixed to it. We know,
however, that Wilhelm von Kaulbach's fresco in the
Berlin museum inspired the composer. The subject
of Kaulbach's picture is the legend that after the
bloody struggle on the Catalaunian Plain, in 451,—
between Attila and his forces on the one side and
the Roman Aëtius and the Visigoth Theodoric and
theirs on the other side,—the fallen warriors continued
the battle in the air. Like the painter, the musician
wished to represent the event as a strife between
Heathendom and Christianity resulting in the victory of
the Cross. Two melodies are, as it were, the standards
of the contending forces, *Crux fidelis* gaining the day.

In the twelfth symphonic poem, *Die Ideale* (The Ideals,
1857; 1859), which is based on Schiller's poem of that
name, Liszt proceeds in a way quite different from those
he follows in his other works. Instead of a general
programme or a single title, he takes nine groups of
verses and prefixes them to as many continuous sections
of the composition. The pith and drift of Schiller's
poem may be stated thus : The sweet belief in the dream
creations of youth passes away ; that for which we once
ardently strove, and which we lovingly embraced with
heart and mind, becomes the prey of pitiless reality ;
already midway the boon companions—love, fortune,
fame, and truth—leave us one after another, and only
friendship and activity remain with us as comforters.

But the composer departs in several points from the poet's data. In a note to the tenth and concluding division of the work, the *Apotheosis*, he says : ' The holding fast and at the same time the continual realizing of the ideal is the highest aim of our life. In this sense I ventured to supplement Schiller's poem by a resumption, in the closing *Apotheosis*, of the motives of the first division in a jubilantly emphasized form.' In justification of an alteration Liszt could have cited Jean Paul Richter, and even Schiller himself, who called the conclusion tame, although a faithful picture of human life. We have to note further that the musician does not give the verses in the poet's sequence, that he makes use of eight lines omitted by Schiller in the ultimate amended form of the poem, and that, lastly, the composer marks the four main divisions of the work by the superscriptions *Aspiration*, *Disillusion*, *Activity*, and *Apotheosis*. Or, as Liszt puts it in a letter to Hans von Bülow : ' Following closely Schiller's poem, the musical composition divides itself, after the introduction, into three main strophes : (1) Aspiration, (2) Disillusion, and (3) Activity, the motives of which, reappearing in an emphasized form, furnish the content of the poet's Apotheosis.'

In addition to the twelve symphonic poems discussed, there has to be mentioned a thirteenth, a short work of the composer's old age (1881 ; 1883), which has not obtained much attention from the public, and was but lightly regarded by Liszt himself. Writing to Gevaërt he describes the score as ' assez courte, et sans *chevilles*.' A pen-and-ink drawing by Count Michael von Zichy inspired *From the Cradle to the Grave* (The Cradle, Struggle for Existence, To the Grave). In a letter to the Count, Liszt says : ' You make me a grand present. Your drawing is a wonderful symphony. I will try to put it into notes, and then dedicate the work to you.'

Liszt's symphonies differ from his symphonic poems in that they consist of separate divisions instead of a continuity of closely connected movements ; and they differ from the old symphonies in the number and internal economy of the divisions. The first of Liszt's two symphonies is the *Faust* Symphony, the full title of which runs *A Faust Symphony (after Goethe) in three Character Pictures*—(1) Faust; (2) Margaret; (3) Mephistopheles, and a concluding chorus, ' All that is transient is but a semblance,' for grand orchestra and men's voices. The three character pictures were composed in 1853-1854, the chorus in 1857 ; and the score of the whole was published in 1861. As the title indicates, the composer does not roam with the poet through heaven, earth, and hell, and represent in speech and action a crowd of creatures of all kinds and degrees, but confines himself to the three principal personages and the portrayal of their inward being. But the title does not indicate that the second and third divisions not merely portray Margaret and Mephistopheles, but also complete the portrait of Faust ; and that incidents of the action are not wholly excluded, as, for instance, the consultation of the flower oracle in the second division shows. The first character picture brings before us in speaking motives and themes the brooding and inquiring, the restlessly chafing, the love-longing, and the triumphantly enthusiastic Faust. The second character picture presents to us the sweet, simple Margaret at first alone, and then in conjunction with Faust, whose entrance is marked by his love-longing theme ; Margaret's

'He loves me, he loves me not, &c.,' with the final exultant 'He loves me' forming a very brief episode. The third character picture is that of the spirit who ever denies. It opens with jeers and diabolical laughter (*Allegro vivace ironico*). No entirely new themes are produced, but Faust motives and themes are introduced in grotesquely metamorphosed forms. Also the Margaret theme appears again. The choral *Coda* is not consistent with the scheme of character pictures. But no doubt the composer disliked the idea of concluding with the strident dissonance of the heartless mocking Mephistopheles. Hence the harmonious resolution by the mystic chorus from the second part of *Faust*: 'All that is transient is but a symbol, the insufficient becomes an event, the indescribable here is done, the eternal womanly draws us upward.'

The second of Liszt's symphonies, usually called *Dante* Symphony, but the full and correct title of which is *A Symphony to Dante's Divina Commedia* for grand orchestra and soprano and alto chorus (1855; 1858), consists of only two divisions respectively entitled *L'Inferno* and *Il Purgatorio*. The composer originally intended to have, like the poet, a third division. 'You are reading Dante,' Liszt writes to Wagner on June 2, 1855. 'That is good company for you. For my part, I shall furnish you with a commentary to this reading. For a long time I have been carrying a *Dante* Symphony about with me in my head [see p. 296]; in the course of the year it is to be finished—three divisions: Hell, Purgatory, and Paradise; the first two purely instrumental, the last with chorus.' The objections to a Paradise strongly urged by Wagner in all probability induced Liszt to alter his plan. As the work stands,

the second division concludes with a *Coda*, that may be
described as an outlook towards Paradise, or as a
presentiment of it.   The score has prefixed to it a long
interpretative Introduction, which, although not written,
was authorized, prompted, and approved by the composer.
The writer of it, Richard Pohl, points out that a
composer worthy of a theme like Faust must be something more than a tone-painter (in the material, bad
sense of the word); his concern ought to be with something that neither the word with its concrete definiteness
can express, nor form and colour can actually realize,
and this something is the world of the profoundest and
most intimate feelings that unveil themselves to man's
mind only in tones.   None but the tone-poet can render
the fundamental moods.   But in order to seize them in
their totality, he must abstract from the material
moments of Dante's epic, and can at most only allude to
a few of them.   On the other hand, he must also abstract
from the dramatic and philosophical elements.   These
were Pohl's, and, we may presume, Liszt's views on the
treatment of the subject.   At the beginning two motives
are heard which play important parts in the first
division.   The trombones and tuba open the Inferno
with the 'Through me you pass into the city of woe.
Through me you pass into eternal pain.   Through me
among the people lost for aye.'   And the trumpets and
horns follow with the direful 'All hope abandon, ye who
enter here.'   The dread gate passed, we find ourselves
in a demoniac turmoil (*accelerando*), in which become
distinguishable the madness, hopelessness, fury, and
curses of the damned (*Allegro frenetico*).   The only
relief in these protracted horrors is afforded by the
beautiful episode of Paolo and Francesca da Rimini.

' No greater grief than to remember days of joy when
misery is at hand.' In the introductory *Andante* of the
second division, the Purgatory, the composer had in his
mind Dante's experiences after issuing from Hell : the
sweet hue of eastern sapphire, the serene aspect of the
pure air, the beautiful planet that made all the orient
laugh, and the trembling of the ocean (*il tremolar della
marina*). What follows speaks of infinite longing for
godliness, of a growing feeling of unworthiness and
weakness, of humility, contrition, and repentance, of
redemption by prayer. With regard to the *Coda*, the
writer of the preface justly remarks that the art cannot
sing heaven itself, only the earthly reflection of it in
the heart of those whose souls· are turned heavenward.
' When the holy glow of divine Love has kindled the
heart, every pang is extinguished ; the heart is lost in
the heavenly bliss of resignation in God's mercy ; from
the individual Magnificat it proceeds, joining itself to the
whole universe, to the general Halleluja and Hosanna.'
With the grand chant and the shouts of rejoicing, sung
by the women's or boys' chorus, accompanied by the
orchestra, the work ends ecstatically.

The Two *Episodes from Lenau's Faust* for grand
orchestra — (1) *Der nächtliche Zug* (The nocturnal
procession), and (2) *Der Tanz in der Dorfschenke* (The
dance in the village inn), also called *Mephisto Waltz*,
—were composed in 1858-1859, and published in 1862.
The following ingredients, extracted from the poem,
will give an idea of Liszt's soul- and body-painting,
his picturing of the inward and outward, in the first
romantic composition. Heavy dark clouds, profound
night, sweet spring feeling in the wood, a warm
soulful rustling in the foliage, fragrant air, carolling

x

of the nightingale. Faust rides alone in sombre mood, the farther he advances the greater the silence; he dismounts. What can be the approaching light illuminating bush and sky, what the sweet solemn singing? A procession with torches, of white-dressed children carrying wreaths of flowers in celebration of St. John's Eve, followed by virgins in demure nuns' veils, and old priests in dark habits and with crosses. When they have passed by and the last glimpses of the lights have disappeared, Faust buries his face in his horse's mane and sheds tears more bitter than ever he shed before. An episode of a very different nature is the *Dance in the Village Inn*, the *ne plus ultra* of weirdness and unbridled sensuality in the whole domain of music, and one of the most remarkable *tours de force* of imagination, combination, and instrumentation. Mephistopheles takes the instrument from the hands of the tame fiddler, and draws from it indescribably seductive and intoxicating tones. The amorous Faust whirls about with a full-blooded village beauty in a wild dance : they dance, and dance, and dance, in the room, out of the room, in the open, to the wood—the sounds of the fiddle grow softer and softer, and the nightingale warbles his love-laden song.

Only one word of one more work, the *Todtentanz* (*Danse macabre*), *Paraphrase on the Dies Iræ* for Pianoforte and Orchestra. It was composed in 1849-1850, revised in 1859, and published in 1865; but the seed was sown in 1838 at Pisa. Liszt told his biographer that when he saw Andrea Orcagna's fresco, ' The Triumph of Death,' in the Campo Santo, he was so greatly moved by the *naïveté* and profoundness of this creation that *Dies iræ* sounded within him with overwhelming power and blended with all the modulations of the thought which the Italian master put into line and colour. Liszt hesitated to publish 'such a monstrosity' as his 'Dance of Death,' but Hans von Bülow allayed his doubts. The work is certainly a gruesome treatment of a gruesome subject.

In the foregoing pages I have shown what Liszt has done in the way of symphonic programme music. The reader who has attentively followed me must have seen that as regards quantity the master's output is very considerable, and that as regards choice of programme it is as a rule unexceptionable. Only ignorance of the composer's intentions and false attributions can find in these works anything that is absurd or illegitimate, anything that lowers or denaturalizes the art. The subjects are always noble and poetical, and the parts of them chosen for interpretation or illustration are musical, or at least within the reach of music. Saint-Säens rightly denies and ridicules the accusation that Liszt sought to set philosophical systems to music ; and stoutly maintains that he translated into music none but poetical ideas. However ready Liszt was to make use of the picturing of the outward as an auxiliary, the picturing of emotional impressions, states, and evolutions was his main object. Let us not overlook that if the painting of the outward is of the right things and of the right sort, it can stir the inward, can produce a powerful effect on the imagination and the emotions by association, analogy, and symbolism. The impression we receive from *Mazeppa* consists of something more than the perception of swift motion. But in making these remarks I do not mean to assert that Liszt's choice of subjects might not sometimes have been more wise, or, let us say, less risky. In programme music, subject and

music can never be quite coincident, quite concurrent—
if they could be, the programme would be superfluous—
but the difference in the extent, in the coincidence,
of the two had better not be too great. Again,
certain subjects—for instance such as the *Inferno* and
Prometheus—may demand an excessive sacrifice of the
beautiful to the characteristic.

Unquestionably and immeasurably more important,
however, than the question of choice of subject is the
question of the composer's creative endowment. No
wonder that opinions as to Liszt's vary infinitely,
and sometimes are as far apart as the south and
north poles. Lina Ramann sees in the master's
works nothing but what is sublime, perfect, and
incomparable ; to Hanslick, on the other hand, Liszt
was one of those natures, endowed with genius,
but sterile, who are impelled by artistic ambition to
mistake inclination for vocation. Few are likely to agree
with the uncritical raptures of the biographer or the
equally uncritical antipathies of the Vienna critic. Real
acquaintance and unbiassed examination will assuredly
lead to an intermediate position. Owing to the neglect
of the symphonist Liszt in the concert room, and the
prevailing prejudice against him, this position cannot,
however, be reached without taking the trouble to go
in search of him, and sympathetically, or at least with
an open mind, cultivating his acquaintance. Those who
have done so agree to a surprising degree in their
judgment of him—not in their estimate of the individual
works, but in their estimate of the total character and
value of his productions. Even the admiring and
thoroughly sympathetic friend and disciple Saint-Säens,
who holds that the symphonist Liszt is the great and

real Liszt, admits that although the master's works are immense, they are unequal, and that a selection has to be made. On the other hand, connoisseurs uninfluenced by personal bonds and artistic leanings, such as Riemann, Kretzschmar, Weingartner, Ambros, Lobe, and others, acknowledge Liszt's creative power while pointing out its limitations. Of a scornful rejection of his works, of a sneering at impotence, formlessness, &c., there is no trace in their utterances. Kretzschmar sees in the master's works freedom, daring, and sureness in the fundamental lines of the formal structure, and regards them as original achievements which represent an intellectual and artistic formative power of extraordinary force. But the same writer notes also that most of the symphonic poems approach in form the free fantasia so frequently employed by Liszt in his transcriptions and rhapsodies. Weingartner remarks that, as in Brahms a brooding reflective element, so in Liszt a rhapsodic one takes the upper hand; an improvising manner often bordering on incoherence (*Zerrissenheit*) being a characteristic of most of Liszt's works. In connection with these remarks on the rhapsodic nature of the master's compositions, we ought to note Riemann's just observation, that Liszt has an intensive feeling for logic.

On turning from the form to the matter, we meet with much more that is liable to objection. It is impossible not to perceive that his compositions are to a larger extent the result of excogitation than of spontaneity, and unduly influenced by his æsthetical views; nor can we fail to be struck by the exuberance of his style, which loves to display itself in a too flowery, over-emphatic, exclamatory, and not unfrequently bombastic, and even hollow rhetoric. Except that it is more

logical, his musical style is a pretty exact likeness of
his literary style. Indeed, we have here another
exemplification of the saying *le style c'est l'homme.*
'*Liszt*' writes Saint-Säens, '*est l'âme magyare, faite
d'un savoureux mélange de fierté, d'élégance native et
d'énergie sauvage.*' Yes, Magyar pride, native elegance,
and wild energy count for much in the character of
Liszt and his music. But although it counts for much,
it does not by any means count for all. Liszt was an
extraordinarily complex being, and full of irreconcilable
contrasts. The son of a Hungarian father was also the
son of a German mother; the man who at the most
impressionable period of his life came chiefly under the
influence of French culture, opened his mind and heart
also to the culture of Germany, of Italy, and to some
extent of England; the artist who believed in Beethoven,
Weber, Schubert, and Wagner, appreciated also Berlioz,
Chopin, and the Italian melodists. No wonder that
Liszt was an eclectic. Indeed, his style, although
swarming with individual mannerisms, is less homo-
geneous than the styles of most of the great composers.
The eclecticism of his melody has repeatedly been
pointed out, but not only there is it clearly perceptible.
Liszt, in writing to Brendel on September 7, 1863,
remarks, after referring to an axiom of the latter's
('the artistic nature, if it is genuine, corrects itself
as a consequence of contrasts') : — 'May it come
true with me! So much is certain, few have laboured
so much at the long-lasting business of self-correction
as I have, the process of intellectual development having
in my case been, if not impeded, made specially difficult
by so many various accidents and incidents. Twenty
years ago, a clever man said not inaptly to me:

"You really have to deal with three men in you who run counter to each other—the sociable salon man, the virtuoso, and the thinking and creating composer. If you manage properly one of the three, you may call yourself a lucky fellow."' But Liszt was not so simple a being as the clever individual made him out to be. Instead of three, he had at least half-a-dozen men contending within him. Besides those mentioned above, there were among others—the man of religion, the scheming diplomatist, the self-sacrificing friend, &c. The many volumes of his letters that have been published (letters addressed to Wagner, to H. von Bülow, to the Princess Wittgenstein, to an anonymous lady friend, to contemporaries of all sorts and conditions, &c., &c.) make that evident. Much may also be learned from his literary works; but in that connection it has to be remembered that others had often a hand in them—for instance, the Princess Wittgenstein was actually his collaborator.*

Liszt's greatest achievements are certainly the two symphonies. To me the *Faust* Symphony seems to be his most successful work, both for the freshness of the ideas and the clearness of the development. Others, however, prefer the *Dante* Symphony. Weingartner regards the latter as the acme of Liszt's productivity, as perhaps more harmonious (*einheitlich*) and powerful than

---

* On at least one occasion she was more than a collaborator. As Liszt told me himself, the much enlarged new edition of his *Chopin* was her work. He made some attempts at a revision; but they failed to please her. He then said to her: 'Do it yourself, and do whatever you like.' She was of course his partner in the writing of the first edition as she was in the writing of all his literary work done during their connection. All the fine writing about Poland is by her, who was a Pole. In view of these facts it is rather amusing to see the Princess's poetic outpourings quoted as the oracles of the genius Liszt.

Faust. Equally appreciative words come from Ambros, who calls it 'this grand, serious, and genuinely ethical work.' The majority of votes, however, are cast for *Faust.* Indeed, *Dante* is hardly ever performed; for which, no doubt, the nature of the first division is accountable. The purest forms in Liszt's symphonic compositions, according to Saint-Saëns, are *Gretchen* (Margaret, the second division of *Faust*), *Il Purgatorio* (the second division of *Dante*), and *Orpheus*, the fourth symphonic poem. General acceptance of this proposition may be expected. Most will also agree with the statement that *Hamlet*, *Prometheus*, and *Héroide funèbre* are the weakest of the twelve symphonic poems. As to the relative value of the others, I feel disinclined to express an opinion. It would be only adding another dissentient voice to the many that have already made themselves heard. *Les Préludes*, *Orpheus*, *Tasso*, *Mazeppa*, *Festklänge*, *Ideale*, *Ce qu'on entend sur la Montagne*, and *Hungaria*, are performed oftenest. Although Liszt's symphonic compositions have been before the public for about half-a-century, they have not become popular. I do not think that the verdict thus given will ever be reversed. Their shortcomings are too many and too serious; they contain far too much crudity, hollowness, and ugliness. But notwithstanding their inferiority in spontaneity, sobriety, and formal beauty, to the symphonies of the great classics, Liszt's works are too full of originality, *Geist*, enrapturing beauties, and striking expressiveness, to entirely deserve the neglect that has been their lot. Be, however, the ultimate fate of his works what it may, there will always remain to Liszt the fame of a daring striver, a fruitful originator, and a wide-ranging quickener.

CHAPTER III.

SIXTH PERIOD CONTINUED.

WAGNER.

Many a reader will be surprised to find Wagner in this company. Did he not condemn programme music, and denounce the insufficiency of instrumental music of the absolute kind? No doubt he did. But what decides a man's position? Is it what he says, or what he does? However, even apart from this question, and confining ourselves to what Wagner said, the case is by no means so simple as most people think. If it is difficult to present Berlioz's views on programme music in his own words, it is still more difficult to present Wagner's. But for a different reason. Berlioz wrote too little on the subject, Wagner too much. It is, however, the quality rather than the quantity that gives trouble. The various circumstances in which he expressed his opinion affected his voice, which at one time was trenchant, at another equivocal, and at a third somewhat conciliatory.

RICHARD WAGNER, born in 1813, received a good general education at the Dresden Kreuzschule, Leipzig Nicolaischule (both secondary schools), and Leipzig University. Although he was early attracted by and occupied himself with music, he had no training in the art until 1830, when he went through a half-year's course of harmony and counterpoint under Weinlig. The lessons he got in 1827 from Gottlieb Müller hardly count: they gave satisfaction neither to master nor pupil. Among the compositions written before his

studies with Weinlig there is an overture in B flat,
performed at the Leipzig Theatre in 1830, of which
Heinrich Dorn, the conductor, said, not without much
exaggeration, that 'it bore in it the germs of all those
grand effects which at a later date were to set the whole
musical world by the ears.' The compositions written
by Wagner under Weinlig's direction and for some time
after his tuition were of a more sober cast and had none
of the individual peculiarities described by Dorn. These
works comprised a sonata for pianoforte (1831), which
was printed; several overtures, one to Raupach's tragedy
King Enzio, and one entitled *Polonia* (1831 and 1832),
and a Symphony in C major, which was performed at
Prague and at the Leipzig Euterpe and Gewandhaus
concerts. At that time Wagner was under the spell
of Beethoven, but he had also a love for Mozart's
instrumental music, instilled into him by Weinlig.
His professional career began as chorus-master at
Würzburg (1833), and conductor at Magdeburg (1834),
Königsberg (1836), and Riga (1837). During this period
began also his career as a composer for the stage. In
1834 he composed, under the influence of Beethoven,
Weber, and Marschner, *Die Fœn*, an opera that remained
unperformed until 1888; and in 1835-1836, under the
influence of the modern French and Italians, *Das
Liebesverbot*, once performed in the latter year at
Magdeburg. Then followed the Paris episode (1839-
1842), with the disappointment of high hopes and the
suffering of great hardships. The performance of *Rienzi*,
an opera in the main fashioned after the Spontini and
Meyerbeer patterns, at the Dresden Court Theatre in
1842, his appointment there as conductor, the production
of his more and more original operas *The Flying Dutchman*

in 1843, and *Tannhäuser* in 1845, and the composition
of the still further advanced *Lohengrin*, seemed to open
a prospect of a most happy future. But the political
insurrection of 1849, in which Wagner was involved,
brought about a revolution in his career, leading in the
first place to his flight and banishment from Germany.
The next years of his life, spent, like many more, in
Switzerland, are chiefly notable for the publication of
æsthetical writings, in which he contends for a new art
and for new art-conditions. In the years 1849-1851
appeared *Art and Revolution, The Art-work of the Future,
Art and Climate, Opera and Drama*, and *A Communication
to my Friends*. After these theoretical discussions of
his ideas, he returns with renewed vigour to composition
—to the four parts of the *Ring des Nibelungen*, and
between them to *Tristan und Isolde* and *Die Meistersinger*
in which he realized his mature ideal, and to which he
added later on *Parsifal*.

When Wagner had resolutely set out on his career as
a dramatic composer, he entirely ceased to write
independent instrumental music. In the years 1835-
1836 he wrote two more overtures, entitled *Columbus* and
Rule, Britannia, and, lastly, in 1840-1841, the first
movement of a *Faust* Symphony, which after a revision
was subsequently published as *A Faust Overture*. I
said 'lastly,' although there is yet to be mentioned
another orchestral composition not connected with any
of his music-dramas, the *Siegfried Idyll* of 1870; but
this is an occasional composition and was originally
intended only for domestic use.

Before justifying my claim for Wagner as a composer
of programme music, in spite of the fewness of his
independent orchestral works, most of which, moreover,

are to all appearance of the absolute kind, we must make ourselves acquainted with his views on the matters bearing on this point. All, however, that can be done is to indicate the main features of these views, and to cull a striking remark here and there. To reproduce everything that bears directly and indirectly on the subject, and to sift the truths from the luxuriating sophisms, would require a book, not a few pages of a chapter. To the reader who is swayed rather by his logical than by his poetical faculty, Wagner's views of art, society, history, and biography, must seem a wonderful phantasmagoria in which reality appears strangely illuminated and irrecognizably distorted. The great poet-musician deludes himself and others the more easily by his sophisms as they are hidden under language abounding in allegories, personifications, similes, and metaphors. Almost all his statements are figurative, and for him figures carry with them conviction. To convince himself and others that the *Gesammtkunst* (the universal art, the union of all the arts) is the true and complete art, the art which ought to supersede the single arts, he argues that singly the human capacities are limited, but that united they are self-sufficient and unlimited. From this very questionable statement he jumps to the extraordinary conclusion that the lifeless, motionless single arts live only an artificial, borrowed life, and that, instead of giving, as in the triple union (dancing, music, and poetry), blessed laws, they receive coercive rules for mechanical movement. But whose logic is proof against the persuasiveness of the following poetical picture? 'As we gaze on this entrancing measure of the truest and noblest Muses of artistic man, at one time we see the three lovingly entwined; at another, this or that

one disengaging herself, as it were to show the others
her beautiful form in complete independence, merely
touching with her finger-tips the hands of the others;
again, the one, charmed by the sight of the double-form
of the closely entwined sisters, bowing before them; next,
the two, carried away by the charm of the one, greeting
her admiringly; until, at last, all three, firmly entwined,
breast to breast, limb to limb, grow in an ardent kiss
into one blissful living form. Such is the loving and
living, and the wooing and winning of art, of the one,
ever the same and ever different, separating in super-
abundant wealth, uniting in ineffable happiness. This
is the free art. The sweetly and strongly urging impulse
in this measure of the sisters is the impulse to freedom;
the love-kiss of the entwined, the bliss of the freedom
won. The solitary individual is unfree, because limited
and dependent in unlove; the associated individual is
free, because unlimited and independent through love.'
Love plays a busy part in Wagner's æsthetics, more
especially sexual love. Its principal appearance is in
the general definition of the characters of poetry and
music, which are respectively described as male and
female, as generative and conceptive. The dangers
of this enthusiastic fantastical rather than calm
philosophical (we could also say, this interested rather
than disinterested) treatment of æsthetics, must be
obvious. Unless the disciple searches for the logical
thread under every rose-bush and flowering shrub, he
cannot tell where he may be led to by his floriculturist
guide. A figure is never a proof, often a misrepresentation, and always a begging of the question.

After telling us that in the ancient Greek lyric and
dramatic art, poetry, music, and dancing were united,

Wagner proceeds thus : ' Just as in the building of the
Tower of Babel, when their speech became confounded
and mutual understanding impossible, the nations
separated in order to go severally their own way ; so,
when the national solidarity broke up into a thousand
egoistic peculiarities, the art species separated from the
proud heaven-scaling edifice of the drama, in which they
had sunk their common quickening understanding.'
Passing over the poet-musician's myths of the rise and
meaning of harmony and counterpoint, for an account
of which time and space are lacking, we proceed to a
more important matter.

According to Wagner the march and dance form is
the immovable foundation of all pure instrumental
music ; or, in other words of his, the basis of the
symphonic art-work is identical with the dance-tune.
' The overture and every other independent piece of
instrumental music owes its form to the dance or march ;
and a series of such pieces, as also a piece in which
several dance forms are combined, has been called a
symphony. The formal kernel of the symphony is still
in our day to be found in the third movement, the
minuet or scherzo, where it suddenly appears in the
greatest *naïveté;* to tell, as it were, the secret of all the
movements of the form.' Wagner protests that he does
not wish to depreciate the form, but it is nevertheless
with the intention of depreciation that he attaches the
stigma of dance and march music to everything that is
not Wagnerian dramatic music. He seems to say : ' Let
the instrumental composer do what he likes he can
produce nothing but the dance-like and march-like.'
Nay, even in the last years of his life he says quite
plainly that this basis of the symphony stamps the

character of Haydn's and Beethoven's works, which consist only of interlacements of ideal dance-figures, and bear throughout the character of a sublime serenity. We have here a strange confusion of ideas and misrepresentation of facts. No wonder that they lead Wagner into many contradictions. As there is a relationship between molluscs and vertebrates, so there is a relationship between dances and symphonies. Still the difference between them both in matter and form is very great. To give the true explanation of the resemblances between the little and the highly developed, we must say that they are different exemplifications of the same formal principles, principles derived from psychical laws that govern all independent music, *i.e.*, all music that is not a mere accompaniment of another art; principles which leave scope for infinite variety and do not interfere with the expression of any kind of content whatever. Moreover, is not Song as well as Dance one of the foundations of developed instrumental music ?

A few additional quotations will show still more distinctly that I am not wilfully misunderstanding Wagner.

' In Haydn's symphony the rhythmic dance melody moves with all the cheerful freshness of youth : its interlacements, dissolutions, and reunion, although executed with the greatest contrapuntal skill, nevertheless present themselves hardly as anything more than the result of such a skilful procedure, nay, rather as something in character like a dance regulated by imaginative [*phantasiereichen*] laws : so warmly are they suffused with the breath of joyous human life.'

' It was Beethoven who opened up the boundless capacity of music for the expression of the all-powerful

impelling and longing . . . . But if his faculty of
speech was boundless, so also was the longing which by
its eternal breath animated this speech. How, then,
proclaim the end, the satisfaction of this longing, in the
same language which was nothing but the expression of
this longing? . . . The transition from a mood of
infinite excitement and longing to one of joyous
satisfaction can necessarily not take place otherwise
than by the absorption of the longing in an object. In
accordance with the character of infinite longing, this
object can only be a finite one that presents itself
distinctly, both sensuously and ethically. . . . What
inimitable art did not Beethoven employ in his C minor
Symphony to steer his ship out of the sea of infinite
longing into the haven of fulfilment! He was able to
raise the capacity of music almost up to the expression
of moral resolve, but was not able actually to give
utterance to it . . . with reverent awe he avoided
throwing himself again into the sea of that unallayable
longing. He turned his steps towards the cheerful
happy people he saw encamped on the green meadow by
the fragrant wood under the sunny sky, frolicking,
kissing, and dancing [the sixth, the *Pastoral* Symphony]
. . . But these were mere " recollections " [one of
Beethoven's finally rejected titles ran : Pastoral
Symphony, or Recollections of Country Life], not the
immediate sensuous reality. Towards this reality he
was impelled with all the yearning natural to the artist.
. . . In the A major Symphony all the storm and
stress, all the longing and raging is turned into a blissful
exuberance of joy, which with bacchanalian omnipotence
carries us through all spaces of Nature, through all
rivers and seas of life, jubilantly self-conscious wherever

we tread the bold measure of this human sphere-dance. This symphony is the apotheosis of the dance itself: it is the dance in its noblest aspect, the most blissful act of bodily motion as it were ideally incorporated in tones. . . . From the shore of the dance Beethoven threw himself again into that infinite sea—from which once he had taken refuge on this shore —into the sea of unallayable heart-longing [the ninth, the Choral Symphony] . . . The last symphony is the redemption of music from her own peculiar element and her incorporation in the universal art. It is the human gospel of the art of the future. Beyond it no progress is possible; for upon it there can follow only the perfect art-work of the future, the universal drama [*das allgemeinsame Drama*], to which Beethoven has forged for us the key.'

Wagner's theory that Beethoven's ninth symphony was and must be the last symphony, that the master had recourse to the word because of the bankruptcy of absolute music, may easily be shown to be wrong in every sense and respect. Beethoven's own notes and opinions, and the subsequent history of the art, disprove its correctness. In writing to a publisher Beethoven refers to the work in question simply as 'a new grand symphony which has a finale with vocal solos and choruses on Schiller's immortal song to *Joy*, in the manner of the pianoforte Fantasia with Chorus (Op. 80), but much grander.' The master, then, did not look upon it as anything new or extraordinary, not as anything revolutionary and epoch-making. Czerny informs us even that Beethoven regarded the introduction of the choral element into the symphony as a mistake. Further, Beethoven, after the ninth symphony, began to

Y

sketch a tenth, and wrote several string quartets. So much for Beethoven. And what has happened since? The symphonies of Mendelssohn and Schumann, composed more than half a century ago, are still highly appreciated and greatly enjoyed; the symphonies of Brahms, although opinions differ in regard to their exact rank among the masterpieces of the kind, are looked upon by all but a minority of extreme partisans as noble works of art; the symphonies of Tchaikovsky, especially the *Pathetic*, have in recent years made a profound impression; Gade, Raff, Volkmann, Saint-Saëns, and many other great if not supreme artists have not lived or are not living in vain; more or less departing from the classical form, Berlioz and Liszt produced in former days, and Richard Strauss produces in our day symphonies and symphonic poems that cannot be set aside by the *ipse dictum* of a self-sufficient art-reformer and art-producer. Sganarelle's reply to his goldsmith friend rises to one's lips: ' *Vous êtes orfèvre, monsieur Josse.*' It is an everyday experience to hear artists depreciate their fellow-artists' works and ways. We must not allow ourselves to be befooled by their blind and narrow egoism. We must tell them that we are grateful for all the beautiful things they give us, but that we cannot forego the pleasures we receive from the beautiful things of others.

But let us look a little more closely into Wagner's ideas regarding instrumental music. ' That the expression of a quite definite, clearly intelligible individual content was in truth impossible in this language, which is capable only of expressing feelings in their generality, could not be detected until that instrumental composer appeared in whom the desire to express such a content became the consuming, ardent life-impulse of all his artistic creation. The history of instrumental music from the time this desire manifests itself is the history of an artistic error, which, however, did not end, like that of the operatic *genre*, with the demonstration of the incapacity of music, but with the manifestation of a boundless power. The error of Beethoven was that of Columbus, who merely meant to seek a new way to the old, already-known land of India, and discovered a new world instead.' After stating that the contemporaries and successors of Beethoven could not show the least inventiveness, Wagner remarks : ' Beethoven makes upon me the impression of a man who has something to say which he cannot clearly communicate ; his modern successors, on the other hand, appear as men who communicate to us, often in the most charming manner, that they have nothing to tell us.'

Wagner treats at length and on various occasions of Berlioz, but with such an extravagant fantasticalness, such a wild, irresponsible deliriousness, that it would serve no useful purpose to do more than just indicate the main points of his views. ' Berlioz is the immediate and most energetic offshoot of Beethoven on that side from which the latter turned away as soon as he proceeded from the sketch to the picture. Berlioz inherited from Beethoven almost nothing but the often hastily dashed-off daring and glaring strokes of the pen [later on described as ' strangely crabbed '] in which the latter noted down quickly and without critical selection [poor Beethoven !] his attempts at discovering new means of expression.' Although endowed with unusual musical intelligence, and always consumed by a truly artistic longing, Berlioz was soon lying ' hopelessly

buried beneath the confused mass of his machines.'
In short, Beethoven's symphonic successors are of no
account whatever, and Wagner begins where Beethoven
leaves off. The shortcomings of Beethoven as seen by
Wagner are most clearly revealed in the following
passage. ' In the works of the second half of his artist-
life, Beethoven is for the most part unintelligible—or
rather liable to be misunderstood—just where he wishes
to express most intelligibly a particular content. He
passes beyond the absolutely musical which by an
instinctive convention is acknowledged as comprehensible
(that is, beyond what has, in expression and form, some
recognizable similarity to dance and song), in order that
he may speak in a language which often appears to be an
arbitrary manifestation of a whim, and, lacking a purely
musical connection, is only bound by the bond of a poetic
intention, which could not, however, be expressed in
music with poetic distinctness. Most of Beethoven's
works of that period must be looked upon as instinctive
attempts to form a language for his longing, so that they
often seem to be like sketches for a picture, as to the
subject, but not as to the intelligible arrangement of
which the master had made up his mind.'

So far the reader has had presented to him Wagner's
opinions before Liszt produced his symphonies and
symphonic poems. Did he change them afterwards?
The answer to this is not easy. In his letters to Liszt,
Wagner is too busy with his own works and troubles to
occupy himself with those of his friend; but on several
occasions he speaks of Liszt's symphonic compositions,
and does so with a heartiness that leaves no doubt as to
his sincere admiration of them, and their stimulating
effect on him. On making the acquaintance of six of

Liszt's scores, he writes on July 12, 1856, that he
received from them the electrical shock which the grand
produces on us, and calls Liszt a wonderful man and a
unique phenomenon in the domain of art.   Urged by
the Princess Wittgenstein to make his opinion of Liszt's
symphonic works more fully and widely known, Wagner,
with great reluctance, wrote a letter to her intended for
publication, a letter which appeared as an article and as
a pamphlet in 1858.   Now this letter must give to the
unbiassed reader the impression of a politic equivocation.
The writer seems to have undertaken the task against
his inclination, for he says as little as possible about the
subject, and in this little studies, above all, ambiguity.
Of the sixteen pages not two are really concerned with
the works to which they are supposed to be devoted.
But here we are confronted by a curious complication.
When it comes to the ears of Wagner that people regard
the letter as 'evasive,' he is greatly surprised, and
inveighs against their incredible denseness, superficiality,
and triviality.   Nevertheless, if he did not wish to be
evasive, he ought to have blamed rather his own want of
explicitness and lucidity, and if he really wished to
approve of Liszt's symphonic poems, he ought not to
have forgotten them and their composer in his eagerness
to set forth his ideas about Liszt as an interpretative
artist, and about music and instrumental music in
general.   Here are the most important passages given
verbally or substantially : ' He who with irresistible
rapidity has made up his mind as to the worth of this
phenomenon, and the uncommon wealth of musical
power which confronts us in these compositions—
presented as it were by the wave of a magician's wand—
may again be bewildered by the form, and, his first

doubt having been about the possibility of our friend's vocation as a composer, be brought to a second doubt because of the unfamiliar.'—'I forgive everybody who has hitherto doubted the thriving of a new art-form of instrumental music, for I must own to having so fully shared that doubt as to join with those who saw in our programme music a most unsatisfactory phenomenon. In this connection I found myself in the droll position of being numbered with the programme musicians and of being thrown into the same pot with them.' From some of his curiously turned remarks we may extract the opinion that programme music is a legitimate *genre*, and Liszt's symphonic poems excellent works of art, good in form and admirable in content. But in no place does Wagner say so in plain words. With the exception of a reference to the genius shown by Liszt in the speaking distinctness of his musical conceptions, which manifests itself strikingly even in a few opening bars, all the straightforward praise is given to the virtuoso and musician generally. 'Do you know a musician who is more musical than Liszt? Who possesses the powers of music more abundantly and profoundly than he? Who feels more subtly and delicately?' &c. The only other unambiguous point in Wagner's letter is 'joyful admiration' of the invention of the happy designation 'symphonic poems,' which necessarily implies the invention of a new art-form.

If what has so far been noticed were the only utterances of Wagner on the subject, we might, notwithstanding their equivocalness, incline to the belief that the master's first opinion of instrumental music, and of programme music in particular, was altered by the achievements of Liszt. But there are later utterances, utterances of the last years of his life, which make it clear that there really was either no such change, or after such a change a reversion to his early position, or to somewhere very near it. A sentence like this : ' The extravagances to which Berlioz's demoniac genius led, were nobly subdued by Liszt's incomparably more artistic genius to the expression of unspeakable soul and world events '—may leave us in doubt. It is otherwise with the following sentences gathered from different parts of the same essay, that on the Application of Music to the Drama. These will elucidate his final ideas. ' The programmatic instrumental music, on which "we" used to look shyly and askance, brought much that was new in harmonization and in theatrical and pictorial (landscape and even historical) effects, and by means of an extraordinary virtuosic art of instrumentation accomplished all this with a striking pregnancy . . . . This tendency led to the gain of new capacities ; but it was seen that unspeakable aberrations, which threatened seriously to injure the genius of music, could be prevented from affecting the further course of the exploitation of these capacities only by the frank and resolute turning of this tendency to the drama.'

The importance of these remarks lies in the acknowledgment of the services of programme music in the development of the art, and the recognition of its serviceableness in the music-drama, where indeed Wagner has proved himself one of the most powerful, perhaps the most powerful composer of programme music. However much he repudiated his inclusion in the ranks of composers of programme music, he must nevertheless have a place assigned to him there. For his deeds rise against his words and convict him.

In reviewing these deeds we need not dwell on his
early instrumental works; and not only because they
have merely a biographical interest, but also because
they keep within the traditional grooves of absolute
music untinged or only slightly tinged by poetic
programmes.   Thus his symphony of 1832, the untitled
overtures of 1830 and 1831, and the *Rule, Britannia*
Overture of 1836, may be classed as strictly absolute
music: whereas the overture to the play *King Enzio* of
1832 and *Columbus* of 1835 had no doubt the kind of
programmatic character to be found in Beethoven's
overtures to plays.   Of the overture *Polonia* of 1832, we
know only that it was inspired by the heroism and
failure of the Polish insurrection that then engaged the
sympathy of Europe, and was brought near to the
composer and his fellow-citizens by the many distressed
fugitives that passed through Leipzig.   We cannot
consult the music of these overtures, and the available
information about them is scanty, vague, and even
contradictory.   Most of what we learn refers to *Columbus*.
This work has been described in contemporary criticism
as heterogeneous in its parts, Beethovenian in conception,
and modern, almost Belliniish in its externals, the
composer having made use of all possible sensational
and stimulating means (*Spectakel und Reizmittel*).   If
these remarks are by no means luminous as to the
general nature of the composition, they leave us in
almost complete darkness as to its programmatic
nature.   The only glimmer of light is in the expression
' Beethovenian conception.'

Apart from these early works of merely biographical
notability, there are among Wagner's works only two
orchestral compositions unconnected with his dramas—

A Faust Overture (written in 1840, and re-written in 1855) and the *Siegfried Idyll* (1871). Of the former and more important of these, which came into existence in Paris in January, 1840, Wagner relates : 'From my profoundly dissatisfied inner self I bore up against the repugnant reaction of the external artistic activity [attempts at French lyrics] by the rapid sketch of an orchestral piece which I called an overture to Goethe's *Faust*, but which was to be really only the first movement of a great *Faust* symphony.' The rest of the history of the overture can be traced in the Wagner-Liszt correspondence, where also a clear and satisfactory account of the composer's intention is to be found. In 1848 Wagner sends the overture to Liszt at the latter's desire, but says that he no longer likes it. From a letter of Liszt's, dated October 7, 1852, we learn that he had performed the overture and intended to do so again, that he thinks it worthy of Wagner, but that he could welcome either a second middle section or a quieter, more sweetly-coloured treatment of the middle section—a contrast, something tender, something Margaret-like being desirable. In replying to these remarks on November 9, 1852, Wagner furnishes a complete programme of the work : 'You have found me out in telling a lie when I tried to make you believe that I had written an overture to *Faust*. Very rightly you have felt what is wanting—the woman. No doubt you would at once understand my tone-poem if I called it Faust in Solitude.' He then relates that his original intention was to write a whole Faust symphony, and that the first movement was the 'solitary' Faust, in his longing, despairing, and blaspheming, the *womanly* hovering before him only as an image of his longing, not in its

divine reality, and it is this insufficient picture of his
longing which he despairingly dashes to pieces.'
The second movement, he goes on to say, was to
introduce Gretchen, the woman. 'I had already the
theme—but it was only a theme. The whole was
abandoned—I wrote my *Flying Dutchman.*' Although
Wagner did not see his way to accepting Liszt's advice
and introducing the woman, he was alive to the necessity
of a revision. Instigated by the completion of Liszt's
Faust Symphony, he set about this work in 1855. He
wrote a wholly new score, with new instrumentation and
an expansion and weighting of the middle part (second
motive), by which the mood is more fully developed.
The composer called the work now *A Faust Overture*, and
adopted as a motto the following lines from Goethe's
poem:

'The God that in my breast is owned
Can deeply stir the inner sources;
The God, above my powers enthroned,
He cannot change external forces.
So, by the burden of my days oppressed,
Death is desired, and Life a thing unblest!'

The above is from a letter dated Zurich, January 19,
1855.

In a letter written a few days later, he says 'there
cannot be any question of Gretchen, but always only of
Faust himself:

"A sweet uncomprehended yearning
Drove forth my feet through woods and meadows
free."'

The overture was published with the title and motto
given in the above cited letter of January 19, 1855.

In Wagner's *Faust* Overture we have then an objective character picture.* In the *Siegfried Idyll*, we have a subjective mood picture. The latter composition, written soon after the completion of the music-drama *Siegfried* and a year or two after the birth of his son Siegfried, was intended as an aubade for his wife's birthday in 1871. The prefixed dedicatory verses to her may be said to be the programme. At any rate some of its lines indicate the spirit and meaning of the work clearly enough. They tell us that by this music the composer gives thanks for wife and son, and that in it the serenity of the existence he then enjoyed becomes tone. They tell us also of the intermingling of life and art, of love and labour, a reflection of which is seen in the material out of which the composition is evolved—on the one hand, a popular South German cradle song (*Schlaf, Kindchen, balde, Vöglein flieg'n im Walde*), and, on the other hand, peace and love motives from *Siegfried*. 'My son and my work,' says Wagner in a letter of his, 'are thriving together.' In short, the *Siegfried Idyll* is a waking dream woven of past joys, present happiness, and future hopes.

We next have to consider the introductory pieces—overtures and preludes—prefixed to Wagner's dramatic works. Leaving out of account the two early attempts, *Die Feen* and *Das Liebesverbot*, and also passing by *Rienzi* (the overture to which is effective enough, but not sufficiently poetic), we come to three compositions of which the composer himself wrote exhaustive interpretations (he calls them Programmatic Elucidations) intended for concert purposes — namely, the overture to the

---

* As the composer, no doubt, identifies himself with Faust, the objectivity may be said to be a subjectivized one.

Flying Dutchman and *Tannhäuser* and the prelude to *Lohengrin*. The object of the master's remarks on the first of these pieces is, however, not so much to give an exposition of the overture and tell the hearer exactly what he will find there, as to set forth the subject of the opera and thus put the hearer in a position to understand and appreciate the orchestral introduction. A somewhat abridged translation will suffice.

'The Flying Dutchman's dreadful ship scours along storm-driven; it makes for the land and lays-to where its master has been promised to find salvation and redemption. We hear the pitying strains of this annunciation of salvation, which sounds to us like prayer and lament. Sombre and without hope the doomed man listens to them; weary and longing for death he steps ashore, whilst the crew, faint and tired of life, bring the ship to rest. How often has the unhappy man gone through the same experience! How often has he steered his ship through the ocean billows to the inhabited shore, where once every seven years it is permitted him to land! How often did he imagine that he had reached the end of his torments! And ah, how often, woefully disappointed, had he to set out again and recommence his frantic ranging of the ocean . . . . The terrors of the sea, at which, in his thirst for wild adventures he used to laugh, now laugh at him. They cannot harm him. He has a charmed life and is doomed to rove the ocean desert for treasures that afford him no satisfaction, and never to find what alone could redeem him. . . . From the depth of his misery he calls for redemption. In the horrible solitude of his existence only a woman can bring him salvation. Where, in what land, does the deliverer dwell? Where is the feeling heart that beats for sufferings such as his? Where is she who does not flee from him with fear and trembling, like those cowardly men who terrified cross themselves at his approach? A ray of light breaks through the night. It pierces his tormented soul like lightning. It is extinguished. It flashes again. The seaman keeps his eye fixed on the loadstar, and stoutly steers towards it through flood and wave. What so powerfully draws him is a woman's look, full of sublime pity and divine sympathy. A heart has unlocked its unfathomable depth to the immense sufferings of the cursed man. It must sacrifice itself for him, break out of compassion, in order to annihilate at the same time itself and his sufferings. At the sight of this divine apparition the unhappy man breaks down, dashed in pieces like his ship. But while the latter is engulfed by the sea, he rises from the waves healed and holy, led by her who victoriously saved him to the dawn of sublimest love.'

In the Programmatic Elucidation of the *Tannhäuser* Overture we have a real setting forth of the contents of the piece. Everything in the programme appears clearly, fully, and in the same order in the music. The programme is so excellent in every respect that long as it is, it must be given in its entirety.

'At the beginning the orchestra lets us hear the song of the pilgrims: it approaches, swells into a mighty outburst, and at last passes away.—Evening twilight: dying sounds of the song. It is nightfall, and magic lights and sounds steal on our senses: a rosy mist rises, voluptuous sounds of jubilation reach our ears; confused movements of a weirdly lustful dance become visible. These are the seductive spells of the Venusberg

which at dead of night manifest themselves to those
in whose breast burns the fire of sensual desire.—
Attracted by the alluring vision, a tall, manly form
approaches : it is Tannhäuser, the minstrel. He
intones his proud, jubilant love-song, joyous and
challenging, as if to draw to himself the voluptuous
enchantment by compulsion. Wild shouts of joy
answer him : the rosy cloud grows more dense
around him, entrancing perfumes envelop him and
intoxicate his senses. Now he perceives before him,
reclining in seductive twilight, an unspeakably lovely
female form. He hears the voice which, sweetly thrilling,
hails him with the siren call that promises the darer the
satisfaction of his wildest wishes. It is Venus herself
who has appeared to him. Then heart and senses burn,
a glowing, consuming longing inflames the blood in his
veins : he is impelled with irresistible force to approach,
and before the goddess herself he now, in the utmost
ecstasy, intones his jubilant love song in her praise. As
it were by this magic call, the wonders of the Venusberg
open before him in all their brilliance : tumultuous
jubilation and wild, voluptuous cries arise on all sides : in
drunken exultation the Bacchantes come noisily rushing
up, and, tearing Tannhäuser along with them in their
furious dance, lead him into the arms of Venus, who
embraces him, and carries him along with her into
unapproachable distances, into the realm of non-existence
[*des Nichtmehrseins*]. A hubbub passes like the Wild
Hunt, and soon after the storm subsides. Only a
voluptuous wailing is still whirring in the air, and a weird
whispering, like the breath of unblessed sensual love,
hovers over the place where the entrancing, unholy
enchantment manifested itself, and over which night

now again spreads her wings. But morning already begins to dawn: from afar is heard once more the approaching pilgrims' song. As this song comes nearer and nearer, as advancing day dispels night, the whirring and whispering in the air, which before sounded like the woeful lamentation of the damned, rises to a more and more joyful billowing, until at last, when the sun appears in his splendour, and the pilgrims' song with mighty enthusiasm proclaims salvation to all the world, and all that is and lives, the billowing swells into a blissful outburst [*Rauschen*] of sublime ecstasy. It is the jubilation of the Venusberg itself, redeemed from the curse of unholiness, which we hear in the song. Thus move and leap all the pulses of life to the song of redemption; and the two divided elements, spirit and sense, God and Nature, embrace each other for the holy uniting kiss of love.'

Leaving out all the rest of the Elucidation of the *Lohengrin* prelude, the strictly expository part of the contents of the piece, the subject of which is the Descent of the Holy Grail (the precious vessel used at the Last Supper, and in which the crucified Saviour's blood was preserved), runs thus:

' To the entranced gaze of highest supermundane love-longing, the serenest blue celestial ether seems at first to condense itself into a wonderful vision, hardly visible and yet magically captivating the eye: in infinitely tender lines, gradually growing in distinctness, the miracle-ministering host of angels appears, descending imperceptibly from on high with the holy vessel in their midst. As the vision becomes more and more distinct and moves more and more visibly towards the earth, intoxicatingly sweet perfumes are exhaled

from it : entrancing vapours flow down in golden clouds,
captivate the beholder's senses, and fill his thrilling
heart to its inmost depth with a wondrous devotional
emotion.   Now blissful pain, now fearful happy joy darts
through his breast; all its suppressed germs of love,
awakened to a wonderful growth by the vivifying spell,
swell out with irresistible might—but, expand though it
may, it is near to bursting with mighty longing, with the
impulse to self-sacrifice and dissolution, such as human
hearts had never felt before.   And yet this feeling revels
again in the highest and happiest joy, when, approaching
closer and closer, the divine apparition displays itself
before the glorified senses.   And when at last the
holy vessel itself in its miraculous reality, nakedly
and plainly, is presented to the sight of those deemed
worthy; when the Grail sends forth far and wide the
sun-rays of sublime love, like the effulgence of a
heavenly fire, so that all hearts within the radiance of
the eternal glow tremble : then the gazer's senses fail
him, he sinks down in adoring annihilation.   But upon
him, lost in the blissfulness of love, the Grail now pours
its blessing, with which it consecrates him as its
knight : the shining flames become subdued to a milder
glory, which now spreads over the earthly valley like a
breath of unspeakable delight and tender emotion, and
fills the adorer's breast with never-divined blissfulness.
In chaste joy the host of angels, looking down smilingly,
soar upward again : the fountain of love, dried up on
earth, they have brought anew to the world ; the Grail
they have left behind in the keeping of pure men, into
whose hearts its contents had poured themselves as a
blessing : and the noble host disappear in the brightest
light of the celestial ether, whence they had descended.'

Who, after reading these Programmatic Elucidations, can help smiling at Wagner's disclaimer of being a composer of programme music? But even if he had not written them, and had not left programmatic sketches of three other compositions, his authorship of the Programmatic Elucidations of Gluck's Overture to *Iphigenia in Aulis,* and Beethoven's *Heroic* and *Choral* Symphonies and *Coriolanus* Overture would rule him out of court as a witness against programme music. Moreover the *Faust* Overture and what he says about it in his letters are alone sufficient to preclude the admissibility of a plea of 'not guilty.' All this, however, is nothing compared with what an examination of his music dramas discloses, especially of those in which he has most fully realized his ideals, namely, the *post-Lohengrin* ones. As the form of the programme—whether it is printed, spoken, sung, pantomimed, painted, &c.—does not matter, seeing that it cannot affect the nature of the music, one is driven to ask : 'What is the music of these dramas but programme music?' For the programme music is not only in the overtures, preludes, and purely orchestral interludes, but throughout the whole extent of the dramas, which indeed may be described as orchestral symphonies with accompanying vocal, pantomimic, and scenic programmes, only here and there interspersed with orchestrally accompanied recitatives. To declare that these symphonies are merely cunning but unmeaning combinations of tones, that they have only æsthetical, not emotional and intellectual significance, would be doing the composer a great injustice, an injustice which he himself would have repelled with greater vigour than anyone else could do. We noticed that Wagner acknowledged the indebtedness of the

z

composers of music-dramas to the composers of orchestral music with verbal programmes. In fact, his position seems to have been that the objectionableness of music with a programme disappears when the programme is the action of a drama, when it consists of the words and gestures of the *dramatis personæ*, the stage scenery, and the representation of elemental and other conditions and occurrences. Without sharing Wagner's prejudice against other kinds, one may readily admit that his programme music, in which what is heard and seen on the stage supplements the expression of the inward and the description of the outward in the orchestra, is not only a legitimate but also a very beautiful kind. Or, to look at it from the usual and more correct point of view, we might say that the programme music in which the transactions in the orchestra supplement those on the stage is also a beautiful kind. The argument in favour of this kind is of course that the constant companionship of the several arts makes the mutual perfecting of their several imperfections at any moment possible. Against it may be adduced that combination necessarily entails limitation of individual freedom.

In Wagner's music-dramas we find all kinds of tone-painting. To select a few from thousands of examples of external tone-painting, both direct (*i.e.*, of things audible) and indirect (*i.e.*, of other things—visible, &c.—by analogy), I may mention: the uncouthness of the giants; the winding insidiousness of Loge, whose element is the flames; the hammering of the dwellers in Nibelheim; mist, thunder, and rainbow (*Rheingold*); —the storm; the ride of the Walkyries; the crackling, sparkling, and flickering of the fire-spell (*Walküre*);—

Siegfried's forging of the sword, with its puffing of the
bellows, hammering, hissing of the hot iron in water,
&c.; the forest sounds of the *Waldweben;* and the
crawling and bellowing of the dragon (*Siegfried*).   Then
we have the depicting of the supernatural by strangeness
of tonal combinations, be it by extraordinary highness,
lowness, softness, or loudness, or by extraordinary
harmonies, melody, or tone colour.   Striking and
familiar examples are the Venusberg witchery in
Tannhäuser, the Grail vision in *Lohengrin*, and the
Tarnhelm spell in the *Ring of the Nibelung*.   But of far
greater importance than the external tone-painting is
the internal tone-painting, the picturing of the moods,
emotions, and thoughts of the *dramatis personæ*, which
indeed forms the bulk of the whole music.   As of this
kind almost every page is full, it would serve no useful
purpose to give examples.   To convince himself that
there is painting not only of stationary moods and
general, clearly-defined emotions, but also of the subtlest
psychological processes, the reader may be referred to
two among innumerable instances—the opening scene of
the first act of *Die Walküre*, and the opening of the third
scene of the last act of *Die Götterdämmerung*.   In the
latter the dreams and forebodings of Gutrune afford an
excellent opportunity for a most effective and poetical
utilization of *Leitmotive* (guiding, *i.e.* characteristic,
motives).   Of these *Leitmotive* it may be said that, if
aptly and sparingly used, they are a valuable enrichment
of the resources of the art, but that, if too lavishly used,
they fetter the spontaneity of the composer, and overtask
the receptivity of the hearer.   Although not the inventor
of the contrivance, Wagner was the originator of its
systematization as we find it in his later music-dramas,

where these recurring characteristic motives play an important part both as means of expression and in the texture of the style, where indeed musical composition assumes more and more the form of a network of *Leitmotive.*

When words and actions accompany the music, they form of course the programme, that is, explain what the music leaves unexplained. In the case of interludes, such as the Dead March in *Die Götterdämmerung*, *Waldweben* in *Siegfried*, and the Good Friday Spell in *Parsifal*, the key is furnished by what was said or done before, or is going on during the performance of the interludial music. But how about the music before the raising of the curtain? If the overtures and preludes have a meaning, as Wagner's certainly have, we must look for the programme in what follows. Accordingly we find that the preludial matter does one of two things : (1) it gives a summary of the main features or the gist of the whole drama, or (2) forms only an introduction to the first scene of the following act. Now, is it not inconsistent to say that absolute music is helpless, and then use it as if it were helpful? We may indeed assume that Wagner in writing programmes to the overtures to *The Flying Dutchman* and *Tannhäuser*, and to the prelude to *Lohengrin*, confessed his inconsistence. I note this inconsistence for the purpose not of blaming the composer, but of regretting that he did not do as much for every one of his preludial compositions. Fortunately programmatic sketches have been found among the master's papers (published in the posthumous volume of his writings—*Entwürfe, Gedanken, Fragmente*) of the preludes to *Tristan und Isolde*, *Parsifal*, and the third act of *Die Meistersinger*. The last of these, perhaps more than anything else, throws much light on his methods and his position as a composer of programme music.

Of the four parts of the *Ring of the Nibelung*, the fourth, *Die Götterdämmerung*, is preceded by only a few bars forming an integral portion of the scene of the Norns, which itself is a prelude to the drama proper. The longer instrumental prelude to *Siegfried* depicts the musing of Mime, who is first on the scene. This piece is extremely interesting, but requires either a programme or a careful study of the whole tetralogy. The prelude to *Die Walküre* is a grand and fear-inspiring storm, which really belongs to the action of the first scene. Have we to regard the prelude to *Das Rheingold* as an introduction to the following sub-fluvial scenes, or as a basis of the tragic action of the whole tetralogy and presentation of a profound philosophical idea? Hans von Wolzogen writes : ' The introduction consists of a colossal pedal point on E flat, the long-sustained solitary fundamental tone of which at the beginning symbolizes that primeval state of perfect rest and undisturbed unity. The joining of the equally-sustained fifth to the fundamental tone forms the transition from this purely musical symbolism to the musical representation of the mythical symbolism, that is, the representation of the primeval state as the primeval water element.' And so on in a way that may not be so clear as one could wish. But whatever view be preferred, the prelude, which from beginning to end has only one harmony, the tonic-triad of E flat major, is both as an appropriate introduction and as a composition a wonderful feat. It grows from the undeveloped to the more and more developed, from darkness to light, from uniform dulness to varicoloured splendour, and fills the hearer with a feeling of inexplicable mystery, with a divination of awakening life in the watery element.

Leaving undiscussed the preludes to other acts than the first, though some offer great temptation, I proceed to the three pieces we hear so frequently at concerts. They are examples of the kind that give a summary of the main features, or the gist of the whole drama to which they are prefixed. Thus the *Meistersinger* overture brings before us the Mastersingers' Guild, their proud banner, the bustle of festive Nürnberg, and amidst all this the love-making of Walther and Eva. Wagner's remarks on this composition in his pamphlet *On Conducting*, although they are not programmatic, will be read with advantage. Among the significant hints is that of the passionate, clandestinely-whispered declaration of love (melody in E major).

In the prelude to *Tristan und Isolde* there is unfolded a picture of the principal phases of the hero and heroine's romantic love—its ardent longing, death-defiance, and ecstasy. Here are the main portions of Wagner's sketch. '. . . world, power, fame, splendour, chivalry, fidelity, friendship, all are gone, only one thing still remains: Longing, longing unquenchable, ever anew self-begetting desire—languishing and thirsting; the sole redemption—death, extinction, never-awakening. . . . As the theme could not possibly be exhausted, the musician lets the insatiable desire swell out only once, but in a long articulated train, from the bashful confession, the most tender devotion, through timid sighing, hoping, and fearing, lamenting and wishing, rapture and torments, to the most violent efforts, in

order to find the breach which would open for the heart
the way into the ocean of infinite love bliss.   In vain !
Fainting the heart droops, to languish in longing, in
longing without attaining, as every attaining produces
only new longing, until in the last prostration the
presentiment of the highest bliss of attainment dawns
upon the dying eye : it is the bliss of dying, of being no
more, of the last redemption, the passing into that
wonderful realm from which we swerve farthest when
most violently striving to enter it.   Shall we call it
death ?   Or is it the nocturnal wonder-world, out of
which, as the legend has it, the ivy and the vine grow up
in close embrace on the grave of Tristan und Isolde ? '

Divine love forms the subject of the prelude to *Parsifal*.
The motives on which the composition is based are taken
from the scene of the Love Feast of the Knights of the
Grail.   The words connected with the three motives,
the second of which is only briefly referred to, explain
the character of the contents.   Here they are in the
order in which they occur in the prelude.   ' Take my body
and eat; take and drink my blood.   Thus be our love
remembered.'   ' Uncover the Grail.'   ' His love endures,
the dove up-soars, the Saviour's sacred token.   Take the
wine red, for you 'twas shed ; let Bread of Life be broken.'
In the poet-musician's sketch, from which I shall now
quote, only the first and the last of these motives are
noticed.   The two themes are respectively entitled
' Love ' and ' Faith.'   The strains of music connected
with the words ' Take my blood, take my blood, for our
love's sake ! ' and ' Take my blood, take my body that
you may remember me,' are each separately repeated by
angels' voices floating away.   The second theme sets
forth promise of redemption through faith.

'Faith declares itself firmly and pithily, increased, willing even in suffering. To the renewed promise responds faith, soaring down from the most ethereal heights—as if on the wings of the white dove—occupying the human heart more and more largely and fully, filling the world, the whole of nature, with mightiest strength, then again gently calmed, glancing upward towards the celestial ether. And now once more the plaint of loving compassion rises from out the awe of solitude. The fear, the holy agony of the Mount of Olives, the divine sorrow of Golgotha—the body grows pale, the blood flows forth, and now begins to shine the heavenly blissful glow in the cup, pouring out over all that lives and suffers the joy of the divine grace of the redemption by love. . . . Once more we hear the promise, and—hope.'

After examining his case as we have done, it is impossible to evade the conclusion that if Wagner is not one of the band of composers of programme music, he bears an extraordinary resemblance to them. Another conclusion from which we cannot escape is that he learned something from the earlier composers of programme music, and that the later ones learned and may still learn a great deal from him. About whatever else we choose to dispute, we must be at one about this: that Wagner immensely increased the expressional resources of music, indeed increased them more than any musician before him. Though his powerful and wonderful attempt at a solution of the insolvable operatic problem may pass like a fashion, slowly adopted and for a time passionately followed, the instrumental portions of his dramatic works, whether descriptive of the outward or expressive of the inward, will live, and long outlive the vocal portions. Even when all Wagner's compositions

shall have ceased to be performed, he will still continue
to live in the art; for the discoverer of so many new
tonal expressions for the intensities and subtleties of
emotion, for the sweetness, brilliancy, and awfulness
of natural phenomena, and for the magnificent display of
the pride and pomp of gods and men, cannot die with
his works. If you like a paradox, consider this : Would
not the dramatist Wagner have been a composer of
pure instrumental music, if he had not confessedly been
in need of a strong external impulse whenever he wished
to do his best ?

BOOK V.

CONTEMPORARIES AND SUCCESSORS OF THE
PROGRAMMATIC PROTAGONISTS OF THE LAST TWO
PERIODS (1830-1900).

CHAPTER I.

IN FRANCE.

The new ideas, forms, and methods of Berlioz, Liszt,
and Wagner did not put an end to the old ideas, forms,
and methods.   But although programme music in the
classical forms continued to be cultivated side by side
with programme music in freer forms, it could not but
become in the course of time more and more influenced
by the new views and processes.   And as the later style
of programme music influenced the earlier, so both these
kinds of instrumental music influenced absolute instrumental music, bringing about either an actual diminution
of absoluteness, or the semblance of such, that is, the
composer either having an unrevealed programme in his
mind or deporting himself as if he had.   In the latter
case, where there is mere aimless parroting of language
regardless of meaning, the outcome is of course lamentable.
To such composers rightly applies Wagner's taunt that
they adorn themselves with the feathers fallen from the
programmatic storm-birds.

Perhaps the best way of making the vast survey
indicated in the title is to have recourse to a grouping
by nationalities.   An exhaustive enumeration of all that
has been written, which would be equally useless and

impossible, is of course not intended. Indeed, nothing
more is aimed at than a general view of the state of
matters obtaining during the period in question. I shall
confine myself to pure instrumental music, and as a rule
not further refer to operas, oratorios, &c. Choral symphonies and symphonic odes cannot however be excluded.

Let us begin with France. Cultivation of dramatic
music still largely preponderates there over that of every
other kind. But during the last three or four decades
of the 19th century the French, both the composers and
the public, have shown an increasing interest in pure
instrumental, especially orchestral music. As late as
1858 Berlioz wrote that there were then only two
societies in Paris that concerned themselves with high-
class concert music—the one was the old Société des
Concerts du Conservatoire, and the other the very young
Société des Jeunes Artistes, the latter conducted by
Pasdeloup. These two societies gave fortnightly concerts
for only three or three and a-half months of the year.
In addition to them, Berlioz thought, might be mentioned
Arban's Promenade Concerts with mixed programmes.
All of these, however, cultivated the old recognized
classics. Pasdeloup used to say to the complaining
young French composers : ' Write symphonies as good as
those of Beethoven, and we will perform them.' Two
earlier promoters of orchestral music ought not to be
forgotten — Valentino, the founder and conductor of
Popular Classical Concerts (from 1837 to about 1840),
and Seghers, the founder and conductor of the Société
Sainte Cécile (1849-1854), who introduced Schubert and
Schumann to the Parisians. In 1861 Pasdeloup founded
the Concerts Populaires de Musique classique, and in
1871 Colonne the Concert National, which afterwards

became the Association Artistique. The large towns of the provinces followed the example of the metropolis, and the opportunities thus afforded to composers of hearing instrumental music and getting works of their own performed stimulated them to greater activity.

In accordance with the national bent the French show a decided predilection for the dramatic and the picturesque in pure instrumental as in other music. Untitled overtures and symphonies, especially symphonies, are of extreme rareness. Very rare also are sonatas, trios, quartets and other chamber music. Picturesque suites, impressions, scenes, and rhapsodies, interspersed with a picturesque symphony here and there—these are the kind of things that abound among the instrumental productions.

The most notable French masters of orchestral music next to Berlioz are Félicien David, César Franck, and Saint-Saëns. That a composer of so little pith as FÉLICIEN DAVID (1810-1876), a producer of so few decidedly successful works, should have made the impression and exercised the influence he did is strange, although not inexplicable. He brought to market certain talents and experiences just at the right psychological moment. After being a choir-boy, pupil of a Jesuit College, apprentice in a lawyer's office, and student at the Paris Conservatoire, he joined the Saint-Simonians, and in 1833, when the sect was judicially broken up, went with some other members as an apostle of Saint-Simonianism to the East. From Turkey, the first stage of his Eastern travels, he was expelled and deported to Smyrna, next he proceeded to Egypt, travelling as far as the Red Sea, thence traversed the desert to Beirout, took ship there, and returned to France in 1835. He now published *Mélodies Orientales*, collected by him on his travels, and several *Romances*, some of which pleased, and composed a symphony and string quintets. But it was not till 1844 that he emerged from obscurity. On December 8 of that year he gave in the Salle du Conservatoire a concert of his compositions, concluding with *Le Désert*, a composition denominated symphonic ode (*ode-symphonique*). It was this work that made him famous. There have been few successes like it. Schumann began his often-quoted first criticism of Chopin with : 'Hats off, gentlemen, a genius.' Maurice Bourges opened his report of David's concert in the *Revue et Gazette Musicale* in similar terms : 'Room, gentlemen, room! Open your ranks! Give way! Once more, room, large and comfortable! For see here : a great composer is born to us, a man of singular power, of an extraordinary stamp, one of those rare talents that fascinate at one stroke a whole audience, that rouse them imperiously, master them, force from them cries of enthusiasm, and achieve in less than two hours an astounding popularity.' The writer assures the reader that there is no exaggeration in his statements, and confidently predicts that the composer of this original score will thenceforth sparkle in the musical pleiads of the century, and perhaps be the dominating star in it. Distinguished critic as Bourges was, and estimable composer as he proved himself, we may hesitate to accept this as the general judgment. The opinion of one man, be he ever so competent and sincere, proves nothing. But this was not a one man opinion, but the practically unanimous opinion of Paris. In the present case no musician's opinion can be more interesting than that of Berlioz, which was as enthusiastic as Bourges's. ' If there were

in Paris a lyrical Pantheon exclusively consecrated to the
representation of monumental masterpieces,' he wrote in
Les Débats of December 15, 1844, 'this Pantheon would
have been illuminated last Sunday up to the top, for a
great composer had just appeared, and a masterpiece had
just been unveiled.' He addressed 'the new poet' thus:
'Yes, David, what you have done is very grand, very
new, very noble, and very beautiful. We came to hear
you with absolute impartiality, without prejudice, with
coolness, without any idea of what was before us; and
we were struck with admiration, touched, carried away,
overwhelmed. You called forth acclamations, tears, and
that commotion of the soul, whose surface talent can
ruffle, but which genius alone can shake down to the
bottom.'

When in the following year Félicien David gave concerts
in Germany and Austria, he met with great success, at
least as far as the public was concerned. The composer
himself says in a letter addressed to a Leipzig friend that
the success of his six concerts at Vienna fulfilled all his
wishes; and that if the critics differed from the public,
it was no doubt because he did not bribe them. An
examination of some of these adverse criticisms
shows, however, that the composer was mistaken. For
although they may have accentuated rather the
weak than the strong points of David's work, they
certainly indicated weaknesses that really existed. Also
on leading musicians the French master made a good
impression. Mendelssohn is said to have been pleased
with David's second Symphony, in E flat major,
which was performed at his concerts along with
Le Désert; and Schumann is said to have spoken
of the latter work with 'surprising commendation.'

Hauptmann voices very well the opinion of the majority of the more thoughtful musicians of the time, and also that of the critics, when he writes: 'Félicien David's *Le Désert* is rather pretty, and I like to defend it against those who try to make out that it is naught. It lacks elaboration. To make such a thing depends not so much on merit as on natural disposition. On the one hand, it is much more agreeable to be moved lightly than to be tormented by an inflated style; but, on the other hand, one does not care to hear anything of this sort again and again, like a quartet of Haydn or a sonata or fugue of Bach. It is a pretty mood out of which nothing further can come than what one gets the first time.' The simultaneous presence of Berlioz and David at Vienna gave rise to a good epigram : Berlioz is a genius without talent, David a talent without genius.

To turn from opinions about the thing to the thing itself. The symphonic ode *Le Désert* consists of a series of musical scenes introduced and connected by spoken words; the interpretative media being a reciter, an orchestra, a chorus, and solo voices. The work is divided into three parts : the first presents the desert in its silent infinitude, the approach of the caravan, a storm, restored calm and resumption of the march; the second part, the desert at night, recreations, and meditation; the third part, the desert at sunrise and departure of the caravan. It is the orchestral pieces and accompaniments, not the hymns and songs, that interest us in our present inquiry, and of them less the orientally coloured march, dances, and Arab fantasia, than the picturing of the desert silence, the storm, and the sunrise, although the influence exercised by the former was not less than that exercised by the latter. Let us hear what Berlioz has to say about the last three points. 'The stringed instruments sound softly a sustained tone, which by being prolonged without end, without movement, without harmony, without *nuances*, produces immediately in the mind of the hearer the image of the desert. Here [after some words of the reciter] the orchestra exhales some vague snatches of melody, then falls back into its vague immobility.' As to the storm, in which orchestra and chorus co-operate, 'it is as beautiful as the storm in Beethoven's *Pastoral* Symphony. The author has shown there that he knew the orchestra as well as anyone in the world, and that he was its master. It is impossible better to direct, increase, and let loose the instrumental tempest. This *ensemble* is overwhelming without ceasing to be harmonious.' One cannot but be unwilling to disagree with such an expert in these things as Berlioz, but the comparison with Beethoven is inadmissible—the storm in the *Pastoral* Symphony is a more developed and more interesting composition, and above all is much more musical. And now we come to the most remarkable and successful piece of tone-painting, the sunrise, where very rightly, and yet for the first time, the increase and the spreading of light is rendered by the increase and the spreading of sound. Here is Berlioz's description: 'An imperceptible extremely high tremolo of one violin part; a *crescendo;* entrance of a second violin part trembling like the first; entrance of a third, of wind-instruments, of the whole orchestra; torrents of harmony; *voilà le jour!* ' And the critic adds: '*Ah, oui! voilà le jour!* and the whole audience rose to greet it, without thinking of the systematic anathemas of the adversaries of imitative harmony.' It has to be added that David makes use in *Le Désert* of many Oriental melodies. Indeed, there were not a few who said that these borrowed strains were the only good things in the work. Chopin was one of them, and certainly cannot be counted with the believers in the new prophet.

In 1847, Félicien David produced a second symphonic ode, entitled *Christophe Colomb*, but not with the same success. In France it was received without enthusiasm, in other countries it was ignored, and everywhere it was soon forgotten. The parts that pleased most were those in which he more or less repeated the effects of *Le Désert*. The economy of this second symphonic ode is exactly like that of the first. There are four parts : Departure, Night in the Tropics (including a storm), Revolt, and Arrival, or the New World. The resemblance with the earlier work made itself chiefly felt in the second part.

In short, David was a poet, but his powers were very limited. Within the range of them were, on the one hand, tender sentiment and vague sweet dreaming, and, on the other hand, picturesqueness. But with regard to the latter, it cannot be overlooked that it was restricted to certain kinds. The two great successes of his career were the symphonic ode *Le Désert* and the opera *Lalla Rookh* (1862), both of which are Oriental. He lacked the dramatic vein and vigour generally. Hence the failure of his oratorios and the moderate success of his other operas. The length of my account may seem out of proportion with the importance of the master's achievements. This is so no doubt if we look only to the present, but perhaps not if we look also to the past. In the history of the picturesque, especially of national colouring, Félicien David plays an important part, most notably of course in France.

2 A

Of the two other principal French masters of instrumental music, CAMILLE SAINT-SAËNS (*b.* 1835) is not the first born, but the one who first succeeded in winning the ear of the public. In him we have a more many-sided personality than in Félicien David, a man of greater intellectual vigour, and a musician of a more solid and extensive professional training. But along with these excellencies there goes a defect, a want on the emotional side. One is tempted to say that his music has not only the glitter, but also the hardness of steel. At any rate, it is the dazzling qualities of mind rather than the touching qualities of heart that make his music what it is.

Saint-Saëns has a great admiration and affection for Berlioz, and a still greater admiration and affection for Liszt. But this has not prevented him from perceiving Berlioz's shortcomings, and from saying of Liszt that, seen in its totality, his output as a composer seems immense but unequal, that a selection has to be made among his works. But his admiration for this master is very great indeed. What he admires especially is the striking expressiveness, the marvellously rich orchestration, and the abounding melodiousness of his music. He looks upon the Liszt of the post-virtuoso career as the grand and true Liszt. And let us note this. Liszt's symphonic poems showed Saint-Saëns the way, as he himself tells us, to where later on he met with his own *Danse Macabre* and *Rouet d'Omphale*. The younger composer was not content with admiring, but made in France propaganda for the older unpopular master's music, indeed, so strenuously that Liszt feared it had retarded his champion's nomination for the Institut. We should however be led astray if we were to conclude from these facts as to the nature of the French master's music. For his four symphonic poems as well as his other compositions are in form and character different from Liszt's. And this difference arises not merely from his different individuality, but also and chiefly from his thorough study of the classics, Bach included. Before writing symphonic poems, Saint-Saëns wrote chamber music and four symphonies, only two of which have been printed; and after the four symphonic poems, he wrote more chamber music and symphonies. In his early symphonies he is mainly under the influence of Beethoven and Mendelssohn. To their influence that of Schumann is soon added. The habits and taste in form and development thus induced were never fundamentally affected by the later influence of Berlioz and Liszt. And this holds good of the two later symphonies, which in some respects differ from the traditional form.

Now let us examine Saint-Saëns's programmes. They are so short that they may be given in full.

The first of the four symphonic poems is the *Rouet d'Omphale*, Op. 31 (1872), which originally was a Rondo for pianoforte.

'The subject of his symphonic poem is feminine seductiveness, the triumphant contest of feebleness against strength. The spinning wheel is merely a pretext, chosen only for the sake of the rhythm and the general turn of the piece.

'Those interested in the examination of details will see on p. 19 (letter J) of the score, Hercules groaning in the bonds which he cannot break, and on p. 32 (letter L) Omphale mocking at the vain efforts of the hero.'

The second symphonic poem is *Phaéton*, Op. 39 (1873).

'Phaeton got permission to drive in heaven the chariot of the Sun, his father. But his unskilled hands made the horses go astray. The flamboyant chariot, thrown out of its course, approached the terrestrial regions. The whole universe is about to be set on fire when Jupiter strikes the imprudent Phaeton with his thunderbolt.'

The third symphonic poem is the *Danse Macabre* (Dance of Death), Op. 40 (1875), after a poem by Henri Cazalis. The following twelve lines of the poem are prefixed to the composition :

Zig et Zig et Zig, la Mort en cadence
Frappant une tombe avec son talon,
La Mort à minuit joue un air de danse,
Zig et Zig et Zag, sur son violon.

Le vent d'hiver souffle, et la nuit est sombre ;
Des gémissements sortent des tilleuls ;
Les squelettes blancs vont à travers l'ombre,
Courant et sautant sous leurs grands linceuls.

Zig et Zig et Zig, chacun se trémousse,
On entend claquer les os des danseurs.

 . . . . . .

 . . . . . .

Mais psit ! tout à coup on quitte la ronde,
On se pousse, on fuit, le coq a chanté !

 . . . . . .

 . . . . . .

The fourth symphonic poem is *La Jeunesse d'Hercule,* Op. 50 (1877).

'Legend.—Mythology relates that on entering life Hercules saw opening before him two paths—the path of pleasure, and the path of virtue.

' Unmoved by the seductions of the Nymphs and Bacchantes, the hero enters the road of struggles and combats, at the end of which he sees through the flames of the pyre immortality as a reward.'

Three of the four symphonic poems consist either, like the *Danse Macabre*, of a single logically developed movement, or, like the *Rouet* and *Phaéton*, of such a single movement preceded by a short introduction. What the composer intended to express is in these cases clearly stated in the programmes. *La Jeunesse d'Hercule*, on the other hand, consists of an uninterrupted series of movements, and has a more complex and ambitious programme. Not to be unjust to the composer and court disappointment for ourselves, we must look upon Saint-Saëns's symphonic poems as illustrations, not as translations of the programmes. The *Rouet d'Omphale* is an illustration of feminine grace, charm, and mockery; the *Dance of Death*, far from being a terrifying sermon such as the artists of mediæval and later times delighted in painting, is a *jeu d'esprit*, in spite of the rattling bones strangely piquant, not repellently gruesome; *Phaéton* is a magnificent spectacle of light, motion, and final crash, ruin, and extinction; and the *Youth of Hercules* is a succession of mood pictures that may be indicated thus : irresolution (short *Andante sostenuto*, C), character of the path of virtue (a longer *Allegro moderato*, C), seductiveness of the Nymphs (*Andantino*, 9/8), allurements of the Bacchantes (a long *Allegro*, ¢), questionings (short *Adagio*, C), choice of the path of virtue and consequent struggles (*Andante sostenuto* and *Allegro animato*, resuming and developing at length the subject-matter of the second movement), and the funeral pyre and immortality beyond (*Maestoso*, C).

If we read Saint-Saëns's programmes carefully we see that they do not deal with subjects that necessarily call for a profoundly emotional treatment. And if we listen carefully to his music, we find that the composer remains on or near the surface. In short, Saint-Saëns is intellectual rather than emotional, brilliant rather than profound, astonishes rather than thrills, handles with virtuosity his materials rather than the hearts of his auditors. To complete this account there have still to be mentioned certain works for the most part of the national-picturesque kind—*Suite Algérienne*, Op. 60, and *Rhapsodie d'Auvergne*, Op. 73, for orchestra, *Africa*, fantasia for pianoforte and orchestra; and the following publications for pianoforte alone : *Koenig Harald Harfagar*, ballad after Heine (*à quatre mains*), *Romances sans paroles*, *Souvenir d'Italie*, *Les cloches du Soir*, *Caprice Arabe*, and *Souvenir d'Ismaïlia*.

Although France was behind other countries in fully recognizing Saint-Saëns's powers, she did so at last. The composer to whom we shall now turn our attention had not even this belated comfort. CÉSAR FRANCK (1822-1890), a Belgian by birth and a Frenchman by professional training and long residence, remained in obscurity well-nigh all his life, and both abroad and at home. The patriotic nationalism roused by the Franco-German war, which did so much for the reputation of some of the French musicians, did but little for Franck. Since his death, however, his reputation has been spreading, and may to-day be considered as established. The world is now beginning to know him as a master distinguished by solidity, seriousness, and originality, and to look upon him as one of the great composers of choral-orchestral and chamber music. His *Béatitudes* and sonata for violin and pianoforte may be regarded as added to the current concert *répertoire*. Whether the purely orchestral works will likewise come to the front remains yet to be seen. We have here to record the existence of three symphonic poems for orchestra, a titled symphony for orchestra and choruses, and a *poème-symphonie* for solo, chorus, and orchestra. In addition to, and after these works, César Franck composed also an untitled symphony. Here are short accounts of the first five compositions.

Les Éolides (The daughters of Æolus—composed 1876, performed 1877), a symphonic poem, is a delicate airy movement consistently worked out, which has as a programme the following lines of Leconte de Lisle:—

> O brises flottantes des cieux,
> Du beau printemps douces haleines,
> Qui, de baisers capricieux,
> Caressez les monts et les plaines,
> Vierges, filles d'Éole, amantes de la paix,
> La nature éternelle à vos chansons s'éveille.

Le Chasseur maudit (The wild Huntsman—Composed 1883, performed 1884) is a symphonic poem founded on Bürger's ballad *Der Wilde Jäger* (see Walter Scott's imitation, *The Wild Huntsman*). The illustration of this subject demanded, of course, colours very different from those employed in *Les Éolides ;* and César Franck had them on his palette. The contents of the four divisions of the work are indicated by the four paragraphs of the programme.

' It was Sunday morning ; from afar sounded the joyous sound of the bells and the joyous songs of the people . . . Sacrilege ! The wild Count of the Rhine has wound his horn.

'The chase dashes through cornfields, brakes, and meadows. — Stop, Count, I pray, hear the pious songs.—No! And the horsemen rush onward like the whirlwind.

'Suddenly the Count is alone; his horse will go no farther; he blows his horn, and the horn sounds no longer . . . A lugubrious implacable voice curses him :—" Sacrilege ! " it says, " thou shalt be for ever hunted through hell."

'Then flames dart from everywhere . . . The Count, maddened by terror, flees, quicker and quicker, pursued by a pack of devils.'

In *Les Djinns* (Evil spirits of Arab Mythology— composed 1884; performed 1885) the composer employs a pianoforte as well as the usual orchestral instruments —a by no means happy combination, as the hammer instrument does not blend with the bow and wind instruments. Notwithstanding the changes from 2-4 to 3-4 time, this symphonic poem, like *Les Éolides*, is a one-movement composition consistently developed. The programme is not prefixed, it has to be looked for in Victor Hugo's poem (one of *Les Orientales*) to which the title refers. César Franck depicts here the approach, presence, and disappearance of the horrible swarm of Djinns, the hideous army of vampires and dragons, driven by the north wind, that fill the air with infernal cries, howls, and groans, and pass whirling, and whistling, shivering the yew-trees, and all but overthrowing the strongest dwellings.

Psyché (composed 1884; performed 1890), a symphony for orchestra and choruses, contains besides a Prelude, entitled Sleep of Psyche, the following orchestral parts: the Abduction of Psyche by the Zephyrs, Joy of Nature in the Gardens of Eros, Love Scene, Sufferings of Psyche after her disobedience, and Psyche after her pardon.

One other composition of César Franck's remains yet to be commented upon, the Prelude to the second part of *Rédemption*, a work written for solo, chorus, and orchestra, and called a *poème-symphonie*. The Prelude of 1872 was re-written in 1885. The programme runs as follows: ' The centuries pass. Joy of the world, which transforms itself and expands under the word of Christ. In vain the era of persecutions opens, Faith triumphs over all obstacles. But the modern hour has struck. Belief is lost; man, once more a prey to the fierce desire for pleasure, for sterile agitations, has found the passions of another age.'

However noble a piece of music César Franck has produced in this prelude, his programme here exceeds the bounds of musical expression. But be this as it may, I am convinced that the reputation of this composer has not yet reached the highest point which it is destined to reach. Still, too much must not be expected in the case of a composer of his highly reflective, profoundly thoughtful, and reconditely artistic nature.

Besides Berlioz, Félicien David, Saint-Saëns, and César Franck, there lived in France during the last sixty years of the 19th century a considerable number of composers that have made notable contributions to the department of orchestral music; but with them I must deal summarily, although the quantity and quality of their productions might well justify a more detailed and reasoned treatment. If what I give is a catalogue, it is not a dull one; for nothing could be more varied and suggestive. My first task will be to enumerate some of the most important titled symphonies, overtures, and suites, music to plays, symphonic poems, dramatic symphonies, and symphonic odes. And in conclusion a few notes ought to be added on ballets and mimodramas, two forms of musical composition in which the French have not only been supreme, but also originators and leaders. LOUIS LACOMBE (1818-1884) composed besides *Sappho*, a melodrama with choruses, two choral symphonies, *Manfred* and *Ava;* ERNST REYER (*b.* 1823), *Le Sélam*, a symphonic ode (1850) in the style of David's *Le Désert;* EDWARD LALO (1823 - 1892), a *Symphonie espagnole*, *Fantaisie norvégienne*, and *Concerto russe* for violin and orchestra, a *Rhapsodie norvégienne* for orchestra, and characteristic pianoforte pieces; PAUL LACOMBE (*b.* 1837), a symphonic legend and a pastoral suite; THÉODORE DUBOIS (1837-1871), a symphonic poem *Notre Dame de la Mer* and overture *Frithjof;* GEORGES BIZET (1838-1875), an overture *Patrie*, music to Daudet's play *L'Arlésienne*, made into two suites, and the suites *Roma* and *Jeux d'Enfance;* RENÉ DE BOISDEFFRE (*b.* 1838), *Scènes champêtres;* VICTORIN DE JONCIÈRE (*b.* 1839), a *Symphonie romantique*, choral symphony *La Mer*, *Hungarian Serenade*, suite *Les Nubiennes*, music to *Hamlet*, and *Li Tsin (chinoiserie);* EMANUEL CHABRIER (1841-1894), a *Spanish Rhapsody;* JULES MASSENET (*b.* 1842), a symphonic poem *Visions*, symphonic fantasia *Pompeia*, overture *Phèdre*, music to Leconte de Lisle's *Les Erynnies*, *Scènes pittoresques*, *Scènes dramatiques*, and other suites (*Hungarian*, &c.); AUGUSTA MARY ANN HOLMÈS (1847-1894—of Irish extraction), symphonies *Orlando furioso*, *Lutèce*, and *Les Argonauts*, and symphonic poems *Irlande* and *Pologne;* BENJAMIN GODARD (1849-1895),

a *Legendary*, a *Gothic*, and an *Oriental* symphony, a
dramatic symphony, *Tasso*, for soli, chorus, and orchestra,
and *Scènes poétiques;* VINCENT D'INDY (*b.* 1851),
Wallenstein, a symphonic poem (called a Trilogy,
consisting of three separate parts entitled *Wallenstein's
Camp* [*Allegro giusto*] *Max and Thekla* [*Andante,
Allegro*], and *Wallenstein's Death* [*Très large, Allegro,
Maestoso*]), *Jean Hunyade*, a symphony, *Saugefleuri*, an
orchestral legend, *La Forêt enchantée*, a symphonic
ballad, *Istar*, symphonic variations (illustrative of a story
from the Babylonian epic Izdabar), the overture to *Antony
and Cleopatra*, and the suite *Tableaux de Voyage;* PAUL
and LUCIEN HILLEMACHER (resp. *b.* 1852 and 1860),
a symphonic poem *Les Solitudes*, and a suite *The Golden
Wedding;* FERNAND DE LA TOMBELLE (*b.* 1854),
Impressions nationales, *Livre d'images*, *Suite féodale;*
ALFRED BRUNEAU (*b.* 1857), a symphonic poem for
voices and orchestra, *Penthésilée;* PIERRE DE
BRÉVILLE (1861), a symphonic poem, *December
Night*, and overture to Maeterlinck's *Princesse Maleine;*
CHARLES DEBUSSY (1862), *Prélude de l'après-midi
d'un Faune* (to Mallarmé's poem), and the orchestral
pieces *Nuages* and *Fêtes;* and GUSTAVE CHAR-
PENTIER (*b.* 1868), *Impression d'Italie, Les Fleurs du
Mal* (after Baudelaire), and the symphonic drama
La Vie du Poëte.

From the above enumeration the reader cannot but
have seen that by far the larger part of these compositions
are rather on than within the borders of programme
music. Among the composers of programme music in
the full sense of the term, VINCENT D'INDY, DEBUSSY,
and CHARPENTIER engage more especially our attention. All three are moderns of the moderns, and all

three divide critical opinion. Vincent d'Indy, the most solid, is also the one most in touch with the old. Debussy, on the other hand, aims at making music as different as possible from anything it has ever been—he aims not at gradual development, but at a cataclysmic revolution. Melody, harmony, rhythm, form, everything has to go into the melting-pot. Debussy's position is that of an ultra-impressionist. He rejects all the old forms, Wagner's included, and is the most radical of the youngest French school, who say : 'We want free speech in free music, infinite melody, infinite variation, and freedom of musical phrase. We want the triumph of natural, free, plastic, and rhythmical music.' As this is not a book of present-day criticism, but of history, it shall be left to the future to pronounce judgment. *Qui vivra verra.*

The programmatic nature of the music to pantomimic ballets is often overlooked and yet is obvious. The libretti of such ballets call for expressive music even more clamorously than opera libretti. Musically well provided ballets have therefore appropriately been dubbed *symphonies dansées.* If we survey the ballet literature of the time we are concerned with, we shall find admirable specimens in AMBROISE THOMAS's *Betty* (1846) and *La Tempête* (1889), Reyer's *Sakountala* (1858), LÉO DELIBES's *Copélia* (1870) and *Sylvia* (1876), WIDOR's *Korrigane* (1880), LALO's *Namouna* (1882), and DUBOIS's *La Farandole* (1883). Closely connected with the pantomimic ballet is the mimodrama, the play without words, where the actors have to make themselves understood by gestures and facial expression. Here have to be named with distinction ANDRÉ WORMSER's *L'Enfant Prodigue,* and RAOUL PUGNO's *Pour le Drapeau.*

CHAPTER II.

IN BELGIUM, ITALY, GREAT BRITAIN, AND AMERICA.

Between the music of Belgium and that of France there is similarity and dissimilarity. The mixture of races and languages in the former country accounts for both. It accounts also for the preponderance of absolute over programmatic and picturesque instrumental music. In recent times Belgium has not in a marked degree drawn on herself the attention of the world by musical works, at least not by larger instrumental compositions. This statement, however, does not imply a denial of the production of much that is estimable and even noteworthy. JOSEPH JANSSENS (1801-1835), a pupil of Lesueur, interests us as an early cultivator of programme music in Belgium. He composed a symphony *Le Lever du Soleil.* Of those that come after him may be noted ADOLPHE SAMUEL (1824-1898) and his choral symphony *Christus* and orchestral suite *Roland à Roncevaux;* PETER BENOIT (*b.* 1834) and his choral symphonies the *Reapers* and *Hucbald,* and his music to the plays *Charlotte Corday* and *William of Orange;* THEODORE RADOUX (*b.* 1835) and his symphonic tone-pictures *Ahasuérus* and *Le Festin de Balthazar;* J. B. VAN EEDEN (*b.* 1842) and his symphonic poem *La Lutte au XVIᵉ Siècle;* JAN BLOCKX (*b.* 1851) and his overture *Rubens;* SILVAIN DUPUIS (*b.* 1856) and his symphonic poem *Macbeth;* and PAUL GILSON (*b.* 1865) and his symphony *La Mer.*

There is much difference as to the proportionate amount of programme music produced by the different countries. To consider only the three that for a long time have been looked upon as the chief music producers. The sensuous Italians keep aloof from programme music; the intellectual French cultivate it with predilection; and the sentimental Germans occupy an intermediate position. Race plays an important part in this matter. Of course in Italy we find a dearth of all kinds of instrumental music since the days of the great violin schools. The most notable master in the 19th century known also outside Italy was ANTONIO BAZZINI (1818-1897), a violin virtuoso as well as a composer of a great variety of music, and for many years the head of the Milan conservatorio. Among his works are a symphonic poem *Francesca da Rimini,* a choral symphony *Senacheribbo,* and overtures to Shakespeare's *King Lear* and Alfieri's *Saul.* Strange to say, GIOVANNI SGAMBATI (*b.* 1843), a pupil of Liszt, has given to the world not symphonic poems, but absolute music in the form of chamber music and untitled symphonies. Of programmatic and picturesque contributions of latter-day composers it will suffice to mention an Italian Rhapsody by ETTORE PINELLI (*b.* 1843); *In the Heidelberg Castle,* a suite by EUGENIO PIRANI (*b.* 1852); and *Leonore,* a symphonic poem by ANTONIO SMAREGLIA (*b.* 1854). In GIUSEPPE MARTUCCI (*b.* 1856), one of the most important of Italian instrumental composers, we have again a composer of absolute music.

A composer who hardly wrote any pure instrumental music at all ought nevertheless to find a place here on account of much of the orchestral matter in his later operas. I mean of course GIUSEPPE VERDI

(1813-1901), the greatest Italian composer of the second half of the 19th century, and one of the foremost European masters. His career is remarkable for the unique range of continuous development. What a distance from *Nabucco, I Lombardi,* and *Ernani,* to *Aida, Othello,* and *Falstaff!* Verdi, who did not lag behind Time, assimilated much; but it was real assimilation, not mere adoption, and moreover assimilation by a powerful, masterful organization. You can never say Verdi imitated this, that, or the other composer. But, no doubt, he learned from many.

From Italy to Great Britain is a tremendous leap. Here we are in an altogether different atmosphere, among a people that with regard to music has had a history, and tastes, views, and ways totally unlike those of the southern people. This, however, is by no means tantamount to saying that England is unmusical, as foreigners used to be inclined to think. But it must be admitted that these foreigners had some excuse, for, like *bonus Homerus,* good old England has at times been found nodding. The last English musician mentioned in this book was Henry Purcell, who died towards the end of the 17th century. The 18th century, which produced good anthems, glees, and ballads, was barren or nearly so in other respects. Of orchestral music it gave us nothing notable, of clavier music little. Without fear of losing anything we, who are in quest of programme music, may pass straight on to the 19th century. The first interesting composer we meet is WILLIAM STERNDALE BENNETT (1816-1875). Has it ever been observed that his music has none of the qualities that are generally regarded as peculiarly English, for instance, a certain sturdiness? The fact is, the qualities of his music are the outcome of his individuality, and not of a nationality, be it his own or any other. No one has spoken with more affection, enthusiasm, and insight of Bennett than Schumann, who calls him an out-and-out Englishman, a poetic, beautiful soul, an angel of a musician, a superb artist, and finds in his music beauty of form, depth, and clearness, and ideal purity.* Bennett's titled productions comprise four overtures—*Parisina*, Op. 3, *The Naiads*, Op. 15, *The Wood Nymph*, Op. 20, and the fantasy-overture *Paradise and the Peri*, Op. 42, music to Sophocles's *Ajax*, Op. 45, and two works for pianoforte. Of the four overtures the second and third are the most famous. They are known all the world over, and are standing items of the classical concert *répertoire*. As they are the *ne plus ultra* of grace, delicacy, and sweetness, this is not surprising. Schumann says of Op. 15 that it needs not much imagination to think, while hearing it, of playful bathing naiads. As to Op. 20 he would have preferred the title *Pastoral Overture* to that of *Wood Nymph*, but he had no doubt that the composition breathed the purest and brightest poetic life. The fantasy-overture *Paradise and the Peri* engages our special interest by its having not only a title but also a somewhat more explicit programme in the form of short quotations from Thomas Moore's poem. These quotations are prefixed to the several continuous parts of the

* Schumann's boundless enthusiasm, however, was never universally shared. Even his devoted Clara positively declined to agree with her beloved on this point. Indeed there were many, especially among the disciples of the new German school, notably Hans von Bülow, who thought Schumann's estimate greatly, nay, ridiculously exaggerated. The lack of robustness and passionate emotionalism in Bennett's music no doubt account for the difference of opinion.

composition, which has not the orthodox overture form, but is divided into an Introduction and three Scenes. The poetic mottoes are as follows :—

INTRODUCTION.

'One morn a Peri at the gate
Of Eden stood, disconsolate.'

FIRST SCENE.

'While thus she mus'd, her pinions fann'd
The air of that sweet Indian land,
Whose air is balm ; whose ocean spreads
O'er coral banks and amber beds.'

SECOND SCENE.

'Her first fond hope of Eden blighted,
Now among Afric's Lunar Mountains,
Far to the South, the Peri lighted.'

THIRD SCENE.

'But nought can charm the luckless Peri ;
Her soul is sad—her wings are weary.

.   .   .   .

Yet haply there may lie conceal'd
Beneath those chambers of the Sun

.   .   .   .

The charm, that can restore so soon,
An erring spirit to the skies.'

One of the two or three works for pianoforte to be considered here is Op. 10, *Three Musical Sketches*, respectively entitled *Lake*, *Mill-stream*, and *Fountain*, which, says Schumann, are, as regards colouring, truth to nature, and poetic conception, genuine Claude Lorraines in music—living, sounding landscapes. In fact, the great critic and composer held that as to

2 B

tenderness and *naïveté* of presentation they surpassed
everything he knew of *genre* painting, and that, like a
genuine poet, Bennett had caught nature in some of her
most musical scenes. Only in one of his pianoforte
compositions, as also only in one of his orchestral
compositions, does the English master add more than a
title.   The exception is the pianoforte sonate Op. 46,
which bears the title *The Maid of Orleans,* and the four
movements of which have both special titles and one
or two or three lines from Schiller's play prefixed to
them—one movement, the third, having also a special
motto for its second subject.

(1.) *In the Fields.*

' In innocence I led my sheep
Adown the mountain's silent steep.'

(2.) *In the Field.*

' The clanging trumpets sound, the chargers
rear,
And the loud war-cry thunders in my ear.'

(3.) *In Prison.*

(*a*)   ' Hear me, O God, in mine extremity,
In fervent supplication up to thee ;
Up to Thy heaven above I send my soul.'

(*b*)   ' When on my native hills I drove my herd,
Then was I happy as in Paradise.'

(4.) *The End.*

' Brief is the sorrow, endless is the joy.'

The hater of programme music need neither stand off,
nor approach Bennett's works with suspicion ; for even
in the sonata the composer does not allow the programme
to interfere with the classical qualities of the form.

Moreover, those four sonata movements are neither more nor less than four character- and mood-pictures. Unfortunately it has to be added that *The Maid of Orleans* is not a happy example of Bennett's art.

From Schumann's writings may be gathered an additional piece of information regarding Bennett as a composer of programme music. The critic says of the Romance in G minor of the third Concerto, Op. 9, in C minor : ' Even without knowing, as I did know from the poet himself, that, while composing, he had in his mind the idea of a female sleep-walker, every feeling heart must at the performance have experienced all that is touching in such a scene. As if afraid to awake the dreamer on the high roof, no one dared to breathe ; and if sympathy in some passages was, so to speak, anxious, it was softened by the beauty of the vision into artistic enjoyment. And here occurred that wonderful chord, where the sleep-walker, out of all danger, seems as it were reposing on a couch illumined by the rays of the moon. This happy trait determined one's opinion of the artist, and in the last movement one abandoned oneself undisturbed to the pleasure to which the master has accustomed us, whether he leads us to war or peace.'

In conclusion it may yet be mentioned that among Bennett's unpublished compositions are two overtures entitled *The Merry Wives of Windsor* and *Marie du Bois.*

GEORGE ALEXANDER MACFARREN (1813-1887), who, although born three years before Bennett, gained his reputation later, had more of the typical Englishman in his character and music. In the matter of programme music Beethoven's was also Macfarren's standpoint. He himself writes : ' Beethoven's purpose . . . was

to give utterance to impressions rather than to present
pictures, and such is the legitimate scope of music,
which is not an imitative but an expressive art.' We
have to take account here only of Macfarren's concert
overtures *The Merchant of Venice, Romeo and Juliet,
Chevy Chase, Don Carlos*, and *Hamlet*. These are noble
themes. But how is it that these works are so entirely
neglected and forgotten? Do they really deserve this
fate? Or does the neglect arise from a caprice of taste,
from a change of fashion? It is a pleasure to remember
that Hans von Bülow, the progressive and slashing, and
at the same time impulsive and capricious critic, said
in 1877 of the conservative Macfarren: 'The present
Nestor-representative of English music is in Germany
undeservedly far less known than his predecessor [as
Principal of the Royal Academy of Music], the friend
and pupil [not pupil] of Mendelssohn, Sir William
Sterndale Bennett . . . . He is a composer that
should not be ignored on the Continent . . . . His
is perhaps a less finely polished musical nature than
Bennett's, but one more sympathetic to me personally,
because healthier, more muscular, more rich in colour,
more sanguine. There is nothing hysterical, molluscous,
and nebulous in his music; on the other hand there is
in it pregnant expression, concise form, and pronounced
individuality, not without originality. Although he is
an Englishman, I should like to describe him in contradistinction to Bennett as a Scotchman.' This account
of Macfarren as a composer of programme music would
not be complete without a specimen or two of his
programmes. The master's synopsis of the intent and
purpose of his overture to *Romeo and Juliet* runs as
follows :

' The following points of the play suggested this
Overture : The Montagues and Capulets—the Nurse—
the Lovers and their passion—Mercutio—the Feud—the
Interdiction—Mercutio wounded—the entombment of
Juliet—Romeo at the Grave—the catastrophe.'

A longer analysis of his overture to *Hamlet*, Macfarren
wrote for the programme of a concert of the New
Philharmonic Society (1856) :

' This Overture was suggested by the following points
in the tragedy : Hamlet's melancholy—aggravated by
the frivolities of the court—yielding to his love of
Ophelia—his foreboding of the purpose of the ghost's
visitation—the ghost's appearance to him—he addresses
it—the spirit of the murdered king reveals the secret of
his death, and exhorts his son to avenge him—he
adjures his companions not to relate what they have
seen, and the ghost invisible calls upon them to swear—
this awful scene is opposed by the revelry of the court—
in the midst of this, the ghost's revelation is ever
present to Hamlet—it distracts him from his love of
Ophelia—the scene with her in the gallery—the play-
scene, where his melancholy is disguised under the
pretence of riotous gaiety—the scene with the queen in
the closet, where, urged by the same intention that
prepared him for the ghost's disclosure, he presses upon
her the subject of his melancholy—the frivolity of the
court again obtrudes itself upon him—he leaves for
England, thinking of Ophelia and of the ghost—he
returns, remembering her love, to learn of her madness
and her death—this excites him for the present time to
action—in the midst of his phrensy he remembers the
ghost's exhortation—the cause of his melancholy, which
has always made him a passive reflector, is now his

motive for desperate action—the last scene, where he dies, knowing the ghost's admonition to be fulfilled.'

In HENRY HUGO PIERSON (1815-1873), an Englishman who settled in Germany, we meet a more decided programmatist. Besides oratorios, operas, and other works, he wrote overtures entitled *As you like it, Romeo and Juliet, Julius Caesar,* and *Romantic,* a symphonic poem *Macbeth,* and music to the second part of Goethe's *Faust.* With the last-mentioned work he obtained his greatest success; in *Macbeth* he proved himself an ultra-programmatist. The translation of the German title runs as follows :—' Symphonic poem to the tragedy "Macbeth" by Shakespeare, Op. 54.' However, there is not only a title but about twenty quotations from the play, which in some places give the score the appearance of a melodrama. Whatever be the excellence of details, the matter and form of the whole preclude the likelihood of a change in the indifference with which this composition has hitherto been treated.

Let us note in passing a *Forest* Symphony, the third of five symphonies, composed about the middle of the 19th century by the prolific amateur composer JOHN LODGE ELLERTON (1801-1873), and six symphonies and two overtures by the much-travelled violinist, ALFRED HOLMES (1837-1876), who in 1864 took up his abode in Paris—*Jeanne d'Arc* (with vocal solos, 1867), *The Youth of Shakespeare, The Siege of Paris, Charles XII., Romeo and Juliet, Robin Hood, The Cid,* and *The Muses.*

And then we come to what has been called the Renaissance of English music, to the time of a more general musical activity, of more liberal views, of wider and more varied sympathies, and of greater independence, a change brought about by a group of composers born in the forties and early fifties, among whom the chief were Arthur Sullivan (1842-1900), A. C. Mackenzie (*b.* 1847), C. H. H. Parry (*b.* 1848), Arthur Goring Thomas (1851-1892), Frederic H. Cowen (*b.* 1852), and Charles Villiers Stanford (*b.* 1852). Not all of these come within the scope of our inquiry. GORING THOMAS distinguished himself in opera and other vocal works, and his few instrumental compositions were outwardly at least absolute music.

Among SIR C. HUBERT H. PARRY'S instrumental works there is an early overture entitled *Guillem de Cabestanh*, and a later symphonic overture with the even more daring title *On an unwritten Tragedy ;* but his four symphonies are without any indication of a poetic subject. The composer's sympathies are easily discoverable from his writings on music, especially from *The Art of Music*, the *Summary of Musical History*, and the articles in Grove's *Dictionary of Music and Musicians*, in all of which the greatest stress is laid on design. Sir Hubert sees in the development of music three stages respectively distinguished by supremacy of design and abstract beauty, by balance of abstract beauty and expression, and by the pursuit of the characteristic to the neglect of the purely artistic. Beethoven is the chief representative of the second stage, but at the same time points and leads to the following one. In the third stage, where Berlioz and Liszt were leaders, the preponderant tendency in the musical as in all art is towards ' variety and closeness of characterization . . . Art comes down from its lofty region and becomes the handmaid of everyday life . . . Though realism is admissible as a source of suggestion, the object of the expressive power of music is not to represent the outward semblance of anything, but to express the moods which it produces and the workings of the mind that are associated with them. . . . Of a conspicuously different type were the wild theories of a certain group of enthusiasts, whose eagerness to solve artistic problems was in excess of their hold upon the possibilities and resources of the art. They emphasized unduly the expressive aims of Beethoven and thought it possible to follow him in that respect without regard to his principles of design.' The main ground of Sir Hubert's accusation and condemnation is that 'they rejected the deeper principles along with some of the superficial conventionalities' of the sonata form.

The titled instrumental compositions of SIR CHARLES VILLIERS STANFORD are more numerous than those of Sir C. H. H. Parry. Of his five symphonies the second, third, fourth, and fifth are respectively entitled : *Elegiac; Irish; Thro' youth to strife, thro' death to life;* and *L'Allegro ed il Pensieroso;*—and one of his overtures, composed for the Armada Tercentenary, bears the title *Queen of the Seas.* To conclude, however, from this that Sir Charles has a pronounced leaning towards programme music would be a mistake. He admits that musical creation can be inspired by a poem or a picture or some abstract poetical view of a concrete idea, and that the above-mentioned works had some such source of inspiration. But while he believes in Beethoven's view of 'working after a picture,' he also believes in his practice of not defining what the picture is, at any rate in detail. Accordingly he holds that absolute music (as distinguished from lyrical and dramatic music) should be able to tell its tale without a title, able to stand as music pure and simple if its title were destroyed ; and that no rigid or detailed explanations can be given without narrowing the effect of the compositions, and limiting their expression. Sir Charles says that he never sets himself to analyze the causes of the music that comes into his head.

ARTHUR SULLIVAN (1842-1900) writes in a letter dated Belfast, 1863 : ' The whole of the first movement of a symphony, with a real Irish flavour, came into my head.' Sir A. C. Mackenzie, after pointing out the absence of vividly and strongly coloured national and racial characteristics, remarks : ' As in the case of Mendelssohn's famous *Scotch*, Sullivan's *Irish* Symphony is rather the result of impressions produced by the scenery, the temperament, and the literature of the people, the general atmosphere in fact, than an artistic reproduction of the country.' However, it was not the composer who gave to the symphony the epithet *Irish*. Sullivan's *In Memoriam* overture was called forth by his father's death, and written within a week of it. Other notable overtures are *Marmion*, *Macbeth*, *Di Ballo*, and that to the second part of *The Light of the World*. And then the reader has still to be reminded of the music to several plays—to *The Tempest*, a remarkable Op. 1, to *The Merchant of Venice*, *The Merry Wives of Windsor*, *Henry VIII.*, *Macbeth*, and *King Arthur*.

The programmatic movement is more heartily joined in by the other composers named by me. Most prominent among SIR ALEXANDER C. MACKENZIE'S contributions to this kind of music are the highly poetic Op. 29, *La Belle Dame sans Merci*, ballad for orchestra, to which the whole of Keats's poem is prefixed ; and the sprightly, humorous overture to Shakespeare's comedy *Twelfth Night*, in the course of which six quotations from the play appear as superscriptions. Mackenzie's Op. 41, *The Dream of Jubal*, a poem with music for soli, chorus, orchestra, and accompanied recitation, deserves special notice because of the latter element. The composer takes pleasure and is felicitous in the melodramatic treatment, as is further proved by many excellent pianoforte accompaniments to poems, especially of a humorous cast. In addition to the above works have to be mentioned the overtures *Cervantes* and *To a Comedy*, the music to the plays *Ravenswood*, *Marmion*, *The Little Minister*, *Manfred*, and *Coriolanus*, and the national tone-pictures the *Britannia Overture*, the orchestral suite *London Day by Day*, *Scenes in the Scottish Highlands* for pianoforte (*On the Hill-side ; On the Loch ;* and *On the Heather*), *From the North* for violin and pianoforte, also for orchestra, and two *Scottish Rhapsodies* and one *Canadian Rhapsody*.

Although Sir A. C. Mackenzie often writes absolute music, and never attempts to follow strictly a poem or drama in its actual sequence of events, yet he has an inclination to programme music. He finds that writing with some definite subject in his mind is more fascinating and easy to him—a picturesque or dramatic figure, the general outline of a poem or play, any given local colour or atmosphere, invariably cause him to work with greater rapidity than he would do without such a mental impression. With some such picture or character before him, the corresponding musical ideas present themselves quickly, without strain and effort, and the contour of the whole piece easily shapes itself after a comparatively short study of the subject chosen for illustration. In the first movement of his suite

London Day by Day, there is to be found quite a series of impressions, each of the eighteen variations being intended to represent in miniature some phase of street life (military band, hawkers' cries, &c.) within hearing of the Westminster chimes, which form a *basso ostinato* upon which the whole piece is built. The *Finale* tells of Hampstead Heath and Bank Holiday. His *Belle Dame sans merci* aims at giving a general impression of Keats's ballad rather than a musical replica of it. The overture to *Twelfth Night*, the composer thinks, might perhaps more fitly have been called *Malvolio*, since its programme is limited to the illustration of a single incident in the play—namely, the successful trap laid for him by the mischievous crew. The finding of the letter begins the piece, and a parallel passage expressing Malvolio's threat, to be ' revenged on the whole pack,' logically ends it. The body of the work (*Allegro con brio*) is an attempt to describe the characteristics of the principal performers in the trick; and its second subject (the fair Olivia), of which a modified version has already appeared during the reading of the letter in the introduction, provides an easy contrast to the vivacity of the chuckling schemers. The composer points out that in this piece he kept closely to the accepted form of an overture, although each section became considerably lengthened out, by reason of the programme, which seemed to him to demand ' expansion,' particularly in the development section. Generally speaking, Sir A. C. Mackenzie acknowledges the legitimacy of, and is thankful for, both absolute and programme music, but deprecates programmes that travel beyond the province and possibilities of musical expression, and further deprecates formlessness, although he believes that Liszt's method of metamorphosis of themes may be to some extent a substitute and help to satisfy the sense of form. The composer explains his liking for programme music by his liking for every kind of stage music, which after all, as he rightly remarks, is nothing else but programme music.

FREDERIC H. COWEN'S programme music takes us to different regions. The third of his six symphonies is denominated *The Scandinavian*, and its second movement (*Andante*) bears the superscription 'Summer night on the Fjord.' But although the other movements have no superscriptions, they do not fail to raise thoughts in the mind of the hearers; for all are poetic and romantic. His fourth and sixth symphonies are entitled *Welsh* and *Idyllic*. Another work (unpublished and, as the composer says, practically defunct) is denominated *Niagara, a Characteristic Overture*. Cowen shows a predilection for, and at the same time a wonderful aptitude and virtuosity in, the depicting of the delicate and graceful, as is demonstrated by his suites *The Language of Flowers* and *In Fairyland*, and by *The Butterfly's Ball*. But he treats also emotional themes, as in *A Phantasy of Life and Love*.

After writing the foregoing, I applied to Dr. Cowen for his views and intentions, and he was so kind as to make the following interesting confessions. 'Generally speaking the *Scandinavian Symphony* was influenced more by general impressions of the country—its ruggedness, its historical associations, and its folk melodies, by which I endeavoured to impart local colour. The *Adagio*, however, is meant to convey a definite idea of a moonlight night on a Fjord. The *Scherzo* has a vague suggestion of a sleigh ride. The *Finale* is an impression

of the sturdiness of the ancient Scandinavian gods.   In
the *Welsh Symphony* I aimed at nothing more than local
colour, and the *Idyllic Symphony* gives merely a vague
picture of rustic simplicity.   The *Adagio* of the latter
work, however, might suggest a quiet, peaceful afternoon,
undisturbed by mundane thoughts; and the *Finale* has
something of the character of a village festivity.   The
Phantasy of Life and Love is a mood, or a variety of moods
—the strenuousness of life, the desire for love, and the
weirdness and humorousness of things in general.   In
all the above I have never intended labelling any
particular phrase or passage, the whole being more the
result of some *Stimmung* [mood of the soul].   With
regard to the following, however, matters are somewhat
different, as they are meant to convey, and I hope do
convey, more or less definite ideas to the hearer.   For
instance, in *The Language of Flowers* and *In Fairyland,* all
the movements are intended to suggest the ideas indicated
by their titles and sub-titles—such as *Daisy* (Innocence),
Dance of the Witches, &c.   *The Butterfly's Ball* is an
ethereal dance suggested by an old nursery rhyme of
" The Butterfly's Ball and the Grasshopper's Feast." '

Of FREDERICK CORDER (*b.* 1852), a less persistent
pursuer of the Muse than the British composers already
mentioned, we will note the overtures *Ossian* and
Prospero (with the motto, ' What harmony is this?
My good friends, hark ! '—Act III., Scene II., of *The
Tempest*), the idyll *Evening on the Seashore,* and the
suites *In the Black Forest, Scenes from The Tempest,* and
Roumanian, and instrumental accompaniments to
recitations (*The Witch's Song,* &c.).   Mr. Corder says he
believes in brains and handicraft, and does not believe
in much else; that although on one or two occasions

favourably influenced under stress of emotion, he cannot but own that his best efforts—such as the *Witch's Song* —have been the outcome of mere merciless brain-cudgelling.   In fact, he mistrusts the assertions of composers who gush about inspiration.   He goes so far as to say that when he writes he tries to avoid all conscious connection with outside thoughts and influences, however *emotional* the composition may be.   To express emotion he makes use of the technique of emotion, of conventional modes of utterance, as it were of universal idioms.   'When one tries to paint the feeling of a poem in music, one must employ the mechanical means which knowledge and experience have taught us will produce on the minds of others the desired effect.   The subtle and just use of these mechanical means we call artistry, and the coarse and vulgar use of them claptrap.' Mr. Corder is fond of paradox and persiflage.   I see traces of this in the exposition of his theory of composition.   Disgust with childish amateurish idealism, with impotent ambitious botching, need not make us fall back on rank materialism, on *le compositeur machine* (to parody Lamettrie's *L'homme machine*) and *la musique mécanique* (however ingenious) as a *summum bonum.* After all, there is such a thing as enlightened magisterial idealism.

Before parting from the generation with which for a while we have been occupied, I shall yet mention a concert overture, *Morte d'Arthur*, by SIR FREDERICK BRIDGE (*b.* 1844), and an orchestra picture, *Clouds and Sunshine*, and a symphony, *A Summer Night*, by FREDERICK CLIFFE (*b.* 1857).

With the later born composers the programmatic tendency becomes more and more intense and absorbing,

and not only does it become more intense and absorbing,
it also reveals itself in new, extraordinary, and even
eccentric ways, both in subject and in form.   Of course,
there are exceptions, among whom DONALD TOVEY is
a notable one; but they do not invalidate what I asserted
as to the general tendency.   The composer who comes
next on the scene is HAMISH MacCUNN (*b.* 1868), who
made an impression with the concert overture *Land of
the Mountain and the Flood*, the orchestral ballad *The
Ship o' the Fiend*, and the ballad overture *The Dowie
Dens o' Yarrow*.   WILLIAM WALLACE (*b.* 1860) has
given us both a good philosophical definition of
programme music (in a paper on *The Scope of Programme
Music*, read before the Musical Association), and some
highly interesting specimens of it.   The definition is:
'Music which attempts to excite a mental image by
means of an auditory impression.'   The specimens are:
the symphonic poems *The Passing of Beatrice* and
Sir William Wallace, the symphonic preludes *Amboss
oder Hammer* (on Goethe's *Kophtisches Lied*), *The
Eumenides*, the *Rhapsody of Mary Magdalene*, &c.   Mr.
Wallace is not in sympathy with the composers destitute
of constructive power who resort to the symphonic poem
as a refuge.   He declares that a musical work, however
poetic the subject, has always to be judged primarily
from the point of composition; and claims for his own
works the possession of construction and a certain form,
consistent working out and avoidance of irrelevancies.
His position can be made clear by the following two
quotations.   'When a composer deals with an objective
idea, he is limited in his expression, and too close an
adherence to a literary text will preclude any strict
musical structure, unless it so happens that the poetic

idea is laid out on lines corresponding to musical form. When the idea is subjective, the music can conform to technical requirements, and can be worked out on lines exactly similar to those in the treatment of absolute music.   For the elaboration of definitely named emotional ideas can be just as consistent, just as academic, just as absolute, if you will, as the elaboration of indefinitely named and abstract emotional ideas.'— 'Resting secure in his conviction that the various musical forms have reached their highest technical development, he [the composer of to-day] strives to impart to his work some new, some modern quality, and this he discovers by giving to his composition a definite poetic significance.'

GRANVILLE BANTOCK (*b*. 1868) is looked upon in England as an extremist among composers of programme music, and critics have often maltreated him because of his supposed utter materialism.   In this as in so many cases popular beliefs turn out to be popular prejudices. The composer himself states that much, in fact nearly all, of his later work may be said to have a literary origin; but that he feels himself much more concerned with the human and emotional element than with any attempt to portray or reproduce in music the effects of Nature or descriptive events—that, in fact, he is not conscious of much external influence, of being affected by the material aspect of things.   In *The Witch of Atlas*, however, and to some extent in *The Great God Pan*, his thoughts have certainly been directed to Nature, though, in the first instance, inspired by the poems respectively of Shelley, Browning, and other poets.   In short, Mr. Granville Bantock conceives that the right kind of programme music is inspired by broad, human

emotions and the great thoughts of literature. It seems
to him that whereas absolute music is merely a
decorative or architectural design of tone upon tone, or
the development of purely musical thematic material,
the object of a programme composer is to convert the
literary idea into musical expression. As to form,
Mr. Granville Bantock holds that it must vary
according to the subject, and that in programme music
the composer may break away from the orthodox and
conventional forms of absolute music and create new
forms in keeping with his ideas. Other compositions of
this most daring and prolific of the younger generation
of composers of programme music are the overture
Eugene Aram, the symphonic overtures *Cain* and
Belshazzar, and the tone-poems *Thalaba the Destroyer,*
Dante (visions of Hell, Purgatory, and Heaven, his
Exile and his Death), *Fifine at the Fair* (after Browning),
Hudibras (after Butler), and *Lalla Rookh* (after Moore).
Granville Bantock had the intention of writing two-
dozen symphonic poems illustrative of Southey's *Curse
of Kehama,* but afterwards gave up the idea. Of this
vast theme, there remain only two Oriental Scenes—
No. 1, *Processional,* and No. 2, *Jaga-Naut.*

It would take too long to mention all the programme
music produced in recent times; but I must name a few
of the producers—Arthur Hervey, Walter Handel Thorley,
Herbert Bunning, Learmont Drysdale, William H. Bell,
Percy Rideout, J. Holbrooke, and Frederick Delius. We
cannot be equally brief with SIR EDWARD W. ELGAR
(*b.* 1857), the composer who since the beginning of the
new century has in so high a degree drawn upon himself
the attention of England and the Continent. Earnest
and intense, and ultra-modern as he is, he could not

2 c

but be a composer of programme music, and as such he has proved himself in his overtures *Froissart*, *Cockaigne*, and *In the South*, in the orchestral Variations and other pieces, and still more strikingly in the instrumental constituents of his vocal‑instrumental compositions, especially in those of *The Dream of Gerontius* and *The Apostles*. ‘Instrumental accompaniments,’ being a misnomer, ought to be regarded as an obsolete term in speaking of modern works, where the voice or voices are oftener the accompanying parts than the instruments. Sir Edward’s instrumental compositions, although programme music, have, however, no other programmes than their titles. *Cockaigne* (In London Town) and *In the South* explain themselves. *Froissart* was suggested by Claverhouse’s remarks about Jehan Froissart’s *Chronique* in the 33rd chapter of Walter Scott’s *Old Mortality :* ‘His chapters inspire me with more enthusiasm than even poetry itself. And the noble canon, with what true chivalrous feeling he confines his beautiful expressions of sorrow to the death of the gallant and high‑bred knight, of whom it was a pity to see the fall, such was his loyalty to his king, pure faith to his religion, hardihood towards his enemy, and fidelity to his lady‑love!’ . . . Peculiarly interesting from the programmatic point of view are the orchestral variations on the ‘Enigma’ theme. R. J. Buckley writes in his *Sir Edward Elgar :* ‘The theme is a counterpoint on some well‑known melody which is never heard [and remains unrevealed by the composer], the Variations are the theme seen through the personalities of friends, with an *intermezzo* and a *coda* [*finale*].’ The friends are indicated by the names Ysobel, Troyte, Dorabella, Nimrod, in one case by three asterisks, and in most cases by initials. Sir Edward is a lover of nature and of books. He holds that a musician needs education and outdoor life. And one of his ideas is that there is music in the air, music all round us, that the world is full of it. Of the *Introduction and Allegro*, Op. 47, for strings, the composer relates that he thought out the theme of this composition in Cardiganshire, ' on the cliff, between the sea and the blue sky,' while there came to him indistinctly the distant sound of singing. The overture *In the South* contains impressions received in Italy, more especially ' on a glorious afternoon in the Vale of Andora, with streams, flowers, and hills ; the distant snow mountains in one direction, and the blue Mediterranean in the other.'

America, as far as music is concerned, may be described by a European as a *terra incognita*. Whether this ignorance is blameless or not, is a question too delicate to be taken up rashly. In any case, however, we can plead in excuse lack of opportunity to hear and see American compositions, especially orchestral and choral-orchestral ones. As I like neither to simulate a knowledge I have not, nor to depend entirely on second-hand knowledge, I shall pass over JOHN KNOWLES PAINE (*b.* 1839), ARTHUR FOOTE (*b.* 1853), GEORGE WHITFIELD CHADWICK (*b.* 1854), FRANCK VAN DER STUCKEN (*b.* 1858), and others, and confine myself to the consideration of a single composer, one who both by the quantity and quality of his instrumental music must raise the curiosity and interest of the student of programme music. EDWARD MacDOWELL (*b.* 1861) is incontestably and pronouncedly a poet, and a certain dreaminess is a predominating feature of his poetry. His music reminds one of the expression that is so striking in his portraits—the quiescent, abstracted, inward look. It suggests also improvisations of a poetic soul in the twilight—exhalation rather than composition. While everything in it is exquisite in feeling and expression, one may miss in MacDowell's music a vigorous abundance, variety, and organization of thought. The dreamer in him tends to neutralize the actor. The composer's more impassioned, more tumultous moments prove rather than disprove what I say.

The most successful of MacDowell's achievements are probably his songs. Next to them come certainly his pianoforte works. But he also composed works for the orchestra. MacDowell confessedly wanted to write 'suggestive music,' and his music cannot leave us in doubt as to whether his programmes were suggestive to himself. But the suggestiveness was general rather than particular, idealistic rather than realistic, and above all dreamily, visionarily poetic. Among the pianoforte pieces we find *Forest Idyls*, *Six Idyls* (after Goethe), *Little Poems*, *Les Orientales*, *Marionettes*, *Moon Pictures* (after Hans Christian Andersen), *Fireside Tales*, and the three most important series, Op. 51, 55, and 62, the *Woodland Sketches*, *Sea Pieces*, and *New England Idyls*. In addition to the general titles the composer gives his pieces special titles, and mostly prefixes to them some verses. The special titles enable us to see further into the poet's laboratory. They are in the case of the *Woodland Sketches :* 'To a Wild Rose,' 'Will-o'-the-Wisp,' 'At an old Trysting Place,' 'In Autumn,' 'From an Indian Lodge,' 'To a Waterlily,' 'From Uncle Remus,' 'A deserted Farm,' 'By a Meadow Brook,' and 'Told at Sunset.' Among the special titles of the

Sea Pieces are : ' To the Sea ' (' Ocean, thou mighty
monster '), ' From a Wandering Iceberg ' (' An errant
princess of the north,' &c.), 'A.D. 1620,' ' In mid-
ocean,' &c.   In the *New England Idyls* occur among
others the following special titles : ' An old Garden,'
' In   deep   woods,'   ' To   an   old   White   Pine,'
and ' From Puritan Days.'   Subjects of a different
nature are dealt with in the *Marionettes*—they are :
' Soubrette,' ' Lover,' ' Witch,' ' Clown,' ' Villain,' and
' Sweetheart.'

MacDowell has written a *Tragic,* a *Heroic,* a *Norse,*
and a *Keltic* Sonata.   Of the meaning of the first sonata
the composer gives no further hints.   To the second he
prefixes the motto " Flos regum Arthuris,' and writes :
' While not exactly programme music, I had in mind
the Arthurian legend when writing this work.   The first
movement typifies the coming of Arthur.   The *Scherzo*
was suggested by a picture of Doré's showing a knight in
the woods surrounded by elves.   The third movement
was suggested by my idea of Guinevere.   That following
represents the passing of Arthur.'   To the *Norse* Sonata
MacDowell has prefixed a number of verses of which I
shall quote four :—

> ' Rang out a Skald's strong voice,
>   With tales of battles won ;
>   Of Gudrun's love
>   And Sigurd, Siegmund's son.'

To the *Keltic* Sonata are prefixed these verses :
> ' Who minds now Keltic tales of yore,
>   Dark Druid rhymes that thrall,
>   Deidré's song and wizard lore
>   Of great Cuchullin's fall.'

And the composer characterizes his music as 'more a commentary on the subject than an actual depiction of it.'

Besides writing a pianoforte concerto, MacDowell wrote for orchestra two suites and some symphonic poems. The first Suite, Op. 42, consists of the pieces 'In a haunted Forest,' 'Summer Idyl,' 'The Shepherdess' Song,' and 'Forest Spirits'; and the second, the *Indian* Suite, of 'Legend,' 'Love Song,' 'In War-time,' 'Dirge,' and 'Village Festival.' More interesting for the student of programme music are the other orchestral compositions—the two pieces *Hamlet* and *Ophelia*, Op. 22, the second symphonic poem, *Lancelot* and *Elaine* (after Tennyson), Op. 25, and the two pieces *The Saracens* and *The Lovely Aldá* (after the *Song of Roland*). As to Op. 25, MacDowell remarks : ' I would never have insisted that this symphonic poem need mean " Lancelot and Elaine " to everyone. It did to me, however, and in the hope that my artistic enjoyment might be shared by others, I added the title to my music.' This and other remarks of the composer's have a curious, somewhat apologetic ring about them. With regard to one quoted above, the reader may feel inclined to ask : 'What then is *exactly* programme music ? '

CHAPTER III.

IN DENMARK, NORWAY, SWEDEN, BOHEMIA, AND RUSSIA.

The Dane NIELS W. GADE (1817-1890) was the first voice from the North European nations that made itself heard in the republic of music. His Op. 1, the overture *Echoes from Ossian* (1841), gave a first taste of northern colour and atmosphere. But nationalism merely tinges Gade's compositions, and only some of them, the early ones. In fact, his countrymen blamed him for going over to Germany, for denationalizing himself. The accusation was unjust. One may be true to one's country without speaking its brogue or obtruding its peculiarities. Gade never adopted its brogue, and soon fulfilled Schumann's hope that he would not allow the artist in him to be submerged in his nationality, but would display his aurera borealis imagination in its richness and variety, and cast his eyes as well on other spheres of nature and life. Besides Op. 1, three more of Gade's overtures have titles—Op. 7, *Im Hochland* ('In the Highlands'), Op. 37, *Hamlet*, and Op. 39, *Michael Angelo* There are, further, five pieces for orchestra, entitled *A Summer-day in the Country*, ('Early,' 'Stormy,' 'Forest Solitude,' 'Humoreske,' and 'Evening, merry life of the people'), Op. 55, and pieces for the pianoforte —*Aquarellen*, Op. 19, *Northern Tone-Pictures*, Op. 4, &c.; among his less known works there is an overture entitled *A Mountain Excursion in the North*. On the other hand, there are eight symphonies, an overture, and other works without titles. Indeed, Gade's programmatic

tendency is not very pronounced. It falls greatly short
of Beethoven's and Mendelssohn's. Liberally gifted with
the sense of the pleasingly beautiful in line, colour,
form, and sentiment, he lacked Beethoven's imposing
intellectual depth and emotional force as well as
Mendelssohn's fascinating life-like picturesqueness. In
some respects, however, there was a close spiritual
relationship between Gade and Mendelssohn. To form a
true idea of the man, it will be well to remember his love
of the two sister arts of music, painting and sculpture,
and especially his early and life-long admiration for the
Danish poet Oehlenschläger (1779-1850), the reviver
of the old Northern myths and legends and sympathizer
with much in the contemporary German romanticists.
The motto of his Op. 1 shows in what spirit Gade entered
upon his career : 'Formulas hold us not bound, our art's
name is poesy.'

Some of the younger generations of Danish composers
have gone further in this direction. EMIL HARTMANN
(1836-1898) wrote a 'Tragedy Overture' and entitled it
Eine nordische Heerfahrt ('A northern War Expedition';
also called 'The Vikings'), and gave to the second of
his three symphonies the title of *Aus der Ritterzeit*.
ASGER HAMERIK (*b.* 1843), who spent much of his
time in America, produced not only five Northern Suites,
a *Poetic*, a *Tragic*, a *Lyric*, a *Majestic*, and a *Serious*
Symphony, but also an *Opera without Words* for pianoforte. To mention one more Danish composer. Among
the works of VICTOR BENDIX (*b.* 1851) there are two
symphonic poems—*Fjeldstigning* and *Summer Sounds
from Russia*.

The obtrusive northern nationalism has come from
Scandinavia, and especially from Norway. It seems to

have been RICHARD NORDRAAK (1842-1866) who
introduced into the art-music of his country the
peculiarities of Norwegian folk-music. He died young,
and although he wrote, besides other things, music to
two of Björnson's plays, he would probably not have
been heard of outside Scandinavia had he not inspired
or infected with his idea a young contemporary composer
of nearly his own age who was destined to live and
effectively apply his principle. This composer was
EDWARD H. GRIEG (*b.* 1843). Unlike Gade, Grieg
revels in his country's brogue, is obtrusively national,
and remains true to his nationalism. We have of him
no symphonies and no untitled overtures. But we
have an untitled concerto and several sonatas full of
national idiotisms, colour, scenery, life, and sentiment.
We have of him further an overture *In Autumn,* music
to Ibsen's *Peer Gynt,* Op. 46 (formed into two Suites),
Three Pieces (*Introduction; Intermezzo, Borghild's
Dream;* and *Triumphal March*) to Björnson's drama
Sigurd Jorsalfar, Op. 56, a Suite *Of Holberg's Time,
Elegiac Melodies* for string orchestra (*Heart-wounds* and
Spring), the melodrama *Bergliot* (the poem by Björnson),
Op. 42, and several interesting series of pianoforte pieces
—*Poetic Tone-Pictures, Humoresken, From the Life of the
People* (Sketches of Norwegian life), *Norwegian Peasant
Dances,* and ten books of Lyric Pieces, and among
the titles of the pieces contained in these series we
find such as *Watchman's Song from Macbeth, Dance of
the Elves, On the Hills, Bridal Procession passing by,
Butterfly, Erotikon, Prayer and Temple Dance, To
Spring,* and *March of the Dwarfs.* The speaking nature
of Grieg's music precludes the assumption that his
compositions are mere formalistic tone-combinations and

the titles fanciful additions without serious significance. To be convinced of the truth of this, we have only to listen with open ears and mind to miniatures like the *Watchman's Song from Macbeth* and the *Dance of the Elves.* And who could fail to perceive the programmatic character of the *Peer Gynt* music ? In the melodramatic *Bergliot* the music is of course patently and necessarily programme music. But the untitled compositions too have tales to tell. He must be a dullard indeed who is not impressed, for instance, by the sea life depicted in the first movement of Op. 8, the Sonata in F major for pianoforte and violin. In short, Grieg's concerto, sonatas, and pieces make us hear, see, and feel land and sea, woods and heaths, flats and mountain-tops, fresh breezes, thick fogs, rocking waves, rushing water, flapping sails, merry dances, melancholy musings, wild rollicking, stories of heroes and goblins, and much more.

Let it not be thought that the secret of Grieg's more than transient success lies in his adoption of the idiotisms of Norwegian folk-music. No doubt they give piquancy and colouring, have a pictorial and ethnographical value, but so extensively and obtrusively used are a source of weakness rather than of strength, result in mannerism rather than in style. You cannot with impunity make the inessential the essential, and the rudimentary the norm of the developed. There are people who imagine that thus a national art-music may be produced; but that is a fatal mistake. If folk-music has virtues, it has also limitations—limitations in the range of thought and feeling and in the means of expression. There is nothing more futile than the endeavour to produce a national art-music by imitation of folk-music and its peculiarities : a national art must be based on the broader and deeper foundation of humanity, on 'the essential passions,' to use an expression of Wordsworth's; it must grow out of the hearts and souls of the individuals that constitute the nation; it must be spontaneous, natural, and sincere. Look at the great masters of the art! Although full of national character, they have none of the tricks of folk phrase and gesture,* and consequently are universal as well as national in the higher sense of the word, have a medium of expression suitable to the whole range of human thought and feeling.

Gade, who approved warmly of Grieg's first sonata for violin and pianoforte (Op. 8, in F major), was quite right when, after hearing the second (Op. 13, in G major), he said to the composer : 'The next sonata you must really make less Norwegian.' It was a pity that Grieg, instead of perceiving the excellence of the advice, defiantly replied : 'On the contrary, the next will be more so.' Both sonatas are thoroughly Norwegian. But there is a difference between their nationalism : whereas in the earlier work the spirit impresses us, in the later the letter oppresses us. National tricks of phrase and vocabulary, which arrest the attention and delight the ear, soon weary and pall. With less obtrusive nationalism the spirited, piquant pianoforte concerto (Op. 16) would have maintained its vogue longer than it has done. And thus it has been or will be with some of Grieg's enthusiastically received pianoforte pieces. Happily for him and us, the master does not often mainly depend on these externalities. Wherein, then,

* Their occasional use of such does not upset the argument. To take an exceptionally strong case. Those who dub Haydn a Croatian composer overlook the German and the broadly human elements that form the great bulk of his music.

lies the secret of Grieg's more than transient success to
which I alluded ?   It lies in the poetic nature of the
man—a nature that derives its character from his
individual constitution in the first place, and only in
the second place from the inspiration yielded by his
country and people.   In short, what of his music will
live, will live thanks to Grieg the poet, not to Grieg the
Norwegian.

The more classically inclined and less strikingly
individual and less obtrusively national JOHANN
SEVERIN SVENDSEN (*b.* 1840) has produced, besides
two untitled symphonies and other things, an Introduc-
tion to Björnson's *Sigurd Slumbe,* Op. 8, *Carnival in
Paris,* Op. 9, *Zorhayde,* a legend, Op. 11, *Wedding-feast*
('Northern Carnival '), Op. 14, an Overture to *Romeo and
Juliet,* Op. 18, and also four Norwegian Rhapsodies,
Op. 17, 19, 21, and 22.   Programme music more of the
Berlioz type has come from the pen of JOHANN
SELMER (*b.* 1844)—*Scène funèbre, Northern Festival
Procession, Finnish Festival Sounds, Among the Hills,
Carnival in Flanders,* and *Prometheus.*   Of the younger
Norwegian composers, OLE OLSEN (*b.* 1850), who
follows ultra-modern tendencies, wrote two symphonic
poems—*Asgardreigen* and *Elfentanz*—and music to
Erik XIV., but also an untitled symphony; whereas
CHRISTIAN SINDING (*b.* 1856), who eschews both
obtrusive national idiotisms and titles (except occasionally,
indeed extremely rarely, in his pianoforte pieces),
distinguishes himself honourably by concerted chamber
music and other compositions in the large forms.

Sweden has not drawn the attention of the world on
her music in the same measure as Norway, and, at least
in the department of orchestral music, has been less

fruitful. It may suffice to name here ANDREAS
HALLÉN (*b.* 1846), the author of two symphonic poems
Sten Sture and *From the Waldemar Legend.* In the
neighbouring Finland, we will also note only one master,
JEAN SIBELIUS (*b.* 1865), whose growing fame has
for some time been spreading far beyond the borders of
his own country. Although the list of his compositions
contains two untitled symphonies, it evidences unmistakably the master's leaning towards programme music.
For we find there the legends *The Swan of Tuonela*
(from the folk-epos *Kalevala*) and *Lemminkâinen travels
homeward*, the tone-poems *A Saga*, *Finlandia*, and
Spring Song, the overture and suite *Carelia*, the suite
Pelleas and Melisande, and music to Ad. Paul's drama
King Christian II.

Although the extraordinary talent and love for music of
the people of Bohemia has always excited much wonder, it
is only in recent times that the musical world has become
cognizant of a Czech school with distinct features and
imposing powers. The many earlier Czech composers
that made reputations outside their own countries—such,
for instance, as the 18th and 19th century musicians
J. W. A. Stamitz, the three brothers Benda, Mysliveček,
Wanhal, Pichl, Koželuh, Gyrowetz, J. L. Dussek, Dyonis
Weber, Anton Reicha,Tomaschek, and J. W. Kalliwoda—
were most of them so closely bound up with the musical
life and productivity of other nations, more especially of
Germany and Austria, that they are included in the
history of these countries, the music of which some of
them (notably Stamitz, the Bendas, and Dussek) not only
enriched, but also leavened and developed. This state
of matters has been changed by two composers, now of
world-wide fame, Smetana and Dvořák, who may be

regarded as the outcome of a renaissance of Czech nationalism, a combative reassertion in opposition to German ascendancy and domination.

FREDERIC SMETANA (1824-1884), a genuine Czech, but not an obtruder in and out of season of folk idiotisms, was active both in dramatic and instrumental music. Hardly anything of the former, with the rare exception of *The bartered Bride*, has found its way beyond the frontiers of Bohemia; the latter, on the other hand, has spread abroad, slowly but continuously, and is likely to do so at a faster rate in future. For, as Liszt, deeply moved by Smetana's death, said : ' He was a genius.' As to his artistic faith, we happily have a sufficiently complete confession from his own pen. We can extract it from his letters to Liszt. Although he cannot call himself one of Liszt's direct pupils, he acknowledges him as his master, to whom he owes everything; and declares himself an uncompromising champion of the great masters of the present time (April 10, 1857). Subsequent to a visit to Weimar, he writes in a letter of October 24, 1858, of the powerful impression made on him by Liszt's music, of the necessity of progress in the very way so grandly and truly taught by the Weimar master, of his most zealous discipleship of that master's artistic tendency (*Kunstrichtung*), and of his desire to work for the deliverance of the art from its confining fetters. But let no one conclude that Smetana was a despiser of the older masters, and deaf and blind to the lessons they taught, because he was not content to follow their lines. As a disciple of Liszt he was of course a believer in programme music. He is one of the very few who have written concerted chamber music with a programme, one of his compositions of this

kind, a string quartet in E minor being autobiographical
and bearing the title of *Aus meinem Leben*. The four
movements of which the quartet consists have, however,
no further programmatic indications.* Of greater
interest to us are Smetana's symphonic poems for
orchestra, *Hakon Jarl, Richard III., Wallenstein's Camp*,
and the series of six symphonic poems entitled *Ma Vlast*
('My Fatherland'). They are compositions consisting
of a continuity of movements; but whereas the first three
have only titles, the other six have also a programme
prefixed to them. Of *Richard III.* we find a concise
programme in one of Smetana's letters to Liszt.
The composer says there: 'It consists of one piece
[*Satz*], and the tonal vesture [*Betonung*] clings pretty
closely to the action of the tragedy'—'The attainment
of the proposed aim after the overcoming of all obstacles,
triumph, and fall of the hero.' Two short motives are
quoted as representative of the hero (who acts throughout
the whole), and of the opposing party. Of the first of the
three early tone-poems, composed at Gothenburg, where
Smetana resided from 1856 to 1861, Sir A. C. Mackenzie
says that the Scandinavian *Hakon Jarl* is 'more northern,
more briny and breezy, than any of the many similar
pictures which have (until very recently indeed) been
painted by Scandinavian composers themselves,' that
this piece 'positively *rattles* with the north wind'; and of
the third tone-poem, *Wallenstein's Camp*, the same racy
commentator remarks that it is decidedly the best of the
three and a masterpiece; that it brings us face to face
with the turbulence of camp life in those tumultuous
times; that through the shrieks of laughter, the uncouth

* The sustained *e''''* of the first violin towards the end of the last
movement is believed to be the tone that haunted him in his deafness.

capering and the carousing of the soldiery, we hear the exhortation of the Capucin, thundering his unheeded denunciations; that, in fact, 'all seems to be taken straight from Schiller—and from life.'

The titles and programmes of the six parts of *Ma Vlast* ('My Fatherland') are as follows:

(1.) *Vyšehrad.*—Thoughts engendered in the poet on beholding the famous fortress. The glorious life there in its palmy days; subsequent unfortunate struggles, and final ruin.

(2.) *Ultava.* The river Moldau.—The scenes through which the course of the noble river leads — natural beauties, historical buildings, and doings of men, wood and water nymphs, &c.

(3.) *Šárka.* The noble Bohemian Amazon.—The Amazons at war with the race of men. Šárka having had herself bound to a tree, cries; Ctirad hears her and frees her. When she finds the men are tired and asleep after the day's rejoicings, she winds her horn; her comrades come; and all the men are slain.

(4.) *Zčeských luhův a hájův.*—From Bohemia's Grove and Field. A Pastoral Symphony.

(5.) *Tábor.* The castle founded by the Hussites.— The Taborites and their enthusiasm.

(6.) *Blaník.*—The hill in which are sleeping the glorious Hussite champions who will rise again and battle for their country when the time comes.

Smetana stands forth in his *My Fatherland* as a musician of extraordinary imaginative and constructive power, and as a patriot of the genuinely noble ideal, not of the pseudo, blatant, chauvinistic type. If the writers of music may be divided into composers and creators, he ought to be numbered with the latter. The six parts of

his greatest symphonic achievement are poems in the
fullest significance of the word. Like so many geniuses
Smetana starved in early life and never greatly
prospered. Like Beethoven he became deaf, and like
Schumann he died in a lunatic asylum. Struggle, death,
and transfiguration—martyrdom and canonization : this
is a typical fate of the true artist.

Much readier, wider, and fuller than the recognition of
Smetana has been that of ANTONIN DVOŘÁK (1841-
1904), whose great popularity for the first time made the
world aware of Bohemia's national individuality in
matters musical. An out-and-out Czech like Smetana,
Dvořák was fonder of folk idiotisms. Like Smetana he
suffered much hardship in his early career, unlike him
he prospered later on. It was not till the age of thirty-
two (1873) that he came prominently before the public.
After drawing his own country's attention upon himself
by a cantata and an opera, he obtained a stipend from
the government. Next (1877) he gained by a happy
chance the patronage of Brahms, who procured him a
publisher. The publication of the vocal duets *Moravian
Strains* ('Klänge aus Mähren') and the pianoforte duets
Slavonic Dances, afterwards arranged for orchestra,
won for him an almost instantaneous and world-wide
reputation, which was heightened especially by his
Stabat Mater and *The Spectre's Bride*. If we look for
the secret of Dvořák's success we are sure to find it in
the vigour, daring, exuberance, and unconventionality of
his personality, in the bloom, freshness, and wealth of
an imagination strongly tinged with Czech characteristics.
It was only in the last years of his life that Dvořák
became a composer of programme music in the fullest
sense of the word. I pass over without comment

2 D

the pianoforte pieces, *Silhouettes*, Op. 8; *From the Bohemian Forest*, Op. 68; *Poetic Mood Pictures*, Op. 85, &c. Of his five titled overtures—*My Home*, Op. 62; *Husitzka*, Op. 67; *In Nature*, Op. 91; *Carnival*, Op. 92; and *Othello*, Op. 93—it may be said that in most cases, at least in the first three, if the title indicates a programme at all, it is a vague one, and that in all cases opinions will differ as to the extent to which the programme inspired and guided the composer. The same holds good of the fifth symphony, Op. 95, called by the composer *From the New World*, a title which no doubt alludes to something more than to the negro melodies contained in the work. It is different when we come to the five Symphonic Poems, Op. 107-111. All these compositions consist of a continuity of movements, and all but one have detailed programmes based on popular Czech legends by K. Jaromir Erben. The exception is the fifth, Op. 111, the most satisfactory, which has only a title, *Heroic Song* ('Heldenlied'). The programme prefixed to the fourth Symphonic Poem, Op. 110, *The Wild Dove* ('Die Waldtaube') runs thus:

(1.) *Andante, Marcia funebre:* The young widow, weeping, and lamenting, follows the body of her husband to the grave.

(2.) *Allegro*, afterwards *Andante:* A jovial, well-to-do peasant meets the beautiful widow, consoles her, and persuades her to forget her grief and take him for her husband.

(3.) *Molto vivace*, afterwards *Allegretto Grazioso:* She fulfils her lover's wish. A merry wedding.

(4.) *Andante:* From the branches of a freshly budding oak, overshadowing the grave of her first husband—who had been poisoned by her—the mournful cooing of the wild dove is heard. The melancholy sounds pierce to the heart of the sinful woman who, overcome by the terrors of an evil conscience, goes mad, and seeks death in the waters hard by.

(5.) *Andante Tempo I.*, afterwards *Più lento :* Epilogue.

Although there are no references to movements in the programmes prefixed to the three other Symphonic Poems, the composer's procedure is the same—that is to say, he follows the course of the stories. Let us see what is the nature of them. The student of our subject cannot fail to find them interesting. A little abbreviation here and there may be both permissible and advisable.

The Water-Fay ('Der Wassermann'), Op. 107.—In the pale moonshine, on a poplar branch by the edge of the lake, sits the Water-Fay, making himself a coat of green and shoes of red, singing at his work, for to-morrow is his wedding-day. Early in the morning, the village maid, his chosen victim, obeying an irresistible impulse, comes to the lakeside to wash clothes, in spite of her mother's evil forebodings. She falls into the lake, is drowned, and wedded to the Water-Fay, who holds prisoner the souls of drowned men and women. Bewailing her miserable fate, she pours out her passionate desire for home in lullabies to her baby. At last the Fay grants her one day to re-visit the world above, keeping the baby as a pledge of her return. When the time comes to end the sorrowful reunion of mother and daughter, the mother scornfully refuses to let her go. A violent storm arises, something is dashed against the door of the cottage—the headless body of the baby.'

The Midday Witch ('Die Mittagshexe'), Op. 108, has the following programme. A mother threatens her crying child with the Midday Witch, and at last exclaims : ' Here, Nanny, come and fetch the cry-baby.' The door opens, and in comes a shrivelled ghostly woman leaning on a crook-stick. ' Give me the child,' she cries. The terror-stricken mother clasps the child in her arms. But, like a shadow, the Midday Witch draws nearer ; she stretches out her arms towards the child ; the mother falls senseless to the ground. It is midday. When the father comes in from the fields, he finds his wife in a swoon on the floor, and the child on her bosom suffocated.

The Golden Spinning Wheel, Op. 109, has an even more gruesome programme. The king enters a cottage by the wood, sees there a lovely maid, asks her to be his wife, and is told by her to ask her stepmother, who will return from town on the morrow. When the king comes again the ugly old woman tries to persuade him to marry her own daughter, who is the image of the stepdaughter. But the king commands her to bring her step-daughter to the palace next day. The old woman, however, determines to take her own daughter to the king, and together they murder the stepdaughter, leaving the body in the wood, but carrying with them the eyes, hands, and feet. The unsuspecting king marries the daughter. After seven days' feasting he goes to war, enjoining his wife to spin diligently. Meanwhile a wise old man, a mighty magician, finds the mutilated corpse in the wood, and sends a boy with a golden spinning-wheel to the castle, with the commission to sell it for two feet. The young queen is so anxious to possess this wonderful piece of work that she makes her mother ask and pay the price. In the same way the girl's hands and eyes are obtained in exchange for a golden spindle and a golden distaff. With the help of the water of life the magician joins the several parts of the body, and disappears after the maid has come to life. At the end of three weeks the king returns victorious, and the queen shows him the spinning-wheel she has got. But no sooner does she begin to spin than the magic wheel reveals the gruesome deed. Pale with fear she tries to silence the treacherous spindle, but the king insists on hearing all. Then he quickly rides into the wood, and after long seeking finds the maid, marries her, and lives happy ever after.

We may assume that in writing these orchestral compositions Dvořák was not under the delusion that his music could, without words, make intelligible all that is in the stories, and knew perfectly well that all he could do was to *illustrate* legends already known to the hearer. There is, however, a great difference between an illustration that runs parallel with the text (as pictures in a book, or instrumental accompaniments of a vocal composition) and an illustration that comes after the text (as in programme music). In the former case, force and beauty may be added by details of illustration that in the latter case are only sources of obscurity and disorganization. The fundamental questions, then, we have to ask ourselves are these : Do the texts chosen by Dvořák ● readily lend themselves to purely instrumental treatment ? Are they essentially and broadly musical ? Are they profoundly and largely emotional ? I am afraid the answers must be in the negative. And why ? Because the non-musical predominates in them. In the cantata, *The Spectre's Bride*, on the one hand, and the four symphonic poems, Op. 107-110, on the other hand, Dvořák has proved that subjects of the same character may be strikingly effective in vocal-instrumental composition, and leave much to be desired, or be wholly unsuitable for a purely instrumental one. At any rate, the musical world has given its decision by cherishing the cantata and ignoring the symphonic poems.

It will suffice for our purpose if I name only two more Czech composers—the Russianized EDWARD F. NAPRAVNIK (*b.* 1839), with his symphony *The Demon* (after Lermontov) and the symphonic poem *The Orient ;* and the much more important true nationalist ZDENKO FIBICH (1850-1900), who, besides three symphonies and some chamber music without programmes, has written the symphonic poems *Othello, Toman and the Nymph, Spring, Zerboj und Slavoj, Vigiliæ,* and *In the Evening,* the suite *In the Open Air,* the overtures *The Jew of Prague, The Tempest,* and *A Night on Karlstein,* 352 short and fragmentary pianoforte pieces entitled *Moods, Impressions, and Recollections,* and lastly and most notably a melodrama, *Hippodamia* (a trilogy: *Pelops's Wooing ; Tantalus' Expiation ;* and *Hippodamia's Death*), after Jaroslav Vrchlicky's poem. We have here substitution of the speaking voice for Wagner's speech-melody, a natural step to take. But Fibich returned to opera.

In the last decades of the 19th century it seemed as if Russia were becoming the leading and predominating musical nation of Europe, as if the music of the vigorous youthful East were to supersede that of the effete, senile West. Now that the glamour of novelty has passed away, this view can no longer be maintained : we see the weakness as well as the strength of the East, and see also signs of still subsisting vitality in the West. But, although Russia has not produced composers and a musical literature equalling in excellence those of the great epochs, or even, all things considered, surpassing those of her contemporary rivals of other countries, it is undeniable that her composers and musical literature compel our attention, engage our interest, widen our ideas, and influence our art-practice. Henceforth Russia has to be reckoned with in music as well as in politics. She has become one of the great musical powers.

Without forgetting Bortniansky (1751-1825) and other early composers we may say that Russia became an art-producing nation of more than merely national importance with MICHAEL GLINKA (1804-1857). Nothing gauges his significance better than the respect and admiration of his successors. He was one of the five composers whom Anton Rubinstein revered most and whose busts adorned his study, the other four being Bach, Beethoven, Schubert and Chopin. To Tchaikovsky, Glinka was an extraordinary phenomenon, a colossal artistic force. These references to Rubinstein and Tchaikovsky are convenient, as Glinka's operas, which make up the great bulk of his works, are unknown outside Russia, if we except *The Life for the Czar*, which has been a few times performed in other countries. Glinka aimed at writing operas entirely national in music as well as in subject, and wanted his countrymen to feel quite at home in them. In this as well as in the means employed, he was epoch-making in Russia. Like him most of his successors delight in the utilization of Russian folk-melodies and peculiarities of Russian folk-music generally. For ethnographical purposes, for the sake of local colouring and the love of colour *per se*, they also delight, again like him, in the utilization of the folk-music of other nations—Polish, Italian, Spanish, and especially Oriental. That in this way

the composer may fail to reach the heart and soul of the
matter, to compass the heights, depths, and breadths of
humanity, and may even become crude and puerile, is too
obvious to require pointing out. Glinka's purely orchestral
writings are the beautiful expressive music to Koukolnik's
drama *Prince Kholmsky* (overture, four entr'actes, &c.),
and the three well-known delightful fantasias or capricci
on popular airs—the Russian *Kamarinskaja* (1848) and
the Spanish *Jota Aragonesa* and *Une Nuit à Madrid*
(1851). Tchaikovsky says that many touches in the
music to *Prince Kholmsky* recall the brush of Beethoven,
and describes the entr'actes as little pictures painted by a
master-hand, as symphonic marvels. 'A symphonic
picture full of poetry' is Cui's comment on *Une Nuit à
Madrid*. Rubinstein asserts that the *Kamarinskaja* has
become the type of Russian instrumental music, an opinion
shared by Tchaikovsky, who remarks that the whole
Russian symphonic school lies in the *Kamarinskaja*.
Both agree also in thinking that this playful bagatelle is
of astounding originality, in fact, a work of genius. The
relation of these fantasias to programme music would be
an excellent subject for discussion. But so much may
be confidently claimed for them without discussion : if
they are not programme music, they are at least full of
life, humour, character, and colour. In the latter part
of his life Glinka seems to have gone further in the
direction of programme music, for he was occupied with
the idea of a symphonic work (begun in 1852) on
Malo-Russian airs on the subject of Gogol's novel
Tarass Boulba. The master's remark, that his unfettered
imagination needed a text as a positive idea, goes far
towards ascertaining his position with regard to
programme music.

The master that comes next in point of time is ALEXANDER SERGEIVICH DARGOMIJSKY (1813-1869), a composer chiefly of operas and songs. Indeed, of instrumental compositions we have to mention only three symphonic pieces in the comic *genre*—*Kazachok* (a Little Russian Dance), the Russian legend *Baba-Yaga* (the name of a witch whose vehicle is a mortar and whose whip a pestle), also called *From the Volga to Riga*, and the *Dance of Mummers*. Dargomijsky's chief aim and all-absorbing passion was realism. He desired that the sound should actually represent the word. Now, the realism so ardently pursued could not be confined to songs and operas, it would assert itself also in the purely instrumental works. The above-mentioned three orchestral pieces have been described as 'bizarre, grotesque, and bordering on caricature.' This judgment points to the ultra-originality of the man and musician who influenced so powerfully his younger contemporaries and made him the *fons et origo* of the New or Young Russian School, the 'innovators' that audaciously set at defiance tradition and the teachings of the schools. The founder of the New Russian School, however, its centre and enthusiastic stimulator, was the twenty years younger Balakirev, not Dargomijsky—whose connection with it was that of an honoured father and tutelary deity. The principal other members were Cui, Moussorgsky, Borodin, and Rimsky-Korsakov. Rubinstein held that the young Russian School was the outcome of the influence of Berlioz and Liszt, with the addition, for pianoforte compositions, of Schumann. The main features of its creations are, according to him, on the one hand, a perfect mastery of technique and an excellent orchestral colouring, and, on the other hand, an entire absence of design and a predominating formlessness. Taking Glinka for their model, they write, Rubinstein tells us, for the most part on folk-songs and folk-dances, proving thereby the poverty of their own invention and palliating it by the name of 'national art' and 'new school.' Although admiring the power and sincerity of some of the members, Tchaikovsky despised the abortions of others, and laughed at the ultra-liberal tendencies of the school. In return for this they excommunicated Rubinstein by calling him a German composer, and accused Tchaikovsky of pedantry, routine, and backwardness. What is a very notable and characteristic fact, not only in connection with the New School, but with the famous Russian composers of the 19th century generally, is the predominant amateur element, an element that does not make altogether for evil. If it accounts for a great deal of weak craftsmanship, crudeness, and fantasticalness, it also accounts for some of the originality, much of the reckless adventurousness, and the width of outlook and boundlessness of enthusiasm. Glinka remained all his life a well-to-do amateur; Dargomijsky was for four years in the government service; Cui kept true to the profession of military engineering and rose to the rank of lieutenant-general; Moussorgsky was first an officer in the Guards, then devoted himself entirely to music, and finally entered one of the administrative branches of the government service; Borodin gave to music the little leisure he could spare from his duties as a professor of chemistry; Rimsky-Korsakov left the navy, for which he was brought up, at the age of twenty-nine; and Tchaikovsky, who was destined for the legal profession, did not exchange it for music till he was twenty-two years old, shortly after he had entered the St. Petersburg conservatorium.

MILY ALEXEIVITCH BALAKIREV (*b.* 1836) has written only songs and instrumental compositions, and no operas. To his belief in programme music, both his own works and his advice to other composers bear witness. Later on we shall have to advert to his influence on Tchaikovsky, who regarded him as the most important personality of his circle, the inventor of its dogmas, and the possessor of an extraordinary talent stifled by various fatal circumstances before he had done much. The works of his that interest us here are the Symphonic Poems *Russia* and *Tamara;* the overture and entr'actes to *Lear*, the overture on three Russian themes, the overture on the theme of a Spanish March, an untitled symphony, and *Islamey*, an Oriental fantasia for pianoforte. The symphonic poem *Russia*, composed in celebration of the 1,000th anniversary of the Russian nation (the arrival of Rurik the Norman in Novgorod in 862), is based on three national melodies representative of three periods in the history of Russia, and concludes with a prayer for the future welfare of the country.

Tamara has for its programme Lermontov's poem of the same name, which is prefixed in its entirety (twelve four-lined stanzas) to the score, both in the original Russian and in a French translation. There is prefixed further a shorter prose account with verse quotations for use in concert programmes. I shall try to indicate the contents still more concisely. Lermontov's poem possesses all the most fascinating elements of a certain kind of romanticism : An ancient tower in a Caucasian solitude rises from a black rock on the bank of the Terek ; it is inhabited by Queen Tamara, an angel of beauty, a demon of wickedness; the light of the tower and the magic voice of the Queen attract the wayfaring merchant, warrior, and herdsman; the hospitable door is opened by a silent eunuch; the lustful Queen richly apparelled awaits her guest on her soft couch; sounds of wild intoxicated passion, as of a hundred couples of lovers celebrating their nuptials and funerals at the same time, soon fill the lonely walls, then follow silence and darkness; and, finally, at daybreak, the corpse of a youth is carried away by the river, and on the roof of the tower a pale woman sends after him a tender, longing farewell. To complete the local colouring and atmosphere of the picture there is yet required a large admixture of restless waves, nocturnal mist, and groaning wind, to which and to the other horrors the composer pays due attention.

As Alfred Bruneau says, Balakirev is a magician of the orchestra and excels in the descriptive poem and instrumental tale. But although this is so, the composer does not as a rule provide detailed programmes. Happily we have *obiter dicta* of his that reveal the workings of his mind. There is first the information he gave to Mrs. Newmarch concerning the overture on the theme of a Spanish March. ' The first theme is my own, written in the Oriental style, in accordance with the programme which depicts the struggle between the Moors and the Spaniards and the victory of the latter with the help of the *auto da. fé* of the Inquisition. The second theme is the original one of the Spanish March given to me by Glinka.' More interesting, because more of a revelation, is the following passage from a letter addressed to Tchaikovsky : ' I do not know how you compose. As a suitable example for you, I will tell you how I composed my *Lear*. After I had read the

drama, there was kindled in me the desire to write an
overture, and I began to plan—for as yet I had no
material, my enthusiasm being confined to the project.
A *maestoso* Introduction and then something mystical
(Kent's prophecy). The Introduction quiets down, and
a stormy *Allegro* begins. That is Lear himself, the
dethroned but still strong lion. As episodes there were
to appear the figures of Regan and Goneril, and then
the second theme, Cordelia, the gentle and tender. After
that the middle section (storm, Lear and the Fool on the
heath), and then the repetition of the *Allegro :* Regan
and Goneril finally overpowering their father. The
overture ends with a *morendo* (Lear over the corpse of
Cordelia), the repetition of Kent's prophecy, and the
slow, solemn death. You must understand that I had
as yet no definite ideas at all. These came only later
and began to accommodate themselves to the outlined
form. I believe that all this will happen to you also if
you will get up an enthusiasm for the plan beforehand.
Then arm yourself with goloshes and a walking-stick,
and take a walk on the Boulevards, beginning with
the Nikitzky ; let yourself be thoroughly saturated with
your plan, and I am convinced that on reaching the
Sretensky Boulevard you will already have found some
theme or episode.'

Of MODEST PETROVICH MOUSSORGSKY (1839-
1881) hard things have been said : he has been accused
of incorrectness, amateurish craftsmanship, ultra-crude
realism, and lack of the sense of beauty. Nevertheless
he was one of the most gifted and most influential
masters of the Young Russian School, overflowing with
vitality, reckless in his daring, and passionately intent
on expressiveness and descriptiveness. It has been

remarked that he was the only one of the innovators to whom the epithet 'musical nihilist' could be applied with any degree of justice. We meet with an interesting characterization of Moussorgsky in a letter written by Tchaikovsky at the end of 1877. 'You are right in your remark that he is 'played out.' As far as talent goes he is perhaps the most important of all, only his is a nature in which there is no desire for self-improvement, a nature which is too much saturated with the absurd theories of those about him, and by the belief in his own genius. Moreover, his is a rather low nature that loves the uncouth, coarse, and ugly. Moussorgsky coquettes with his lack of cultivation; he seems to pride himself on his ignorance and writes down whatever comes into his head, believing blindly in the infallibility of his genius. And indeed a quite original talent often flashes up in him.' If this cannot be called a sympathetic characterization, it is a striking one, which moreover agrees pretty well with the general judgment. Cui says of his music that it is eminently expressive and descriptive; but that the composer is always ready to sacrifice poetry and musical charm to realism, and does not recoil even from repulsiveness and shocking nudeness. Moussorgsky's achievements in opera (*Boris Godounov*, &c.) and song are much more notable than those in pure instrumental music. In fact, in this respect very little is to be recorded : An *Intermezzo in modo classico*, a *Scherzo*, a *Turkish March*, *A Night on a bare Rock*, and pianoforte pieces, *Ten Pictures from the Art Exhibition*, with special titles ('Children's Fun,' 'The Seamstress,' *Intermezzo*, 'On the Southern Shore of the Crimea,' 'In the Village,' 'Meditation,' 'A Tear,' &c.). But the composer who wrote what I am about to quote deserves a place here.

'To seek assiduously the most delicate and subtle features of human nature, of the human crowd—to follow them into unknown regions, to make them our own: this seems to me the true vocation of the artist. . . . To feed upon humanity as a healthy diet that has been neglected—in this lies the whole problem of art.' We may of course hold that this is not so, but the asseveration is interesting and significant.

ALEXANDER PORPHYRIEVICH BORODIN (1834-1887) was professor of chemistry at the St. Petersburg Academy of Medicine. His meeting with Balakirev in 1862 proved a turning point in his life; only after it did he begin to give his leisure time to the more serious study of harmony and composition. Tchaikovsky did not think that the study amounted to much. 'Borodin, too, has talent, even very great talent, which, however, in consequence of insufficient knowledge, has come to grief. . . . He has not so much taste as Cui, and his technique is so weak that he cannot write a bar without extraneous help.' This, however, was written in December, 1877, ten years before Borodin's death and the composition of his best works. The last and grandest of his achievements was the opera *Prince Igor*. Of openly declared programme music we have of him only one work—the Symphonic Sketch *In the Steppes of Central Asia*, which was originally intended for a representation of *Tableaux vivants*. It is the most popular of his instrumental pieces. But he wrote also two symphonies (1862-1867, and 1871-1877) and two quartets without programmes and titles. The critic Stassov, who looked upon Borodin as 'a national poet in the highest sense of the word,' writes of him: 'Like Glinka, Borodin is an epic poet; he is not less national than Glinka, but the Oriental element plays the same part in him as in Glinka, Dargomijsky, Balakirev, Moussorgsky, and Rimsky-Korsakov. He is reckoned among the composers of programme music. Like Glinka, he can say : " My unfettered imagination needs a text as a positive idea." Of Borodin's two symphonies, the second is the most perfect, and owes its power not only to the matured talent of its author, but still more to the national character with which its very subject invests it. The old heroic Russian form predominates as in *Prince Igor.* I may add that Borodin himself has often told me that in the *Adagio* he intended to recall the old Slavonic *bayans* (a kind of Troubadours, or Minnesänger), in the first movement the assembling of the old Russian princes, and in the Finale the banquets of the heroes, to the tones of the guzla and bamboo flute, amid the enthusiasm of the people.' The programme of the Symphonic Sketch is as follows. ' In the monotonous steppe of Central Asia there are heard the hitherto unknown tones of a peaceful Russian song. From afar comes the trampling of horses and camels, and the peculiar sound of an Oriental melody. A native caravan approaches. Protected by Russian arms it proceeds safe and fearless on its way through the immeasurable desert. Further and further it goes. The song of the Russians and the melody of the Asiatics combine in a common harmony, the echo of which gradually dies away in the air of the steppe.'

Although beginning his musical career as an amateur and with a slight technical outfit, NIKOLAI ANDRE-JEVICH RIMSKY-KORSAKOV (*b.* 1844), soon after exchanging the Navy for music, in 1873, devoted himself to the study of the art with commendable seriousness and energy. Tchaikovsky, with whom he was in correspondence, told him that this laborious training was astounding, and heroic in one who already eight years ago had written a *Sadko* (the symphonic poem, not the later opera). A comparison with Rimsky-Korsakov made him think himself small, pitiable, self-contentedly naif. 'I am an artisan,' wrote Tchaikovsky, 'but you are an artist.' That these were not empty compliments may be gathered from a letter written two years later to Madame von Meck. 'He is an exception (has become so lately) among the generally badly trained Russian composers. It is true that he is self-taught like the others, but some time ago a change took place in him. This man is by nature very earnest, very honest and conscientious. Korsakov is the only one of the school who came to realize, about five years ago, that the ideas preached in his circle had no foundation whatever, that the disparagement of schooling and of classical music, the decrying of authorities and masterpieces were nothing but ignorance. . . . I am still in possession of a letter of that period which touched and moved me much. Rimsky-Korsakov was in despair when he became aware that so many years had passed uselessly, that he found himself on a way that led to nowhere. He asked himself then what he was to do. Of course he had to learn. And he began with such zeal that the school technique soon became to him a necessity. In one summer he wrote numberless counterpoints and sixty-four fugues, of which I received ten to look through. The fugues were faultless, but I noticed even then that the reaction was too violent. Rimsky-Korsakov had suddenly leapt from the disparagement of school to the cult of musical technique. Soon after this appeared his

2 E

symphony and also the quartet. Both works are full of
artistic trickeries, and bear, as you rightly remark, the
stamp of pedantry. Plainly he is in a critical state, and
it is difficult to prophesy how this crisis will end. Either
he will develop into a great master or will be submerged
in contrapuntal ingenuities.' Rimsky-Korsakov's operas
do not concern us. As an instrumental composer
he has proved himself unquestionably—in spite of
three untitled symphonies and two overtures, and
whether they mean much, little, or nothing — a
composer of programme music by the two symphonic
poems *Sadko* and *Antar*, the *Sheherazade*, a *Fairy-tale*,
a *Servian Fantasia*, a *Spanish Capriccio*, and suites
extracted from operas. *Sadko*, an early work, is
a musical illustration of a popular Russian legend, or
rather of a part of one. The programme prefixed to the
score is given in two paragraphs, the shorter first one
being in small type. It runs as follows :

The ship of Sadko, a notable of Novgorod, is stopped on the
open sea. Chosen by lot, Sadko himself is thrown overboard as a
tribute to the King of the Seas. . . . The ship pursues its way.

'Remaining alone among the waves, Sadko, with his
lyre (tympanon), is dragged by the King of the Seas to
his submarine kingdom. He finds himself there in the
midst of a grand feast. The King of the Seas was
marrying his daughter to the Ocean. Having made
Sadko play the lyre, he began to dance, and all the
kingdom imitated him. The Ocean, too, began to stir :
he broke and swallowed the ships. . . . Then Sadko
tore the strings from his lyre, the dance ceased, and the
sea became calm.'

The slow introduction and Coda (*Moderato assai*, 6-4)
depict the calm sea, the main part of the composition

(*Allegro molto* 3-4, and *Allegretto* 2-4) the merry-making, which in the 2-4 time grows wilder and wilder and ends ferociously (*feroce*). The opening of the *Allegro molto*, before the dance begins, is concerned with the dragging down of Sadko. Verve and picturesqueness cannot be denied to the composition. But one may ask oneself whether the picturesqueness does not occupy the composer too exclusively, even at the cost of the musicalness?

The subject of *Antar*, the other symphonic poem, is the Arab chief and poet of the 6th, celebrated in a romance of the 8th century, who in his poem sings of his warlike deeds and his love of Abla. Of this later and more developed work Cui gives the following account—programme and commentary. 'First Part: Antar is in the desert—he saves a gazelle from a bird of prey. The gazelle is a fay, who rewards her deliverer by granting him three pleasures. (The whole of this part, which begins and ends with a picture of the desolate and boundless desert, is worthy of the composer's magic brush.) Second Part: The pleasure of power (an Oriental March, a masterpiece of the finest and most brilliant interpretation). Third Part: The pleasure of vengeance (a rugged, savage, unbridled *Allegro*, with crescendos like the letting loose of furious winds). Last Part: The pleasure of love, amid which Antar expires (a delicate, poetic, delicious *Andante*, where sometimes one wishes greater animation in the passion).'

One of the suites, Op. 57, bears the title Musical Pictures, Suite for orchestra to the legend of *Czar Saltan*. There are three pictures, and to each are prefixed lines by Poushkin. They run as follows: (1) At that time there arose a war. Czar Saltan took leave

of his spouse, bestrode his horse, and enjoined upon
her for his love's sake to take care of herself. (2) The
Czarina sits at home lamenting, but the child grows
big and strong in its prison. (3) The three wonders
of the island in the sea.—As to the *Fairy-Tale*
(Conte féerique), it has prefixed to it lines from the
prologue of Poushkin's *Russlan and Lioudmilla.* They do
not give the subject, but form the introduction to the
telling of a tale, an introduction characterizing as it
were Russian love of fairy-tales and legendary tales of
all sorts. We read there of the tree from which is
suspended a golden chain to which is attached a wise
cat—going to the right she hums a song, going to the
left she tells a tale.

Alfred Bruneau, on hearing *Antar*, praised enthusiastically the searching, powerful, and original painting of
the three great human passions in the last parts of the
work. He thought that there lay the superiority of the
music. ' These sentiments, passing severally through
diverse measures, tonalities, and rhythms, over which
hovers insistently the *phrase-mère* of Antar, are the faithful
reflections of our tormented, vague, and mysterious souls.
Only sounds can render the infinite nobility of the
thoughts that make us act and then die. M. Rimsky-
Korsakov has expressed all these profound *nuances* of
the heart in an eloquent, solid, novel, and bold language.'
In short, Bruneau held that Rimsky-Korsakov was by
nature essentially descriptive, but that he did not stop
short at the exteriority of men and things, that he
interpreted, magnified, and vivified his subjects. It is
interesting and instructive to read in the composers'
preface to his fairy ballet-opera *Mlada* that he
attaches much importance to the descriptive side of

his music, and forbids thunder, wind, and other noises on the stage, as the orchestra is charged with their imitation.

ALEXANDER GLAZOUNOV (*b.* 1865), a pupil of Rimsky - Korsakov, presents himself, notwithstanding some untitled symphonies, as a confirmed composer of programme music. We have of him a symphonic poem, *Stenka Razin,* Op. 15; two fantasias, *The Forest,* Op. 19, and *The Ocean,* Op. 28; two symphonic tableaux, *Through Night to Light,* Op. 5, and *The Kreml,* Op. 30; a *Poème lyrique,* Op. 12; *In Memory of a Hero,* Op. 8; *Idylle et Rêverie Orientale,* Op. 14; *Rhapsodie Orientale,* Op. 29; *Spring,* Op. 12; *Intermezzo romantico,* Op. 69; *Mediæval Suite* (Aus dem Mittelalter), &c. As Stenka Razin is not an individual with whom Western Europe is familiar, it may not be superfluous to mention that he was a robber executed at Moscow in 1671, the hero of many Russian ballads. Alfred Bruneau tells us in his *Musique de Russie* that he was greatly struck by *l'âpreté, la grandeur, la fermeté* of the work. The preface to the Elegy *A la Mémoire d'un Héros* will interest the reader. ' The author has in view an ideal hero, whose life had never been soiled by any act of cruelty, who had fought only for the just cause, that of the oppressed people, and in times of peace had filled his life with acts of justice and general beneficence. The death of this hero is bitterly wept by the people, and a double glory attends him—the terrestrial and the celestial glory.'

More than any one of the Russian composers already discussed, PETER ILITCH TCHAIKOVSKY (1840-1893) has engaged the interest and gained the sympathy and admiration of the musical world. What will be the position finally assigned to him no one can as yet tell.

His reputation has undergone various changes, and may still undergo others. At first it rose slowly, then took a sudden upward leap, and after that declined quickly and considerably. Still, his appreciation even now is high, and, I think, rightly so. For, although not an original and a power of the first quality, he is a distinct individuality, a genuine poet, and a craftsman masterly in counterpoint and virtuosic in colouring. He has not in his symphonic works the sweep of thought of Beethoven, Mozart, and Haydn, not even that of Mendelssohn and Schumann, but he has a wealth of soul-stirring, ravishing, bewitching, and piquant beauties of detail and in miniature. Naturally this deficiency in weight and development of thought is not felt so much in the suite-like middle movements of his symphonies— in the graceful waltzes, fantastic intermezzi, sweet lyrical outpourings, &c.—as in the first and the last movements, where something more monumental is expected. Tchaikovsky loved colour dearly. This love grew upon him, grew upon him so much that in the last years of the master Cui could say of him, with some justification, that the colourist had gained the upper hand over the thinker. But what of the man, the substratum of the musician? Tchaikovsky was extremely sensitive, very retiring, inclined to melancholy, and decidedly a creature of moods. 'There's naught in this life sweet . . . . but only melancholy,' he might have said. His work was his life. Without it, life was impossible. And from his work came what happiness he had. It could be said of him that he was one of the kind to which belonged Goethe's Werther, Chateaubriand's René, Byron's Manfred, Poushkin's Lensky, and Sénancour's Obermann; but it would be necessary to add that his

individuality is unlike any one of these. The comparison
is worthless without the perception of the difference. As
a composer Tchaikovsky was an eclectic. His likings
and dislikings of other masters' music account to some
extent for the character of his own, and point to some of its
qualities. In early life, before his serious studies began,
Tchaikovsky delighted chiefly in Italian opera, and Italian
vocal art continued to have always a great charm for
him. Nor should we overlook that Italy herself became
very dear to him. Whilst having an open ear and warm
heart for Russian folk-music, sometimes using it and
oftener fashioning his own melodies on it, his relation to
it differed from that of the young Russian School, a
school which on account of its neglect of thorough
technical training and respect for the classics, he regarded
with antipathy. He loathed those who, as he said,
thought that novelty and originality consisted in trampling
on all hitherto existing laws of musical beauty. Bach
and Handel did not appeal to him. Beethoven, he looked
up to with respect and wonder rather than with affection.
In him and Michael Angelo he saw the same breadth and
strength, the same daring that touches the limits of the
ugly, the same sombre moods. The characteristic part
of the remark is ' the touching of the limits of the
ugly.' Tchaikovsky's chief love and idol was Mozart.
To him he owed his life's devotion to music. ' I am
in love with *Don Giovanni*, and at this moment,
while I am writing, I could weep for emotion and
excitement . . . In his chamber music, Mozart seduces
me by his purity and grace of form, and wonderful beauty
of part-writing. Here also some passages can draw tears
from me.' This Mozart-worship puts one in mind of
Tchaikovsky's remark that ' the absence of spiritual

relationship between two artist individualities does not exclude mutual sympathies.' While *La Damnation de Faust* was one of the Russian master's favourites, he regretted in Berlioz's works generally unloveliness and poverty of melody, unsatisfactoriness of harmony, and disproportion between his strong luxuriant imagination and his deficient art of invention, between his magnificent intentions and his power of execution. Although never a follower or enthusiastic admirer of Wagner, Tchaikovsky came in later life to some extent under his influence, slightly after the *Ring des Nibelungen*, rather more after *Parsifal*. With Grieg he found himself in full sympathy. Brahms, on the contrary, was his pet aversion. He seemed to him a great musician, even a great master, but cold, nebulous, repellent, pitiably pretentious, coquetting with profundity rather than profound, without poetry, charm, and warmth of feeling, without melodic invention, inspiration, and any creative power whatever. The other contemporary German composers did not fare much better: they were dried up, had nothing to say, imitated either Mendelssohn-Schumann or Liszt-Wagner. On the other hand, he had a genuine love for the contemporary French composers, more especially for Bizet, and next to him for Délibes. He admired their striving after eclecticism, their feeling for proportion, their readiness to depart from the secular routine while keeping within the boundaries of the beautiful. In short, he was charmed by the novelty and freshness of modern French music, and by the absence of pretence of profundity, and the presence of anxiety for musical beauty. Have we not in these judgments a revelation of the composer's nature and an analysis of his eclecticism?

About a large portion of Tchaikovsky's works I shall say nothing—nothing about his nine operas, nothing about his concerted chamber music, songs, and concertos, nothing even about his Trio, Op. 50, *A la mémoire d'un grand artiste* (Nicholas Rubinstein), his Elegy for stringed instruments on the death of Samarin (an actor), his string Sextet *Souvenirs de Florence,* Op. 70, his *Italian Capriccio* for orchestra, Op. 45, his pianoforte pieces *Souvenir de Hapsal,* Op. 2, *The Seasons,* Op. 37 *bis,* the *Children's Album,* Op. 39, &c., although they undoubtedly offer opportunities for comment to the searcher after programmatic lore. The fact is we shall have enough to do with the orchestral pieces of declared programme music and the untitled symphonies and suites. What will occupy us, however, are not comments of the present writer's, but of Tchaikovsky's. And here I will say at once, that in my opinion Tchaikovsky has better described the process of composition in the mind of a tone-poet than any other musician I know—not excepting Schumann, Berlioz, Liszt, and Wagner. It need hardly be added that writing about this process implies dealing with the question of absolute and programme music.

In 1864 Anton Rubinstein gave his pupils of the composition class as a task for the summer holidays the writing of an overture. Tchaikovsky took for his subject a favourite Russian drama of his, *The Thunderstorm* by Ostrowsky, and devised the following programme. 'Introduction, *Adagio*—the childhood of Catherine and her whole life before marriage; *Allegro* (indication of thunderstorm)—her longing after true love and happiness. *Allegro appassionato*—her soul struggles. Sudden transition to the evening on the bank of the Volga : again the struggle, only with the feature of a certain feverish happiness. The premonitions of the thunderstorm (repetition of the motives after the *Adagio* and the further development of that motive). Thunderstorm: the climax of the desperate struggle—death.'

The critic Laroche, a companion of Tchaikovsky during his conservatorium days, relates that among the compositions his friend most enthusiastically admired were Litolff's overtures *Robespierre* and *Les Girondins;* and adds that since his acquaintance with these two works and Meyerbeer's overture to *Struensee,* Tchaikovsky had all his life a passion for programme music.

A year after leaving the conservatorium, two years after the *Thunderstorm* overture, that is in 1866, Tchaikovsky wrote his first symphony, Op. 13, and entitled the whole *Winter Dreams,* and the first two movements respectively *Dream on a winter road* and *Desolate country, gloomy country.* This symphony was followed two years later (1868) by a symphonic poem. The title of this work is *Fatum,* and the programme runs as follows : ' Do you know what old Melchizedek said when, taking leave of life, he was dying ? As a slave man is born, as a slave he sinks into the grave. Death, too, will not tell him why he wandered through this valley of tears, and wherefore he suffered, endured, and wept, and now must disappear.' This motto rather than programme, taken from the writings of Batioushkov, was suggested by an admirer of the composer to Nicholas Rubinstein, who was to conduct the work, and wished for the sake of the public something more than a title. But what motto and music had in common did not seem obvious. Laroche remarked, ' The piece resembles rather a battle, a revolt, or an elemental natural phenomenon than the gloomy monologue of a disappointed old man ! '

The *Romeo and Juliet* ouverture-fantaisie (revised 1870) was composed at the instigation of Balakirev, as a letter of August, 1869, shows.* The founder of the New Russian School followed the writing with great interest, and to him the composer sent both the first sketch and the finished score, which were returned with severe criticisms intermixed with hearty praise. The work was published without a programme. The title-page said only *Romeo et Juliette, Ouverture-Fantaisie d'après Shakespeare.* From Tchaikovsky we learn nothing of consequence concerning the nature of this work. Balakirev speaks of the drawing of Friar Lawrence and of Romeo and Juliet, and the love-ardour, voluptuousness, and longing of the parts dealing with them. Stassov regrets that the composer left out Juliet's nurse. Ivan Knorr calls the representation of the drama graphic. And Cui praises the beauty and superb passion of the melodies, but blames their imperfect inter-connection.

After the second symphony, composed in 1872, followed in 1873 the fantasia *The Tempest.* At a party at Rimsky-Korsakov's in December, 1872, Tchaikovsky asked Stassov to give him a theme for a symphonic fantasia, adding that he preferred something of Shakespeare's. Hardly a week after this Stassov wrote in detail about the subject he proposed. The programme prefixed is as follows : ' The sea. Ariel, an airy spirit, obeying the will of the magician Prospero, raises a tempest. Wreck of the ship bringing Ferdinand. The enchanted island. First and timid love-impulses of Miranda and Ferdinand. Ariel. Caliban. The amorous couple give themselves up to the triumphant spell of the passion.

* The dates of the letters are old style, add twelve days and you get new style.

Prospero divests himself of his magic power, and leaves
the island. The sea.' To see more of the inspiring
influences at work, we will look into the letters in
which Stassov expounds and discusses the subject. 'In
The Tempest all the elements are so poetic and grateful :
at the beginning the sea, the uninhabited island, the
imposing and severe figure of Prospero, and immediately
afterwards grace and womanliness itself, Miranda
like an Eve who has not yet seen a man (except
Prospero), and who is enraptured and surprised at sight
of the beautiful youth cast on land by the storm. They
at once fall in love with each other ; and here, I think, is
to be created the most wonderful poetic picture. In the
first half of the overture Miranda passes but gradually
from her childlike innocence to her maidenly love; in
the second half of the overture both—she and Ferdinand
—would already be seized by the flames of passion.
Around these principal characters, there might be
grouped (in the middle part of the overture) the other
figures : the monster Caliban, the airy spirit Ariel with
a choir of elves. The conclusion of the overture should
represent how Prospero resigns his magic power, blesses
the lovers, and induces them to return to the
fatherland.' A few weeks later Stassov writes : ' You
ask whether the storm itself was necessary ? Certainly,
unquestionably ! Without it the overture would not be
worth anything; without it, the whole programme, too,
must be crippled. I had considered all moments, all
their consequences and contrasts; therefore it would be
a pity to transform the whole story now. I had in my
mind that the sea should appear twice—at the beginning,
and at the end. At the beginning, in the introduction, I
think of it as calm, until Prospero speaks the magic

words and conjures up the storm. But this storm must break out *instantaneously in all its violence*, and not, as usually, become gradually wider and louder. I propose so peculiar a form for the storm because in this case it is raised by magic words, whereas in all operas, symphonies, and oratorios hitherto written it arises from natural causes. After the storm has abated, and its roaring, whistling, thundering, and tumult have died away, the magic island appears in all its wonderful beauty, and the still more beautiful, still more glorious maid Miranda, who, like a sunbeam, walks with light step on the island. Her conversation with Prospero and immediately afterwards with the youth Ferdinand, who surprises and enraptures her, and with whom she at once falls in love. The motive of the falling in love (*crescendo*) should be like an unfolding, like a growing; in Shakespeare it is so described at the end of the first act, and I believe that would be the very thing for your talent. After this I would propose the appearance of Caliban, the animal-like low slave; then further, Ariel, whose programme is to be found in Shakespeare's song (end of the first act) "Come unto these yellow sands." After Ariel, Miranda and Ferdinand must again come upon the scene, but this time full of impetuous passion. Then the imposing figure of Prospero, who resigns his magic power, and takes leave of his past: at last, at the end, again the sea, the calm, still sea, which bathes the lonely island, now abandoned, whilst its happy inhabitants are carried in a ship to distant Italy.'

After the third symphony, composed in 1875, Tchaikovsky produced in 1876 the orchestral fantasia *Francesca da Rimini*, Op. 32, which was published without a programme. On July 27, 1876, he writes from Paris to his brother Modest: 'To-day I read the fifth canto of the *Inferno*, and was animated by the desire to compose a symphonic poem, *Francesca da Rimini*.' Immediately after the completion of the work, he says in a letter of October 14, 1876: 'I have worked at it with love, and therefore believe that I have succeeded in the love part. As to the whirlwind, it might perhaps with advantage be a little more like Doré's drawing. I have not succeeded with it quite so well as I really wished.' Knorr, who alludes to the motives treated by the composer—the dread portal, the gruesomeness of the city of woe, the whirlwind, and the lovers, whose appearance in the surrounding horrors is accompanied by a touching melody—thinks that Tchaikovsky was influenced in this work by Liszt and his *Dante* Symphony. But similarity in the selection of motives, and similarity in their treatment, by no means compel us to draw the critic's conclusion. In fact, both the similarity of selection and of treatment, especially the first, are almost inevitable.

Another untitled symphony, the fourth (1877), comes between the last discussed and the following titled orchestral work, which is the *Ouverture Solennelle* '1812,' Op. 49. Tchaikovsky had not a very high opinion of it. On October 10, 1880, he writes: 'The overture will be very banging and noisy. I wrote it without much love, on which account it is probably without much artistic value.' In another letter he says that it was written at the request of Nicholas Rubinstein for the Moscow Exhibition concerts.

The next programmatic work of Tchaikovsky's is *Manfred*, described on the title-page as a *Symphonie en quatre tableaux d'après le poëme dramatique de*

Byron (1885). The programme runs thus : ' I. Manfred wandered in the Alps. Tormented by the fatal anguish of doubt, torn by remorse and despair, his soul is the victim of nameless suffering. Neither the occult sciences, of which he fathomed the mysteries, and thanks to which the dark powers of hell are subject to him, nor anything else in the world can give him the forgetfulness to which solely he aspires. The recollection of the beautiful Astarte, whom he loved and lost, gnaws his heart; nothing can raise the curse which weighs on the soul of Manfred, he is incessantly a prey to tortures of the utmost atrocious despair. II. The Witch of the Alps appears before Manfred under the rainbow of the torrent. III. Pastoral. Simple, free, and peaceful life of the mountaineers. IV. The subterranean palace of Arimanes. Manfred appears in the middle of the Bacchanals. Evocation of the shade of Astarte. She predicts to him the end of his terrestrial troubles. Death of Manfred.'

Writing on June 13, 1885, to Taneiev, Tchaikovsky says : ' After some hesitation I have decided to write *Manfred*, for I feel that I shall have no rest until I have redeemed my word given last winter to Balakirev. I do not know what will be the outcome of it. In the meantime I am dissatisfied with myself. No, it is a thousand times more agreeable to compose without a programme. When I write a programme symphony I have continually the feeling that I cheat the public and deceive them, that I do not pay with ready money, but with worthless paper rags.' Was this not the expression of a momentary humour? His action in spite of this feeling, and the following remark incline one to think so. After a performance of *Manfred*, on March 13, 1886, he writes:

' I am satisfied with it. I believe it is my best symphonic piece.'

There remain for enumeration only two more works—the fantasia-overture *Hamlet*, Op. 67, without a further programme, composed in the same year in which Tchaikovsky composed his fifth symphony (1888), and the symphonic ballad *Le Voyvode*, Op. 78 (1891), to which a poem of Poushkin's after Mickiewicz is prefixed.

In the Suites there is of course much more to be found than *jeux de sons*, as Tchaikovsky calls the first number of the second suite. Indeed, they consist of character pieces full of life and poetry. The titles suffice to show it—*Dance of the Giants, Scherzo burlesque, Rêve d'enfants, Danse baroque*, &c. As to the sixth symphony (1893), which Tchaikovsky characterizes in a letter as the sincerest of his works, we must take note that only on the morning after the first performance the composer began to consider what to call it, as he did not wish it to bear merely a number. He rejected the titles ' Programme Symphony ' and ' Tragic Symphony,' and at last accepted his brother's suggestion ' Pathetic Symphony.'

But what was really Tchaikovsky's position with regard to programme music ? Was he a composer of programme music only where he distinctly declared it, and purely formalistic everywhere else; or did his programmatic tendency extend farther ? And if the latter was the case, of what nature were the programmes and what was their function in the process of creation ? Tchaikovsky has full and clear answers to these questions. I am sure the reader will not complain of the long quotations in which they are given.

'What really is programme music? As for us two, for me and for you' [he is writing to Madame von Meck], 'a mere play with sounds is a long way from being music—every kind of music is programme music from our standpoint. But in the narrower sense this word signifies such symphonic music or such instrumental music generally as illustrates a definite subject placed before the public in a programme, and bears the title of this subject. . . . I find that the inspiration of a symphonic composer can be of two kinds: subjective and objective. In the former case the personal feelings of joy or sorrow are expressed in the music, similarly as with the lyrical poet, who, so to speak, pours out his soul in poems. Here the programme is not only unnecessary, but impossible. It is otherwise when the musician in reading a poetic work or at the sight of a beautiful landscape is inflamed by enthusiasm to musically characterize the subject that fills him with such ecstasy. In this case a programme is indispensable, and it is a pity that Beethoven has not provided a programme for the sonatas of which you speak. At any rate, from my standpoint, both kinds of music have a right to exist, and I do not understand the people who will admit the legitimacy of only one of them. Of course not every subject is suitable for a symphony, just as not every one is suitable for an opera—nevertheless there can and must be programme music: for would it not be unreasonable to demand of literature that it should ignore the epic element and confine itself solely to the lyrical?'

In reply to S. I. Taneiev who had remarked that the first movement of the fourth symphony made upon him the impression of a symphonic poem, of programme

2 F

music, Tchaikovsky wrote on March 27, 1878, as follows:—

' As to your remark that my symphony sounds like programme music, I agree with you. Only I do not see why that should be a fault. I am afraid of the contrary, that is to say, I should be sorry if symphonic works were to flow from my pen which express nothing, but consist merely of chords and a play of rhythms and modulations. Of course my symphony is programme music, only it is quite impossible to formulate its programme in words; it would have a ludicrous effect and give rise to ridicule. But should not this be the case with a symphony, the most lyrical of all forms? Should it not express all that cannot be expressed in words, but which fills the soul to overflowing and calls for expression? Moreover, I must confess to you that in my simplicity I had believed that the thought of this symphony was so clear that its meaning, at least in outline, would be intelligible even without a programme. Now do not believe that I wish to make a boast of profound feelings and sublime thoughts. I did not in the least endeavour to express new ideas. At bottom my symphony is an imitation of Beethoven's fifth symphony, that is to say, I imitated not its musical content, but its fundamental idea. What do you think— has the fifth symphony a programme? Not only has it a programme, but there cannot even be the slightest difference of opinion as to what the symphony purports to express. Almost the same underlies my symphony; and if you have not understood me, it follows that I am no Beethoven, about which I had never any doubt. I will add that there is in this symphony, *i.e.*, in mine, not a single bar which I have not truly felt and which is not an echo of my innermost soul-life. The middle of the first movement may perhaps form an exception, as in it there are some forced and patched passages, in short, there is fabrication. I know that in reading these lines you will laugh. For you are a sceptic and mocker. In spite of your great love for music you seem not to believe that one can compose from an inner impulse. But wait; your turn, too, will come. You, too, will some day, perhaps very soon, write not at the desire of others, but from inward necessity. Then only will fall on the luxuriant soil of your talent seeds that will bear splendid fruits. In the meantime, however, your soil awaits the seed.'

Although Tchaikovsky says to Taneiev that it is impossible to formulate in words the programme of his fourth symphony, he had found it possible to do so in a letter to his friend Madame von Meck, of February 17, 1878.

'How much pleasure has your letter of to-day brought me! I am unspeakably glad that the symphony [the fourth, Op. 36, in F minor] has pleased you, that while hearing it you felt the same feelings which filled me while working at it, and that my music found its way to your heart. You ask whether a definite programme was in my mind during the composition of this symphony. To such questions my usual reply is "No." Indeed it is difficult to give an answer to this question. How should one interpret all those indefinite feelings which take possession of one while composing an instrumental work without a special name? It is a purely lyrical process. It is the musical confession of the soul, in which much material has gathered and then flows out in tones, as a lyrical poet gives utterance in verse. The difference lies only in this, that music possesses

incomparably richer means and is a more subtle language
for the expression of the incalculably varied moments of
a soul mood.   Usually the germ of the coming work
appears quite suddenly, quite unexpectedly.   If this germ
falls on fertile soil, *i.e.*, if there is inclination for work,
then it takes root with incredible vigour and rapidity,
springs up from the earth, and shoots forth branches,
leaves, and at last blossoms.   I cannot otherwise illustrate
the creative process than by this comparison.   The
greatest difficulty lies in this, that the germ must appear
under favourable conditions.   All the rest comes of itself.
It would be useless were I to try to clothe in words this
ineffable feeling of pleasure which comes over one when
a new thought suddenly arises and growing begins to
assume definite forms.   Then I forget everything, behave
like a madman, everything within me pulsates and
trembles, scarcely have I begun when a thousand details
race through my head.   In the midst of this magic
process it often happens that some shock from without
tears me out of my somnambulism ; for instance, when
suddenly someone rings the bell, or when the servant
enters the room, or when the clock strikes and reminds
me that it is time to break off.   Such disturbances are
absolutely horrible.   Sometimes they scare away the
inspiration for a long time, and I have to seek
it again—how often in vain !   In this case one must have
recourse to cool headwork and technical skill.   Even with
the greatest masters there are to be found such moments,
where the organic connection is wanting and its place is
taken by an artificial joint, so that parts of a whole
appear as it were glued together.   But that cannot be
avoided.   If that mood of the soul of an artist which is
called *inspiration*, and which I just now endeavoured to

describe, were to continue long without interruption, one would not be able to survive a single day. The strings would break and the instrument fly asunder in a thousand pieces. It suffices if the principal thoughts and the general outlines of the composition are not found by means of " seeking," but appear of themselves under the influence of that supernatural, inexplicable force that is called inspiration.

'But I have strayed from my path. *Our* symphony has a programme, that is to say, it is possible to put the contents into words; and I will communicate to you, but only to you, the meaning of the whole work as well as its several parts. Of course I can do that only in outline.

' The introduction is the *kernel* of the whole symphony, the principal thought :—

This is Fate, that momentous power which hinders the desire for happiness from attaining its aim, which takes care that well-being and contentment do not gain the upper-hand, that the heavens do not become free from clouds, a power which, like Damocles' sword, always hangs overhead, which continually poisons the soul. This power is inevitable and unconquerable. There remains nothing but to submit to it and lament in vain :—

The feeling of depression and hopelessness becomes
stronger and stronger, more and more burning. Is it
not better to turn from reality and rock oneself in
dreams ? :—

O joy! What a tender, what a sweet dream is this! A
resplendent human being promising happiness hovers
before me and beckons me :—

How beautiful! The obtrusive first motive of the *Allegro*
is now heard far away. Gradually the whole soul
becomes wrapped in a web of dreams. All that is sombre,
all that is joyless, is forgotten.

'Happiness! Happiness!! Happiness!!!

'No, these are only dreams, Fate scares them
away :—

'Life then is nothing but an eternal change of sombre
reality and flitting dreams of happiness. There is no
haven : you are driven hither and thither by the waves
until the sea swallows you up. This is approximately
the programme of the first movement.

'The second movement shows sorrow in a different
state. It is that melancholy feeling that encompasses
us when we sit at home alone, in the evening, exhausted
by work ; the book, taken up for reading, has slipped from
the hand ; a whole swarm of memories arise. How sad

that so much is already past and gone! And yet it is
pleasant to recall early years. We regret the past,
and have not the courage, not the inclination to begin a
new life.—We are rather weary of existence. We should
like to refresh ourselves and look back, revive many a
memory. We think of joyous hours when the young
blood was still foaming and seething, and found
satisfaction in life. We think also of sad moments, of
irretrievable losses. All this lies already so far, so far
behind us. It is sad, and yet so sweet to brood over
the past.

'In the third movement no definite feeling is
expressed. Here are capricious arabesques, intangible
forms, which whisk through the imagination when one
has been drinking wine and is a little excited. The
mood is neither gay nor sad. One thinks of nothing
in particular; lets the imagination take its own course,
and it delights in drawing the most wonderful lines.
Suddenly there emerges from memory the picture of
a tipsy peasant and of a street song. . . . In the
distance one hears military music passing by. Such
are the disconnected images which come and go in our
brain when we are falling asleep. They have nothing
to do with reality: they are unintelligible, bizarre,
fragmentary.

'Fourth movement. When you find no joy within
you, look around you. Go among the people. See,
they know how to enjoy themselves, they give themselves up fully and wholly to their joyous feelings.
The picture of a popular festivity. Scarcely have you
forgotten yourself, scarcely have you lost yourself in
the contemplation of the joy of others, when the
indefatigable Fate again announces its presence. But

the other mortals do not much concern themselves about
you; they do not even see you; they do not notice at all
that you are lonely and sad. O, how they enjoy
themselves; how happy they are! And you will maintain
that everything in this world is sombre and sad? After
all there is still joy, simple primitive joy. Enjoy the
joy of others, and—you can still live.

'This is all I can tell you in regard to my symphony,
my dear friend. Of course, my words are not clear
and not sufficiently exhaustive. But therein lies the
peculiarity of instrumental music that it cannot be
analyzed.'

This letter is a priceless document, an illuminating
contribution to æsthetics and psychology, and will be
studied long after the master's compositions have been
forgotten. The process of forgetting may be quicker
than we expect, and more extensive than is just. For
although Tchaikovsky's thoughts are not sufficiently
great and powerful, or not sufficiently developed, for the
grand symphonic forms, and his morbid pessimism, with
its concomitant monotonies of rhythm, &c., is productive
of pathological rather than of æsthetical effects, he was
undoubtedly an exquisite composer of *suites de pièces*,
and has left us many delightful and perfect things—as
many of the middle movements of his symphonies and
chamber music, his suites, and pianoforte pieces prove
incontrovertibly.

In conclusion I should like to say this: If we wish to
understand Russian music, we shall do well to make
ourselves acquainted with Russian literature and Russian
pictorial art—with the poems, novels, and dramas of
Poushkin, Lermontov, Gogol (the founders of the modern
truly national Russian literature who so often inspired

the Russian composers), Tourgeniev, Tolstoy, Ostrovsky,
Dostoievsky, and Gorky; and with the paintings of Perov,
Repin, and Verestchagin.   They constitute a psychology
of the Russian people, and will explain what otherwise
is well-nigh inexplicable—the deep melancholy of their
music, its fierce passionateness, its unbridled barbarities,
and much more.   All these are to be found in the
character and the life of the people.

CHAPTER IV.

IN GERMANY.

The writing of the present chapter cannot be called an inspiring task. Without Wagner's sovereign contempt for the music of his time, and Tchaikovsky's belief in Germany's complete exhaustion, one may yet be unable to grow enthusiastic over the theme. The productivity during the period with which we are concerned has been enormous. But how about the really valuable outcome of it? In the latter part of the 19th century the question was often asked : What remains if you remove from the living German composers Wagner and Brahms? And then there were ever so many people who, while heartily admitting the greatness of one of the two, were not so sure of the other—not to mention those who were all for the one and would have none whatever of the other. Now, this exclusive way of looking at men and things is not only unfair. it is absolutely foolish. The men of genius leave room for the men of talent ; and the masters *en grand* for the masters *en miniature*. To be sure for some time past Germany has not been abounding in musical genius of the first or even second order. But if there has been a dearth of powerful original creativeness and of strikingly outstanding individuality, there has been also a goodly provision of artistic ability well deserving our respect and gratitude, ability displaying itself not merely in technical skill, but often also in imaginativeness, sensibility, and poetic charm. The great bulk of crudities, futilities, and vacuities need not trouble us : they are not peculiar to any one period.

One could classify composers into (1) such as write only absolute music, and are uninfluenced by and even averse to the programmatic tendency; (2) such as write programme music, but only in the classical manner and forms; (3) such as go only to a limited extent beyond this standpoint; and (4) such as follow unhesitatingly the lead of Liszt. This classification, although useful, gives rise to difficulties. In the first place it is not possible to draw boundary lines between the different species. But perhaps even a greater difficulty arises from the assumption of the existence of the first of the four. Is there such a thing as absolute music? Are there composers uninfluenced by programme music and averse to it *in practice*? My opinion is that there is no such music, and that there are no such composers. Of course, I am thinking of good music, music we care to hear, music which we really enjoy, *i.e.*, music that affects the mind and heart, and does not consist merely of unmeaning combinations of sounds.

JOHANNES BRAHMS (1833-1897) is generally put forward as the model of a composer of absolute music, in fact, as the most perfect representative of the antipodes of the composers of programme music. Well, I claim him as a composer of programme music. Of course so extraordinary a statement, which to many cannot fail to be shocking and seem absurd, ought not only to be proved by reasoning, but also to be supported by facts. I believe that in listening to Brahms's music a mind unprejudiced as well as sensitive and receptive must have frequently and forcibly impressed upon it the fact that there is in these wonderful tone-combinations something that connects them with life—that is, with the composer's experiences, thoughts, and feelings, with his relations to man and nature. This impression is confirmed and greatly strengthened by a reading of Max Kalbeck's biography of the master. In fact, the author of that work represents Brahms as a more deep-dyed composer of programme music than I should venture to make him out to be. Strange to say, Kalbeck is an uncompromising opponent of programme music. The seeming contradiction, however, is easily understood if we notice that it arises from a misunderstanding of the nature of programme music. He assumes that there is, on the one hand, *Gedanken- und Begriffsmusik* [music that has to do with intellectual concepts], as in symphonic poems, and, on the other hand, *Gefühlsmusik* [music that has to do with feelings], independent of thinking, as in absolute music, music proper. And he remarks of Liszt's music that in it there is an amalgamation with a detailed poetical description. Now, in the first place, feeling is not independent of thought, although a good deal of it is connected with the subconscious. In the second place, programme music, like absolute music, is mainly concerned with feelings. And in the third place, neither Liszt's programmes nor programmes generally (with the exception of some bad examples) are descriptions of what is expressed in the music, but expositions of the subjects illustrated by the music. Moreover, as far as declaration goes, the programmes consist very often of nothing more than a title—take as instances Liszt's *Faust* Symphony and symphonic poems *Festklänge, Hungaria,* and *Hamlet.*

In studying Brahms's position with regard to programme music, we should not overlook his love of nature and literature, and his constant and intimate communication with them. On this point all witnesses are clear and unanimous. Kalbeck rightly lays stress on the influence exercised on Brahms's conceptions by the surrounding scenery, saying that his music was not indoor but outdoor music (*Freilicht und Freiluftmusik*). Of the process of composition, however, we know in Brahms's case less than in that of almost any other great composer. He certainly did not wear his heart upon his sleeve. Indeed, he was extremely reticent on the subject of his travails and the parentage of his children. Nevertheless we know a great deal more than is generally supposed.

As a rule Brahms is content with calling his compositions symphonies, sonatas, trios, &c., or scherzi, capricci, intermezzi, rhapsodies, &c. We meet in his works with only two suspicious titles—Tragic Overture, and Ballad. However it may be in the former case, in the latter case the suspicion is well founded. In fact, we take him *en flagrant délit*, namely that of writing programme music, and even shamelessly owning it. Above the first Ballad of Op. 10 we read : ' After the Scotch Ballad *Edward*,' and a reference to Herder's *Stimmen der Völker*. Kalbeck is of opinion that the other two ballads of the same *opus* have undeclared programmes. Hermann Deiters, a writer with a decidedly classical leaning, says of this Op. 10 : ' Brahms tries even in this early work to build a bridge as it were between instrumental and vocal art, or rather to declare that music without words perfectly suffices him for the expression of what impels him to composition, that to him it expresses the same.' Brahms's ballads, the later ones as well as those of Op. 10, give one the impression not of mere ballads in name, but of real ballads. The case mentioned, however, is not the only one where our

master confesses himself in print a programmatic
profligate. In his first pianoforte sonata, Op. 1, in
C major, Brahms puts above the theme of the variations
(second movement) the words 'after an old-German
Minnelied,' and under it the words of the song. In his
third sonata, Op. 5, in F minor, the composer heads the
second movement, an Andante, with three lines from
a poem by Sternau, and the fourth movement, an Intermezzo between the Scherzo and Finale, with the word
'Rückblick' (Retrospect). These are the openly declared
programmes. Now let us look for the undeclared ones.
Brahms told his friend Albert H. Dietrich that in the
6/8 part of the last movement of the first sonata he had
in his mind the song 'Mein Herz ist im Hochland'
('My heart's in the Highlands'). The composer told the
same friend that the second movement, *Andante con
espressione*, of the second sonata, Op. 2, in F sharp
minor, was inspired by the minnesinger Kraft von
Toggenburg's 'Winter Song'! Kalbeck sees in the third
sonata an innocent love romance, and in its second
movement a love duet bathed in moonlight, the actors of
the romance being the composer and a *soubrette* of the
Hamburg Opera. He also suggests that in writing the
opening of the first movement of the first sonata, Brahms
may have had in his mind the words 'Auf! Hinaus in
das Leben' ('Up! and plunge into life'), which fit the
music rhythmically and emotionally as well as do those
already mentioned in connection with the last movement.

It is not surprising that E. T. A. Hoffmann's musical
characters and thoughts on music, which affected
Schumann so powerfully (to witness: his *Kreisleriana,
Nachtstücke, Phantasiestücke*, and literary writings),
made an impression on our young musician with

romantic ideas and unconventional ways and manners. *Princess Brambilla, a Capriccio after Jacques Callot,* inspired him with a string quartet.   Indeed, he identified himself to such an extent with the fantastically enthusiastic Kapellmeister Johannes Kreisler that he had the intention of calling a number of pianoforte compositions *Leaves from the Diary of a Musician, edited by Young Kreisler.*   It was Joachim's dissuasion that prevented the execution of the plan.   Brahms's biographer does not hesitate to describe the B minor Trio, Op. 8, as Young Kreisler's diary of travel, in which are reflected his experiences of a summer on the Rhine in 1853.   In fact, Kalbeck sees in the first ten published works occasional compositions in the sense in which Goethe called his lyrics occasional poems, and thinks that in the directness of expression of his feelings the composer did not trouble himself about symmetry and euphony.

But are the traces of programmes confined to these early works?   By no means!   Before continuing the enumeration of facts bearing on this point, we should note Brahms's relation to the Schumanns—his affection and admiration for the man and musician Robert Schumann, and his respectful worship of Clara Schumann.   Of what nature the latter was and to what pitch it rose, may be gathered from the following words that escaped from Brahms in an unguarded moment of intimate expansiveness :   'I believe I do not esteem and revere her more than I love her . . . . I mean, I shall be no longer able to love a girl, at least I have entirely forgotten them—they only promise us the heaven which Clara opens to us.'   Of the Concerto in D minor, which has been called a monument to Schumann, Joachim relates that the sombre commencement of the first movement was suggested by Schumann's suicidal attempt on the outbreak of his insanity, when he threw himself into the Rhine. The Adagio bore originally the superscription *Benedictus qui venit in nomine Domini.* Of one of the variations of Op. 9 (probably No. 15), Brahms said, 'Clara speaks.' When showing in 1868 his C minor string quartet, Op. 60, to Deiters, the composer remarked: 'Now imagine a man who is about to shoot himself, and to whom there remains no other choice.' And in sending the MS. of the quartet to his friend Billroth, the Vienna Professor of Surgery, he wrote: 'I communicate the quartet to you only as a curiosity—as it were an illustration to the last chapter of the man in blue dress-coat and yellow waistcoat.' This is an allusion to Goethe's description of the dead Werther near the end of his romance. 'Only music,' says our anti-programmatic programmatist, 'could free the youth matured by sorrows from the burden of his experiences: Werther-Manfred [Brahms] conjured up Astarte [Clara], and sketched the Allegro of the C minor symphony.' Clara undoubtedly played an important part in the early life and works of Brahms.

Influences of another kind are the romantic old castle and park of Detmold, and the neighbouring woods and hills. Kalbeck cites the Serenades Op. 11 and 16 as witnesses. Of the Adagio of the first of them, the Serenade in D major, he says: 'The most beautiful summer-night seems to descend when the low string instruments and bassoons begin their dark, waving, but hesitating and faltering song. One seems to hear the earth quietly breathing in her sleep, and the softly blowing wind so cautiously gliding over her as if afraid to awake the clouds.' In the Scherzo of the same work,

' the gnomes and elves of the wood play their mad pranks and dip their exuberant sportiveness in a melancholy minor, in order to mock a couple of sentimental sons of the Muses' [Brahms and his companion, the violinist Bargheer]. The same writer thinks he perceives in the pianoforte quartet, Op. 26, memories of the Düsseldorf Music Festival of 1855—in the Adagio : moonlight ; quiet wave-motion of the broad, sparkling Rhine ; occasional dimming of the glitter by a fragrant breeze ; nightingales.

Now it may be said that what is true of young Brahms may not be true of the mature Brahms. And, no doubt, as he grew older, he became a severer critic of himself, and more exacting as to the formal and technical qualities of his work. But I cannot imagine that the master builder and the tone-smith in him ever altogether ousted the master thinker and tone-poet, although the activity of the latter may have been somewhat circumscribed by the former. The absence of programmatic information in regard to the later works does not prove a change in the composer's attitude towards the nature of the musical content. His silence is perfectly accounted for by his growing reticence, which, as far as the inner man was concerned, completely isolated him, even from his most attached friends. I cannot but think that in the tonal combinations of a composer of Brahms's colossal inwardness (*Innerlichkeit*) —to use an expression of Adolf Jensen's—there must be some meaning. Of course, in speaking of programmes in connection with Brahms, I am not thinking of Berlioz, Liszt, and Strauss programmes, but of programmes such as Tchaikovsky describes in writing about his fourth symphony, and as Beethoven is partly known and partly believed to have had in his mind.

2 G

The variety among programmes is indeed very great: they differ in kind and degree, and are different not only in the works of different composers, but also in different works of the same composer. If those were right who see nothing in Brahms's music but a mere formal play, an æsthetic exercise, we should be at a loss what to think of so much that is speaking in the master's works —for instance, not to go farther, in the later pianoforte pieces, the Rhapsodies, Fantasias, Ballads, &c. Surely, so sincere and earnest an artist as Brahms would not descend to the unintelligent mouthing of expressive phrases, to the haphazard parroting of the language of passion, so justly pilloried by Wagner, and unfortunately so common among the composers without the grace of God. And again, must we not be puzzled by the totally different characters of the four symphonies—to mention only one of the different classes of instrumental music in the larger forms—and by the evident logical evolution to be found in them, unless we assume that at the bottom of the sounds there are states of the mind, and trains of thoughts and feelings, necessarily conditioned by remembered, imagined, or actual experiences ? That the mature Brahms himself believed in a beyond of æsthetical combinations may be gathered from a remark he made to Richard Heuberger. In the course of a severe criticism of some of the young composer's attempts, he repeatedly and emphatically pointed out that these were purely technical matters, with which the poetry of musical creation had nothing whatever to do. Of the Sextet in G major, Op. 36, Deiters says : ' It is the tone-poet who here speaks. He shows us a meditative mind animated by pictures of the imagination, endeavouring to rise by an effort from its inwardness with a vigorous resolve to venture out into the fulness of life, where, however, new uncertainty and disquiet will not be wanting.' Of course we are familiar with the discussions of critics who talk glibly of the poetry and the emotional expression of compositions, and yet shrink with horror from the idea of these things having any actuality. Evidently there is some confusion in their minds. Their words and their doctrines are certainly contradictory.

Closely connected with the subject of expressiveness is that of popularity. The latter depends upon the what and the how of the former. Compared with the width of the appreciation of Haydn, Mozart, Beethoven, Schumann, Chopin, and others, that of Brahms is extremely limited. It is confined to the Teutonic countries, is high only in Germany, and even there is restricted to certain temperaments. To explain this simply by saying that the few are the select that alone can understand an exceptionally superior nature is begging the question. History teaches us that the few are not always the wise, learned, and refined ; on the contrary, it teaches us that they are often the crazy, ignorant, and vapid. And, then, the above mentioned more popular composers appeal to the really select few as much as and even more than to the motley many. The fact is, while the following of a select few implies the presence of one or more good qualities in the admired object, the unresponsiveness of the many implies the absence of qualities perhaps not less or even more precious. We may get nearer the solution of the problem—I do not say we shall reach it—if we remember that both the French and the Russians will have none of Brahms, and can find out why they will not. Now what qualities do these nations prize most highly? The answer will in all probability name such qualities as are not characteristic of the rejected master. The French love clearness, brightness, liveliness, pointedness, elegance, and symmetry: the Russians love strong colours, strong contrasts, strong passionateness, in short, strength that makes light of regularity and refinement of form, and does not shrink from downright barbarism and even brutality. Thus we obtain something like definition by means of elimination. In discussions on Brahms there is always heard a great deal about profundity, which some people seem to think is measurable by the difficulty of comprehension and the minus quantity of ingratiating power. Now, of two men, one may be clear, striking, and engaging, and the other the reverse, and yet the former may be as profound, nay, may even be more profound. Compare Beethoven and Brahms. Which of the two is the more profound? Compare the Beethoven of the last quartets and sonatas and the mature Beethoven of the less recondite works. Are you sure the former is more profound than the latter? The difference between Brahms and the more widely popular great masters seems to me to be this: Brahms is more reflective, more brooding, more anxiously weighing, more laboured; has less spontaneity, less copiousness, less elemental striking power, less natural grace and lucidity. These hints offered as a contribution towards a characterization of Brahms, help us to form a notion of the expressiveness of his music, and to distinguish it from the expressiveness of the music of others. It is to be hoped that no one will see in this characterization an attempt at depreciation. The foregoing has been written with a full belief in the greatness

of Brahms, by a true admirer of the master—an admirer
of his nobility, earnestness, and sincerity, of his intense
thoughtfulness and quiet heartiness, of his love of perfect
craftsmanship, and of his pursuit of ideals regardless of
public opinion and pecuniary profit. And if you ask:
' Ought we not to be thankful that Brahms was what he
was ?' then my answer will be a sonorous : ' Yea, and a
thousand times yea!' For, being what he was, he
produced works endowed with precious qualities nowhere
else to be found and otherwise impossible.

The musician on whom we have allowed our attention
to dwell so long calls up a contemporary who, since the
eighties of the last century, has, as a symphonist, been
pitted against him—I mean ANTON BRUCKNER
(1824-1896). Brahms composed four symphonies,
Bruckner eight and three movements of a ninth. Both
began writing symphonies when already well on in life :
the former came forward with his first symphony at the
age of forty-three (1876), the latter at the age of forty-
two (1866). But Brahms had already published sixty-
seven works, including important chamber and choral
compositions, and was famous ; whereas Bruckner had
as yet written nothing of consequence, and was unknown.
It was not till the performance of his seventh symphony
at Leipzig, in 1884, that the world deigned to take notice
of Bruckner. And even then, although the world did
take notice of him, it was not conquered by him.
Indeed, his works are still very little played—out of
Germany hardly at all—and the opinions concerning
them are as contradictory, and as nebulous and
inconclusive as it is possible for opinions to be. Owing to
the rare opportunities of hearing Bruckner's symphonies
performed, and the rare opportunities not having

come my way, I do not wish to speak about these compositions otherwise than with hesitation and reservation. Wagner said of Liszt's symphonic compositions : ' It is all very well to read such things, but the real salt, what is decisive, what solves all doubts, we can after all enjoy only through actual hearing.' This is even more true of Bruckner's than of Liszt's symphonic work. And now we come to our usual question : Is Bruckner a composer of programme music ? There are only three or four facts that point in that direction. The fourth symphony is entitled ' Romantic.' And, although there is no other title, and no programme whatever in the printed scores of the symphonies, an autograph of the later version of the fourth symphony is known in which the Trio of the Scherzo bears the superscription *Tanzweise während der Mahlzeit zur Jagd* (Dance tune during the repast at the hunt) ; and a copy of the Finale exists with the added designation *Volksfest* (Popular festivity). On what authority the parenthetical title *Jagd* (Hunt) appears above the Scherzo in the pianoforte arrangement I do not know ; but its appropriateness cannot be doubted. Bruckner always referred to the second movement (*Adagio*, in C sharp minor) of the seventh Symphony as the *Trauermusik um den hochseligen Meister* (Funeral music for our late blessed Master). He used to say that he composed it on receiving the news of Wagner's death ; and when it was pointed out to him that the movement was finished four months before that event, he mended his statement by saying it was a presentiment of the death that gave the impulse. It is worth noting that he preferred the designation *Tondichter* (tone-poet) as applied to him to that of *Tonsetzer* (composer). To give an example of

the contradictoriness of opinions, alluded to : One
writer characterizes Bruckner's symphonies as showy,
having outwardness rather than inwardness, and lacking
inner logic ; while another writer describes them as
attempts to monumentalize improvisations, as confessions
that reveal the inmost heart of the composer, as subjective,
intimate tone-speech that often assumes the form of
monologues. An important element in the development
of the composer and the constitution of his music is
undoubtedly the powerful influence of Wagner. But to
say, as some critics have said, that Bruckner introduced
Wagner's dramatic style into the symphony is a
misapprehension of the facts. Bruckner took from the
Bayreuth master only externalities—his use of instruments as regards number and grouping, his peculiar
polyphony, his harmonic innovations, and certain effects
thereby producible. He did not adopt the spirit that
created and legitimized these means, and did not
engineer them with a consistent conscious aim in view.
Now let it not be thought that in Bruckner's music there
is nothing but a stupendously clever technical display ;
no, there is a great deal more in it, in fact, it is full of
impressions and visions of immense grandeur and superlative brilliancy, and others of childlike joyousness and
devoutness.   But notwithstanding the overwhelming
grandiosity of his music, Bruckner was not an intellectual
and emotional force, least of all an intellectual force.
It is this deficient intellectuality, the outcome of which
was vagueness and inconsequence of thought and feeling,
and lack of measure and concentration, in short, lack of
self-command, that distinguish him from Wagner, and
distinguish him also and in a still higher degree from
his other great contemporary, Brahms.   It is difficult to

guess what the author of the above-quoted phrase, 'monumentalization of improvisations' may have meant, but, taken in one sense, it gives a meaning consonant with the opinion just expressed—namely, in the sense of fixing and perhaps elaborating the uncontrolled and semi-conscious daydreams and the wholly subconscious sensations that with musical people are apt to vent themselves in free outpourings on the pianoforte or organ. If the supposition is correct, Bruckner has to be ranked with the composers of absolute rather than of programme music. A knowledge of the dominant facts of Bruckner's life will help us to recognize the elements of his constitution as a composer. What we have specially to note is this: (1) his birth in Upper Austria (1824); his destitute childhood; his callings as choir-boy, poverty-stricken village schoolmaster, organist of the monastery St. Florian (where there was a magnificent organ) and, after a triumphant competition, of the Linz cathedral (1855); his subsequent short visits to Vienna for lessons from the contrapuntist Sechter (hitherto he had been practically self-taught) and two years' study of composition and instrumentation with Otto Kitzler of the Linz theatre (1861-1863); his introduction to the music of Wagner; his appointment as Court Chapel organist and professor of counterpoint, composition, and the organ at the Vienna conservatorium (1867); and (2) the other more vital facts, his undying attachment to his beautiful native country and congenial fellow-countrymen; his profound impressions from these sources and from the ecclesiastical solemnities of the Catholic religion, more especially at St. Florian (where he wished to be buried); his love for the organ and its grand, varied, and overwhelming effects; his remaining

at heart and in appearance a peasant and schoolmaster
to the end of his days; his indifference to other arts and
literature; and his abject self-abasement before people
of position, including critics and conductors. Rusticism
and ecclesiasticism were the main elements in the
character of the man, the latter of the two furnishing
the higher ideal. It was chiefly for the expression of
his deeply and strongly devout Roman Catholicism that
the artist used his phenomenal musical endowments and
acquirements, his harmonic, contrapuntal, and orchestral
virtuosity. Consequently there was a great deal of
truth in speaking of 'the scholastic vesture, sounding
mysticism, and *musicized* cathedrals' in the rich romanticism of Bruckner's symphonies. In short, we may
assume that, in so far as Bruckner's works had unrevealed
programmes, these were as a rule subconscious or
sporadic and inconsequent.

In the brief survey now to be made of the German
composers of instrumental music who, besides those
already discussed, played prominent parts during the
period in question, we shall deal first with those who
either proceeded entirely on the lines of Beethoven,
Mendelssohn, and Schumann, or adhered to them in the
main while coming to some extent under the influence
of Berlioz, Liszt, and Wagner, the extent being in some
cases no more than a bolder choice of subject. The
latter class appears of course later in the field, and only
gradually increases in number and distinctness. It will
also be seen that the cultivation of the programme
symphony is less early and less general than that of the
programme overture.

JULIUS RIETZ (1812-1877), a conductor of high
repute — Mendelssohn's colleague and successor at

Düsseldorf, subsequently conductor at the Leipzig theatre and Gewandhaus, and finally at the Dresden opera—was also an esteemed composer. His compositions, excellent in workmanship and classical in style, comprise overtures entitled *Hero and Leander* (Schiller), *The Tempest* (Shakespeare), and *Comedy Overture.* A more interesting, if not more worthy, personality is that of FERDINAND HILLER (1811-1885), a fine pianist, a good conductor and teacher, a clever, many-sided, and indefatigable composer, and a writer on music both elegant and witty. In Paris, from 1828 to 1835, he enjoyed the friendship of Berlioz, Chopin, and Liszt, of Cherubini, Meyerbeer, Rossini, and Bellini, and familiarized himself with the romanticism of the time and country. But he was also a friend of Mendelssohn and later on of Schumann. After occupying posts as conductor at Dresden and Düsseldorf, he became director of the Conservatorium and conductor of the Gürzenich concerts at Cologne (1850-1884), and before very long was the recognized musical head of the Rhineland. His friendship for Berlioz and Liszt did not make him love their music. Among the opponents of Liszt and Wagner not one was so uncompromising and dangerous as Hiller. It will suffice to record three of his works: the symphony with the motto *Es muss doch Frühling werden* (Spring must come at last), *An Operetta without Words* for pianoforte (four hands), and the *Rondo* of a pianoforte concerto, composed at Paris, in which he endeavoured to portray the charming actress Léontine Fay, and, as Mendelssohn told him, succeeded in doing so. Of the serious ROBERT VOLKMANN (1815-1883), whose admirable chamber music, symphonies, &c., deserve to be oftener heard than

they are nowadays, we must note at least his overture
Richard III. (Shakespeare), and the pianoforte pieces
Visegrád (twelve musical poems: The Oath, Sword
Dance, The Banquet, Love-song, Wreath of Flowers,
Bridal Song, The Fortune Teller, a Pastoral, The Lay
of the Hero, The Page, Soliman, and At the Tower of
Soliman), the Musical Picture Book (four hands), and
the Hungarian Sketches (four hands).

To CARL REINECKE (*b.* 1824) Schumann proved a
magnet. This we may see in the latter's correspondence.
Indeed, beyond this standpoint Reinecke never passed.
As conductor of the Leipzig Gewandhaus concerts (1860-
1895) he made that institution a stronghold of classicism
into which Liszt and Wagner and their followers could
not penetrate, and to which even Brahms was admitted
only late and reluctantly. Among Reinecke's refined
compositions the following ones cannot but interest us:
the overtures *Dame Kobold* (Calderon), *Aladin, Zenobia*
(drama by J. L. Klein), and overture and *entr'actes* to
the opera *Manfred,* the second symphony, *Hakon Jarl*
(Oehlenschläger), the *Dramatische Fantasiestücke,* Tone-
Pictures for Orchestra, and twenty-five pianoforte pieces
and songs for the young, *From our four Walls.* More
closely connected with Schumann were ALBERT H.
DIETRICH (*b.* 1829) and JOSEPH JOACHIM (*b.* 1831),
who together with their friend Brahms were in affectionate personal relation with the admired master, and
ever since have remained true to his memory. Classical
to the backbone and to the heart's core, they abhorred the
tendencies of Liszt. Though bound to Liszt by friendship, contracted during a four-years' stay at Weimar
(1849-1853), Joachim wrote to him from Hanover in 1857,
with what pain may be easily imagined: 'Your music

is for me quite inaccessible. It is opposed to everything my faculty of apprehension has absorbed as nourishment from the spirit of our great masters since my earliest youth.' In 1860, Brahms, the instigator, Joachim, J. O. Grimm, Bernhard Scholz, Dietrich, Bargiel, Kirchner, and others intended to publish a declaration against Liszt and other leaders and disciples of the New German School, and their noxious theories and products. The plan miscarried, owing partly to the difficulty of agreeing on the wording, and partly to the unauthorized publication of the original proposal. Of Dietrich we have one titled overture *Die Normannenfahrt;* of Joachim five, *Hamlet, Demetrius* (Hermann Grimm), *Henry IV., To a Comedy of Gozzi* (after reading two of the Italian's comedies), and *To the Memory of Kleist;* and three pieces for violin and pianoforte, Op. 5, respectively called *Lindenrauschen* (Rustling in the linden trees), *Abend-glocken* (Evening bells), and *Ballade.* Schumann writes in a letter to Joachim about the *Hamlet* overture as follows : 'As I went on reading, it seemed as if the scene became more and more illuminated, and Ophelia and Hamlet stepped bodily forward. There are affecting passages in it, and the whole is presented in a strikingly clear and grand form.' WOLDEMAR BARGIEL (1828-1897), related to Schumann both by family connection and by congeniality, named three of his overtures *Prometheus, Medea,* and *To a Tragedy.* Another composer that could claim kinship with Schumann, although only spiritually, was THEODOR KIRCHNER (1823-1903). His few concerted chamber works failed to arrest the attention of the musical world, but his poetic pianoforte pieces made many friends. The mere titles, simple and unpretentious as they are, have an attractive suggestiveness about them : *Miniatures, Album Leaves, Sketches, Aquarelles, Pen-and-Ink Drawings, Legends, Village Stories, Romantic Stories, Night Pictures* (ten character pieces), *Florestan and Eusebius, New Scenes of Childhood,* and *Neue Davidsbündlertänze,* &c. The last three and other titles, as the reader has of course noticed, point to Schumann. The older master had no mean opinion of the younger, who, as may be mentioned in passing, was one of the first pupils of the newly-founded Leipzig Conservatorium. Schumann found in Kirchner a 'music-soul,' and thought his things 'genial' (in the German sense of having the quality of genius).

ADOLF JENSEN (1837-1879), too, was an heir of Schumann, but one who profited also by the accumulations of the later composers, especially Wagner, and had a stronger, more distinct individuality than Kirchner. His exquisite songs, which form by far the larger part of his contribution to musical literature, we pass over, as we are concerned only with his instrumental music—his pianoforte pieces *Romantic Studies, Inner Voices, Wanderbilder, Idyls, Scènes carnavalesques, Wedding Music* (four hands), and *Erotikon.* But I wish to draw your attention specially only to the last. On January 10, 1872, Jensen wrote to a friend as follows : 'Everything fatigues me [he was consumptive]. The most salutary occupation for me is reading. It soothes me to look into the misty grey distances which the phantasy of the ancient poets opens to us. The inexhaustible treasures of ancient Greek literature, which it is my endeavour gradually to raise, afford me particular satisfaction. For a change I betake myself to the domain of Oriental poetry ; read also Shakespeare or what treats of him, Holberg, Grabbe, and many others. In short, it is a pleasant rambling

through the infinite.' The influence of Jensen's reading
on his creations is most strikingly exemplified by the
seven pieces entitled *Erotikon*, which he composed about
the time he wrote the letter from which I quoted, and
which are not only respectively named *Kassandra, Die
Zauberin* (The sorceress), *Galatea, Electra, Adonisklage*
(Lament for Adonis), *Eros,* and *Cypris,* but are also
provided   with   mottoes   from   the   works   of
Æschylus, Theocritus, Sophocles, and Bion.   The
Romantic Studies, which are studies in romanticism, not
technical exercises, have, like the pieces of the *Erotikon,*
both titles and poetical mottoes.   The composer says of
these ' small musical poems ' in the preface that they are
intended to illustrate musically scenes from the life of a
true friend, a deep-souled personality endowed with warm
feeling, noble sentiment, and calmest resignation.   And
adds : ' It is hardly to be expected that these attempts
will win for themselves the sympathy of all.   A predominant inclination distinctly expressed therein will no
doubt prevent this—namely, the inclination to the
fantastico-enthusiastic, to the mysterious ; nevertheless,
it has here, as in art generally, its justification.
The six pieces, Op. 48, entitled *Erinnerungen*
(Recollections) have prefixed to them a poetical
motto.

GEORG VIERLING (1820-1901), a classically-
disposed and nurtured composer, better known by his
choral than by his orchestral works, chose as subjects
for his overtures *The Tempest, Mary Stuart* (Schiller),
Die Hermannsschlacht (H. Kleist), and *In Spring*. Two
of them are subjects that have a perennial charm for
composers : Spring and Shakespeare's *Tempest*.   We
meet with them more frequently than with any others.

But certain other affections of programmatically inclined tone-poets cannot fail to reveal themselves in these notes. CARL GOLDMARK (*b.* 1830), whose chief ambition trends to the music drama, has nevertheless distinguished himself by orchestral works. Besides the overtures *Sakuntala* (Kalidasa), *Penthesilea* (H. Kleist), *In Spring*, *Prometheus Bound*, and *Sappho*, we have of him the much played symphony entitled *The Rustic Wedding*, in which, however, the programme is of a less exalted nature and oftener forgotten than in the overtures. Moreover, the so-called symphony is much rather a suite of five pieces bearing the subtitles *Wedding March*, *Bridal Song*, *Serenade*, *In the Garden* (where there is love-making), and the *Dance*. Goldmark does not in his orchestral music follow in the steps of Berlioz, Liszt, and Wagner, but he has learned from them. AUGUST KLUGHARDT (1847-1902), a pupil of the classics and learner of the moderns, entitled the first of five symphonies *Lenore*, the second of two suites *Auf der Wanderschaft*, and four Overtures *In Spring*, *Sophonisbe*, *Festival Overture*, and *Triumphal Overture*. HEINRICH HOFMANN (1842-1902) composed a *Frithjof* symphony, a suite *Im Schlosshof* (In the castle court), a *Hungarian* Suite, a scherzo *Irrlichter und Kobolde* (Will-o'-the-Wisps and Goblins), and four-hand pianoforte pieces with promising titles like *Italian Love Novel*, *Love's Spring*, *The Trumpeter of Säkkingen*, *Eckehard*, *Pictures from the Steppes*, and *From my Diary*. All these highly pleasing compositions are by no means severely programmatic, not even the symphony. The four movements of the latter work are entitled *Frithjof and Ingeborg*, *Ingeborg's Lament*, *Lichtelfen und Reifriesen* Light-elves and Frost-giants — *Intermezzo*), and

Frithjof's Return. HEINRICH VON HERZOGEN-BERG (1843-1900), whom we know as an ultra-classical writer, was in his younger days under the influence of Wagner, and then ventured, but only once, to write a programme symphony, Op. 16, *Odysseus,* the four movements of which dealt with *Irrfahrten* (Wanderings), *Penelope, Circe,* and *The Suitors.* Of ARNOLD KRUG (*b.* 1849) may be mentioned the orchestral compositions *Othello* (a Symphonic Prologue), *Gretchen im Kerker* (Margaret in prison), *Liebesnovelle* (A love novel), and *Italian Sketches of Travel* (for strings) ; and of HANS HUBER (*b.* 1852), a *Tell Symphony,* Op. 63 (an appropriate theme for a Swiss composer), a *Böcklin* Symphony, Op. 115 (a no less appropriate theme for a resident of Basel, the birthplace of the great painter), a serenade entitled *Summer-night,* a *Roman Carnival,* and a *Comedy Overture.* Among the works of JEAN LOUIS NICODÉ (*b.* 1853), a highly-gifted and nobly-striving composer, in whom old schooling and modern feeling are felicitously blended, we find three symphonic poems, *Mary Stuart, The Chase after Happiness,* and *Gloria,* the last with a concluding chorus ; Suites, entitled *Pictures from the South ; The Sea,* a symphonic Ode for male chorus, solo voice, orchestra, and organ ; and charming poetic pianoforte pieces.

ANTON RUBINSTEIN (1829-1894), denied by his countrymen, the Russians, and by them made over to the Germans, has consequently to be considered here. The justice of this action is questionable. For, although his sympathy with the young Russian School was limited, he was not anti-Russian, on the contrary, was a thorough admirer of Russian folk-music and of Glinka, the father of modern Russian art-music. Fortunately for us he has explained his position to programme music. ' I am not altogether a partisan of programme music,' he writes. ' I am for the programme that has to be guessed and to be poetized into the composition, not for the programme that is given along with it.   I am convinced that every composer not merely writes notes in some key, *tempo*, and rhythm, but lays into his compositions a psychical mood, *i.e.*, a programme, in the justifiable hope that the performer and the hearer will apprehend this programme. Sometimes the composer gives a general name, that is he gives the performer and hearer a clue, and more is not necessary, for the circumstantial programme of moods cannot be rendered by words.   Thus I understand programme music, but not in the sense of reflective tone-painting of definite things or events.   This is only admissible in the sense of the *naïf* and the comic.' Within the latter come, according to Rubinstein, the pastoral (as in Beethoven's sixth symphony), and the romantic, fantastic representation of elves, witches, fairies, nixies, gnomes, demons, spirits, &c., which are not imaginable without a programme.   In fact, he goes so far in his programmaticism as to call music a language, and to communicate to us his programmes of Beethoven's Op. 81 (the sonata ' Farewell, Absence, and Return ') and Chopin's Ballade in F major.   But what compositions of Rubinstein's have clues ?   His *Ocean* Symphony, Op. 52 (now of seven movements), his symphony ' In Memory of the Grand Duchess Helen,' Op. 107, the tone-picture *Russij*, the *Heroic* Fantasia, the musical character-pictures *Faust*, Op. 68, *Ivan IV.* Op. 79, and *Don Quichote*, Op. 87, and the overture *Antony and Cleopatra*—not to mention pianoforte pieces. Taking into account the impulsive character of the man

2 H

and the executant, his way of composing and the nature
of his compositions, we cannot imagine Rubinstein to
have been anything but a composer of programme music.
He wrote on the spur of the moment, driven by an inner
force; he could not, as he told me, criticize, file, and
brood over his compositions. They were indeed
improvisations, and had the virtues and vices of
improvisations.

Among the most popular and important programme
symphonies after Liszt's revolt and before R. Strauss's
triumphal progress are two works by composers issuing
from the old school—Abert's *Columbus* and Rheinberger's
Wallenstein. There can be no doubt that these
successful examples encouraged imitation. It is
noteworthy that both composers wrote two such works,
and that the earlier was the more successful and the
more pronouncedly programmatic. JOHANN JOSEPH
ABERT (*b.* 1832), a pupil of Tomaschek of Prague, from
1852 double-bass player in the Stuttgart orchestra and
from 1867 to 1888 first conductor, was chiefly a composer
of operas, but produced in 1864, after an earlier untitled
symphony, a symphonic poem, *Columbus,* which at once
found favour and for some time was much played, and in
1894 a *Spring* Symphony, which excited less interest.
The praise lavished upon the earlier work embraced
excellence of form as well as beauty of conception,
richness of colour, and mastery of technique. Eight
years before the publication of *Columbus,* Liszt mentions
in a letter to the Princess Wittgenstein 'Abert, a young
composer of merit, and *très bien pensant.*' From this
we may gather that Abert showed some appreciation of
Liszt's achievements, but ought not to conclude that he
adopted his principles and procedures. Even without

the testimony of the music, one fact would suffice to prove the wrongness of such a conclusion—namely, the performance of *Columbus* at the Leipzig Gewandhaus and other conservative concert institutions. But the character of the music and the title itself prove incontrovertibly that Abert was neither a revolutionary nor an innovator.   Here is what we read on the title-page and over the four movements : ' *Columbus :* Musical Sea-Picture in form of a Symphony.'   (1) Feelings at the Departure (*Allegro*) ; (2) Doings of the Sailors (*Scherzo*) ; (3) Evening on the Sea (*Adagio*) ; (4) Good Signs, Revolt, Storm—Land (Finale. *Allegro non troppo*).

Of JOSEF RHEINBERGER (1839-1901) Liszt would hardly have said that he was *bien pensant*. If we divide composers into classicists and romanticists, Rheinberger has to be numbered with the former.   For in him the classic temperament predominated over the romantic, and did so more and more as he advanced in years. Moreover, his romanticism differed from the later developments in being neither violent, extravagant, voluptuous, fantastic, nor transcendentally sentimental. No doubt Rheinberger learned much and assimilated something from Schumann and Chopin ; but he did not come under their sway, did not swear fealty to them. Berlioz, Wagner, and Liszt had no perceptible influence upon him.   Health, simplicity, and clearness pervade everything he wrote.   His music is diatonic rather than chromatic, and eschews the piquancies, eccentricities, and intricacies of melody, harmony, rhythm, and instrumentation now and for some time in fashion. Rheinberger's contrapuntal skill proves that he studied J. S. Bach assiduously, his natural, flowing, translucent style seems to indicate that Mozart was his ideal.   But for certain qualities also Weber and Beethoven must have strongly attracted him. Has the reader to conclude from the above that Rheinberger's style was antiquated? No! For, although keeping apart from some of the tendencies of the age, he was nevertheless of the age. At any rate this holds good of his best work. Nothing need be said here of his well-known and highly-prized organ sonatas, his estimable but now neglected concerted chamber music, the oratorio *St. Christophorus*, the pianoforte pieces, and a large mass of vocal and instrumental music of all sorts. What concerns us are the following few compositions : *Wallenstein*, a symphonic tone-picture, Op. 10 (1866) ; the *Florentine Symphony*, Op. 87 (1875) ; the Overtures to Shakespeare's *Taming of the Shrew*, Op. 18 (1866), and to Schiller's *Demetrius*, Op. 110 (1878) ; Introduction to Calderon's *The Wonderful Magician*, Op. 30 (1865) ; and the pianoforte composition *Fantasiestück* with a poetical motto from Julius Hammer, Op. 23 (1866). Three of these compositions, and among them the most important, are of the year 1866, which seems to have been the time when his programmatic leaning was strongest. The symphonic poem *Wallenstein* opens with a prelude (*Allegro*), where amidst the bustle of war appear the proud imperious Wallenstein and the devoted lovers Max and Thekla, and fear-inspiring bodings of fate make themselves heard. The second movement (*Adagio*) is superscribed ' Thekla,' the third ' Wallenstein's Camp ' (a *Scherzo*, the *Trio* of which has for its subject the Capucin's Sermon), and the fourth 'Wallenstein's Death' (*Moderato, Allegro vivace, Allegro*). The form, being largely determined by the poetic ideas, has not quite the cut of the classical symphony, but the thematic treatment and the style are undoubtedly

classical.   As to the conception of the work, it is
powerful, picturesque, and expressive and impressive.
The vivacity and humour of Wallenstein's Camp made
this movement particularly popular.

Before we turn our attention to the immediate
disciples of Liszt, those who were in close personal
relation with him, I must say a few words on two
interesting personalities, one of whom acted on the
promptings of his own revolting spirit before Liszt, and
the other of whom had revolutionary temptations and
inclinations simultaneously with Liszt.   Who now knows
HERMANN HIRSCHBACH (1812-1888) ?   Nay, how
many knew him at the time of his greatest activity ?
Although he composed to the end of his days, and
published about fifty works, few have been publicly
performed, and all of them have been rarely heard and
read.   And yet, he must have exercised a not inconsiderable influence : partly by his compositions, partly by his
writings on music, and partly by what Schumann said
about him.   His compositions comprise many string
quartets and quintets and other concerted chamber
music, fourteen symphonies, and several overtures.   His
Op. 1 is a string quartet with mottoes from *Faust* and
the general title *Pictures from Life;* the symphonies
bear titles such as *Life Struggles, Recollections of the Alps,
Faust's Walk,* &c. ;   and the overtures treat of
Goethe's *Götz von Berlichingen,* Shakespeare's *Hamlet*
and *Julius Cæsar,* &c.   Hirschbach's writings on music
appeared in various publications, notably in Schumann's
Neue Zeitschrift and in the *Musikalisch - Kritisches
Repertorium* (1844-1845), of which he himself was the
founder and editor.   His confession of faith is to be
found in the preface to his symphonies Op. 46 and 47.

' My lodestar, from the first moment I began independent creation, was characterization.   Then [1836] it was no longer possible to advance instrumental music solely by the development of craftsmanship [*kunstvoller Entwickelung*].   One had to be satisfied with maintaining the polyphonic style in chamber music, where it was employed, at the same high level.   But in this way nothing was lost : besides the inexhaustible wealth of thought of our art, there remained the sharper stamping and grander conception of the characteristic content. Inevitably connected with this was the enlargement and the treatment in various other ways of the free forms. As long as twenty-four years ago I loudly declared the principle : *The content determines the form.*   It has always seemed to me frivolous to fling the hearer from one mood into another, as if art were merely a joke. No, to sustain and exhaust a mood, even the most serious, unless the play demanded it otherwise, that has been my task, a task however, for which are required, besides thematic means, a far-reaching inventiveness.'   Two remarks from his article : *For what purpose does one compose instrumental music?* (*Neue Zeitschrift*, August 10, 1838) may further illustrate Hirschbach's standpoint. ' No one becomes a profound instrumental composer who has not a profound mental life. . . . Genuine instrumental music, in the highest and deepest sense, must be so constituted that, though not urgently requiring a verbal indication of the content, it yet really admits of it.'

Schumann wrote twice on Hirschbach in the *Neue Zeitschrift*, addressed many letters to him, and mentions him with enthusiasm in other letters.   The first account of his discovery of this genius occurs in a letter

addressed to Clara Wieck on July 13, 1838. It is
characteristically ejaculatory. 'A great phenomenon
has passed my way this week. You must have seen the
name in the *Zeitschrift* [as a contributor] : Hirschbach.
He has much of Faust, of the black-art in him. The
day before yesterday we played quartets of his ; in
writing defective, in invention the most colossal [*das
Ungeheuerste*] I have as yet met with. In his tendency
some resemblance to myself—states of the soul. But
he is more passionate, more tragic than I. The forms
are quite new, likewise the treatment of the quartet.
Some things moved me profoundly. Where there is
such an overwhelming imaginativeness one overlooks
slight faults. Besides this an overture to *Hamlet*, ideas
for an oratorio, *Paradise Lost*. The quartets are scenes
from *Faust*. There you have a picture. Along with this,
profoundest romanticism combined with simplicity and
touching truthfulness.' To the composer, Schumann
wrote about the same time : 'Your striving seems to me
the most colossal I have met with in recent artistic
tendencies, and is supported by great powers. But I am
doubtful as to some things, especially as a musician.'
In the report of the private matinée at which three
quartets and a quintet of Hirschbach's were played (see
Neue Zeitschrift, August 14, 1838), and in the criticism
of the quartet, Op. 1 (May 17, 1842), Schumann repeats
most of what he wrote in those letters, but of the new
things he says, some deserve to be quoted. 'Words
cannot describe how his music is fashioned, and all that
it pictures ; his music is itself speech. . . . soul-
speech, truest music-life. . . . A longing impulse,
a crying for rescue, an incessant onward rushing, and
between them blissful figures, golden meads and rosy

evening clouds. . . . I saw also an overture to *Hamlet*, a grand symphony of many movements, and a second half finished, which is to be continuous throughout—all of them fantastic, full of vital energy, in the forms deviating from everything hitherto known, if I except Berlioz, and a few orchestral passages such as one is accustomed to hear only from Beethoven when he is in the mood to take up arms against the whole world and annihilate it. . . . One sees the composer wishes to be called a poet; he wants everywhere to evade stereotyped forms; Beethoven's last quartets he regards as beginnings of a new poetic era, in which he intends to pursue his labours; Haydn and Mozart lie far, far behind him.' Hirschbach's revolutionary progressiveness is so much the more wonderful as most probably he knew not a note of Berlioz when he began his ambitious but unsuccessful career. The case considered by itself is interesting enough, but it becomes a hundredfold more so when we think of the influence Hirschbach may have exercised on the composers who were better able to arrest the attention of the public—for instance, Liszt and Wagner. Words are seed-corns that often are sown and grow up unnoticed.

HENRY LITOLFF (1818-1891), the brilliant pianist and composer, admired in both capacities, but especially in the former, offers a striking contrast to the obscure and unheeded Hirschbach. If Litolff was a genius, no better proof could be brought forward in confirmation of Lombroso's theory as to the connection of genius with degeneracy and insanity. Look at his restlessness, nervousness, fitful energy, and twitching face! Think of his love of sensationalism, alternations of feverish activity and torpid slothfulness, marriages and divorces, acquaintance with lunatic asylums, migrations and wanderings! However let us also note his Alsatian extraction, London birth and education, and long residences in Paris and Brunswick. Litolff was unquestionably a musician of great talent; but he did not get a proper training in composition when young, and afterwards had not the will and perseverance to make up for the want of it by hard and systematic study. Nevertheless he improved to some extent by practice and force of genius. As a composer he first made himself a reputation by pianoforte concertos, for which he invented the title *Concerto Symphonie.* This was in the forties of the 19th century. The success of these works—he wrote five—is difficult to understand if one looks at them now. No doubt the fire, vivacity, and bravura of his playing counted for much in the success, and the same qualities in the music for the rest. However, we need not dwell on these compositions, nor on his successful pianoforte pieces and more or less unsuccessful operas. What we have to consider are his overtures, especially those to two tragedies by W. R. Griepenkerl—*Maximilian Robespierre* and *Die Girondisten.* These two overtures were composed about 1850, and go by the names of *Robespierre* and *Les Girondins.* As a reformer we cannot take Litolff so seriously as he took himself. ' Yes,' he wrote to Liszt on June 24, 1857, ' on the threshold of your home I will shake off the dust of mediocrity which for so long has been clinging to me, and through you and with you pull down, uproot, destroy, and rebuild.' These are grand words and big sentiments, which, however, in the mouth of Litolff sound ridiculous. He had not even the strength to perform the negative part of the operation, not to speak of the positive. But, on the other hand, it cannot be denied that Litolff's compositions had a stirring, stimulating effect on many of his contemporaries. From the first his critics pointed out the combination of good and bad qualities in his work. The bad qualities oftenest mentioned are eccentricity, love of violence, and lack of self-command. The generally regretted mixture of the baroque and extravagant with the beautiful, and the monstrous and morbid with the well-thought and well-felt, was the outcome of his desire and determination to be original. Fétis, who was not blind to Litolff's faults, allows him to have been an eminent poet by imagination, inspiration, and spontaneity of ideas; although he saw in him a colourist rather than a thinker. We get a good description of the general character of Litolff's style when Liszt writes of his friend's *Les Girondins* and the *Ouverture triomphale* that they are far from lacking talent, but belong somewhat to the flamboyant style, which seemed to him played out (*flambé*) as far as music was concerned. A less qualified appreciation of the overture *Robespierre* comes to us from young Hans von Bülow (1850), not an altogether impartial judge, but a noteworthy contemporary voice. He says that this overture, which received everywhere universal and unanimous praise, was, though not a Beethoven overture *à la Egmont*, a very clever (*geniales*) piece of music with unmistakable flashes of thought, full of interesting instrumental effects, and also a harmonious whole—which surprised him, as he found Litolff generally disjointed and digressive. The reader remembers no doubt that young Tchaikovsky raved about *Robespierre* and *Les Girondins*, and that these and Meyerbeer's overture to *Struensee* implanted in him a taste for programme music. In short, Litolff was a kind of electric machine that vivified and invigorated those who came in contact with it.

Liszt's revolutionary activity as a composer about the middle of the 19th century, the enthusiasm of the devoted band of disciples gathered around him at Weimar, his and their propagandism of the new doctrines by means of the Press generally and the *Neue Zeitschrift für Musik* (under Brendel's editorship) particularly, and last, but not least, the master's vast diplomatic correspondence by which throughout Europe and even beyond the seas partisans were enlisted, fortified, and stimulated—all this would lead one to expect that the outcome must have been a flourishing school of composition that realized and developed the ideas and ideals of the beloved master and found far and wide attention and recognition. Strange to say, nothing like this came to pass. From all the strenuous striving there resulted not an imposing school of composition, but a tragedy of negation and impotence. The men of creative talent among Liszt's disciples did not pursue the master's lines, and the men who did had not the capacity to produce anything worth having. There is, however, this to be noted if we are not to misunderstand and misjudge the case. Liszt was not a teacher in the common sense of the word, he was much rather a stimulator and inspirer, and as such he no doubt did much even for those who struck out into roads and paths diverging from his. Nor should we overlook that much of Liszt's preaching against traditionalism, conventionalism, and all dead formalism, and for poetry in the content, freedom in form, harmony, and colouring, and correspondence between content and form, has borne fruit, and has done so not only within the circle of his adherents, but far beyond it, nay, well-nigh everywhere, the very camps of his most implacable opponents not excluded. Nevertheless the fact remains that Liszt's example as a producer of instrumental music in the larger forms, as a composer of symphonic poems, in short, as a symphonist, was not immediately followed in such a way and to such an extent as to admit of one's speaking of a Liszt school of composition. To test the correctness of this assertion, let us consider the master's chief disciples, those that were most highly endowed, most intimately connected with him, most zealous in his service, most prominent in the eyes of the world— Cornelius, Bronsart, Bülow, Draeseke, and Raff. I omit Tausig because he does not count as a composer.

Of the five disciples mentioned PETER CORNELIUS (1824-1874) had the greatest originality, and was the most genuine poet. But with all his admiration for and self-sacrificing devotion to Liszt, in spite of the latter's undoubted influence on him, and notwithstanding his decided modernity, Cornelius did not follow in the footsteps of Liszt—he did not compose a single symphonic poem, or indeed any symphonic work at all, and confined himself to solo and choral songs, Masses, and operas, in the later of the operas coming under the spell of Wagner. If we inquire into the reason of this difference between disciple and master, we shall find it partly in the difference of their individualities and natural endowments, but to a large extent also in the five years' previous training under the famous Dehn, that thorough-going teacher of the old school. The case of HANS VON BRONSART (*b.* 1830) is not identical, but similar. He, too, was a pupil of Dehn's before coming to Liszt; he, too, had individuality and creative power, although in less degree and less abundance. Among the small number of his known works the chief are a Trio, a Sextet, a pianoforte Concerto, a *Spring Fantasia* for orchestra, a symphony with chorus entitled *In the Alps*, and a second symphony entitled *Powers of Fate*. Of these only the Trio, Concerto, and Fantasia succeeded in gaining a modicum of attention, and with it much respect for the composer. It will be noticed that the titles point to programmes such as even composers of so-called absolute music look upon with indulgence and even approval. Another composition of Bronsart's, however, which Bülow mentions in a letter, is more boldly programmatic—a fantasia for pianoforte, *Melusina*, after Moritz von Schwind's series of pictures. It is published as Op. 9, but denominated *Ein Märchen* (A legend), not a fantasia.

HANS VON BÜLOW (1830-1894), so supremely eminent as an interpreter, both as a pianist and as a conductor, was sterile as a composer. His overture to *Julius Cæsar*, Op. 10, symphonic poems *Des Sänger's Fluch* (after Uhland's ballad *The Bard's Curse*), Op. 16, and *Nirwana*, Op. 20, and *Four Character Pictures* for orchestra, however respectable, have not in the slightest degree contributed to the treasury of living musical literature. But what must deeply interest us is, that the thorough-going disciple and champion of Liszt became in later years the defender of Mendelssohn, the apostle of Brahms, the worshipper of the supreme trinity, the three great B's (Bach, Beethoven, and Brahms), and the disparager of much he once highly prized, his master's symphonic works included. With regard to his writing of programme music there is a curious piece of information to be gathered from the Liszt-Bülow correspondence. Liszt writes : ' What do you think of this title : " Symphonic Prologue to *The Robbers* (or to Byron's *Cain*) ? " ' And a footnote supplies the following comment : ' Probably the work meant is that afterwards called *Nirwana.*' One would hardly have expected the high-priest of programme music to assist a disciple in finding a title and subject illustrative of a work already composed. This smacks rather of the unregenerate ways of unbelievers, half-believers, and mountebanks. Nevertheless the proceeding is excusable, nay, may be quite legitimate if done in the right spirit and with sufficient care. Moreover, the work in question was real programme music, being originally written to an unpublished tragedy, *Ein Leben im Tode* (A Life in Death) by Carl Ritter. But a reference to an unknown play would have been useless to the hearer. Hence a substitute had to be found—either a known play of a similar character, or, better, a suggestive title. Liszt expresses himself to Hans von Bülow in high terms on *Nirwana.* He calls it noble, profound, firmly knit (sometimes even rather knotty), but does not expect a good reception for it, the poetic data and the region in which the composer's thoughts move being outside the habitudes of the theatre and concert public. FELIX DRAESEKE (*b.* 1835), a pupil of the conservative Julius Rietz at the Leipzig Conservatorium, became one of the Weimar circle, but only for a time. Subsequently he turned away from what has been called the antiformal tendencies of the New German School, without, however, losing hold of its harmonic, modulatory, and other modernities. Characteristic of his early period is that he wrote in the periodical *Anregungen für Kunst, Leben und Wissenschaft* (edited by Franz Brendel and Richard Pohl) of 1858 and 1859, analyses of Liszt's

symphonic poems, and characteristic of his second
period that he wrote a two-volume treatise on
counterpoint and fugue, called *The Strict Style* (1902).
The list of Draeseke's works has an out-and-out classical
aspect.   There are three symphonies, the third of which
is called *Sinfonia tragica*, and three overtures, two of
which are respectively to Calderon's *Life a Dream* and
H. Kleist's *Penthesilea*, and the third is a *Jubilation
Overture*.   These are the only signs of the programmatic.
The rest of his works consist of concerted chamber
music, a concerto, a concert piece, oratorios, operas, a
requiem, &c.   As to the fifth and most important of the
Liszt circle at Weimar, he differs from those already
discussed in that he was at no time a believer in the
composer Liszt and his doctrines and methods.

JOACHIM RAFF (1822-1882) was destined by his
parents for the church or the school, by his genius
for the art of music, and his genius gained the
day in spite of the most formidable obstacles.   As a
composer he had no other teacher but himself.   That
alone would have been enough to deter an aspirant even
of more than average will-power.   Now add to this,
poverty and the necessity of laboriously making a scanty
living.   In 1843 Raff sent a couple of compositions to
Mendelssohn, and asked for a straightforward opinion,
pointing out that his adoption of music as a profession
would mean giving up his employment and breaking with
his family.   Mendelssohn's reply was warmly encourag-
ing.   He recognized in him unquestionable talent, and
proved the sincerity of this expression of opinion by
recommending the compositions for publication to
Breitkopf & Härtel.   Even more important than this
event proved a walk from Zürich to Basel, undertaken in

the summer of 1845, through downpours of rain, for the purpose of hearing Liszt. The great virtuoso, struck by the enthusiasm and amused by the appearance of his dripping admirer, at once took an interest in him, made him his travelling companion for some months, and then procured him a post in Eck & Lefebre's pianoforte warehouse at Cologne. While in this position Raff made the personal acquaintance of Mendelssohn, who invited him to come to Leipzig. Mendelssohn's death, however, destroyed this hope. He then (1847) went to Stuttgart, giving there lessons, writing for the music papers, composing, and working hard at self-improvement. Two years later he left Stuttgart for Hamburg, where he found employment with the music-publisher Schuberth. During all this time Raff had been in correspondence with his patron and counsellor Liszt. His close connection with him as assistant began towards the end of 1849 and lasted till 1856. Raff next settled in Wiesbaden, and remained there, teaching and composing, till 1877, when he was appointed director of the Frankfurt Hoch Conservatorium, a post which he held to the end of his life.

The relation between Liszt and Raff was peculiar— it had on both sides much genuine respect, affection, and good-will, but also some disrespect, suspicion, and contrariety. It lacked the quality of ease, indeed was disturbed by a positive element of discomfort. This state of matters arose from disparity in their characters, positions, and abilities. There was, on the one hand, Liszt, aristocratic and idealistic as a man, famous and high-placed as a musician, and ambitious and self-confident, but ill-trained, as a composer; on the other hand, Raff, boorish and homespun as a man, unknown and low-placed as a musician, and equally ambitious and self-confident, but of skilful craftsmanship, as a composer. Liszt could not forget that he was the patron and employer of Raff, nor Raff that he was the subordinate and dependent of Liszt. And again, Liszt, who, conscious of his genius, originality, and poetic inventiveness, no doubt looked down upon Raff, could not but feel his own technical inferiority; whereas Raff, we know, proudly felt his superiority in this respect. Some extracts from letters will throw further light on the relation of the two men, and expose to view Raff's standpoint with regard to Liszt's position as a composer. However, I must not conceal my suspicion that Raff's strong self-satisfaction leads him now and then—unconsciously no doubt—to lay on a subjective colouring that interferes somewhat with objective truth. These letters appeared first in the German periodical *Die Musik* (vol. i., 1901-1902), and most of those of Raff's are intimate effusions addressed to a dear old lady friend. Toward the end of 1849 Raff writes from the small watering-place Eilsen, where his assistantship began :

' Last week I expurgated Liszt's first concert-symphonique, and to-day I was occupied with the copy and translation of the remodelled Field article.— Then follows the instrumentation and fair copy of an overture entitled *Ce qu'on entend sur la Montagne*, the first symphonic poem composed after a lengthy programme in verse.'

' I confess that I find Liszt extraordinarily changed. He accepts my criticisms most patiently, and shows that he wants still to learn. Chrism and holy-water, as the Roman Catholics say, are therefore not wasted upon

2 I

him. His intention is to devote two or three years
to quiet preparation for the career of a composer, and
then to come forward in Paris.'

'My labours for Liszt, it is true, are endless. But, as
you know, I am not afraid of a heap of paper. . . . I
have just made a fair copy of his first concerto and his
two concert-overtures [Symphonic poems] *Ce qu'on
entend sur la Montagne* and *The four Elements* [*Les
quatre Eléments: La Terre, Les Aquilons, Les Flots,
Les Astres;* after a poem by Aubray—a composition out of
which was developed *Les Préludes*], partly orchestrated.'

'I was just occupied with the instrumentation of
Liszt's *Héroide funèbre,*' writes Raff in January, 1850,
from Weimar, 'and the broad, gloomy motives, to which
I was yet to give the sombre instrumental tints which
call up in us thoughts of the last events of us all,
penetrated my soul. . . . My melancholy had
reached a high degree, and to this circumstance I owed
some technical inspirations which drew from my friend
exclamations of joy and surprise.

'My relations to Liszt have entered on a second stage
. . . At Eilsen and also at first here [Weimar]
my friend displayed a certain self-confidence which
was to imbue me with the conviction of how little
I was really necessary to him. In everything he seemed
to let me know that anyone could do for him what he
required, that my only superiority was in my fairer
copies, and that beyond this not much was wanted. . . .
One day Liszt took courage, and asked me to orchestrate
something for him. When this had been done
satisfactorily, he went somewhat further, and now we
have come to this, that whole passages in Liszt's new
works are as little acquainted with the pen of the author

as certain passage-work in my Op. 15 originated from Joachim Raff.

'Now I am busy with the remodelling of the *Tasso* overture, out of which I intend to make him [Liszt] a symphony in two parts.'

The foregoing extracts show the nature of the work Raff did for Liszt, who, we may be sure, found his younger friend and assistant, what on one occasion he calls him, ' a thoroughly capable splendid fellow.' Now we must see what was Raff's view of Liszt as a composer, which is a much more important and interesting subject of inquiry.

' I am determined to have some little influence—this I must have—on Liszt's newest works ; and, thanks to his intelligence, he has already perceived that this is as it should be,—because four eyes can see better than two —and accepts readily observations which he used to repugn. The Princess [Wittgenstein] calls me an unfeeling man who cultivates art only as a science, not from the standpoint of inner poesy. Heavens!—I, on the other hand, say it is time that Liszt should cease to play the orchestra on the pianoforte and the pianoforte in the orchestra .   .   .   to wholly banish from the art one of its most useful parts, counterpoint, and to make a real heap of stones of the edifice of beautiful forms which we have inherited, extending a song to nineteen pages, and in other things being sometimes at a loss for sufficient material.'

'Should I,' he writes to Liszt on December 31, 1850, ' some day be less satisfied with your artistic achievements than I wish and hope, depend upon it, my heart will never cease to be nearest your heart.'

When, seven years later, Liszt applied to Raff, then no longer his assistant, for analyses of his symphonic poems, the latter wrote to a friend: 'He did not ask that his works should be praised, but only wished me to supply an objective exposition of the technical structure and poetical content. In a three hours' discussion I stated mainly that I did not agree with his tendencies.' The upshot was that Raff did not write the analyses. Raff published his confession of faith in a *Letter to the Editor of the Neue Zeitschrift für Musik* (February 11, 1853). He there says that he has felt the need of seeking the *terra firma* of a neutral ground, as productive activity cannot find support in either of the negations presented by the extreme parties—by those who oppose what goes farther than Beethoven and even what goes so far as the works of his last period, and by those who are exclusive partisans of R. Wagner, and deny the right of existence to specific music, *i.e.*, music apart from the drama.

After Raff's opinion of Liszt, let us have Liszt's of Raff.

'Your true friends must seriously draw your attention to the probable bad consequences of the gigantic fertility of your genius, and remind you of moderation and aim' (October 28, 1846).

'The five or six pieces of yours published by Mechetti show strikingly talent, ideas, versatility in form, and a comprehensive knowledge of what has been written for the pianoforte during the last sixteen years' (November, 1846).

A few years later, after a performance of a composition by Raff at one of Liszt's musical gatherings, the host remarked to those present: 'He has learned something,

and can do something. Depend upon it! in a few years
he will be high up.'

The first two of these three extracts refer to a very
early period of Raff's career, yet even then Liszt put
his finger on the weak and strong points that remained
the same throughout Raff's life. Overproductivity, however, was not, as we shall see, the only cause of the fate
that so soon overtook the composer Raff. What was
this fate? Early in the last quarter of the 19th century,
one of the most distinguished, and at the same time
most sane and solid musicians and critics of England,
Ebenezer Prout, declared that Raff was one of the three
German composers that stood in the front rank, head
and shoulders taller than their fellows, the other two
being Wagner and Brahms. The fame of the first has
been short-lived. No one would now pronounce his
name in the same breath with those of the two other
masters. Indeed, although Raff's published works
number considerably more than two hundred, and
comprise compositions of all kinds, his name on programmes has for some time been a very rare phenomenon.
The explanation seems to be this : Raff, a composer of
inexhaustible inventiveness and wonderful fluency of
expression, of masterly craftsmanship in counterpoint,
form, and instrumentation, was not an inspired poet,
not an original individuality, not a grand personality.
Moreover, pedantry made him sometimes indulge in
unseasonable contrapuntal sportiveness (canons, &c.) ;
and an irrepressible passion for work even more than the
need of making money prevented him from waiting for
the propitious moment and from selecting his ideas. But
as Raff, besides being intellectual, was poetical, although
not a poet, was a distinct individuality, although not a

strikingly original one, was an estimable personality, although not a grand one, it must be admitted that the neglect of his more than respectable achievements is not quite deserved. But that, I am afraid, may be said both of all successes and all failures : even time, the supreme court of appeal, does not know how to hold the balance. As to my explanation, it is incomplete. Riemann is right when he says : ' it is true that Raff's works are unequal ; but it would be difficult to give an explanation of the fact that, for instance, the *Forest* Symphony, too, does not " sound " nowadays.' Or let us rather say : ' that it now fails to impress the public as it used to do.'

Among Raff's pianoforte pieces we find titles like these : ' Angele's last day in the convent,' a cycle of twelve pieces, Op. 27 ; ' Messengers of Spring,' twelve pieces, Op. 55 ; ' From Switzerland,' a fantastic eclogue, Op. 57 ; ' Am Giessbach,' *Etude*, Op. 88 ; ' Dans la nacelle,' *Rêverie-Barcarolle*, Op. 93, ' La Cicerenella,' new carnival, Op. 165 ; and ' Les Orientales,' eight pieces, Op. 175. Everyone knows ' La Fée d'amour,' Op. 67, for violin and pianoforte (or orchestra), made so popular by Sarasate. Of Raff's eight String Quartets, the seventh (Op. 192, No. 2) is entitled *Die schöne Müllerin* (The beautiful maid of the mill). Four overtures have for their subjects *Romeo and Juliet*, *Othello*, *Macbeth*, and *The Tempest*. With two exceptions (Nos. 2 and 4) Raff's eleven symphonies have programmes. Their titles are as follows: (1) *An das Vaterland* (To my Fatherland) ; (3) *Im Walde* (In the forest) ; (5) *Lenore ;* (6) *Gelebt, gestrebt, gelitten, gestritten, gestorben, umworben* (Lived, strove, suffered, struggled, died, and was glorified) ; (7) *In the Alps ;* (8) *Spring Sounds ;* (9) *In Summer ;* (10) *In Autumn ;* and (11) *Winter.*

It would take up too much space to analyze all these compositions or even all these symphonies. I shall confine myself to a few remarks on the first, third, and fifth. A preface sets forth what are the ideas expressed in the five divisions of the symphony *An das Vaterland*: in the *Allegro*, free aspiration, thoughtful meditation, moral refinement, and gentleness and conquering endurance, to which four ideas correspond four subjects; in the *Scherzo*, youths and maidens go joyfully forth into wood and meadow to the sound of the horns and the cheerful folk-song; in the *Larghetto*, the charms and pleasures of home life are depicted; in the *Allegro dramatico*, repeated attempts at national union frustrated by the hostilities of the enemy; in the *Andante*, sadness; in the *Larghetto*, hope; and in the *Allegro*, victory and union. The two best known and most popular of all Raff's symphonies are the third and fifth. *In the Forest* has four movements which form three divisions : (1) In the day-time—impressions and feelings; (2*a*) In the twilight —dreaming; (2*b*) Dance of dryads; (3) In the night-time —the still life in the forest, coming and going of the Wild Hunt with Hulda and Wotan, daybreak. The *Lenore* Symphony is of course based on Bürger's ballad; but the composer supplements in the first two of the three divisions what the poet presupposes. Only the last division illustrates the poem itself. The content of the three divisions is as follows: (1) Happiness in love (*Allegro* and *Adagio*); (2) Separation; (3) Reunion in death.

From what has been said it may be gathered that the programme acted on the form as well as on the content of Raff's compositions. But it has to be noted that the form, however modified, is classical, *i.e.*, based on the

example of the great classics and their followers. While
Liszt's theory and practice had undoubtedly a considerable influence upon Raff, it is equally clear that his
programme music differs from Liszt's, both in programme
and music, both in content and form, but in form
especially. In short, Raff, although connected with the
New German School, was not of it. This was evidenced
not only by his musical compositions, but also by his
writings on music—for instance, *Die Wagnerfrage* (The
Wagner question; 1854), and still more in his article on
Mozart in the *Signale* (1856). These caused some heart-
burning among the party to whom he ostensibly belonged.
Moreover, Raff's daughter assures us that her father
was a sincere reverer of the classics and especially of
Mozart.

To the five famous disciples of Liszt and champions
of the New German School there has to be added a sixth
who, although less prominent in the eyes of the world,
and less regarded by his leaders and fellow combatants,
was nevertheless destined to do more for the propagation
of Liszt's ideas than all the five together ever did.
ALEXANDER RITTER (1833-1896), violinist and
composer, studied music at the Leipzig Conservatorium
and in Dresden, became (after marrying a niece of
Wagner's) a member of the Weimar orchestra in 1854,
and conductor at the Stettin Theatre in 1856; lived
subsequently at Dresden, again at Stettin, at Würzburg
(with two interruptions) from 1863 to 1882, at Meiningen
(as a member of the orchestra under Bülow's direction),
and at Munich. His Op. 1, a String Quartet, was
·published in 1865. Many songs followed. But his
reputation was not made until in his fifties, when two
one-act operas of his were performed with considerable

success, *Der faule Hans* (1885) and *Wem die Krone?*
(1890). Ritter's name appears very frequently in the
letters of Liszt and his following. He evidently was
much liked as a friend, but apparently was not estimated
at his full value as a musician. There are no allusions
to his compositions, if a letter of Bülow's is excepted, in
which two concertos are criticized, on the whole very
favourably. The writer remarks (October 29, 1860):
' I had always credited your musical brain with great
receptive genius ; as to your productive imagination I
mistrusted it. You have given me an opportunity to
change my erroneous opinion, to overthrow it.' Strangest
of all is that when Liszt writes in 1867 a letter of recommendation for Ritter, he praises him as a violinist and
as a conductor, extols his extensive musical knowledge,
notes his intimate relations with celebrated virtuosi and
composers, but says not a word about his being a
composer. That he lacked energy, perseverance, and
stability, developed his powers slowly, wrote reflectively
rather than spontaneously, was modest, reticent, in
short, the reverse of pushing, may account fully for the
little notice taken of him by the public, but cannot
altogether account for the ignorance and indifference of
his friends. And yet to the observer of the ways of the
world the mystery disappears when he learns that
Ritter not only was modest but also thoroughly
unselfish, made no claims on the patronage of his great
friends, and thought himself fortunate in and super-
abundantly enriched by his intercourse with them.
Liszt and Wagner had the most decisive influence on
Ritter's artistic development, without, however, destroy·
ing his individuality—as is proved by his operas and by
his songs, which latter excellent judges declare to be the

best part of his artistic output. All his life Ritter was a
convinced believer in programme music in Liszt's sense.
He held that all genuine music is programme music
—Beethoven's symphonies as well as Liszt's symphonic
poems — and fought with ruthless energy against
Hanslick's thesis of tonal moving forms. While
enthusiastically admiring Liszt and Wagner, contending
for their cause to the neglect of his own interests, even
of his creative work, he had little sympathy with Berlioz.
He recognized the French master's bizarre genius, but
would not admit him to be the equal of Liszt and
Wagner. Besides songs and operas Ritter wrote
symphonic poems. Most of them belong to the last ten
years of his life. Here are their titles, with a few notes
added : *Seraphic Fantasia; Erotic Legend; Olaf's
Wedding-dance* (the ultimate outcome of an operatic
subject carried about with him for many years);
Sursum corda, a storm and stress fantasia (an old
man's retrospect on his artist life, described with
youthful passion); *Good Friday and Corpus Christi
Day;* and *Emperor Rudolph's Ride to the Grave,* after
Kerner's poem (written under the influence of his
wife's death and presentiments of his own). It has been
said that both formally and programmatically Ritter
goes beyond Liszt. This, however, is emphatically
contradicted by most authoritative judges. As these
works of Ritter's have been but rarely performed and
probably in Germany only, it is impossible to prophesy
what their future will be. But whether it be popularity
or oblivion, historical immortality is secured to Alexander
Ritter as the intermediary between Liszt and Richard
Strauss, between the New and the Newest German
School.

To RICHARD STRAUSS (*b.* 1864), the much discussed, the problematic, we must now turn our attention. On certain points all the world is at one—on his virtuosic craftsmanship, his supreme mastery over all the resources of the art, his diabolical cleverness, and even his genius. But agreement ceases when we come to the consideration of the application of the craftsmanship, mastery, cleverness, and genius. Then opinions may be found as far apart as the poles, and even as heaven and earth. Then we may see ecstatic delight on the one hand and downright disgust on the other, and hear praise and blessings on the one hand and condemnation and curses on the other. In Strauss's career as a composer there are clearly distinguishable two periods, the second of which was brought about not by evolution, but by revolution, and not by an inner, but by an outer impulse. Many ask now: Will there be a third period, and how will that be brought about? Strauss's musical training, which ran parallel with his secondary school and university education, was on classical lines, and during the short first period of his creative career he adhered to these lines. As belonging to this time and style we may indicate Op. 1-15, and add to them Op. 18, the most notable works of which are the Sonata for violoncello and pianoforte, Op. 6; the Serenade for thirteen wind instruments, Op. 7; the Symphony, Op. 12; the Quartet for pianoforte and strings, Op. 13; and the Sonata for violin and pianoforte, Op. 18. In 1885 Strauss went to Meiningen, and there he made the acquaintance of Alexander Ritter, by whom he was converted and imbued with the principles responsible, indirectly if not directly, for the sensational works that have made the world stare and stand agape. From Dr. Arthur Seidl, the friend to whom Strauss dedicated his *Till Eulenspiegel,* we learn some interesting particulars about the composer's mental development and tendencies.   He tells us of their hearing at the Munich University courses of lectures on æsthetics (Carrière), Schopenhauer (Fr. Jodl), and the history of culture (Riehl) ; and how in 1889, at the time of his friendship with Ritter—in the Wagner-Liszt period of his artistic development, and the Schopenhauer period of his intellectual development—Strauss suddenly struck up as it were a new tune, Dostojevski's *Raskolnikov* raising his enthusiasm and inciting him to psychological analysis and dissection, and Gerhart Hauptmann (still in the ante-'Weber' days*) keenly interesting him on account of the progressive-naturalistic technique in the painting of the *milieu,* the presentation of human character, and the refinement of dialogue.   Some years later, at the turning-point of his life, there occurred a veering round from Schopenhauer to Nietzsche, in whom he became absorbed and found deliverance and recovery, or—shall we say ?—freedom and health (*Loslösung und Genesung*).   Strauss's attention was further arrested by John Henry Mackay and his novel *The Anarchists,* by Karl Henckell and his social lament 'the times are forceful, they bring distress to heart and brain,' and by the poet R. Dehmel, the poet, dramatist, and prose-writer Detlev von Liliencron, and the prose-writers Julius Hart and Otto Julius Bierbaum.   In short, Strauss bathed in the troubled waters of modernity, and came out an ultra-modern.   A circumstance alluded to above deserves more than an allusion, and authoritative information enables me to speak of it more fully.   When in 1885 Strauss came to Meiningen, Hans von Bülow introduced him to

---

* *Die Weber (The Weavers)* is one of Hauptmann's plays.

his old friend Alexander Ritter, whose opinions we
know already. The latter was not slow to perceive the
extraordinary talent of his new acquaintance, but also
his conservatism and youthfulness in more respects than
years. That Strauss was not as yet favourably impressed
by Wagner's music may be easily accounted for by his
father's violent anti-Wagnerism. Ritter set himself
the task of showing the young man the way to clear
and develop his views; of stirring up, not merely the
musician, but the whole intellectual man, to artistic
activity; and of awaking in him the notion that in order
to attain an object it is necessary to have a mental grasp
of it. By means of Wagner's literary works Ritter
revealed to Strauss the ideas which inspired that master's
art-work. Nor was Ritter's influence confined to matters
musical. It extended, for instance, to Schopenhauer's
philosophy. The strength of Ritter's conviction and the
ardour of his propagandism were irresistible; indeed,
they were so great as on one occasion to draw from
Strauss the remark that they were 'directly suggestive,'
in the hypnotic sense. The acquaintanceship of the
two men soon grew into intimate friendship. At
Meiningen and at Munich, they were in close
and almost daily intercourse; and when Strauss
took up his abode at Weimar a lively, long-continued
correspondence followed. Later on, unfortunately, an
estrangement arose, which, however, had nothing to do
with Strauss's artistic development, as some supposed.
Strauss told the writer of the interesting article on him
in *The Musical Times* of January, 1903: 'Ritter was
exceptionally well read in all the philosophers ancient
and modern, and a man of the highest culture. His
influence was in the nature of a stormwind. He urged

me on to the development of the poetic, the expressive in music, as exemplified in the works of Liszt, Wagner and Berlioz.' In short, Ritter stamped him, as Strauss himself declares, as a progressive musician.

Passing over the songs and operas, and even over his melodrama *Enoch Arden*, Op. 38 (recitation and pianoforte accompaniment), let us proceed to the symphonic works for orchestra of the second, the programmatic period; and be it noted at once that the nine compositions in question are not uniform in style, but progressive in regard to complexity, intensity, and expressiveness. In speaking here of progressiveness I leave it an open question whether the progress leads to greater or less perfection, to a desirable or undesirable end.

(I.) *From Italy*, symphonic fantasia, Op. 16 (1886; 1887).* This work need not detain us; it is really a suite of four characteristic pieces, respectively entitled *In the Campagna, Amid the Ruins of Rome, By Sorrento's Strand*, and *Scenes of Popular Life in Naples*. We have here characteristic pieces of mood and scene with which conservative composers have made us familiar; in fact, the programmes indicated by the titles go but little beyond those of the composer's Op. 9, called by him *Mood Pictures:* (1) *On the still wood path;* (2) *At the lonely spring;* (3) *Intermezzo;* (4) *Dreaming;* and (5) *Heath Picture.* Of course, the means of expression and the force, sweep, and realism of the expressiveness are very much greater in the later work. As the composer himself says: ' My symphonic fantasia *Aus Italien* is the

---

* Where two years are given, the first is that of composition, and the second that of the first performance. Where only one year is given, it is that of the first performance.

connecting link between the old and the new method.'
In the composition next to be considered quite a different
state of matters obtains.

(II.) *Don Juan*, tone-poem (after Nicolaus Lenau),
Op. 20 (1888 ; 1889).   Prefixed are three passages,
altogether thirty-two lines, from Lenau's dramatic poem
of the same name.   The gist of the three passages may
be briefly given as follows: (1) Don Juan's desire to rove
through the immeasurable charmed circle of variously
attractive womanhood, and die in a kiss on the lips of the
last ; (2) Mortifying individuals he worships the species;
a woman's breath that to-day seems to have the
fragrance of spring, may to-morrow be to him like the
air of a dungeon ; pressing forward to new and ever new
victories as long as youth's fiery pulses fly ; (3) The
beautiful storm is stilled, the combustible material
consumed, and the hearth has become cold and dark.—
The printed programme gives only a few slight
indications of the programme in the mind of the composer.
In the latter were many particulars not in the former.
Besides the generalities of infinite amorous desire,
ceaseless alternation of passionateness and satiety, and
final exhaustion, there are in the music three adventures
with women of unlike character, and a duel with the
father of one of them, by whose weapon Don Juan falls.
The fatal sword-thrust, represented by a piercing
dissonant high trumpet note, is famous.

(III.) *Macbeth*, tone-poem (after Shakespeare's drama),
Op. 23 (1887 ; 1891).   This work was composed four
years before its publication, and before the composition
of *Don Juan*, and consequently is the first of the master's
symphonic poems, and properly dedicated to Alexander
Ritter.   Beyond the title, that is beyond the wide

reference to the drama, there is little to indicate the
particularities. This little consists of the word 'Macbeth'
above the sixth bar; and further on these words of Lady
Macbeth : ' Hie thee hither, that I may pour my spirits
in thy ear, and chastise with the valour of my tongue
all that impedes thee from the golden round, which fate
and metaphysical aid doth seem to have thee crown'd
withal.' If a brief account of the work as a whole is
wanted, we may call it an illustration of Macbeth's
character and soul-struggles.

(IV.) *Tod und Verklärung* (Death and Transfiguration),
tone-poem, Op. 24 (1889 ; 1890). This work, like
Don Juan, has a programme prefixed—thirty lines in four
divisions, forming a complete poem. (1) In a poor little
room, dimly lighted, and awfully and ominously silent,
except for the ticking of a clock, there lies on his bed,
fallen asleep after an exhausting desperate struggle with
death, a sick man, with a smile on his face as if he were
dreaming of childhood's golden time. (2) Before long
the battle begins anew between the desire for life and
the power of death, but without victory on either side;
and again there is silence. (3) Sleepless, as in a fever
delirium, the sufferer sees passing before his inner eye
the rosy dawn of innocent childhood, the more daring
sport of youth, and the ardent striving of manhood that
turns obstacles into stepping-stones to higher things, the
storm and stress continuing until the hour of death that
now strikes. (4) From heaven descends towards him,
resounding grandly, what he had longingly sought here
below: World-redemption and world-transfiguration.
The programme of *Tod und Verklärung* is not only a
more sufficient guide than that of *Don Juan*, but also
the most musical of all Strauss's programmes.

(V.) *Till Eulenspiegels lustige Streiche* (Tyll Owlglass's merry pranks). Nach alter Schelmenweise—in Rondeauform (After the old rogue-manner—in rondo form); Op. 28 (1895; 1895). The 14th century hero of tricks and drolleries, whose fame still flourishes, and whose immortality is secured by words coined after him not only in the German, but also in the French language (*espiègle* and *espièglerie*), is supposed to have been a rustic born at Kneitlingen in Brunswick, who, after a vagabond life in many countries and cursory trials at many trades, died of the plague at Mölln in Lauenburg (four leagues from Lübeck), in 1350. His tombstone may still be seen. It is, however, of the 17th century, but may be the renewal of an older one. The history of his achievements was not written by himself, and when it was written many achievements of others were added to his own. It appeared first in Low German (1483), afterwards in High German (Strasburg, 1515). The latter may be the work of Thomas Murner. Now what has Strauss done with this rude but vigorous and vivacious *Volksbuch?* When Dr. Franz Wüllner gave the first performance of *Till Eulenspiegel's merry pranks* at Cologne, he asked the composer for an explanatory programme. Strauss replied : ' It is impossible for me to furnish a programme to Eulenspiegel. Were I to put into words the thoughts which its several incidents suggested to me, they would seldom suffice, and might even give rise to offence. Let me leave it, therefore, to my hearers to " crack the hard nut " which the Rogue has provided for them. By way of helping them to a better understanding, it seems sufficient to point out the two Eulenspiegel motives [they appear at the beginning of the work], which in the most manifold disguises, moods, and situations pervade

2 K

the whole up to the catastrophe, when, after he had been
condemned to death (a descending major seventh—F to
G flat), Till is strung up to the gibbet. For the rest, let
them guess at the musical joke which a rogue has
offered them.' The reason given for his reticence does
not carry conviction with it. This the composer seems
to have felt himself, and he may also have felt the
unwisdom of a policy of concealment. At any rate he
subsequently changed his mind, and gave to his
commentator Wilhelm Mauke a score in which the names
of most of the motives were entered with pencil. Here
they are. (1) Prologue. ' Once upon a time there was
a rogue.' (2) Of the name of " Till Eulenspiegel." (3)
That was a mischievous sprite. (4) Away for new
pranks. (5) Wait! you hypocrite! (6) Hop! on
horseback through the midst of the market women!
(7) With seven-league boots he makes off. (8) Hidden
in a mouse-hole. (9) Disguised as a pastor he overflows
with unction and morality. (10) But the rogue peeps
out from the great toe. (11) Before the end, however,
a secret horror takes hold of him on account of the
mockery of religion. (12) Till as cavalier exchanging
tender civilities with pretty girls. (13) With one of
them he has really fallen in love. (14) He proposes to
her. (15) A polite refusal is also a refusal. (16) [Turns
away in a rage.] (17) Swears to take vengeance on the
whole human race. (18) Philistine motive. (19) After
proposing to the Philistines a couple of monstrous
theses, he abandons the dumbfounded ones to their fate.
(20) Great grimace from afar. (21) Till's *Gassenhauer*
(vulgar street song). (22) [Watched by catch-poles,
and collared by the bailiff]. (23) The judgment. (24)
He whistles to himself with indifference. (25) Up the

ladder ! There he is swinging, his breath has gone out,
a last quiver. All that is mortal of Till is ended. (26)
[Epilogue. What is immortal, his humour, remains.]'
To this has to be added only one remark, namely, that
the Straussite commentators hold that the composer had
more in his mind than he confessed in the above, that
he aimed at something higher than the mere illustration
of a rogue's pranks.

(VI.) *Also sprach Zarathustra* (Thus spake Zarathustra),
tone-poem (treated freely after Friedrich Nietzsche),
Op. 30 (1896 ; 1896). It seems strange that a musician
should go for a subject to a philosopher's book. But
going to Nietzsche is not the same as going to Aristotle,
Descartes, or Kant. Nevertheless the venture was
strange. Zarathustra cannot be numbered with those
literary works that yearn for musical treatment. For,
although the poetical element in it may be predominant,
it is impossible to eliminate the unmusical philosophical
element without obscuring and denaturalizing the
former. An explanation by the composer hardly
improves the situation, as it fails to reduce the amount
of philosophy implied. Strauss wrote in 1896 : ' I did
not intend to write philosophical music or portray
Nietzsche's great work musically. I meant to convey
musically an idea of the development of the human race
from its origin, through the various phases of development,
religious as well as scientific, up to Nietzsche's idea of
the *Uebermensch* [superman].' Nietzsche's Zarathustra,
who has nothing whatever to do with the Persian
Zarathustra (Zoroaster), is a superman and a preacher
of the gospel of the superman. ' Man is a something
that must be overcome. What have ye done to overcome him . . . . What is the ape for man ? A

laughing-stock or a sore shame. Man must be the same for the superman, a laughing-stock or a sore shame . . . . I conjure you, my brethren, remain faithful to the earth, and do not believe those who speak unto you of super-terrestrial hopes! Poisoners they are whether they know it or not.' Apart from what Strauss left untouched, there is this difference between the book and the symphony: Nietzsche brings before us a complete superman; Strauss, one in course of development. As to the contents of the composer's work his expounders are by no means at one. According to Arthur Hahn, Strauss begins with depicting a man who inquires into the solution of the world problem and the riddle of existence, and seeks in vain salvation in religion, in the whirlpool of life, and in science, all of which shows as much Faustian as specific Nietzschian spirit. The symphonist, we are told, depicts for us the development of the higher man to the Zarathustra personality; and his work is an artistic deposit from his subjective meditations and thoughts on Nietzsche and his book. Dr. Arthur Seidl will hear nothing of the 'Faustian longing for knowledge,' nothing of the stupid wearisome 'solution of the world riddle'; but he, too, dwells on the preliminary degrees, the stages of feeling in the process of purification by which the tone-poet leads the growing Zarathustra to the perfection of the superman. But what indications does the composer give us of the programme in his mind? On the one hand, there is a preface, a quotation of the opening of Nietzsche's book, but this is in no way a programme. On the other hand, however, the composer supplies something like a programme by superscriptions that occur in the course of the work. Here they are with a

few elucidations in square brackets : (1) Of the Back-
worlds Men [the believers in a beyond of the worlds].
(2) Of the great Longing. (3) Of Joys and Passions.
(4) The Grave-Song [over his earlier self]. (5) Of
Science. (6) The Convalescent. (7) [The Dance Song.
The superman has thrown off the burdens of the
common man]. (8) The Night Song, or Drunken Song.
['Eternity of all things is sought by all delight . . .
So rich is delight that it thirsteth for me, for hell, for
hatred, for shame, for the cripple, for *world*, for this
world! Oh, ye know it.']

(VII.) *Don Quixote* [Introduction, theme with variations, and Finale]. Fantastic variation on a theme of
chivalrous character. Op. 35 (1897 ; 1898). There is no
programme prefixed to this work ; and, apart from the
title, the composer vouchsafes only two programmatic
indications—namely, two superscriptions in connection
with the theme : 'Don Quixote, the Knight of the Rueful
Countenance,' above the first half, and 'Sancho Panza'
above the second. The Introduction may be regarded as
a picture of Don Quixote before the days of his knight-
errantry, a picture of the state of his mind, full of the
ideas imbibed from his beloved romances of chivalry. In
the variations are described some of the achievements
of the Ingenious Gentleman, Don Quixote of la Mancha.
The following programme has been devised for them.
How far the composer is responsible for it, I do not know.
(1) First Sally, Dulcinea del Toboso, and adventure of
the Windmills.   (2) Don Quixote charges a flock of
sheep, believing them to be the army of the mighty
Emperor Alifanfaron.   (3) Colloquies between the knight
and his squire.   (4) Don Quixote's assault of the pilgrims
bearing a covered image, which he took for a great lady

carried away by force. (5) The knight's watch of his arms. (6) Sancho Panza's assertion that a certain vulgar peasant woman was Dulcinea, and Don Quixote's indignation. (7) Ride through the air, while, with bandaged eyes, they were in reality remaining stationary on a wooden horse. (8) The enchanted bark. (9) Encounter with the two sorcerers, who, however, are only harmless priests. (10) Combat with the Knight of the shining Moon. Finale : Don Quixote's end. These variations are fantasias on a theme, not variations in the original acceptation of the word. This might be concluded, without looking at the contents, from the great differences in the length. But, of course, no one would expect from Strauss Haydn-Mozart variations, which indeed lie a long way behind us, as even Beethoven and Brahms make obvious. It has been said that Strauss's *Don Quixote* was a reaction from the high idealism of *Zarathustra;* but it has also been said that it is something more than a mere series of comic scenes. Here, then, in connection with Strauss's fantastic variations, repeats itself the old discussion about the deeper meaning of Cervantes's book, the fundamental idea of which, according to some, is the eternal contrast between the spirit of poetry and prose, between ideality and reality.

(VIII.) *Ein Heldenleben* (A hero's life), a tone-poem. Op. 40 (1898 ; 1899). This work has no printed programme nor any other programmatic indications. The ideas in the composer's mind, however, are not difficult to divine or even to understand ; and moreover have been indicated by authorized commentaries. The general outline is as follows : (1) The Hero. (2) The Hero's Opponents. (3) The Hero's female companion.

(4) The Hero's battlefield. (5) The Hero's works of peace.
(6) The Hero's renouncement of the world and perfection.
Ein Heldenleben has given rise not only to prose commentaries, but also to a descriptive, or rather transcriptive
poem, the author of which is Eberhard König. Notwithstanding the realistic battle-picture contained in
the composition, and the idealizing and generalizing
features in the conception, we cannot be far off the
truth in saying that Strauss himself is the hero of
Ein Heldenleben.

(IX.) *Sinfonia Domestica*, Op. 53 (1904). The
dedication is significant : ' To my dear wife and our boy.'
The title and the dedication are the only hints we get
as to the composer's programme. This 20th century
symphony, which in form and content has nothing of
the 18th and 19th century symphony, is a family idyll
in which husband, wife, and child are the sole *dramatis
personæ.* It is a picture-book of domestic portraiture
and incidents, conceived and executed with a happy,
admiring, and proud husband and father's sympathy
and enthusiasm. We might also call it : Family joys,
woes, contrarieties, and humours. An interviewer of
Strauss relates that it illustrates a day in the family life
of Madame, Monsieur, and Bébé. The authorized
synopsis of the work (which consists of a continuity of
movements) runs as follows :—

Introduction and development of the three principal
groups of themes : Themes of the husband ; themes of
the wife ; themes of the child.

Scherzo : Parental happiness ; the child at play ;
lullaby (the clock strikes 7 p.m.).

Adagio : Doing and thinking ; Love-scene ; Dreams
and cares (the clock strikes 7 a.m.).

Finale : Waking and merry dispute (double fugue); joyful conclusion.

The time has not yet come for a final judgment on Richard Strauss. In twenty years, perhaps in ten, we shall be able to speak with the calm, if not with the absolute impartiality, which a fair judgment presupposes. As yet the object is too new, too strange, too near, to justify the hope of attaining such a desideratum. A few critical remarks, without any pretension to finality, may, however, not be out of place and unwelcome to the reader. There are two of Strauss's symphonic poems that have found wider acceptance than any of the others. These two are *Death and Transfiguration* and *Till Eulenspiegel.* As both works are decidedly modern in feeling, form, and means employed, it cannot be said that the people who prefer them are old-fashioned. We have therefore to look for another explanation, and I think we shall find it, in the case of the former work, in the thoroughly musical nature of the subject and in the sincerity of the treatment. *Till Eulenspiegel,* on the other hand, is a *jeu d'esprit,* one of the cleverest and most delightful imaginable, and eccentricities and extravagances would there be readily forgiven if they required forgiveness. The objections made to Strauss's music arise from the increasing admixture of unmusicalness and insincerity in his compositions, which undoubtedly contain so much that is truly beautiful and truly expressive in the best sense. As every one knows, it is widely believed that the master himself looks upon his tone-poems as huge jokes played upon the public. I have heard many musicians—by no means of the pedantic, reactionary, and milk-and-water kind— express this view with conviction. Strauss denies the

insinuation ; and, of course, we must accept his word.
But it is his own fault that the belief has sprung up and
spread. He seems to have an irresistible itch to provoke
the amazement and the horror of the multitude. He
seems to have retained in him something of the
burschikos character, something of the young university
student, who, revelling in the belief of his superiority,
looks down upon those he calls Philistines, and never
tires of laughing and tilting at them. But, alas ! the
superiority of these young men has mostly no better
foundation than self-deception, and the so-called
Philistines comprise in reality not only dullards but also
wise men, men that know the measure of things, and
have learned to winnow chaff from grain. Indeed, this
feeling of superiority is a rest of childishness that is
generally thrown off when the youth becomes a man, or
at least when the man reaches years of discretion.
The spirit that dictated the extravagances of tone-
painting, material and metaphysical—for instance,
the cacophonies of the battle in *Ein Heldenleben* and
the bleating sheep variation in *Don Quixote*, and the
conundrums of *Zarathustra*—may also be seen in an
unpublished title and a published note. Strauss
originally intended to give *Till Eulenspiegel* this sub-title :
‘ Symphonic Optimism in *fin de siècle* form ; dedicated to
the 20th century.’ And a note to a song, which ends a
semitone higher than it begins, runs thus : ‘ Singers
who wish to perform this little composition before the
termination of the 19th century are at liberty simply
to ignore the new signature and remain comfortably
in the opening key, so as to soothe their artistic
conscience in regard to the formal correctness of the
conclusion.’ The out and out admirers of Strauss, the

enragés, call this sort of thing _genial_, that is, look upon it as a mark of genius ; whereas in reality it is, as has already been said, something very different, which might be euphemistically described as too excessively youthful. However, of the _Kraftgenies_, the storm and stress geniuses, for a while gaped at by the many and exalted by easily inflammable brains, time and history have the habit of making short shrift. But we should not leave un-noted what I am now going to mention. Strauss may say, as many a one has said before him, 'Heaven preserve me from my friends.' The claims they make for him make him ridiculous. Thus Paul Riesenfeld, who had written a 'soul-analysis' of Richard Strauss, writes that the composer expostulated with him, and told him that he had interpreted into him (Strauss) too much philosophy, and thereby had led many a one into the temptation of seeking still more and more philosophy in his works. Indeed, Strauss maintains on the contrary that he is 'altogether and always a musician for whom all programmes are only suggestions for new forms and nothing more.' Of course, Strauss, to escape from Scylla, falls here into Charybdis. He exaggerates, I am glad to say. If he spoke quite truly, he might be a musician, but could not be a tone-poet, and the use of the word tone-poem would be a sham. Strauss, however, expressed the same view to a London interviewer who signs himself 'C. K.'* He said : 'The poetical programme serves but to give an impulse to the discovery of new forms. The programme is a poetical help in creating new shapes. To use an extreme illustration, one might draw inspiration from this pianoforte

---

* The account of a later American interviewer is also in agreement with C. K. s.

stool. You have to find the musical equivalent for the poetical programme.' On being asked whether he sketched a definite programme, Strauss replied: 'Yes, with a view to giving it musical shape. You must not forget, however, that it is a musician who casts the programme. After all, poetry and music work hand in hand; music may represent any feature of life.' Of course, we cannot hold Strauss responsible for every word of this report; nor is an informal conversation in the course of a crowded day the best mode of setting forth one's æsthetic principles, which setting forth is, even under the most favourable conditions, a most difficult and risky proceeding. But taking the above quotations to be in the main correct, we cannot but be struck by the stress laid on forms and shapes, and the lack of differentiation in the subjects of the programmes. The pianoforte stool, even as an extreme illustration, is an unfortunate example. Perhaps the meaning of the obscure saying is that the composer chooses and constructs his programmes with a view to a musically effective collocation of parts. The following remarks of Strauss's, coming from a tone-poet, are somewhat puzzling, although of course the first statement is supremely true, and should be taken to heart by admirers of the chaotic: 'The musical poem must have hands and feet, so to speak; must be ship-shape musically considered. Let him who likes look on it merely as a musical work of art. In *Don Quixote*, for instance, I show how a man goes mad over vain imaginings. But I do not wish to compel any listener to think of Don Quixote when he hears it. He may conceive it as absolute music if it suits him.' Strange, a *tone-poet* who does not care whether his ideas are understood or not!

Strauss says truly that a composer must be a master of his craft, must not only have something to say, but also know how to say it. He, however, enunciates doubtful, nay pernicious doctrines when he continues thus : 'For me absolute beauty or ugliness does not exist in music. What is truly and sincerely felt, and then faithfully and properly reproduced, is beautiful. Ideas of beauty are constantly changing. I may now directly aim at expressing the ugly in music ; the achievement may be considered beautiful ten or fifty years hence. The question is, Does the composer succeed in musically representing what he aims at, even that which is ugly ? Therein lies æsthetic justification. Amateurishness is ugly.' The concluding part of this statement will be readily accepted. But is masterliness always beautiful ? I should say, it may be always admirable, but certainly is not always beautiful. The use of the ugly in art is limited and must be qualified. Not every ugliness is admissible, and every ugliness admitted has to be æstheticized. This calls up a remark of Strauss's on dissonance. He is reported to have said : 'What we consider a dissonance to-day, may seem smooth beauty to some of those who will come after us, or appear tame and pallid to others. The taste of the ear varies and changes in development.' This is, on the whole, true enough, but the statement does not present the problem fully. Dissonance is endurable in so far as it is intelligible, that is, in so far as its relationship to consonance is understood (felt) by the hearer. The power of this intelligence is increased by experience. We learn to dispense with the preparation of dissonances, and to put up with delayed resolutions. What is unintelligible to one generation may be perfectly intelligible to another. From this, however, it does not follow that it is impossible to make too great a demand on the endurance and the intelligence of the ear. And, then, dissonance by itself, unrelated dissonance, will always be unintelligible and unendurable. Neither genius nor time can raise dissonance to the independence of consonance. The rules of the schoolmaster can be overthrown, not the laws of nature. Now, in the notorious battle of *Ein Heldenleben*—to take one of many examples—the composer treats dissonance as independent, self-sufficient, and the unavoidable result is noise not tone, a charivari not music, indeed nothing that even by the greatest stretch of the imagination can be called music. The effect produced is certainly realistic, and Strauss's battle may be more like a real battle than any musical battle picture ever conceived. But *cui bono?* What art-lover is the richer or the better for it? Where is its æsthetic justification? Who wants a realistic reproduction of discord unrelieved by harmony, ugliness unrelieved by beauty? Not the sane and healthy. Besides this specially glaring and specially outrageous case of misapplication of genius and maltreatment of a noble art, we meet with innumerable objectionable cases of a milder and more passing nature—with things that cannot or ought not to be expressed, with ways of expression that are not in accordance with the nature of music, which must obey the law of dissonance and cannot very well do without tonality. As to what cannot be expressed, take, for instance, the conclusion of *Zarathustra*. The contradictory tonalities B major and C major are intended, we are told by the commentators, to signify a purely intellectual concept, the world problem still facing man at the height of his knowledge and wisdom. But the music is not the expression of the thought at all, for thought and expression have here only one subsidiary quality in common, that of opposition and exclusiveness. In short, Strauss has made use of an arbitrary non-conventional symbolism, which leaves the hearer unlimited freedom of interpretation. Regarded as absolute music, the passage in question cannot be defended : it is justifiable only by a poetic idea—but this idea should be at least guessable, and if it is not, ought to be verbally indicated by the composer. Strauss, ignoring the laws of dissonance and tonality, has, however, not only written series of dissonant intervals and chords, and any consecution of keys, he has also done what goes far beyond these ventures, he has even combined different keys simultaneously (like D and E flat), has combined what of necessity is mutually exclusive. If in this way a *valuable* effect is produced without the hearer becoming conscious of the device, its legitimacy might *perhaps* be admitted for discussion; but if the hearer becomes conscious of the device, discussion is out of the question and no words of condemnation can be strong enough. Strauss has furnished cases of both kinds.

Related to the abuse of dissonance is the mania for increasing the orchestra, chiefly for the purpose of making it more uproarious and ear-splitting. In a *Heroic* Symphony we may perhaps find excuse for 4 flutes, 3 oboes, *cor anglais*, 3 clarinets, 1 bass clarinet, 3 bassoons, 1 double bassoon, 8 horns, 5 trumpets, 3 trombones, 1 tenor tuba and 1 bass tuba, a strong force of percussion instruments, and the usual strings ; but we cannot help wondering at the employment in a *Domestic* Symphony of even a greater number of instruments—including, besides the strings, 2 harps, 4 flutes, 2 oboes, 1 oboe d'amore, 4 clarinets, 1 bass clarinet, 4 bassoons, 1 double bassoon, 4 saxophones, 8 horns, 4 trumpets, 3 trombones, 1 bass tuba, 4 kettle-drums, triangle, tambourine, glockenspiel, cymbals, and big drum. There must be something wrong here. The suspicion of mania arises quite naturally. The disproportion between means and subject is ridiculously extraordinary. Not long ago I read a letter of a composer who clamoured for more instruments in the orchestra, in order to obtain a greater variety of colour. The public, which is getting tired of colour and nothing but colour, begins to clamour for design, above all for ideas. Moreover, variety and beauty of colour depend more on treatment than on number. Study the great masters of the brush, oh ye ambitious musical colourists! You will see that their greatness is not calculable by the number of colours on their palettes.

The root of the mischief with Strauss and other composers of to-day is in the false ideal they worship, in that boasted modernity, of which there is a particular German species. The fundamental fault of it—in music perhaps more than in literature and the other arts—is extravagance in thought, sentiment, and imagination, in line, mass, colour, sonority, and form. The worshippers of modernity regard as commonplace and unworthy of the attention of any but Philistines, the normal, natural, healthy, simple, temperate, graceful, harmonious, and well-balanced; and take delight in the abnormal, eccentric, morbid, complicated, violent, delirious, grotesque, swaggering, strutting, flamboyant, noisy, colossal, wildly jagged, and even monstrous. Modernity, not Nietzsche, is the parent of the superman, and the music that boasts of its modernity is his music. As to that magnificent superman—with the abolished God, the transvaluation of all values leading to a beyond of good and evil, and the ultra-individualism of the strong and its *Herrenmoral* that is a law unto itself—he is but a poor, pitiable creature, a weakling with a swelled head. These moderns would say something never said before and say it in an altogether new manner. This, no doubt, is the highest an artist can achieve. But it cannot be done by will, it must come spontaneously. No excess, no extravagance can make up for the want of spontaneous originality, nay, it will even kill or spoil the originality that exists. Force and freedom are noble qualities, but the former should not be brute force brutally exercised, and the latter should be freedom to do good, not to do evil. Notwithstanding the truths and half-truths of Nietzsche's work, notwithstanding the beauties and half-beauties of Strauss's, the former as philosophy and the latter as music are as a whole indigestible. At best each is, historically considered, but yeast for leavening or lymph for inoculation. In itself it is corruption, disease. Nietzsche ended his life in a lunatic asylum. For Strauss may be predicted a better fate—a phase of full maturity and perfect sanity.

There have been and there are composers who speak disdainfully of an existing style, simply because they are without the talent and training that would enable them to succeed in it. They are in the position of the fox in the fable who called the grapes sour that hung too high for him. Strauss is not one of these. He has proved by his early works that he can write effectively in the old style, and he has proved by his newer works that he has the stuff in him to develop that style. This we see from the heightened expressiveness of his music, emotionally and descriptively, and from the virtuosic and truly masterly handling of all the resources of the art. Consequently we look upon him with hope and great expectations, and implore him not to throw away his pen, not to return to earlier methods, but to proceed onward in a soberer spirit and a more single-hearted manner, in short, to commence his third period, where will be manifested the natural Strauss, purified from the dross that still clung to the gold in the second period.

We now come to a contemporary and ultra-modern personality of a very different cast. GUSTAV MAHLER (*b.* 1860), the famous conductor, is also a notable composer, in fact, the symphonist who among the younger men has next to Strauss caused the greatest sensation. That he was a pupil of Bruckner's is not insignificant. The works that concern us are four in number, and bear the plain designation of ' symphony.' The executive forces of the second symphony comprise, besides a large band of instrumentalists, two solo voices and a chorus, and those of the third, which is more especially regarded as programme music, a solo voice and vocal choirs of different constitution. Mahler revels in expanse and volume, at least does so from the second symphony onward. As Weingartner remarks, those who at the Berlin performance of his symphony called the first movement a monstrosity (*Unding*), may not have taken in at all the principal theme in its vast dimensions, and consequently still less the developments. But the same authority points out the thoroughly musical character and strong emotional qualities of

2 L

Mahler's works as well as their colossal breadth and the
enormous apparatus employed. The reader has made
some acquaintance with Strauss's views of music and
programme music in particular, and cannot but have
found them rather reckless and uncertain. He will fare
still worse with Mahler's vague and groping effusion on
the same subject. The following curious remarks of
his refer to the second symphony in C minor (1895).
'You are right,' he writes to Dr. Arthur Seidl, 'my music
has ultimately recourse to the programme as a last
ideal elucidation, while with Strauss the programme lies
before him as a task . . . When I conceive a grand
musical structure I always come to a point where I am
obliged to call the "word" to my aid as bearer of my
musical idea. Somewhat like this it must have been with
Beethoven in his ninth symphony; only that his time
could not yet furnish him with the suitable materials—
for, at bottom, Schiller's poem is not able to formulate
the unheard-of that was in his mind . . . . What
took place in connection with the last movement of my
second symphony (in C minor) is simply this—I searched
through the whole world of literature up to the Bible
in order to find the redeeming word . . . . Deeply
significant for the nature of the artistic creation is the
way in which I received the inspiration. Even then I
entertained the intention of having recourse to the
chorus in the last movement, and only the fear that
this might be regarded as an external imitation of
Beethoven made me hesitate again and again. At this
time Bülow died, and I attended the funeral service in
Hamburg. The frame of mind in which I sat there
and thought of the departed one, was very much in the
spirit of the work I carried about with me. Then the

choir in the gallery intoned the chorale *Auferstehen*
(Thou shalt rise again, rise again from the dead). This
struck me like lightning, and everything became clear
to me. For this lightning the creative artist waits—
that is the 'holy conception.' What I then experienced
I had next to create in tones. And yet, if I had not
already borne this work within me, how could I have
experienced this? . . . . And so it is with me
always : only when I experience do I poetize in tones;
only when I poetize in tones do I experience . . . .
Schopenhauer somewhere makes use of the simile of
two miners who dig into a lode from opposite sides,
and then meet on the subterranean road. This seems
to me to describe my relation to Strauss excellently.'
To supplement this information let me add first that
Mahler is an enemy of explanatory programmes and
programme-books. This, however, prevents neither
himself from composing what may rightly be called
programme music, nor others from writing comments on
the compositions which he leaves without comments. I
shall not follow the commentators, but confine myself to
a few brief remarks. The fourth of the five divisions of
the second symphony contains a novelty, a song, entitled
Urlicht (Primeval light), the words of which are taken
from *Des Knaben Wunderhorn*. In the last division
enters the choral element already alluded to in the above-
quoted confession of Mahler's. It has been said that
whereas in the second symphony the composer arrives
at the idea of a future life, he introduces us in the third
(F major) to the problem of life in nature—the development of natural force from the most rigid matter to the
highest articulation. This work has two divisions,
respectively of one and five parts. In the third part of

the second division a contralto voice sings Nietzsche's
words: *O Mensch! O Mensch! . . . . Doch alle
Lust will Ewigkeit, will tiefe, tiefe Ewigkeit,* the roundelay
at the end of the Drunken Song in Zarathustra. Besides
the contralto voice there are heard in the fourth part a
boys' choir and a three-part female choir. Here again
the composer goes to *Des Knaben Wunderhorn* for the
words, choosing this time '*Es sungen drei Engel einen
süssen Sang.*' Of the fourth symphony (G major), a
friend of the composer's says: 'Years ago Mahler had
composed the song "*Das himmlische Leben.*" Moved by
the delightful childlike representation of this heavenly
life, he felt transported into a like supremely serene,
distant, and strange sphere, and developed symphonically
the thematic material that arose out of the quite peculiar
world of feeling.' The curious mental processes indicated
by Mahler's confession and the notes that follow offer
food for reflection, but need not detain us now. However, I will not conceal the fact that they in no way
excite my admiration.

Another famous conductor and contemporary of
R. Strauss is FELIX WEINGARTNER (*b.* 1863).
His compositions have obtained a *succès d'estime,* but
hardly more. They consist of operas, songs, concerted
chamber and orchestral works. Among the last are two
symphonies and two symphonic poems—*King Lear* and
Die Gefilde der Seligen (The abodes of the blessed).
Arnold Böcklin's picture of the same designation in the
Berlin National Gallery inspired the second of the latter
two works. From Weingartner's book on the *Symphony
after Beethoven* we see that he is neither a fanatic for nor
against programme music. 'Seen from a very high
point of view, there are perhaps after all not two

tendencies, but only one.' That is to say, not absolute
and programme music, but only good music. He rejects
the perverse, artificial, and therefore inartistic offshoots
of both tendencies, thinking them closely akin and
equally bad.

And now a few brief additional notes on notabilities.
HUGO WOLF (1860-1903), the now celebrated composer of songs, whose life came to an end so prematurely
and, what is sadder still, in a lunatic asylum, wrote a
symphonic poem, *Penthesilea,* inspired by Heinrich
Kleist's drama of that name, a poem Wolf admired
passionately. Of ENGELBERT HUMPERDINCK
(*b.* 1864) there should here be mentioned especially his
great achievement in melodrama, *Die Königskinder,*
where by means of 'speech-notes' (notes with star-
shaped heads) he indicates tempo, rhythm, and cadence
of the declamation. In his prefatory remarks he
says : 'The speech-notes employed in the melodramatic
parts are intended to bring into unison the rhythm and
accents of the heightened speech (the melody of the
speech verses) with the accompanying music.' This
procedure, however, is not only extremely difficult,
perhaps impossible, but even if successfully realized
would not be satisfactory. You must choose between
the accents of speech and those of music ; they cannot be
combined. An older composer, HEINRICH SCHULZ-
BEUTHEN (*b.* 1838), a follower of Liszt, deserves a
place here on account not of the success of his compositions, but of the seriousness of his striving and the
interesting nature of the subjects treated by him.
Besides eight symphonies, some of which have titles
(Fair Elizabeth, Reformation, King Lear, &c.), and a
Heroic and an *Alhambra Sonata,* he has written the

symphonic poem *Die Toteninsel* (inspired no doubt by Böcklin's picture ' The Isle of the Dead '), the overtures *Chriemhilda's Woe and Revenge*, the *Dionysian Procession of Bacchantes*, and *Pan and the Wood Nymphs*, and the orchestral pieces *Ball Episodes*, *Mediæval Popular Scenes*, *Am Rabenstein* (At the place of execution), and *Indian War Dance*. Another of the distinguished among the multitude of scantily encouraged strivers is AUGUST BUNGERT (*b.* 1846), whose dramatic tetralogy *The Homeric World* and plan of founding, in imitation of Bayreuth, a *Festspielhaus* of his own at Godesberg, on the Rhine, have been the subjects of much talk. Here we have to do only with an overture *Tasso* and the symphonic poems *Auf der Wartburg* and *Das hohe Lied der Liebe*. Of the many young composers who write programme music I shall mention only six more—FRITZ VOLBACH (*b.* 1861) and his symphonic poems *Easter* (for organ and orchestra), *Es waren zwei Königskinder* (There were two royal children) and *Alt Heidelberg du Feine* (A spring poem) ; FRIEDRICH KLOSE (*b.* 1862) and his symphonic poem in three parts, *Life a Dream* (for orchestra, organ, female voices, and declamation), and the dramatic symphony *Ilsebill ;* MAX SCHILLINGS (*b.* 1868) and his symphonic prologue to *Œdipus*, the symphonic fantasias *The Ocean glitters* and *The Sea-morning*, and the melodramatic treatment of Wildenbruch's *Hexenlied ;* LEO BLECH (*b.* 1871) and his symphonic poems *The Nun, Consolation in Nature*, and *Forest Excursion ;* SIEGMUND HAUSEGGER (*b.* 1872) and his *Dionysian Fantasia* and symphonic poems *Barbarossa* (1902) and *Wieland the Smith* (1904) ; and ERNST BÖHE (*b.* 1880) and his four tone-poems entitled *The Travels of Odysseus.*

My account of programme music will be appropriately brought to a close by the views of one of the youngest of the above composers, the son of Friedrich von Hausegger, the author of that excellent book *Musik als Ausdruck* (Music as expression).

Siegmund von Hausegger distinguishes between descriptive programme music, which represents external occurrences, and programme music that has its origin in poetic suggestions, and expresses internal occurrences. He exemplifies the two kinds respectively by Berlioz's *Symphonie fantastique*, and Liszt's *Faust* Symphony. Whilst confessing himself a believer in the second kind, he admits that the boundaries of the two are often confused, and that the way to the second is often only found circuitously by the first. 'My compositions,' Hausegger informs me, ' are always in closest connection with my experiences. These experiences, however, are for the most part not something spontaneous, but as it were the ultimate outcome of a strongly marked funda-mental mood dominating a whole period. Thus I wrote the *Dionysian Fantasia* at the special suggestion of the first conscious apprehension of the creative Dionysian moment as it was revealed to me by Nietzsche's *Geburt der Tragödie* (The Birth of Tragedy), but at the same time also as a comprehensive expression of the transcen-dentalism of my youth. Again, as the outcome of national enthusiasm, caused by brutal attempts of the Slavic majority to suppress German nationality in Austria, I wrote the symphonic poem *Barbarossa*. And, lastly, in the year of my betrothal, I wrote *Wieland der Schmied*, as a glorification of the inner deliverance by love!' Hausegger explains his attitude towards the programme as follows. 'By an experience a current of feeling is set free that yearns to vent itself. That this current may not spread out indefinitely, but be embanked, and made to take a direction visible to everyone, recourse is had to a poetic train of thought that transforms the meaning and nature of the experience that gave the first impulse into a poetically perceived picture. This train of thought is for the music a form-giving principle, but only in so far, I think, as its rhythm may be identified with that of the musical fundamental mood. All the purely intellectual and purely pictorial, which would influence the form of the music in a manner foreign to its nature, has to be excluded. Hence external occurrences concern music only in so far as they are phenomena of psychic occurrences, in which case it is the task of music to express the latter, but not to depict the former. The development of my *Barbarossa* plan may serve as an example. First there came to me the general suggestion from life: the contentions between the Germans and Slavs, which awoke my national enthusiasm. This feeling remained unfruitful in me until there resulted from it its vesture in the poetic symbol of the Barbarossa legend — the distress of the people, the longing after deliverance, desperate but vain struggling, the weird romanticism that hovers around the magic hill, the touchingly sublime picture of the sleeping hero (who represented to me the glory and grandeur of the German people) surrounded by his faithful ones, the impressive moment when the hill opened and the Emperor heading his hosts rode forth into the young day and clanging fanfares announced freedom to the enslaved people, the decisive battle, and, at last, triumph and the invigoration of the German spirit—all this represented to me a total of

suggestions so definite that the feelings awakened by
them could give birth to my composition. Thus the
first quite general suggestion determined what I wrote;
and the second suggestion, derived from a series of poetic
ideas, how I wrote. — For my work as a composer nature
impressions have always been of the greatest influence;
but the reading of philosophical and literary works has
also repeatedly incited my productivity.'

Many notable names are absent from this book, a few,
very likely, by oversight, most, however, for good reasons.
Robert Franz was not mentioned because he wrote
hardly anything but songs, and no instrumental music;
and Franz Lachner and Max Bruch because they did not
offer matter for comment. Others are in one or the
other of these cases. Others again were ruled out by the
limitation of space and time. In Max Reger (*b.* 1873),
one of the most powerful musical personalities of the
present day, we have the exceptional appearance of a
composer who is under the influence not of Liszt,
Wagner, and R. Strauss, but of Bach, Beethoven, and
Brahms, and who eschews programme music and until
quite recently had not meddled with the orchestra. A
rara avis indeed. Only after eighty or more other works
there comes at last an orchestral one, a symphony, but
not a programme symphony. The programmatic
tendency has not yet led him beyond *Pièces pittoresques*
and *Silhouettes*. There is, however, an older composer
whom I now regret not to have included, although I had
not forgotten him at the proper time. I mean the Italian
Benedetto Marcello (1686-1739), the most illustrious
amateur composer, who in the history of musical
expression ought to have assigned to him a distinguished
place. How much might not have been said of the

striking expressiveness of his fifty Psalms for one, two, three or four voices, with a thorough bass for the organ or harpsichord, and here and there with the further accompaniment of *obbligato* stringed instruments! May I hope to obtain the reader's pardon for this and other shortcomings?

EPILOGUE.

He who for the first time views the route over which we have travelled, cannot but be bewildered by the sight of the weltering chaos that presents itself to him. With continued attention, however, the observer discovers running through the whole of this apparently hopeless confusion of movement in all directions and of all kinds, one constant tendency, the twofold development of the art—the purely technical development for virtuosity's sake, which has its origin in the joy of display and the pride of conquering difficulties, and the development for expression's sake, which has its origin in the craving to give vent to what moves heart and mind. Whether the cultivation of imitation of outward things belongs to the former or the latter branch of the tendency, or partly to the one and partly to the other, depends on the nature and object of the imitation, on whether it is mechanical or emotional, the outcome of pride or affection.

In view of the contrary historical and psychological facts, it is impossible not to characterize as absurd the assertion that music is a purely formalistic, non-expressional art. Even the rudimental music of savages testifies to expressional as well as æsthetical aims, and on scanning the records of the antique and medieval civilizations we find them abounding in expositions and eulogies of the emotional and ethical powers of the art. This, however, lies outside the four centuries dealt with in these pages. What I have reported of Josquin Deprès, Lasso, Palestrina, Marenzio, Thomas Morley and others, must have convinced the reader that in the 16th century music was something more than an art of beautiful proportions, of sounding arabesques. But up to that time the development of music as an art of expression had been slow. The quickened and ever more quickening rate of this development did not begin until the latter part of the 16th century, with the rise of accompanied solo song and the efflorescence of instrumental music. Then opened the era *par excellence* of the invention of expressive melodic and rhythmic figures and harmonic and colouristic combinations. Vocal and instrumental music stimulated and aided each other. But pure instrumental music, which afterwards outstripped vocal music, at first lagged behind, remaining longer to a large extent a playing with sounds. Monteverdi (1567-1643) may be named as the earliest composer of notable expressive instrumental music. All the really great masters that followed, and innumerable minor ones, contributed more or less to the development of the same side of the art, Beethoven (1770-1827) being the first who unfolded the expressional capabilities of music in all their emotional and intellectual width, depth, force, grandeur, and sublimity. After him the question as to the nature of music was no longer an open one. His works were a revelation. And the lead given by him could not be ignored by his successors with impunity.

In regard to the development theory, we should, however, neither overlook certain facts nor be disturbed by them. The study of history certainly informs us that with the increase of the means of expression, the wisdom of employing them does not at all keep pace. In our advanced age we still meet with notions and performances that ought to be possible only in the childhood of the art. Some prejudices—both to the credit and the discredit of the art—seem never to die; and it is difficult to say which are the most baleful, those of over-estimation or those of under-estimation. How many composers really take the trouble of thinking out the problem on the solution of which depends the degree of success, and even the success or unsuccess of their efforts? It is to be hoped that the thoughts of the great composers and others on the nature of music, collected in this volume, may be helpful to their successors, and draw the attention of not a few to vital matters of which otherwise they might remain unaware.

Programme music in its widest sense is co-extensive with expressive music; in its narrower sense it is a species of this genus. Taking for granted that music can express something, the question arises, What can it and what can it not express? After the many professional opinions already given, I shall, for a change, quote one by a layman, and that layman no less a person than the incommensurable Goethe, one of the half-dozen or fewer greatest and wisest men the world has produced. On February 16, 1818, he writes to Adalbert Schoepke: ' To the question as to what the musician may depict, I venture to reply: Nothing and everything. He may imitate nothing as he receives it through the external senses; but he may represent everything he feels as the effect of these external sense impressions. To imitate thunder in music is not art, but the musician who excites in me the feeling as if I heard thunder would be very estimable. So we have also unmistakable expression for perfect rest, for silence, even for negation—perfect examples of which I have at hand. I repeat: To evoke moods of the soul, without using the ordinary external means, is the great and noble prerogative of music.' Apart from the interest it has for us on account of the source it comes from, this definition deserves our respectful attention and grateful acceptance. It points out that the true vocation of music is the expression of the inner, not the imitation of the outer phenomena. But, although the outer phenomena should never be the main concern of the composer, they may, if artistically idealized and kept in proper subordination, be of great value to him. Goethe's reply, however, good as far as it goes, does not go far enough. Certainly, it does not cover all that can be said, and indeed ought to be said, about the boundaries and the strengths and weaknesses of music. While music is pre-eminently strong in the depicting of the emotions themselves, it is lamentably weak, nay impotent, in the setting forth of their circumstantiality, their localization, in short, their who, why, where, when and whither. Now, cannot the composer in some other way supply what is lacking, and thus obtain the full benefit of the peculiar strength of his art? Adam Smith (not in his *Wealth of Nations,* but in his essay on *The imitative Arts*) says : ' It would be a strange picture which required an inscription at the foot to tell us, not only what particular person it meant to represent, but whether it meant to represent a man or a horse, or whether it meant to be a picture at all, and to represent anything. The imitations of instrumental music may, in some respects, be said to resemble such pictures. There is, however, this essential difference between them, that the picture would not be much mended by the inscription; whereas, by what may be considered as very little more than such an inscription, instrumental music, though it cannot always even then, perhaps, be said properly to imitate, may, however, produce all the effects of the finest and most perfect imitation.' We need not enter here on a discussion of the imitation theory of the British 18th century philosophers.* It will suffice for our present purpose to note Adam Smith's assertion of the importance of the inscription, *i.e.*, of the programme, which, however, in painting is not so unimportant, certainly not in our day, as the philosopher seemed to think. Ruskin, in a letter to the Editor of *The Times* (May 5, 1854), after giving a beautiful interpretation of Holman Hunt's *The Light of the world*, says: 'I believe there are very few persons on whom the picture, thus justly understood, will not produce a deep impression. . . . It may, perhaps, be answered, that works of art ought not to stand in need of interpretation of this kind. Indeed, we have been so long accustomed to see pictures painted without any purpose or intention whatsoever, that the unexpected existence of meaning in a work of art may very naturally at first appear to us an unkind demand on the spectator's understanding. But in a few years more I hope the English public may be convinced of the simple truth, that neither a great fact, nor a great man, nor a great poem, nor a great picture, nor any other great thing can be fathomed to the very bottom in a moment of time; and that no high enjoyment, either in picture-seeing or any other occupation, is consistent with a total lethargy of the powers of the understanding.'

It is strange that there are still composers who think that those who endeavour to express something in their art lower its dignity. As if an art of arabesques were

* See what is said about imitation as a means of expression on p. 2 of this book.

something nobler than an art of thought and emotion. Would they consider poetry consisting of ingenious collocations of sound quantities and qualities superior to poetry that is concerned with the things of the mind and the heart ? And if not, why is the converse to hold in music ? It is stranger still that there are composers who approve of programmes in their own minds, but disapprove of revealing them, preferring them to be guessed by the hearer. One wonders whether it never strikes them that this is turning works of art into conundrums, and giving to the hearer's imagination unrestricted liberty to roam where chance may lead it. But it is strangest of all that there are composers of programme music of the most convinced and advanced type who content themselves with a title, conceal their programme, and express their indifference as to whether their music is listened to as absolute or as programme music. Unreasonableness and inconsistency cannot go farther. If the composers declare that they use the programmes simply for their own inspiration, I decline to accept this as an excuse. The hearer has the right to ask for a clue to the inexplicable mysterious things he hears. He is quite entitled to say to those high and mighty geniuses (who are too ready with their *car tel est notre plaisir*) that when they wish to express more than simple moods, when they wish to depict a multiplicity of details, complicated relations, recondite symbolisms, and abstract ideas of all sorts, when, in short, they wish to express what music can only partially express, they are in duty bound to furnish the necessary verbal supplement. Indeed, it seems to me that there can be no other common-sense view on the question of programmes than this : Whenever the composer ceases to write formal music and goes beyond the expression of simple moods, the programme is not only legitimate, but even obligatory. Objections to programmes arise from prejudice, from a misunderstanding of what is really intended by them and implied in them.

Programme music, as we have seen, is of all kinds. There are even such things as unconscious programmes. A creative musician—I am not speaking of composers in the literal sense—may unintentionally reproduce in a work an emotion, thought, or picture that at the time has possession of him. As to the conscious programmes, they may be of all degrees of vagueness and distinctness. They may also be subjective or objective. A master of the most subjective of the arts, however, will do well to subjectivize his object, which is done in two ways—by realizing in himself the experiences of the object where that is animate, and by realizing the impression received from the object where that is inanimate. It is not always easy to distinguish between absolute and programme music. The former term, unless used in the sense of pure instrumental music (in contradistinction to mixed vocal-instrumental music), ought to be regarded as obsolete in modern music. For absolute music in the sense of formal music, music unconnected with any ideas, hardly exists nowadays. Presence of a programme on, or absence from, the title-page proves nothing. What decides the matter is its presence in or absence from the music. But sometimes the term absolute music is in our day applied to music which has a programme of more or less vagueness. This I can illustrate in an interesting manner by a quotation from a letter of Fritz Volbach, the composer, conductor, and writer on music. Writing to me about a symphony he

2 M

is composing, he says: ' It is without a programme, absolute music. First movement: A defiant struggle for deliverance—as it were in Schiller's sense. Second movement: What is the good of fighting? *Carpe diem!* Let us enjoy ourselves! But pleasure is as brittle as glass. Third movement (*Largo*): Holy night descends; solemn peace; longing for God. Fourth movement (*Finale* built on an old Alleluia theme): Hymn of Redemption.—In short, what everyone experiences in himself; what one is again and again impelled to express—not much, and yet everything.' Those who condemn programme music altogether do not know what they are about. If they had their way, a large portion of our treasury of noble music would be non-existent. Musical genius is of various kinds as well as various degrees. For some composers a programme is a necessity if they are to do their best—their powers have to be roused. Löwe was such a one; Wagner was another. But how much and how felicitously was not even so genuinely musical a nature as Mendelssohn's affected by a programme! Nay, do not the most genuinely musical of all composers—Mozart as an opera composer and Schubert as a song composer—prove the efficacy of programmes? But ideas, which stir the living, are powerless with the dead. Programmes may stimulate genius, but cannot produce it. Unfortunately, barren composers do not understand this, or rather they do not know that they are sterile. They use stimulants, fail nevertheless, and alas! bring programme music into disrepute. But the programme question, that is, the question what music can and the musician ought to deal with, is enormously difficult and supremely important. When a composer of the 18th century, in

setting the words ' Twelve Apostles followed Jesus,' made
the parts enter one after the other in a long procession ;
and another, in setting the words ' There is none among
us who doeth right,' wrote a series of consecutive fifths—
they had recourse to symbolism. The reader may laugh
at these examples and call them childish, but he will
find equally perverse ones in grand compositions of
present-day composers. Battle symphonies are not so
common as they used to be ; it would, however, not
greatly surprise me to meet with a title similar to that
of a work of the respectable Hanoverian musician A. F. C.
Kollmann (died in London, 1829), *The Shipwreck, or the
Loss of the East Indiaman ' Halsewell.'* Nor should I be
greatly surprised to hear of a Motor Car Symphony, as I
saw a quarter of a century ago a critique of a *Bicycle
Sonata* by Stanislaus Elliot (*Allegro :* The first attempt.
Andante : His despair and return. *Scherzo :* His second
attempt. *Rondo :* Success at last).

A programme is of course a factor in determining the
form of a composition, but not the sole factor. Another
factor is the nature of the art ; and a third, the constitution of the human mind. Formlessness is altogether out
of the question. Form, and not only form, but beautiful
form, is a *sine qua non* of art. Not unfrequently,
however, discussions on form resolve themselves into the
assertion that form in instrumental music means sonata
form. Now against this it is impossible to make too
emphatic a protest. The sonata form is undoubtedly a
most beautiful form, but it is only one exemplification of
the laws of mind that are at the root of all good form.
There was good form before the sonata form, and there
will be after it. Moreover, the classical masters,
especially Beethoven, have not recoiled from remodelling

that form in a way that left nothing or little of its fundamental features (key-relation, number of subjects, recapitulation, &c.). That excellent musicians grown up in the sonata form, indoctrinated in it, and writing in it, preach a monoform religion, does not prove anything. I cannot help remembering that arch-classic Moritz Hauptmann's jubilation on escaping from the tonic-dominant-tonic see-saw of modern music into the freedom of 16th century music. The foregoing, however, must not be read as an apology for all the formal novelties produced under the device of Progress, Genius, and Poetry. It has always struck me as strange that Liszt and Wagner, who fought with such prowess for nature and freedom in art, should adopt methods that have so much artificiality and restrictiveness about them as the former's highly-developed system of metamorphosis of themes and the latter's excessively developed system of *Leitmotive.*

To give an historical account, not to draw a moral, was the object of this book. Still, the facts before us point to a moral. To me at least it is clear and certain that all good music has a programme, taking the term in its very widest signification. What indeed distinguishes the fugues and canons of J. S. Bach from those of A. A. Klengel? Is it not the humanity behind the craftmanship? How is it that Beethoven stirs us more powerfully and profoundly than any other symphonic composer? Is it not because of the emotions and ideas his tonal forms arouse? Undoubtedly the forms of art must be beautiful. But the artist whose forms are nothing but forms will always leave his auditor or spectator cold. *Pectus est quod facit disertos.* The added interest of expression may be traced even in decorative art by comparing the rigid straightlined geometrical designs with those in which graceful serpentining lines allude as it were to features in man, animals, and plants, living beings that engage our sympathies. A thoughtful survey of music cannot fail to lead us to the conclusion that bad programme music is bad because it has too little of the qualities of good absolute music, and bad absolute music is bad because it has too little of the qualities of good programme music. At least this is what we mostly find. But programme music may also be bad because it meddles with matters uncongenial and even foreign to music. Programme and artistic form do not exclude each other. Rightly understood we may then say that programme music is the only high-class music.

And now a question in conclusion. Can we congratulate ourselves on the present state of our art and the progress we have been making? If we can boast of improvement, it is, I think, only technical improvement in some directions. In all other respects we are getting poorer and poorer and are face to face with imminent bankruptcy. The road on which we are travelling offers no prospect—the increase of complexity and sensationalism cannot go on for ever. We must strike out in a different direction. There was a great revolution in music about 1600. We may therefore without unreasonableness expect another—the present age is ripe for it and longing for it. And what do we want? Simplicity, sanity, spontaneity, and, above all and including all, beauty—natural, gracious, persuasive beauty.

INDEX.

[A consistent system of writing proper names is impossible where many nationalities are concerned. Slavonic names give much trouble—especially the Russian—owing to the different ways of transliteration to be found in different countries. The familiar spelling of some well-known composers has here and there been preferred to the correct—for instance, Dussek and Tomaschek.]